REUNION WITHOUT COMPROMISE

The South and Reconstruction: 1865–1868

MICHAEL PERMAN

Assistant Professor of History, University of Illinois at Chicago Circle

To Helen

With gratitude,

Michael.

7 . i. 75.

CAMBRIDGE
AT THE UNIVERSITY PRESS
1973

Published by the Syndics of the Cambridge University Press
Bentley House, 200 Euston Road, London NW1 2DB
American Branch: 32 East 57th Street, New York, N.Y.10022

© Cambridge University Press 1973

Library of Congress Catalogue Card Number: 72-86418

ISBNs:
0 521 20044 X hard covers
0 521 09779 7 paperback

Photoset in Malta by St Paul's Press Ltd and
printed in the United States of America

Contents

Contents

Part 3 : Seeking Southern cooperation, 1866

Part 4 : Demanding Southern acquiescence 1867–1868

Preface

Although there have been numerous general studies of the Confederate States during Reconstruction, there has been little or no attempt to analyze and understand the policies adopted and the course pursued by the men who held office in the Southern States at the end of the war. Historians have given scant thought to the political needs and goals of the defeated Southern leadership; they have assumed these were so obvious or inconsequential that further examination was unnecessary. Yet, without examining the preoccupations of the Southern politicians who were in power during 1865 and afterwards, a vital element in the fight for reunion is overlooked. This distortion, however, is exactly what has been allowed to emerge. Much energy has been spent analyzing the policies of the President and the Congress, while little attention has been directed at those in the South whom they sought to reorganize and reconstruct.

This is especially surprising since the group of politicians who held office and therefore wielded political power in the South were central to all of the plans for reconstruction discussed in Washington from 1865 to 1868 while Federal terms and policies were being formulated. The post-war status and position of the Confederacy's political leadership was what Northern policy-makers believed reunion and reconstruction were all about. Should the post-bellum South continue to be led by the men who had held positions of power and leadership during the Confederacy and in the years previous to it when secession was being debated? Or should it be governed after the war by some of these former leaders only, namely those who had publicly opposed secession and been critical of the Confederate government? Or should all previous officeholders be removed from power, regardless of distinctions and differences among them, and a new group, unacquainted previously with political power, be installed instead of them? This was the nub of the problem. Suffrage for the freedmen was secondary; it was a weapon which could be used in the post-war struggle to curb the Confederate leaders, but it could never take priority over the matter of political office and its tenure in the post-war South.

That their present possession of political power and their future access to it were at issue was quite apparent to the Confederate leaders. But this privileged power could not be conceded; and it would not be, so long as they were in a position to exercise any opinions on the matter or to take any steps to ensure its continuation. To pursue any other course would be a voluntary abdication of power. Moreover, additional pressure to defend their hold on power was applied through their knowledge that in the predicament which their section faced, economically devastated and socially disorganized, political ingenuity was all that they possessed to offset or moderate the effects of defeat. Maneuvering from a minority-position had been Southern practice in the last decades of the ante-bellum period; the skillful employment of these tactics was absolutely necessary now that the conditions for a permanent reunion of the sections were in the process of being arranged. Weaker than in 1861 and without the option and threat of secession, the South's political leaders had to bargain as vigorously as possible on their section's return to the Union. They might lose everything or they might lose only a little and for a short time. Maybe they could continue in power with minimal further cost. But whatever the outcome, what was at stake were their own individual offices and the political control of the South which the possession of them carried. And these could not be surrendered until the extent of the Federal authorities' determination in this matter had been tested to the maximum.

The way in which the South's leaders (whom I have called 'the Confederates', a term which includes both those who were secessionists in 1860–1, as well as their opponents) responded to the situation in which they found themselves in 1865 and the nature of their attempts to withstand and outmaneuver the proposals emanating from Washington is the subject-matter of this book. And it is my contention that once it is understood what these were, and why, a number of interpretative assumptions will have to be discarded and the parameters and ingredients of post-war sectional adjustment considerably revised.

In the process of collecting the material upon which this study is based I have accumulated many debts to archivists and librarians in a number of locations but, in particular, Washington, D.C., at the National Archives and the Manuscripts Division of the Library of Congress, and, naturally enough, in the Southern States. Without these collections of manuscripts and without the knowledge of them which their custodians possess the writing of history would be impossible. I am very grateful, therefore, to those who collected, sorted, and catalogued these documents and to those who personally introduced me to them. A number of people offered their time and criticism at various stages in the preparation of this manuscript. John Hope Franklin, my dissertation advisor at the University of Chicago, always gave the right kind of personal help and expert criticism. Also very helpful to me was the American historian who was one of the readers consulted anonymously by Cambridge University Press when this manuscript was first submitted. Many of my colleagues and friends in the History Department at the University of Illinois, Chicago Circle, read large portions of the manuscript when it was nearing its final form, and I would like to thank Robert Conrad, Melvin Holli, Gilbert Osofsky, Leo Schelbert, Peter Stanley and Mills Thornton for their assurances and criticisms. I am grateful to Mrs Helen Bailey who has typed the bulk of the manuscript with remarkable speed and accuracy.

Chicago, Illinois　　　　　　　　　　　　　　　　　　　　　　M. P.
October 1972

. . . in our opinion, the real cause which brought the question to the decision of war was the habit of concession on the part of the North, and the inability of its representatives to say *NO*, when policy as well as conscience made it imperative.

James Russell Lowell,
'The Rebellion: Its Causes and Consequences,' 1864

It's easy under existing circumstances to win the first victory and reconstruct these States under the acts of Congress. But this victory is only the beginning of the contest and unless it be a victory openly and fairly won and very decisive in its results, it may prove not only fruitless but absolutely destructive. If hastily or partially done, reconstruction will drag with it a train of evils to this country which can never be remedied.

Report of General John D. Pope, Commanding 3rd. Military District,
in Secretary of War's Report for 1867

. . . and I am waiting for the deepest South to stop Reconstructing itself in its own image. . . .

Lawrence Ferlinghetti: 'I am waiting'

FOR BONNIE

Part 1
Conciliation and conflict

You know the strange perversity of these people and their fierce belief that
what they wish to happen is sure to do so the next day. . .
General John Pope to General William T. Sherman,
Atlanta, Ga., 29 June 1867, W. T. Sherman MSS.

Any plan of reconstruction is wrong that tends to leave these old leaders in
power. A few of them give certain evidence of a change of heart, —by some
means save these for the sore and troubled future; but for the others, the men
who not only brought on the war, but ruined the mental and moral forces of
their people before unfurling the banner of Rebellion — for these there should
never any more be place or Countenance among honest and humane and patriotic people.
Sidney Andrews, The South Since the War
(Boston: Ticknor and Fields, 1866), pp. 391–2

Introduction
Reconstruction as reconciliation

At the close of the war there was a widespread feeling in the Northern press and among public figures that sensitive and generous treatment of the rebels would be more likely to produce reconciliation and a permanent settlement than harsh measures. Prevalent was the assumption that the Confederates and their allies could undergo a change of attitude and accommodate to the facts of their own defeat and of Northern supremacy. To deny the South's leaders the chance to exercise a desire to conform and manifest their loyal feelings was to allow a great opportunity for reunion to go by default. Since slavery had now been abolished, the argument ran, and the existence of slave labor in the South had after all been the only cause of friction between the sections, there was no major obstacle to reunion. By contrast there were some who doubted that the abolition of slavery had ended all but superficial distinctions. But they also were often sympathetic to the adoption of a conciliatory policy on the grounds that if the sections were fundamentally distinct, coercion and interference in the South would obviously be productive of nothing but tumult and further antagonism. So even those people who believed that despite the cessation of hostilities the sections were still basically out of alignment were amenable to policies which were conciliatory.

A key perhaps to the enthusiasm for accommodation with the South was embodied in the analysis developed by the Secretary of State, William H. Seward, who played a major role in forming and implementing the President's post-war program for reunion. Criticism of the Administration's Southern policy had been made to Seward personally by the Comte de Gasparin, an aristocratic French observer of the American political scene who had complained particularly of the omission of provisions for Negro suffrage. In reply, Seward explained the reasoning and purpose behind the policy, which was that 'According to the Constitution those citizens acting politically in their respective states must reorganise their state govts. We cannot reorganize with due adherence to the national authority, including the effective

abolition of slavery.' Toward this end, the government's amnesty was
intended 'to exclude all disloyal citizens and persistent upholders and
defenders of slavery from all part in reorganization,' for 'it was the
wealthy men of the slave states that invested money in slaves, and
made the war into which they conscripted the poor non-slaveholding
loyal white men.' But, beyond withholding amnesty and retaining
'military control until the civil power is reorganized,' the central government could do nothing. Anything more, such as Negro suffrage,
would require constitutional admendment. This, Seward said, 'No one
hinders or opposes, . . . but that involves delay attended with the uncertainty of obtaining promptly, or even of obtaining at all, the required consent of three-fourths of the States. Those who insist upon it
seem to require the Union to be held in its present state of disorganization indefinitely, in order to coerce that consent;' moreover, he added,
'The coercion recommended is a policy of centralization, consolidation, and imperialism, . . . repugnant to the spirit of individual liberty'
and unknown to 'the habits of the American people.' In essence,
Seward had suggested in his 10 July letter, Gasparin misunderstood
the American political system and the nature of the war for 'analogies
can hardly exist between popular insurrections against arbitrary
systems in Europe and the ambitious insurrection in this country
against a popular and free govt.'[1]

Seward's assessment of the post-war situation, and of the proper
way to deal with it, was not idiosyncratic but rather one which was
widely held. Lincoln, Johnson, the Cabinet and most of Congress in
1865 would have agreed with him. It was not surprising then that
James Russell Lowell said he could discern a large body of opinion
favorable to a course which would involve minimal action by the Federal government, and naturally this policy would be conciliatory in
tone and intent. This aggregation of sentiment, he said, consisted of
three groups: those who sympathized with slavery; those 'who hope
even yet to reknit the monstrous league between slavery and a party
calling itself Democratic;' and, a larger segment yet, those 'who seem
to confuse their minds with some fancied distinction between civil and
foreign war. Holding the States to be indestructible, they seem to think
that, by the mere cessation of hostilities, they [the Confederates] are
to resume their places as if nothing had happened, or rather as if this

---

[1] Seward to Agénor Etienne, comte de Gasparin, Washington, D.C., 10 July 1865
and 7 April 1866, W. H. Seward MSS.

had been a mere political contest which we had carried.'[2] Despite this growing body of influential opinion, Lowell warned that 'the public mind should be made up as to what are the essential conditions of real and lasting peace, before it is subjected to the sentimental delusions of the inevitable era of good feelings in which the stronger brother is so apt to play the part of Esau.'[3]

Equally worried at this development was Charles Sumner who warned, in a December article for *Atlantic Monthly*, that 'Clemency has its limitations; and when it transcends these, it ceases to be a virtue, and is only a mischievous indulgence.' These limits had been reached, he explained, when magnanimity began to impinge on or threaten the 'general security,' the guarantee of which was 'the first duty of government.' Furthermore, as a guide to the scope and meaning of clemency Sumner suggested two aphorisms – 'Nothing for vengeance; everything for justice' and 'Be just before you are generous.'[4] A further danger to be cautioned against, Sumner urged, was that in seeking to end hostility and war, the government might escape from Charybdis only to rush upon Scylla. The Scyllas that he could perceive penetrating above the eddies of public discussion were numerous. Among them were 'that old rock of *concession* and *compromise* which from the beginning of our history has been a constant peril;' the cry that States cannot be coerced and that instead their rights must be respected, an anomalous argument after four years of military coercion; the fear that governmental 'centralism' would be the outcome of schemes to interfere in the South and to enfranchise the freedmen, despite the fact that the government had already used immense power to free them; the reminder that 'military power must yield to the civil power and the right of self-government;' and, finally, the solemn protestation that 'we must trust each other,' even though 'In trusting them, we give them political power, including the license to oppress loyal persons, whether white or black.'[5]

But the warnings of Lowell and Sumner were not heeded. Instead, all of the policies pursued by the Federal government after the war em-

[2]James Russell Lowell, 'Reconstruction,' [1865], in Lowell, *The Writings of James Russell Lowell*, 10 vols. (Boston: Houghton, Mifflin and Co., 1981), v, 235–6.
[3]*Ibid.*, p. 237.
[4]Charles Summer, 'Clemency and Common Sense: A Curiosity of Literature; with a Moral,' *Atlantic Monthly*, December 1865, p. 758.
[5]*Ibid.*, pp. 759–60.

bodied conciliation and provided for the cooperation and consent of the Confederate leadership. This applied not only to Johnson's policy but more surprisingly to that of Congress as well. In 1865 the President restored self-government to the Confederates on condition that they would do certain things indicative of their readiness to coexist in the Union and of their fitness to govern their own section. In its alternative proposal, the Fourteenth amendment which was formulated a year later, Congress left with the South and its better judgement the option of acceptance or rejection. And since the details of Congress' terms were highly threatening to the Confederate's security and position of the leading Southerners, there was far less incentive to approve than there had been in 1865. Even Congress' second, and more severe, set of terms, the Reconstruction Act of 1867, included in its provisions procedures for the Confederates to register either their cooperation and approval or alternatively their opposition.[6] Refusing to countenance reconstruction by men and groups from outside the South's traditional rulers because that would imply coercion and dictation, the conservative and moderate Republicans insisted continually, over the objections of the radicals, that Southern reorganization had to be engineered with the cooperation and concurrence of the very men their legislation intended to curb. When challenged on this point, the moderates would reply that, as Johnson had also argued in 1865, they were employing a mixture of consent and coercion, reconciliation and reconstruction, and they were not simply conciliating the Confederates. But nonetheless they were deluding themselves since the success of their schemes depended on Confederate assent, no matter that this was obscured by elements of coercion and demand. Furthermore, by leaving sufficient options to the South, the Republicans invited responses similar to Herschel V. Johnson's reaction to the Reconstruction

[6] A recent dissertation on the Reconstruction Act, Larry G. Kincaid, 'Legislative Origins of the Military Reconstruction Act, 1865–1867,' Ph.D. dissertation, Johns Hopkins University, 1968, argues that the law was substantially a result of successful bargaining by the moderates rather than the radicals. That the moderate John Sherman felt that his position had been sustained in the legislation was indicated in a letter to his brother on 7 March 1867, in which he remarked that 'The bill was much injured by the additions in the House but after all there is nothing obnoxious to the South in it but general suffrage. This they must take [the moderates, according to Kincaid, had by 1867 accepted Negro suffrage as a necessity] and the only question is whether they will take it in their own way by their own popular movements or whether we will be compelled at the next session to organize provisional governments.' W. T. Sherman MSS.

Act when he had exclaimed: 'Our oppressors can put chains upon us, if they will, seeing us impotent and prostrate at their feet; but let us consent to it never.'[7]

Involving the Southern leadership in a policy which required their consent while at the same time it contemplated their removal from power was not the only irony in the Federal approach to reconstruction. One of the advantages of conciliation, its advocates argued, was that it would ensure a speedy settlement of the post-war problem. Yet because it required Confederate consent, a policy of conciliation always left terms open-ended; therefore they were never final nor were they, in any real sense, terms. This was quite evidently so because the Confederates whenever possible rejected them and forced Congress to prepare further measures and devices. Therefore, rather than speeding settlement this approach kept it on ice for about three years. By contrast, the kind of propositions envisaged by the radicals would at least have removed the ambiguity and obscurity which pervaded the relationship between the sections. Early and unequivocally, the status of the South and the North's expectations of it would have been defined. And at that point it would not have mattered so much that the radicals' program would take a good amount of time to run its course, involving as it did military rule, restriction of Confederate power, universal suffrage, and perhaps some kind of land distribution. Matters actually developed differently, however, and a moderate Republican, Jacob D. Cox, was to regret years later that 'The worst thing in the whole reconstruction business was the way in which new terms were imposed and nothing made a finality.'[8]

Considerable blame for this weakness in Federal reconstruction policy lay with the assumption that a real reunion demanded reconciliation at the expense of reconstruction. In recent years, historians of the Reconstruction period have also been receptive to these same arguments for conciliation which, at the time, gained influence and yet caused such havoc. Widely known as the revisionists, these historians have rewritten and reinterpreted the period by rejecting the views of the previously dominant school which had been presented during the first decades of this century. Through popular works like Claude Bowers'

[7]Johnson to Messrs John G. Westmoreland, James F. Alexander etc., Augusta, Ga., 11 July 1867, H. V. Johnson MSS.
[8]Jacob D. Cox to James Ford Rhodes, the historian, Oberlin, Ohio, January 1899, Jacob D. Cox MSS.

The Tragic Era and George F. Milton's *The Age of Hate*, the earlier
school of interpretation had, by the 1930s and 1940s, permeated not
only the universities but the national culture as well. Basically it was a
pro-Southern interpretation of Reconstruction, with President
Johnson and the radical Republicans emerging as misunderstood
courageous hero and vengeful hypocritical villains respectively. Yet
although the revisionists, to their credit, have reversed this sentimental
and erroneous casting of roles, many of them have, in the process, committed what would appear to be a grievous error of judgment. Like the
Civil War revisionists of the 1940s, who argued that the war was
avoidable, the Reconstruction revisionists of the 1950s and 1960s
have suggested that radical reconstruction was not inevitable, that the
differences between the sections were negotiable, and that a formula
was available for reconciling the needs and fears of both Congress and
the Confederate South. Rather than arguing, as their predecessors had,
that the South *should* not have been coerced and reconstructed, they
have asserted that it *need* not have been. Although sympathetic to the
radical Republicans, the revisionists have nonetheless proposed that on
a moderate set of proposals a settlement could have been reached,
thereby rendering unnecessary the less conciliatory demands espoused,
and later implemented, to some extent, by the radicals.

The revisionists have therefore focused their attention on the early
years of Reconstruction, in particular 1865, when, they argue, the
defeated South was more amenable than at any later time to terms.
Since they had been defeated and ruined, the Confederates expected
terms from the North and were, to a considerable degree, malleable.
This was also a moment, they say, when the radicals could have been
satisfied with a firm but generous policy which at least guaranteed
legal and civil equality to the freedmen. Of course a moderate and conciliatory policy was proposed at this juncture by President Johnson
but it failed. And in view of the favorable circumstances for a settlement acceptable to all the protagonists why was the vital opportunity
lost? This perplexed the revisionists and so they proceeded to subject
the episode to careful scrutiny in order to discover why what was intended as an intersectional compromise failed to mature.[9]

[9]The major revisionist works which have emphasized this feature most obviously and persistently are Eric L. McKitrick, *Andrew Johnson and Reconstruction* (Chicago: University of Chicago Press, 1960); Kenneth Stampp, *The Era
of Reconstruction, 1865–1877* (New York: Vintage Books, 1967); LaWanda
and John Cox, *Politics, Principle, and Prejudice, 1865–1866* (Chicago: The

A number of general explanations were offered, all of them very cogent. First of all, the revisionists argued, Johnson's program, while in approach it was suitable and correct, was ineptly and carelessly administered. Requirements were not clarified, demands were not insisted upon, and communication was lax, imprecise and unconvincing. Second, the details of the policy took inadequate account of the views of the radical Republicans, even of many of the moderates, and in consequence its results were rejected by Congress when it refused to seat the Southern representatives in December 1865. At that moment, with political dexterity on the President's part, the Republican Party could have aligned itself with Johnson's approach and policy. Another explanation was that Johnson had immense power at his disposal but he failed to use it. As President just after a war, he could have wielded sufficient influence that both Congress and the South could have been brought into line. And finally, the failure, later in Reconstruction, to produce an intersectional settlement based, as all consensuses must be, on moderate terms, was attributed to a considerable degree to the degradation and abuse encountered by

Free Press, 1963), and David Donald, *The Politics of Reconstruction, 1863–1867* (Baton Rouge: Louisiana State University Press, 1965).

In his *Reconstruction: After the Civil War* (Chicago: University of Chicago Press, 1961), John Hope Franklin is more critical than most revisionists of the general approach taken by Johnson. He inclines towards an explanation of the failure of Presidential policy based on the shortcomings of its assumptions and fundamentals rather than on the inadequacy of its specifics and manner of implementation. But the treatment is very broad and general (as is appropriate to the kind of book he was writing) and it does not provide an explanation which is sufficiently thorough or adequate. With regard to Congress' proposals, Franklin does not apply the sorts of considerations he uses for Johnson's policy; indeed he does not view them in terms of success or appropriateness or adequacy.

Another revisionist, William Brock, in *An American Crisis: Congress and Reconstruction, 1865–1867* (London: Macmillan and Co. Ltd., 1967) has, however, dissented from the general approach taken by his colleagues. He has argued that 'Reconstruction was an ideological struggle, and the crisis must be understood in emotional terms and not merely as a record of personal rivalries, conflicting interests and political maneuvers' (*Ibid.*, p. 14). His assessment as to why Reconstruction was a failure was presented in terms, not of the weakness inherent in a particular approach to the problem, but of the tragic proportions of the situation in which Congress found itself, beset as it was by ideological, constitutional and institutional obstacles and limitations. In other words, the problem the nation faced was fundamental in its proportions. With much of this I agree but I am not so fatalistic as Brock in attributing Reconstruction's deficiencies to situational ironies and to tragedy.

the moderates because their position was so closely identified with the combative and unattractive personality of Andrew Johnson.

This analysis of why a harmonious settlement did not emerge in 1865 has been very persuasive. Yet there are a number of major objections to it which need to be raised. The first of these is that in this interpretation too much emphasis is placed on deficiencies in administration and political manipulation, as if by a more astute and pragmatic use of the devices available to him the President could have made a success of his policy. Yet it was the policy itself not simply its implementation which was at fault. It was the goal and the formulation of the program that ensured its failure to produce a more compliant South; Johnson's shortcomings merely aggravated the difficulty. A second observation centers on the revisionists' accentuation of the role of an individual, Andrew Johnson, in explaining the failure of 1865. This is to reduce a massive problem involving the institutions and very nature of American society at its moment of greatest crisis to a matter of individual shortcoming. With this perspective the differences between the sections take on an air of unreality, for it is assumed that the give-and-take of pragmatic politics are operational. Not only does politics rarely work in that fashion, but, after a four-year war and about fifty years of sectional hostility, conditions and attitudes prevailed which made it even less likely to do so. To focus attention, then, on an individual and his deficiencies as the reason why the customary procedures did not succeed (the implied assumption being that normally they do) is to oversimplify a complex problem, to blame individuals for institutional and even societal shortcomings, and to suggest that American society and its political system had not broken down fundamentally in the 1860s. Ironically, it was because Andrew Johnson and vast numbers of influential men in the North also felt that nothing much had happened as a result of the war that they pursued the conciliatory policies they did and believed the status quo ante bellum was the only basis on which reunion could be accomplished. Actually many of the revisionists have concurred in these assumptions and have therefore taken Johnson to task not because he was out of touch with political reality so much as because he was not a sufficiently astute political operator.

But the most important reason why the revisionists' analysis is inadequate as well as erroneous is that it does not take into consideration the attitude of the Confederates towards Washington's policies. Yet the Confederates were crucial to the success of any sectional settlement. By not taking into account their needs and interests, discussion of the possibility of a settlement on moderate terms is unreal and speculative. Debate over what might have been, a dubious exercise at the best of times, becomes even more so because of this oversight. Curiously, very little attention and detailed examination has been given to the Confederates by historians of Reconstruction whether of the revisionist or of the pro-Southern schools. The latter did sympathize with the white Southern predicament in the Reconstruction period but they accepted as given the reasonableness and the merit of their response to it. Neither they nor the revisionists went beyond this to scrutinize carefully the political calculations and strategies involved in the maneuvers of the Southern leaders during the crucial period from 1865 until 1868 when Washington was devising its terms for readmission and reunion.

The purpose of this book is to introduce and delineate this vital aspect of the problem. Discussion of the possibilities for an intersectional compromise, whether in 1865 or at any other time before the South was readmitted, is speculative unless the needs and interests, the assumptions and goals, of the Confederates are known and taken into account. And it is my contention that, unless the South's leaders were coerced and their wishes and inclinations countered, the prerequisites of the men who led that section and with whom terms would have to be arranged were such that no settlement or compromise such as the revisionists envisaged was possible. Moreover, with the option of consent or rejection continually held out to them, the legitimacy of their resistance was established and, contrary to the assumptions of its proponents, this approach provided a disincentive rather than encouragement for the Confederates to comply and thus reciprocate Northern conciliatoriness. Therefore it mattered little how well or how inadequately such policies were implemented; their assumptions were erroneous and flawed.

Conciliation presupposed a disposition or ability on the Confederates' part to concede and compromise. To some extent this was possible for the Southern leadership did yield on a number of points in 1865, but, beyond these, concession was regarded as capitulation and consequently beyond consideration. For the essential differences between the leaders both of the Republican Party and of the South could not be submitted to negotiation; they could not be reconciled. Therefore the persistent attempt to produce terms and requirements to which the Confederates could agree, or rather yield a voluntary assent, was bound to be a waste of energy. Reasonable, moderate, well-intentioned men might try but they were obstinately ignoring reality. The South's rulers, although militarily defeated, economically ruined and politically vulnerable, were not a negligible force, nor were they prepared to ignore their vital interests in pursuit of reunion at any cost. In fact their predicament made them less malleable, not more. Thus, for the Federal government to cover the mailed fist with a velvet glove was not to exhibit statesmanship but to concede the whole issue. And against the warnings of the radicals, this was what it did.

I
Defiant optimism

a: *The South under Northern scrutiny*

'The most important feature attending the regeneration of these States is the temper and disposition of the Southern people.'[1] This was the conclusion of a *Chicago Tribune* editorial published on 26 April 1865. But although the *Tribune* was a newspaper associated with the radical wing of the Republican Party, this observation corresponded with the assumptions and priorities of a broad spectrum of Northern opinion-makers and politicians in the early days after Appomattox. It was generally agreed that before proposals could be formulated for dealing with the Confederate States, the attitudes and feelings prevailing there had to be known. Thereby a policy based on evidence rather than ignorance could be devised, with a greater hope that it might eventually succeed. Implicit in the *Tribune*'s comment and in this general approach was a second assumption: that, if possible, the leaders of the Confederacy should be involved in the intersectional adjustment. Terms would be proposed to which the former Confederates would give their assent and compliance; no matter whether the details were harsh or lenient, settlement would not be long-lasting or even possible, it was felt, if the South's leaders were bypassed.

Some in the North hoped with Horace Greeley and his *New York Tribune* that they could make an 'Appeal to the statesmen of the South.' 'You, surely, must realize,' he warned them in June 1865, 'that great changes are at all events inevitable – make them so that they shall seem dictated by your own sense of fitness, not conceded to an unwelcome necessity.'[2] Others were not so sure that this sort of approach was realistic and felt that pressure and persuasion would have to be exerted more forcibly. No one however was fully informed of the Confederates' feelings or of the state of affairs in the South, and so there was a compulsion to find out, to know as precisely as possible, the real mood of the defeated South.

[1] Editorial, *Chicago Tribune*, 26 April 1865.
[2] Editorial, *New York Tribune*, 20 June 1865.

13

In response to this need, there flocked to the war-torn region, behind the Confederate battle-lines, a host of newspaper reporters, special correspondents, and other fact-finding emissaries. Unlike the Treasury's cotton agents or the Federal soldiers, they came, not to tax and police the South, but to observe, analyze, and assess Southern feelings. This procession of commentators and observers was to continue throughout the first two or three years of Reconstruction and even beyond into the 1870s. But the initial weeks after the surrender of the main Confederate armies and the fall of Richmond were the most crucial because it would be on the basis of this evidence that the first post-war overture from the conqueror in the Northern States would be formulated, and this, and the Southern response to it, would considerably influence the tone and future course of relations between the two sections.

Of course this whole problem could have been avoided, or at least could have caused less anxiety, if a mandatory settlement enforced by an occupying army had been imposed upon the South, without concern for the cooperation or evidences of loyalty from the Confederates, a mandatory settlement which would be enforced as the edict of the conqueror and implemented by its occupying military forces. This might have involved the exclusion from power of the Confederacy's political élite for a number of years, suffrage for the freedmen, the division of confiscated and abandoned lands for distribution to the freedmen, and other measures capable of effecting and enforcing a reconstruction of the Southern States. Moreover, the South was powerless to resist: Federal troops were in occupation and Southern armies were being disbanded; the South's agriculture was in disarray and its labor force freed and uprooted; and finally its people were exhausted by war. The South could only succumb to what the North demanded. But that was not the course taken; and only a handful of Northerners even considered it.

Instead the Confederates were to be involved and to participate in post-war reunion and reconstruction. And so the attempt to discover their state of mind had to be made. Yet what would the evidence and data collected by the commentators who traveled in the Confederacy mean? What was the relation between it and the policy to be undertaken? Here lay the dilemma of a post-war settlement based on a mixture of coercion and conciliation, of reunion and reconstruction. For the knowledge of Southern feelings could be inconclusive, even if it were accurate. Furthermore, observations about the mood of the

South could not be isolated and detached from the policy towards that section which the observer already preferred and anticipated and on the basis of which he had carried out his survey.

That the evidence could be inconclusive was apparent when, in the light of what they had learned, policy-makers considered the nature of their response to it. After being informed that the South's mood was one of, let us say, defiance, disloyalty and truculence towards Federal authority, should they then formulate harsh or lenient, coercive or conciliatory, terms? Either alternative would be logical. Harsh and coercive terms could be the only way to chastise and counteract defiance, but equally generosity and appeasement might well transform hostility into gratitude and cooperation. On the other hand, if Southerners were found to be reconciled to Northern power and gave evidence of loyalty and repentence, then once again more than one course of action was possible. Conciliatoriness could be reciprocated on the grounds that if the South were loyal there was then no need to be punitive and severe, or, alternatively, the opposite course could be applied and advantage be taken of Southern malleability so that exacting terms could be required without fear of a truculent reaction or a lapse into sullenness.

This conundrum was best exemplified in the first-hand observations gleaned by Chief Justice Salmon P. Chase and General John M. Schofield and in the Southern policies advocated by each. Chase had sailed to the coastal ports of the South at the request of the new President only a few weeks after Johnson had acceded to the office. In his first dispatch to the White House, written on 7 May from Beaufort, N.C., Chase observed:

All seem embarrassed about first steps. I do not entertain the slightest doubt that they would all welcome some simple recommendation from yourself, and would adopt readily any plan which you would suggest. They would receive, without resistance from any and with real joy in many hearts, an order for the enrollment of all loyal citizens without regard to complexion with a view to reorganization. This would be regarded by all not as an interference but a fatality so far as the order should relate to enrollment of whites, and with almost universal acquiescence by the best citizens, in its whole scope.[3]

[3] Chase to Johnson, Beaufort, N.C., 7 May 1865, Johnson MSS, Series I. The details and significance of Chase's correspondence with both Lincoln and Johnson over reconstruction is discussed by James Sefton in 'Chief Justice Chase as

This acquiescence and submissiveness which Chase noted throughout his tour was also detected by Schofield who was based in North Carolina. On 5 May he wrote from Raleigh:

I hope the Government will make known its policy as to the organs of State government without delay. Affairs must necessarily be in a very unsettled state until that is done. The people are now in a mood to accept almost any thing which promises a definite settlement. 'What is to be done with the freedmen?' is the question of all, and it is the all-important question.[4]

Agreed though they were on the general state of feeling in the South, their recommendations as to the appropriate steps to be taken in view of this were markedly different. For Chase, a submissive South provided the possibility for implementing Negro suffrage and producing a loyal electorate. 'Equal rights,' a radical proposal in the spring of 1865, was Chase's aim and it could be accomplished without disturbing State sovereignty or producing a resentful reaction since Southerners appeared to be compliant and cooperative. With the same opinions about the South, Schofield concluded that this was sufficient proof that punitive terms for the white South such as Chase suggested were not necessary. He told Grant in May that a policy similar to that later enunciated by Andrew Johnson was all that was necessary. A provisional Governor, who would be the Federal general in command, would be appointed for each State; he would prepare the State for a convention, appoint interim State officials, and enroll voters able to take Lincoln's oath of allegiance. Then, said Schofield, 'I would expect a convention, so chosen, to repudiate the doctrine of secession, abolish slavery, and fully restore the State to its practical constitutional relations to the Government of the United States. The people are now ripe for such action. They only ask to know what the government desires them to do, and how they are to do it.'[5]

an Advisor on Presidential Reconstruction, *Civil War History*, September 1967, pp. 242–64.
[4] Schofield to Sherman, Raleigh, 5 May 1865, in W. T. Sherman, *Personal Memoirs of General W. T. Sherman* (2 vols.; New York: Charles Webster and Co., 1892), pp. 356–7.
[5] Schofield to Grant, Raleigh, 10 May 1865, in J. M. Schofield, *Forty-six Years in the Army* (New York: The Century Co., 1897), pp. 373–6. Schofield added that if these stipulations were not met, he would 'regard them as having violated their oaths, would dissolve the convention, and hold the State under military government until the people shall come to their senses.' And here he would have differed from the practice of the President in his policy, for Johnson was not

To Schofield and Chase the Southern people appeared submissive and would accept whatever demands were made firmly and speedily by the North. But their policies and their intentions differed markedly. There was a considerable difference between abolishing slavery and enfranchising the freedmen, yet each man felt opinion was amenable to either possibility. Analysis of the South could be used for whatever policy the observer needed or desired. And both Chase and Schofield had general lines of policy in mind that were characteristic of their customary and reputed viewpoints, the one radical, the other conservative or at the most moderate. So possibly it could be said that the state of the South was almost incidental as a causative factor in policymaking and was instead only a pretext or justification for a previously adopted preference. Perhaps the *New York Tribune* was being penetratingly frank when it observed in August that 'There is a good deal of rambling discussion in the journals of the day respecting the spirit in which the South accepts the result of our late contest. As it is easy to find isolated facts that make for whichever side you may wish to uphold, this sort of controversy may go on interminably.'[6]

A further remark ought to be made at this point regarding the utilization of Southern analysis for justifying pre-selected policies, for the whole enterprise was even more misleading than it already appears. While Schofield and Chase disagreed about the appropriate and preferable policy for the South, perhaps they also disagreed in fact about what they seem to have been in agreement upon. Both considered the Southern people submissive and acquiescent yet possibly their respective use of those words was distinctive. For the degree of submissiveness that Chase required was very much more than Schofield needed. If the South were sufficiently submissive to accept only Schofield's terms, then Chase would not regard that as being submissive at all. So, further complicating the issue was the likelihood that the adjectives and terminology used to describe Southern feelings would be differently understood by different individuals. What did terms like 'loyal,' 'repentant,' 'whipped,' 'submissive,' and their antonyms mean as descriptions of Southern white psychology in the wake of defeat?

In Salmon P. Chase's case, however, there was less debate over accuracy and meaning than in most reports from the South in these early months. For Chase had indicated in numerous letters before he set out

prepared to repudiate his initial policy if it did not produce the required response in the South.
[6]Editorial, *New York Tribune*, 21 August 1865.

for the South Atlantic States that he was determined on Negro suffrage as a prerequisite in Southern reorganization and had made suggestions along these lines to Lincoln as well as Johnson. It was obvious
that the Chief Justice counted on his trip to produce evidence which
could influence the President and facilitate his own predetermined
policy. Early in May, he was informing the President that what he had
suggested to Lincoln on 11 April and to Johnson in the days before
leaving for the South was possible in view of his observation of Southerners and his conversations with them. Yet he had only met a few
Virginia politicians and had not so far set foot on North Carolina soil.[7]
His proposed policy was, he felt, intrinsically sound and effective, and
therefore a compliant mood on the South's part was simply additional
justification, rather than a precondition for moving toward its implementation.

This was a radical proposal, involving mandatory Negro suffrage
and probably a narrow definition of Confederate loyalty, though
Chase was not at all precise on this point. Traveling with Chase to the
South was another Republican who was also radical, Whitelaw Reid
of the *Cincinnati Gazette*, who throughout the voyage was sending dispatches to his paper describing conditions in the South. Reid's analysis
of the state of the South prior to the announcement of the President's
policy matched Chase's a priori assumptions. Yet because none of his
dispatches were written until after 29 May when the President's policy was officially announced in the form of two proclamations, one
defining amnesty, the other describing the manner of Southern reorganization, they were influenced also by the effect which Reid felt the
proclamations had had on the Southern mood. The drift of Reid's
conclusions were that

the National Government could at that time [before 29 May] have prescribed no conditions for the return of the Rebel States which they would

---

[7]Chase to Lincoln, Baltimore, 11 April 1865, J. M. Schofield MSS, where the
Chief Justice suggested that the Pierpont government-in-exile be recognized as
the post-war government for Virginia, and added 'it is not to be doubted that,
on a suggestion from the National authorities, that [the suffrage's] extension
to colored citizens on equal terms with white citizens, is believed to be essential
to the future tranquility of the country as well as just in itself, the Legislature will
promptly act in the desired direction.' Loyalty without distinction of color was
the condition for suffrage rights, and this was reiterated in dispatches from
Beaufort, N. C., on 4 and 7 May 1865, both in Johnson MSS, Series I. Chase
did not specify his definition of loyalty though presumably it would have been
at least as restrictive as Johnson's later amnesty proclamation of 29 May.

not have promptly accepted. They expected nothing; were prepared for the worst; would have been thankful for anything.

In North and South Carolina, Georgia and Florida, we found this state of feeling universally prevalent. The people wanted civil government and a settlement. They asked no terms, made no conditions. They were defeated and helpless – they submitted. Would the victors be pleased to tell them what was to be done? Point out any way for a return to an established mode of things, and they would walk in it. They made no hypocritical professions of new-born Unionism. They had honestly believed in the right of secession. The hatred of Yankees, which had originally aided the conspirators in starting the movement, had grown and strengthened with the war. Neither the constitutional theory nor the personal hate of their lives could be changed in a day, but both alike were impotent; and having been forced to abandon the war, they hoped for the blessing which any peace on any terms might be expected to bring in its train. . . . The whole body politic was as wax. It needed but a firm hand to apply the seal.[8]

But after the North Carolina proclamation, the tenor of Southern feelings began to change, said Reid, until 'By the time we reached New Orleans the change was complete; the reaction had set in.'[9]

Reid's interpretation of the Southern mood and how it had become truculent and non-cooperative as a result of the conciliatory plan outlined by the President was widely accepted by others who followed Reid to the South and who later wrote books about their experiences. Although he had not been in the South before the May proclamations, John Richard Dennett, the young Harvard Law School graduate who was a roving Southern correspondent for *The Nation* from July 1865 to March 1866, believed that 'Then, better than at any other time, the North might have reaped the fruits of war. Even universal suffrage the Southern people would have accepted. Not willingly, more unwillingly, probably, than they accepted the Constitutional Amendment abolishing slavery, but with far less resistance than would be opposed to it now.'[10] Also reiterating Reid's conclusions was John

---

[8]Whitelaw Reid, *After the War: A Tour of the Southern States, 1865–1866* (Torchbook edition; New York: Harper and Row [1866], 1965), pp. 296–7. Reid published his book in June 1866 after three trips to the South, in April, May and June 1865, the fall of 1865, and again in early 1866. His dispatches were printed in the *Cincinnati Gazette* throughout these visits under the pseudonym of 'Agate.'

[9]*Ibid.*, p. 297.

[10]John Richard Dennett, *The South As It Is: 1865–1866*, ed. Harry M. Christman (New York: Viking Press [1866], 1967), p. 360. Dennett's reports appeared in the *Nation* during the fall of 1865.

T. Trowbridge who after a long book full of instances of Southern assertiveness and non-cooperation, concluded: 'At the close of the war, the South was ready to accept any terms which the victorious government might have seen fit to enforce. The ground was thoroughly broken; it was fresh from the harrow; and then was the time for the sowing of the new seed, before delay had given encouragement and opportunity to the rank old weeds.[11] Yet Trowbridge admitted the limitations on this mood of compliance when he observed that 'The loyalty of the people is generally of a negative sort: it is simply disloyalty subdued.'[12]

This assessment, with minor variations and qualifications, became the generally accepted view of radical Republicans and Southern Unionists who opposed the reinstatement of the ruling Confederates which resulted from Johnson's policy. Charles Sumner accepted this when he asserted during July that 'Two months ago the whole South was ready to accept the *rule of Justice*, prescribed by the Declaration of Independence. Now it is perverse, recalcitrant and rebellious.'[13] So did J. J. Giers, an Alabama Unionist, when he testified before the Joint Committee on Reconstruction in January 1866. In terms which were similar to most of the Southern Unionist testimony at the Committee's hearings, he said, 'At the time of the surrender I found the people entirely willing to submit to anything and to everything. . . . If I give the cause of the change in feeling I would blame the President. . . . He has been deceived. . . . I think it has been the mistaken policy of appointing men not loyal that has produced the change in public sentiment.'[14] All the same, nine months earlier, on 14 May 1865, Giers was telling Andrew Johnson that 'The rebellion is crushed, it is true, but I find no change in the sentiments of the people. The old Union people can now avow their sentiments more openly, it is true, but the Secessionists are as bitter and hostile against the Government as ever. If the army were removed today, no Union man would be safe in the counties farther South [of Decatur], nor in many parts

[11] John T. Trowbridge, *A Picture of the Desolated States and the Work of Restoration, 1865–1868* (Hartford, Conn.: L. Stebbins, 1868), p. 584. Trowbridge first published his work in the early summer of 1866. It was then updated and supplemented with the events of 1867 and 1868, and subsequently republished.

[12] *Ibid.*, p. 584.

[13] Sumner to McCulloch, Boston, 12 July 1865, McCulloch MSS.

[14] J. J. Giers, Testimony, *Report of the Joint Committee on Reconstruction* (Washington, D.C.: Government Printing Office, 1866), Part III, p. 15.

of the Country farther North.'[15]

The discrepancy cannot be explained simply by asserting that Giers was a liar, but rather by admitting that not only was the mood of the South a very elusive and subtle subject-matter to assess accurately but also that assessment was very much intertwined with the intended policy and prior assumptions of the observer. Perhaps no clear indication of Southern feelings could be obtained until after specific proposals had been formulated and a Southern response to them had manifested itself. But even then contradictory conclusions as to the policy appropriate in the light of this new evidence could be drawn. So, little that was beneficial and helpful could be gained from studying the Southern mood and trying to base policy upon it. Yet the opposite was in fact the assumption that all policy-makers made. In spite of all the concern about discovering how the Southerners responded to their defeat and to the proposal of Northern terms, the evidence that was culled was used to justify a line of policy already espoused or embarked upon rather than vice versa.

Nevertheless, few in the North were prepared to act upon this in a ruthlessly logical fashion. Few were willing to ignore the feelings of those with political power and influence in the Confederate States and instead to advocate a mandatory and enforced set of stringent peace terms for the South. Even Chase who was in favor of a mandatory Negro suffrage was also amenable to recognizing State sovereignty and accommodating the former Confederates' avowals 'that they would *prefer* to have the reorganization in their own hands and those of *their friends*. . . .'[16] So if the Confederates were to be included and involved in the process of reconstruction, their attitudes could not be neglected. Consequently the elusive search had to continue.

Although beset by all the difficulties already suggested, an attempt can be made to arrive at some sort of generalization about the Southern temper after the war. Among the advocates of a firm, if not punitive, policy toward the South, that is to say, among the radical wing of the Republican Party, the view of Reid and Chase and of many others was that the South was compliant just after the war, and therefore the sort of policy they advocated could have been safely implemented. Yet there is far more evidence from the same source, that is, the radical Republicans, that the South was very far from acquiescent. Newspaper reporters from the *Chicago Tribune*, the *Cincinnati Gazette* and the *New*

[15]J. J. Giers to Johnson, Decatur, Ala., 14 May 1865, Johnson MSS, Series I.
[16]Chase to Johnson, Beaufort, N.C., 4 May 1865, Johnson MSS, Series I.

York Tribune, who were in the Southern States before June and whose acquaintance with the situation was far more thorough than Reid's and Chase's (and of course they cannot be compared with Dennett's and Trowbridge's since the latter were not in the South until the summer), revealed a very different state of affairs. Reid's paper, the *Gazette*, had a particularly strong contingent of reporters – 'H.V.N.B.,' 'S. R. Pierce,' 'Occasional,' 'D. S.,' 'Y. S.,' and 'Quill' – and all agreed that the Southern whites, the Confederates especially, were defiant and unsubdued in the weeks between Appomattox and 29 May.

A perceptive report, submitted by 'H.V.N.B.' from Richmond in early June, observed that 'With the exception of the younger class of hot-headed rebels, the external conduct of all is proper, and shows an outward respect for authority. But underneath this calm, society is seething and boiling, as if a volcano were struggling beneath it. All here is chaos, and designing politicians are very busy with schemes to save all that can be saved of the old order of things. Everything looks as if the South had only laid down the sword and rifle as weapons, and changed the fighting ground to the political arena.'[17] Something similar was discerned by a Southern report reprinted in the *Chicago Tribune* on 2 May: 'The moral power of the rebellion is not evinced in any public demonstration, but is manifested privately, or under such circumstances as will not incur the displeasure of the authorities.'[18] Submission there might be but it was a mask. 'Quill,' however, did encounter overt signs of resentment and truculence. In Brunswick County, Virginia, he noted, 'I cannot consume space in recounting expressions showing an ineradicable hostility to the North.' Submission was evident to the extent that 'they "supposed" they were whipped, or General Lee would not have surrendered.' Of Warrenton, North Carolina, all 'Quill' could say was that 'it was a pestiferous hive of implacable disloyalists.'[19]

Most correspondents, however, perceived the situation in the same way as 'H.V.N.B.' 'E.S.' wrote from Raleigh, 'The *spirit* of the Rebellion is not broken though its power is demolished.'[20] A *New York Herald* correspondent who had toured all the Southeastern States con-

[17]'H.V.N.B.,' Richmond, Va., 13 June 1865, *Cincinnati Gazette*, 17 June 1865.
[18]Correspondence from the South, *Philadelphia Press*, 24 April 1865, cited in the *Chicago Tribune*, 2 May 1865.
[19]'Quill,' in the rear of Sherman's army, Richmond, Va., 10 May 1865, *Cincinnati Gazette*, 18 May 1865.
[20]'E.S.,' Raleigh, N.C., 20 April 1865, *New York Tribune*, 2 May 1865.

cluded in July that the South's submission had so many conditions attached that it was in fact not submission at all. Southerners would in effect announce conditions:

We are whipped, subjugated – anything you please – and never want to see or hear of a soldier again. All we want is a chance to be quiet, and to make a living for ourselves and families. If you see fit to punish us for our past sins we shall be obliged to submit; but, on the other hand, if you wish us to love and cherish the old flag again, and feel that the Union is a blessing, treat us leniently.[21]

On occasion Southern Unionist newspapers would propound similarly critical analyses of the reality of Southern submissiveness. In November, the *North Carolina Standard*, Provisional Governor William W. Holden's paper, commented:

We agree with our contemporary [the *Raleigh Progress*] that there is much disloyalty in the South, but we do not agree that there is more now than there was six months ago; it has been here all the time, but, a few months ago it crouched and snivelled at the feet of the victorious national forces, and now, as leniency and mercy has warmed it into life and the troops have been withdrawn, treason becomes bold and defiant.[22]

A final caution as to the reality of Southern acquiescence was offered by 'E.S.' of the *New York Tribune*. When he heard of Salmon P. Chase's upcoming tour of inspection he sent off a hasty dispatch from Raleigh to his editorial office, warning the Chief Justice that

The temper of the masses in North Carolina is, as yet, unchanged; and as to their aristocratic and Rebel class *par excellence*, they are as haughty, exacting, unsubdued, and, if possible, *more* devilish than they ever were.

One would think we were the subjugated and conquered people, and not the Rebels. They act as if the surrender of Lee and Johnston were made merely to accommodate us – not from necessity; and that they were entitled to particular considerations therefor. I caution you not to take one-half you hear from this quarter touching the fast returning spirit of loyalty, as genuine. . . .[23]

---

[21] *New York Herald* correspondent, Mississippi, 23 July 1865, cited in *Augusta Constitutionalist*, 3 August 1865.

[22] Editorial, *North Carolina Standard*, 18 November 1865. Holden was President Johnson's appointee as Provisional Governor of North Carolina under the Presidential policy announced in May 1865.

[23] 'E.S.,' Raleigh, N.C., 8 May 1865, *New York Tribune*, 13 May 1865.

An awareness of the superficiality and duplicity of the Southern whites' avowal of submission was not missing on Whitelaw Reid either, though he did not apparently feel that this necessitated an alteration of the thesis of his book. On one occasion in the book he had observed that

Little change in the actual Unionism of the people could be seen since the surrender. In the year that had intervened, they had grown bolder as they had come to realize the lengths to which they might safely go. They were 'loyal' in May 1865, in the sense of enforced submission to the Government, and they are loyal in the same sense in May, 1866. At neither time has the loyalty of the most had any wider meaning.[24]

Yet on 31 July 1865 he had sent a report to the *Gazette* in which he admitted:

Whoever has attentively watched manifestations of Southern spirit since the surrender of Johnston's army, needs no argument to be convinced of the truth which, indeed, they themselves, perpetually boast of, that they submitted only because they were overpowered. Their views of the right of the white man to make the negro work for him, were not changed, they were merely overpowered.

We were charitable enough to suppose that being subdued they were at once ready to become good citizens of the Union again. But leopards do not change their spots in a night. . . .[25]

What all of these vignettes of the South's state of mind amount to is the conclusion that very few Republicans of a moderate to radical persuasion who were in the Confederate States immediately after the war believed that the leadership of that section was sufficiently subdued and cooperative to be entrusted with self-government and a mandatory Negro suffrage. The evidence that this feeling really existed in the South, provided mainly by Reid and Chase, is weak indeed. By contrast there is a greater quantity of first-hand evidence which points to the opposite conclusion. Needless to say this does not prove that Southerners were in actual fact unrepentant, untrustworthy, and uncooperative. All it does prove is that most radical or moderate Republicans who had personal experience of the South during the spring of 1865 felt they were. They agreed with the editors of the *Cincinnati*

[24]Reid, *After the War*, p. 578.
[25]'Agate,' Washington, D.C., 31 July 1865, *Cincinnati Gazette*, 3 August 1865.

Gazette in December 1865 that all the reports from the South demonstrated that nothing had changed in the Confederates' feeling toward the Union and Northerners; as far as the Confederates were concerned, all that had been effected by the war was 'that might had crushed right.'[26]

The announcement of Johnson's Southern policy had not therefore produced any great change in the South; it had simply provided the occasion for existing feelings to be manifested. If this were their response to a conciliatory policy like Johnson's, was it then reasonable to assume they would have felt constrained to accommodate to Chase's plan? The Washington correspondent of the *Cincinnati Gazette* would have replied along the lines of a dispatch of 15 December: 'It is true, as the radicals assert, that immediately after the occupation of Richmond, or even two months later, the coerced rebels would have promised anything without a whimper, to be assured their lives only. But there is nothing to show that the promise would have found any support after the disappearance of the symbols of coercion.'[27]

Rather than effecting a change in Southern feelings towards the Federal government, it is more than likely that there was a continuity in the mood prevailing within the Confederacy. The President's announced policy merely provided the catalyst for it to emerge. For whatever the North's policy, once it was known, those sentiments which the newspaper reporters had observed would come welling to the surface.

b: *Southerners consider their own situation*

Appomattox and Durham Station left the Confederate South in 'a state where apathy alternates with despair' as the impact of the 'aggregated calamities of a century overwhelmed the inhabitants of the defeated and ravaged section.'[28] Confronted by a recent past which had brought the decimation of families, the destruction of farms, the burning of cities, the liberation of slaves, and the loss of a war, the Confederates now faced a future in which they had to attempt the almost impossible task of rebuilding what was destroyed with a labor force that they were all convinced would not work except by compulsion. To some, the humiliation and hopelessness of their situation suggested

[26] Editorial, *Cincinnati Gazette*, 23 December 1865.
[27] Washington correspondence, 15 December 1865, *Cincinnati Gazette*, 23 December 1865.
[28] Editorial, *Augusta Constitutionalist*, 30 May 1865.

the advisability of their leaving for Mexico, or Europe, or Brazil, where slavery still existed; for others, the woeful situation led them away from public life into seclusion where they could nurse their grief in private. But for most who remained, the reaction of William F. DeSaussure, a secessionist from Columbia, South Carolina, was typical, mixing as it did regretful capitulation with positive resolve. In July 1865, DeSaussure confided to his brother, 'I am beginning to realize that we are a subjugated race, and sometimes my spirit sinks within me. But we must not give way to this, or our Country is undone for a century, perhaps forever. . . . The contest is over, we are subdued, and I am for submitting in good faith to the result.'[29]

Without functioning governments and without leadership, most Southern whites were unsure what to do, or how and in what direction to channel their interests and energies. Into this vacuum stepped the newspapers, the *Augusta Constitutionalist* explaining this initiative in terms of responsibility and restitution since 'The press of this country did much to get them into trouble, and should spare no effort to get them out.'[30] Their line of approach corresponded with DeSaussure's, the gist being 'Accept the situation and make the best of it!' And it was most clearly summarized by the *Houston Telegraph* when, after a series of vitriolic editorials, it suggested that 'To accept and make the most of the inevitable tendency of things will be far better than blindly to kick against fate or to elapse [*sic*] into despondency at the death and burial of all previous political hopes.'[31]

A futile angry resistance to the fact of defeat or a collapse into inert passivity were equally pernicious according to the *Telegraph*, but that did not imply that unqualified and fawning submission was the only alternative. Acceptance of the situation and turning it to the South's advantage was far from weak-kneed capitulation. During May, the *Constitutionalist* continually reminded its readers of this. On one occasion it offered the reassurance that 'It is neither unwise or unmanly thus to acquiesce in the logic of existing facts, and thus cheerfully pursue the only path left to regain the position lost to us by the fortunes of

[29]William F. DeSaussure to H. W. DeSaussure, Columbia, S.C., 23 July 1865, H. W. DeSaussure MSS. The phrase 'our Country' refers, of course, to the Confederate States, the South.
[30]Editorial, *Augusta Constitutionalist*, 30 May 1865.
[31]Editorial, *Houston Telegraph*, 30 May 1865. This was written before news of the President's Proclamations had reached Texas.

war.'[32] And on another, when a recent Presidential speech had indicated hostility to the South, it exhorted its readers, 'Countrymen of the South! Let us not be spaniels. Though overwhelmed, we have not been dishonored; though overpowered, we have not been silenced; though surrendered, we have not lost the right of protest. Let us cling to each other in this evil hour – and the unanimous protest of a nation in chains will reach with its hoarse murmur even to the throne of Andrew Johnson.'[33]

A stance was to be adopted which presented in public a mood of acquiescence; rejecting both defiance and resigned submission, this posture was nonetheless to involve alertness to the necessity of defending the South from what it regarded as unreasonable demands as well as to the urgency of keeping the section united in its relations with the Northern foe. This line of approach would simultaneously achieve two very basic goals which the South's leaders had to effect if they were to remain in power in the wake of defeat. It would disarm the North and encourage it to experiment with conciliatory policies and at the same time it would prevent differences of opinion and interest from emerging in the South which would enable opposition to the Confederate leaders to burst forth and which in turn Northern policy-makers could exploit.

Agreement on a policy of guarded and responsible acquiescence would enable the Southern leadership to retain its hold on power and deny the North a lever which, if available, could be used to punish the instigators and perpetrators of rebellion. So, for internal reasons, acquiescence could be invoked by the *Constitutionalist* when on 20 May it conceded: 'There may be bitter terms, and an alternative that we never apprehended, but better any condition above that of abject slavery, than a state of society torn by contending factions, rent by partisan interests, and, above all, subject to the tyranny of this and that guerilla [*sic*] chief.'[34] And, for external considerations, there was also justification as when the same paper excused its refusal to publish letters on political questions with the argument: 'We are under military rule, which does not permit a very extensive freedom of expression. Our true

---

[32] Editorial, *Augusta Constitutionalist*, 17 May 1865.
[33] *Ibid.*, 5 May 1865. The speech was given to a delegation from Illinois in April 1865. The *Constitutionalist* felt that the speech was misleading and lacking in frankness because it contained traces of hostility as well as conciliation toward the South.
[34] Editorial, *Augusta Constitutionalist*, 20 May 1865.

course at present is to urge unity of feeling and cheerful acquiescence in all measures of the administration, in order that we may regain and re-establish a civil government.'[35]

Through the newspapers a public position was being enunciated on the political situation facing the defeated South, and it was one which would enable the interests of the traditional rulers, in spite of their ignominious failure to win the war and achieve independence, to identify their own survival with that of the whole section. The fears of John A. Campbell, the Confederacy's Assistant Secretary of War, during March that leadership was not forthcoming were, by the war's end, being put to rest. On that earlier occasion, Campbell had confided to John C. Breckinridge, 'I do not regard reconstruction as involving destruction, unless our people should forget the incidents of their heroic struggle and become debased and degraded. It is the duty of their statesmen and patriots to guard them in the future with even more care and tenderness than they have done in the past.'[36]

Submission and acquiescence in the powers-that-be became a widely adopted stance in the South during the months after the surrender. Unconditional and passive it certainly was not; instead it was resolute and proud, a policy geared to withstand Northern blandishments and resist terms which were considered dishonorable and humiliating as well as to prevent irresponsible and divisive reactions within the South. Along with this avowal of submission it was widely admitted throughout the former Confederacy that they were 'whipped.' Northern observers continually reported the use of this phrase, and its repetition was a marked feature which, because of its indignity, needs explanation. Soldiers frequently admitted to being 'whipped.' On the part of enlisted men who had been forced to fight in a cause that was not their own, this was perhaps a way of indicating their superior officers; and for the officers themselves, because the whipping was usually attributed to the greater numbers rather than skill of the enemy, it offered an excuse and a gratification to martial pride. But this phrase came to be employed by civilians as well; all, it appeared, agreed they were 'whipped.' General John W. Turner was not convinced of the genuineness of the sentiment. When testifying before the Joint Committee on reconstruction, he explained that 'They would say to me,

[35] Editorial, *Augusta Constitutionalist*, 28 May 1865.
[36] Campbell to J. C. Breckinridge, Richmond, Va., 5 March 1865, Groner Collection.

"Well, you have conquered us: we are whipped." Now, I think if a man of generous soul felt deep mortification he would keep quiet on the subject. I have always thought that their feeling of mortification was more superficial than otherwise.'[37]

To admit to being whipped hardly meant an admission of guilt and of total surrender. In fact, such a recognition of defeat when volunteered so freely and with so little repentance may very likely have been part of the strategy of acquiescence which it was hoped would culminate in a Northern realization that the South admitted defeat, had no intention of, or means for, renewing the conflict, and therefore could be treated with leniency. That this was intended by Southerners who avowed their submission and defeat was betrayed by an up-country Senator from North Carolina whom Chief Justice Chase and his party met in Beaufort. After inquiring about sentiment in his State, whereupon he admitted that all felt whipped, one interviewer asked:

'Then they really feel themselves whipped?' 'Yes, you've subjugated us at last,' with a smile which showed that the politician thought it not the worst kind of a joke, after all.

'And, of course, then you have only to submit to any terms the conquerors may impose?' 'No, sir – oh, ah – yes, any terms that could be honorably offered to a proud, high-minded people!'[38]

'Whipped' the Southern armies may have been, but 'whipped' the Southern mind and will were not.

Moreover, on many other grounds, it was very clear that the vocalization of sentiments recognizing defeat and avowing submission had as its intent not capitulation to, but the avoidance of, harsh terms. After admitting that 'Submission with what grace we may is all that is left to us,' the *Houston Telegraph*, on one occasion, proceeded to define submission. 'If submission is made to mean reconstruction on honorable terms,' wrote the editor, 'we may still live and flourish upon this soil as a political power, and a strong support to the United States,' but should the terms be crushing and ruinous, that is to say, unacceptable, then there would be no alternative but emigration. In the same editorial, the *Telegraph* also discussed the meaning of defeat and being whipped: 'It has been left to the wager of battle – we are defeated –

---

[37] Gen. J. W. Turner, testimony, *Report of the Joint Committee on Reconstruction*, Part II, p. 6.
[38] Reid, *After the War*, p. 24.

and that decides the matter, but involves us in no real guilt. We yield the question, and claim as a right, "life, liberty, and the pursuit of happiness."'[39]

Submission was therefore tactical rather than heart-felt, and it was conditional. The conditions could be summarized under four heads, and the first of these was the one indicated by the *Telegraph*. The South, although defeated, still possessed rights and could not rejoin the United States if the guarantees provided by the Union in its Constitution were not assured. This was an argument from principle and was based on the inviolability of contracts. The South, it was argued, had seceded because the Constitution was being infringed; therefore it could not submit again to its jurisdiction if the Constitution were not to be enforced and obeyed by those Northerners who had political and economic control within the nation. As Alexander H. H. Stuart of Virginia told an Augusta County meeting on 6 May, Virginia still had rights under the Constitution 'which have only been suspended during her abortive efforts to sever her connection with the United States.' Therefore Virginians 'should endeavor, as far as we can, to give shape and direction to our own destiny.' Besides, he argued, 'Those who advocate a policy merely passive, seem to act on the idea that we have lost all our rights and must accept such form of government as may be imposed on us. . . . A victorious party may have the *power* to impose an obnoxious form of government on its defeated adversary, but it by no means follows that it has the *right* to do so.'[40]

This argument, based on rights and constitutional principles, was usually advanced by those who had opposed secession in 1861, mostly Whigs, like Stuart, and who therefore argued that individuals, rather than States, had committed treason, the latter course being in fact constitutionally impossible. A few of the leading rebels could conceivably be punished but for the rest of the population of the Confederacy the end of the war involved no inferior status or vulnerability because the States had never left the Union. Only secessionists regarded the Confederacy as a separate nation and therefore as a belligerent, although even for some of them, as the example of the *Houston Telegraph* indicated, it was sometimes expedient to argue the contrary once the war was over.

[39] Editorial, *Houston Telegraph*, 29 May 1865.
[40] Alexander F. Robertson, *A. H. H. Stuart, 1807–1891* (Richmond, Va.: William Byrd Press Inc., 1925), pp. 228–9.

Consideration for the rights of the Confederates could be sought on grounds other than principle. A conciliatory policy would be expedient for the North to pursue because thereby better and more cooperative feelings would be engendered among the defeated and helpless Southerners, and consequently a fraternal and harmonious union of the sections might emerge out of the existing hostility and division. If the North had really fought to save the Union, then it would not only be in its interest, but it would be essential, to ensure that cooperation was the keystone of its post-war policies. Leading Confederates constantly called attention to the folly of harsh penalties and expressed confidence that Northern policy-makers would see where their real interest lay and formulate conciliatory and generous terms. Some even were so forward as to offer suggestions along these lines to the President while petitioning for pardon. Robert M. T. Hunter argued that since the 'restoration of the authority of the Union and the abolition of slavery' were 'established facts' there was no need to demand anything further either of Hunter himself or the South. And with regard to the section as a whole, he continued, 'Supposing them to have been mistaken in their convictions would it be politic or humane to punish them beyond what they have already suffered if there be no necessity to do so in order to maintain the Union and secure the authority of the General Government?' For, after all, 'Has not the spirit of resistance been crushed?'[41] Also advising magnanimity was Howell Cobb who urged on the President the wisdom of a course based on what he regarded as a truism. 'No man will doubt,' he wrote, 'that the man, who is received back into the Union, and feels, that he has been subject to no severe penalty, and has been required to submit to no humiliating test, will make a truer and better citizen, than the one who feels that his citizenship has been obtained by submitting to harsh and degrading terms, which he was compelled to yield to to secure the rights he has acquired.'[42]

On the occasions when this advice was proffered in public, it carried with it warnings, which could be viewed as threats, as to what would ensue if a policy of conciliation were not adopted. In late June after being paroled on the condition that he would work to produce a cooperative spirit in his own State, Joseph E. Brown published an open

---

[41] R. M. T. Hunter, petition for pardon, no date, 1865, Hunter–Garnett MSS.
[42] Cobb to Brig.-Gen. J. H. Wilson, 14 June 1865, forwarded to the President, Johnson MSS, Series I.

letter to the people of Georgia in which he reminded Northerners 'that they are sitting as judges in their own cause' and therefore if they wanted to 'restore unity, harmony and permanent prosperity' they 'must, while flushed with victory, exercise magnanimity to their fallen foes. . . . Otherwise, though held in the Union by force, they could not expect the people of the South and their posterity to meet them in future as friends and embrace them as fellow-citizens.'[43] The *Augusta Constitutionalist* was even more explicit in an editorial of 5 May which declared that 'an austere policy can only be productive of scowls, hatred, hypocrisy, perjury, rapine and a whole Iliad of woes.'[44] And from the *New Orleans Times*, there issued, on the day after Lincoln's death, an indictment of those in the North who 'have so little faith in their fellow-countrymen that we cannot entrust political privileges to those who bore arms against us.' These individuals, said the *Times*, 'had best retire to some other land, where petty-minded bigotry has a better chance for success.'[45] And this came, not from a secessionist paper, but from the organ of Louisiana's Free State Party, the instrumentality for Lincoln's war-time attempts to restore Louisiana to the Union.

There were two other arguments which were continually cited to demonstrate the wisdom and the necessity of a generous policy towards the South. General P. O. Hébert of Galveston pointed out the first of these when he told General Sherman that 'As an agricultural immensely producing country *the South is dead*—for a generation at least,' so 'Surely the most bitter and [un]forgiving at the North should be "satisfied."'[46] Rather than deserving or requiring punishment, the South was desperately in need of help in the form of Northern capital and a 'more reliable' labor force, and that meant white immigrants. Since the South was so impoverished, there was surely no occasion for further damaging the section by confiscation of lands or by continued collection of the cotton tax. Until the South revived, the financial gain from these activities would be paltry and the bitterness they would provoke would far outweigh whatever economic advantage accrued. Surely the Yankee's well-known and much despised economic priorities would be brought to bear on the problem; was it

[43] Joseph E. Brown, Open Letter to the People of Georgia, 29 June 1865, Johnson MSS, box 233.

[44] Editorial, *Augusta Constitutionalist*, 5 May 1865.

[45] Editorial, *New Orleans Times*, 16 April 1865.

[46] Gen. P. O. Hébert to Sherman, Alexandria, La., 8 July 1865, W. T. Sherman MSS.

possible that the North would allow its material self-interest to be overwhelmed by an outpouring of vengeance and hate and in the process the economic well-being of the entire Union be forfeited? The economic was only part of the Northern self-interest to which Southerners appealed and on which they relied. Howell Cobb, in that same letter to the President cited earlier, described Northern self-interest in broader terms. 'Looking to the future interests not only of the Southern people but of the whole country,' he wrote, 'it is desirable that the bitter animosities, which have been produced, should be softened as much as possible; and a devastated country restored, and as far, and as rapidly as practicable to comparative prosperity.' Magnanimity and generosity, 'not often, if ever found, in the hearts of conquerors,' would therefore fuse Northern self-interest, economic as well as political, with a noble moral impulse.[47] How could such a policy be overlooked?

A final consideration which Confederates were not slow to point out as evidence of the wisdom of a moderate Northern policy was that a program of reprisal and proscription, universally applied, would alienate those who were cooperative and drive them into the arms of the irreconcilables. After traversing the interior of South Carolina and observing that the people were orderly and correct in their determination to accept the situation and cooperate, William Lee Trenholm, son of the Confederate Secretary of the Treasury, pointed out that 'If the action of the government is such as to establish party lines, and to drive from the reconstruction ranks men who have heretofore had decided convictions and the honesty and boldness to own and maintain them, these men will be lost upon the side of reconciliation which they are now ready to support earnestly. . . . '[48] By such a policy the North would alienate the emerging sentiment of cooperation and acquiescence which alone could provide the thread for reuniting a harmonious Union.

All of these recommendations and suggestions about the nature of a wise and expedient peace were based upon the desperate need of the Southern rulers for a peace policy which respected the status quo and provided self-determination in the reestablishment of agencies and institutions of civil government. All that was required, suggested John

[47]Cobb to Gen. J. H. Wilson, 14 June 1865, Johnson MSS, Series I.
[48]William L. Trenholm to W. W. Boyce, Charleston, 4 June 1865, G. A. Trenholm MSS.

H. Reagan, the Confederate Postmaster-General, was that the North should 'consent to the existing condition of things, as those who opposed [the government] are compelled to do.'[49] Within these limits the South was indeed cooperative and acquiescent. But if the terms demanded rather than protected, interfered rather than disengaged, then Southerners felt no compunction to comply or cooperate. In that case, they argued, the intent of the North was not reunion and harmony and they were therefore not bound to act as if it were. The only Union which was acceptable to the South and to which they wished to be restored was one based upon sentiments and assumptions of harmony and mutual respect. As Alexander Stephens informed the President when applying for his pardon, 'The only force that should bind them or keep them in bonds should be that force that brought them together in the beginning – the law of attraction, affinity, attachment and devotion. This is the true principle of the strongest adhesion between States thus united.'[50]

If the Union of the States were to be restored, then union and harmony had to be the keynote. The North therefore had to jettison all its feelings of hostility to, and all its disputes of interest with, the South. Otherwise the South would withhold its assent from any kind of arrangement proposed. The spirit of acquiescence so much vaunted was heavily conditional, and the Confederates challenged the North to present terms which were satisfactory and, in the situation as they saw it, correct.

At times, in fact, Southern defiance was overt. Southern leaders absolved themselves of responsibility for what might result in the South if unsatisfactory terms were forced upon them. General Robert E. Lee, for example, told a *New York Herald* correspondent in April that 'should arbitrary or vindictive or revengeful policies be adopted, the end was not yet. There remained a great deal of vitality and strength in the South.'[51] To the same newspaperman General William T. Hardee offered the same explanation when he said: 'They will do it cheerfully [i.e. live peacefully with the North], provided your

---

[49]Reagan to Johnson, Fort Warren, Boston, Mass., 28 May 1865, in John H. Reagan, *Memoirs* (New York and Washington, D.C.: The Neale Publishing Co., 1906), p. 273.

[50]Stephens to Johnson, Fort Warren, Boston, Mass., 8 June 1865, Johnson MSS, Series I.

[51]Gen. Robert E. Lee to *New York Herald* correspondent, *New York Herald*, 24 April 1865, reprinted in *Cincinnati Gazette*, 2 May 1865.

Government does not resort to harsh measures. If it does resort to such measures, I cannot answer for the consequences.'[52]

This feeling was not confined to the military. It was rife in the South, even during the summer when the States held their conventions. If the Northern government was to interfere in Southern affairs and stipulate some of the ways in which matters should be run, then it should be responsible for the administration and execution, and the consequences, of these requirements. Most particularly, the effects of emancipation were pointed to as proof that Yankee panaceas and meddling were calamitous. Southerners had warned that the freeing of a labor force which would not work unless coerced was dangerous; therefore let the North be responsible for the inevitable chaos which would result. And it was in this same spirit of defiance that most of the Confederate Governors, who were removed by Andrew Johnson during April and May, left office. All of them had argued that their continued exercise of power was necessary to provide against the incipient anarchy and economic disorder which surrender and defeat would bring. Writing to the commander of the occupation forces, General Embury Osband, Charles Clark of Mississippi exemplified their truculence when he said: 'I am relieved from the duties of the Chief Executive of the state of Mississippi, and for the grave consequences that may result, the President of the United States has assumed the responsibility.'[53]

This defiant attitude seemed to be widespread. 'Marcel,' a correspondent for *The Nation*, was in South Carolina before and after the President's policy was announced and a Provisional Governor appointed for that State. From Orangeburg, in late July, he reported: 'A few weeks ago the tone was: "We're whipped, and the Yankees have matters in their own hands. We'll step aside and let them 'run the machine' to suit themselves" – and a nice time they'll have of it.' This was a challenge to the North to do its worst. 'Now, on the other hand,' added 'Marcel,' 'there is a disposition to look jealously upon any interference from outside. They say they understand the terms and are willing to live up to them; but they wish to manage their own affairs themselves, and are able to do it.'[54] What 'Marcel' and many others in

[52]Gen. William J. Hardee to *New York Herald* correspondent, in *Cincinnati Gazette*, 11 May 1865.

[53]Governor Charles Clark to Gen. Embury Osband, Jackson, Miss., 22 May 1865, Charles Clark MSS.

[54]'Marcel,' Orangesburg, S.C., *The Nation*, 27 July 1865.

the North misunderstood was that these two sentiments were simply
the reverse side of the same coin. Just because Southerners wanted to
guard the autonomy which the Johnson plan implied it did not mean
that they were suddenly becoming conciliatory and accommodating.
In fact the opposite was true, for with self-government within reach
they were determined to make the most of it and preclude the possibility of Federal intervention or additional demands.

No matter how much Southerners might defy the Federal authorities to inflict a harsh policy, there was still the possibility, until terms
were enunciated, that Washington might in fact take up the challenge.
So, on all sides in the South, there was an eagerness that the government's intentions be made specific as soon as possible. In early May,
for example, the *Richmond Times* and the *Augusta Constitutionalist*
were demanding of the President that he discontinue playing games
with the South by hinting at his policy but instead speedily reveal the
details.[55] Those who were out of power, however, wanted delay and
continued military rule, fearing that if terms were promulgated at an
early stage they would most likely involve either complete, or at least
a considerable degree of, self-government. And this would mean that
there would be no social and political reorganization of the South.
Unionists and loyalists who had remained aloof from the Confederacy
and who now hoped for a new dispensation after the war, men like
J. F. H. Claiborne in Mississippi, and Jeremiah Clemens, J. J. Giers,
George Spencer, who was actually from the North, and others in
Alabama, warned the President of the danger in speedy restoration;
and to their testimony were added the observations and conclusions
of Carl Schurz and others of a radical Republican persuasion in the
North.[56] Some Unionists, such as the Charlestonians, A. G. Mackay
and Frederick Sawyer, felt nevertheless that delay was likely to produce more evil than good. Accordingly, they told Schurz that military
rule would be seen as 'a *quasi* continuance of the war' and therefore as
evidence of an abiding hostility, while delay in specifying post-war
relations between the sections would be productive of anxiety, instabil-

---

[55] Editorials, *Richmond Times*, 13 May 1865 and *Augusta Constitutionalist*,
5 May 1865.
[56] J. F. H. Claiborne to Johnson, Hancock County, Miss., 1 May 1865; Jere
Clemens to Johnson, North Alabama, 21 April 1865; J. J. Giers to Johnson,
Decatur, Ala., 14 May 1865; all in Johnson MSS. Schurz's views are contained
in his letters to Johnson during the summer of 1865, to be found in the Johnson
MSS, Series I.

ity, and a general lassitude. Moreover, said Mackay, it would be fatal to leave the status of the Negro undefined until Southern opinions on the subject had had time to settle; it was better to act soon and firmly in this matter since at all events the Blacks 'must be entrusted to the conscience and good sense of the whites as an experiment.'[57] These preferences for a speedy announcement of Washington's formal disposition towards the inhabitants of the Southern States, no matter how earnestly stated, probably had little effect on the President since it is abundantly clear that immediately after entering office Andrew Johnson had commenced urging on the Cabinet a reconstruction policy which was moderate in scope and which throughout its drafting departed but minimally from the North Carolina proclamation outlined by Lincoln just before his death.[58]

Curiously though, the other features of the Southern posture (the profession of acquiescence and the assertion that a conciliatory policy would best produce a harmonious Union and a cooperative South) did, on occasion, have a positive effect on Northern views and assumptions about the mood of the rebels.[59] On 5 June 1865 the radical Republican *Chicago Tribune* printed an editorial from the *Columbia*

[57] Frederick Sawyer to Carl Schurz, Charleston, S.C., 23 July 1865, Johnson MSS, Series I. A. G. Mackay to Schurz, Charleston, S.C., 20 July 1865, Johnson MSS, Series I.

[58] The debates in Cabinet over Lincoln's North Carolina scheme can be followed in the *Diary of Gideon Welles*, ed. Howard K. Beale (New York: W. W. Norton and Co., 1960), II, 279–82, 299–304; Gideon Welles, *Civil War and Reconstruction*, compiled by Albert Mordell (New York: Twayne Publishers, 1959), pp. 186–204; Benjamin P. Thomas and Harold M. Hyman, *Stanton: The Life and Times of Lincoln's Secretary of War* (New York: Alfred A. Knopf, 1962), pp. 354–8, 402–44, 444–6.

[59] In chapter 7 of his *Andrew Johnson and Reconstruction*, 1960, Eric McKitrick asserts that there was a degree of submissiveness in the South's leaders immediately after the war which was genuine, albeit partially expedient. Basing his conclusions primarily on observations by Whitelaw Reid, arguments by a number of conciliatory members of the Mississippi convention of 1865, and A. S. Wallace, a South Carolina Unionist, McKitrick argues that the South was sufficiently acquiescent as to have been willing to concede even a qualified Negro suffrage if the President had required it firmly. It is my contention, which I hope to prove in this and the next two chapters, that neither the assertion nor the corollary hold true. Moreover, the view that more might have been conceded if the President had been firm is based on speculation only; the context in which terms were posed made a more firm verbal insistence of little consequence since self-government and consent were the premises of Johnson's overall approach.

(S. C.) *Phoenix* under the rapturous headline, 'SOUTH CAROLINA CON-QUERED, Remarkable Article from a Columbia Newspaper.' The editorial was seemingly submissive in tone, explaining the desire and readiness of South Carolinians to establish civil government and have the Federal troops removed and terms quickly announced. But throughout there were expressions and turns of phrase which indicated that this submission was not only qualified and conditional but was also infused with covert threats that certain terms would be unwise and therefore unacceptable to the South.

The *Phoenix* began by indicating the extent of acquiescence and submission:

In the absence of all shows of war and of all the materials for the struggle, in the spectacle everywhere of a people submitting to a fortune, which, however revolting to their pride, is forced upon them by their necessities, in the state of a country torn, ravaged, bleeding and destitute, what is needed over all is rest.

Submission, indeed, but hardly repentant or ungrudging. There was also no guarantee that if self-determination and the status quo were not recognized the South would remain submissive. At the possibility of temporary military rule, the *Phoenix* was adamant:

It will be hardly possible for a people to remain at peace, or be allowed to do so, with armed and probably insolent garrisons quartered among them. Even if the provocations of power dressed in brief authority do not goad them to desperation, they will perpetually tend to raise discontent, to induce feverish restlessness — a perpetual anxiety — a neglect of all regular habits of industry, and a sense of surveillance and annoyance, which in the end, must drive them into exile.

South Carolina was at this moment under military rule and the *Phoenix* was, in fact, daring Northerners to try to 'run the machine' for then they would soon see what disasters would follow. Finally, the editorial pointed out, with mocking sarcasm, the absurdity and wickedness of a severe Northern policy:

It may be that they [the North] would prefer that we should not recover, and that a hard policy will decree that in order to prevent future disaffection, we shall be kept as hewers of wood and drawers of water, under a sort of Egyptian bondage.[60]

[60]Editorial, *Columbia Phoenix*, no date cited, reproduced in *Chicago Tribune*, 5 June 1865.

This was a 'conquered' spirit similar to that observed in Selma, Alabama, by Brigadier C. C. Andrews, a friend of Andrew Johnson. On 11 May he relayed to the President the astonishing assessment that 'The people are glad to have peace on almost any terms. But they prefer gradual emancipation.'[61] Submission on these terms was in fact hardly submission at all, and Andrews' statement is so contradictory as to be meaningless. But that, or something like it, was the extent of the capitulation and 'acquiescence in the powers that be' felt by the former Confederates. Their submissive stance was induced by military necessity and by the realization that social and political order at home and political advantages in the nation might be gained by a strategy which shunned both diehard non-cooperation and listless passivity. But it was a strategy nonetheless, since acquiescence and cooperation were conditional and were limited exclusively to those policies which would recognize the autonomy of, and status quo in, the defeated South, that is to say, only those policies which the Confederates wanted.

c: *The North under Southern scrutiny*

Although he had not been in the South at the time, Andrew Johnson's friend, Benjamin C. Truman, reported, after his Southern tour in the fall and winter of 1865, that prior to the announcement of the President's policy, so he was continually informed, the South had 'lived in a state of the most fearful suspense' with 'a fearful looking for of judgement' and an 'hourly apprehension of the beginning . . . of northern vandalism and hideous butchery.'[62] This was indeed accurate reportage by Truman. What it portrayed accurately, however, was what the reinstalled Confederates were saying in the fall of 1865 about the six weeks after Appomattox, not what were the actual feelings and anticipations at the time itself.

In the fall, conventions were being called in the Southern States and the South's leaders were seeking to reassure their constituencies that if they played their cards right the President's policy would protect rather than persecute the South. Paeans were sung to Andrew Johnson, and his courage, magnanimity and principle were being lauded. And one of the ways in which support was elicited was by pointing out what the President had prevented from occurring.

[61] Brig.-Gen. C. C. Andrews to Johnson, Selma, 11 May 1865, Johnson MSS, Series I.

[62] 'Report of Benjamin C. Truman,' *Senate Executive Documents*, 39th Cong., 1st Sess., II, No. 43.

William Henry Trescot exemplified the general feeling when he told
Governor Perry that the 'Wisdom and courage' of the President's
policy 'has saved us from destruction that would have been as rapid
as it was ruthless.'[63] If this were so, then it was likely that before
the President's policy was revealed the South might indeed have
been fearful and expectant of the worst. The *Raleigh Sentinel* was sure
that this had indeed been so, and an editorial in late October ran:
'The excited state of the public feeling at the North, and the melan-
choly circumstances which shrouded the country at the time when
the destiny of the nation was placed in his [Johnson's] hands,
almost for a moment obliterated all hope of generosity or of justice to
the South.'[64] For many, Johnson himself had been the cause of this
dread and worry. As the *Montgomery Advertiser* wished to remind
everyone, 'That great fears were entertained of a vindictive policy
by the President, is so well established a fact as to find a witness in
almost every Southern man.'[65]

This description of the Confederate South as terrified and fearful
before the President's saving grace was made available was far from
accurate. Angered at defeat, sullen in the face of an exultant foe, uncertain as to the contours of the future, this the South's leaders may
have been.[66] But a vindictive peace was never widely expected before
29 May when the two proclamations announcing the President's
policy were promulgated. It would be quite wrong to assume that the
Confederates and their followers were fearful and submissive as they
faced the apparent likelihood of a severe policy from Washington,
and that consequently the generous plan of the President, once it was
made known, relieved them of their fears and rekindled instead the
fires of secession and hostility as they saw that they were to be treated
with leniency. The 29 May proclamations did not, first of all, come as

---

[63]Trescot to Perry, 24 October 1865, published in *Charleston Courier*, 8 November
1865.

[64]Editorial, *Raleigh Sentinel*, 31 October 1865.

[65]Editorial, *Montgomery Advertiser*, 18 October 1865. Private letters and the
public press abound with plaudits of the President at this time and frequently,
as a corollary, the post-Appomattox mood is described in terms similar to those
quoted so far. Concurrence can be found in the editorials of the *Charleston
Courier* for 9 October and the *Augusta Constitutionalist* for 22 September, for
example. A comparison of this *Courier* editorial with one on 18 April, see below
p. 46, n. 78, will point up the special pleading involved in the depiction during
the fall of a fearful South in April and May.

[66]Editorial, *Augusta Constitutionalist*, 24 May 1865.

an unexpected surprise, and, furthermore, they did not effect so dramatic a change in Southern attitudes.

Before elaborating on these two observations concerning the anticipations of the Confederates about likely Northern policy, it is important that the significance of the 29 May proclamations be put into perspective. It has often been assumed that 29 May marked a point of no return and thereafter the Confederates, realizing that Federal policy was to be conciliatory, were truculent and unsubmissive. If they did react this way it was done with very little prescience or calculation, for, after all, the pronouncements of late May were hardly definitive. It could be argued that the North Carolina proclamation was unique and that for other States with greater numbers of freedmen a different policy involving some kind of Negro suffrage would be necessary. In this context the Mississippi proclamation a week later was far more significant. Moreover, there was no guarantee that the policy of restoring self-government to the South would not involve more requirements than the proclamations indicated; they were not final and definitive pronouncements. And of course the President gave no assurance, nor was he capable of giving it, that this policy was anything more than an experiment which could be modified or annulled if its results were unsatisfactory. Even if Southern leaders were unprepared to consider this, many radical Republicans did, and it was on this vague hope that they frequently withheld sharp criticism of the policy as it evolved during the fall of 1865. And finally, of course, even if the President considered his policy to be irreversible, Congressional politicians might deprive him of this option. Both his assumption that Southern policy was an executive prerogative and his ability to act upon that assumption were likely to be assaulted, possibly with success. There was, in fact, no substantial evidence for the Confederates to believe that after 29 May they were safe and secure. The fact that they did believe this, however, and that they were also quite confident even before that date, does need explanation.

When Southerners surveyed the political scene immediately after their surrender it seemed to them clear that nothing but a conciliatory policy could be entertained by the victorious Federal government. If the North acted upon self-interest rather than passion and tried to weld harmoniously the Union they had fought four years to save, a generous peace settlement would be a sine qua non. Justice, sound sense, wise statesmanship, all demanded conciliation. Upon this self-fulfilling prophecy the South based its conviction that what it desired the North could not but do and that, if it took the contrary course, both sections would suffer. With confidence that Federal policy-makers would see the obvious wisdom in its argument, the *Augusta Constitutionalist* in mid-May epitomized the public stand of the Southern establishment when it pronounced that 'Bloodshed and spoliation dry up the fountains of wealth' and therefore, 'No such policy will suit a shrewd and prudent people, and with just such a people we are united by a correlation of interest. If we suffer, they suffer too, and, like the Siamese twins, the blow that falls upon Chang will tingle through Eng.'

This does not mean, however, that there was no fear and no pessimism whatsoever about the possible drift and tone of Federal policy. In late April the *Houston Telegraph* was sure that Andrew Johnson, a former member of the Committee on the Conduct of the War, would be severe: 'Abolition, confiscation, the gallows, revenge in its most sweeping decrees and direct forms, are all in his heart, and will soon find utterance in his programme.' A few days later, the *Augusta Constitutionalist*, although by no means convinced, felt that a harsh policy might emerge since 'The animus of the President seems to be hatred of the South because there are many here who claim to be of gentle blood.'[67] At about the same time Johnson was prohibiting the recall of the Confederate legislatures by the State Governors whom he in turn disqualified from office. To many this boded ill and William A. Graham, the North Carolina Whig and pre-war Governor, confided his fears to David Swain, also a former Whig Governor, that these actions were 'a gross indignity to the State, and an indication that rude conduct, and harsh measures may be expected.' Furthermore, he added, 'The speeches of the President shew vindictiveness, and I look for Military rule for some time, with test oaths etc.'[68]

Yet, although there were these indications of a fearfulness that harsh terms would be forthcoming, there was enough evidence in Northern behavior, enough straws in the wind, for public figures to be able to derive a good deal of consolation. And where the existence of fear was referred to, it was often in the context of uncertainty as to the government's intentions and with a desire to disarm the North with evidence of Southern impotence and fright, as when the *Richmond Times* on 13 May, discerning that Andrew Johnson adhered to the constitutional view that the Southern States had never left the Union and that he

[67] Editorials, *Houston Telegraph*, 28 April and *Augusta Constitutionalist*, 5 May 1865.
[68] Graham to Swain, Hillsboro, N.C., 11 May 1865, W. A. Graham Collection.

would therefore be unlikely to make severe demands on that section, protested that Federal policy should quickly be revealed so that 'our minds will be relieved of shadows and hobgoblins, and banishment and confiscation, and indefinite terrors and imaginings, which pervade every Southern family because of the suspense which naturally grows out of silence.'[69] This was not a description of Southern reality but a gross parody of Northern intentions and consequently of Southern reactions to them.

If it were an accurate depiction of feelings and expectations in the South, how was it that at the beginning of May, a number of Southern leaders could unite and act as if the opposite were the actuality? David L. Swain was telling William A. Graham, before Governor Vance set off for Washington only to be forestalled a few days later by Federal authorities, that he expected that the Governor, once reinstalled, would call a convention to deal with post-Appomattox and post-emancipation problems and commented of the unpardoned Confederate, Graham, 'I suppose as a matter of course you will be a delegate from Orange County and suspect that my friend Mr. Phillips will be disposed to be your colleague.'[70] The prominent Floridian and former U.S. Senator, David L. Yulee was telling the Secretary of War, Edwin Stanton, just before his arrest, that 'The opinion of the people of the State is very general that the ancient relations held under the Constitution of the U.S. should be resumed. In this I concur with them.'[71] Even Joshua Hill, a leading Georgia opponent of the Confederacy, was urging that Joseph E. Brown, the war-time Governor of the State, be retained in office, and added to this the remarkable assumption that 'A convention will assemble, if permitted, to remodel the State constitution — so as to accommodate political affairs to the restoration of the authority of the government of the United States. The oaths of officials must all be changed, the ordinance of secession be rescinded — and the people in all respects restored to their ancient privileges.'[72] And about this time in early May there was the spectacle of most Confederate Governors, Clark of Mississippi, Murrah of

[69] Editorial, *Richmond Times*, 13 May 1865. Similarly unabashed demands for clarification were made of the President by the *Augusta Constitutionalist*, 5 May 1865.
[70] Swain to Graham, Chapel Hill, N.C., 6 May 1865, W. A. Graham Collection.
[71] David L. Yulee to Stanton, Tallahassee, 14 May 1865, Edwin M. Stanton MSS. 'Ancient relations' probably included even slavery. That was understood as intended by the term which was a piece of euphemistic political shorthand.
[72] Joshua Hill to Sherman, Augusta, Ga., 5 May 1865, W. T. Sherman MSS.

Texas, Allison of Florida, Brown of Georgia, Magrath of South Carolina, Vance of North Carolina, and Smith of Virginia, resuming their executive functions and calling for sessions of their State's Confederate legislatures. When the military, at the behest of the President, forbade these assemblies and denied the authority of the Governors, there was, for a time, a degree of uncertainty as to the President's intentions, as Graham's remarks to Swain, cited earlier, would indicate. But this would not last long and it was never a substitution for the earlier confidence, merely a counterpoint to it.

Among those whom one might have expected to be most fearful and concerned for future Federal policy, there was in fact a minimal anxiety. The Confederate prisoners of war seemed to regard it as inconceivable that their imprisonment might lead to execution or even a life-sentence. From Fort Warren Reagan and Stephens even wrote to the President as if they were equals who had been cruelly maligned and they demanded pardon, explained their lack of guilt, and offered advice as to the course the President should take towards them and their rebellious section.[73] The extensive correspondence to and from Robert M. T. Hunter during the early days of his incarceration also indicated scant concern for the possibility of punitive measures or reprisals. On one occasion this was explicitly stated in a letter to Mrs Hunter of 15 May 1865 in which it was reported that, 'Judge [John A.] Campbell [who was also in Fort Pulaski] thinks there is no cause for uneasiness and is of opinion that Mr. Hunter and his friends should remain as quiet and be as patient as possible – expressing no fear nor apprehension and in fact conversing as little as possible on the subject.'[74] And Campbell himself, noting earlier when he was free that the President was making speeches saying that 'treason is a crime,' wryly observed, 'I think that the administration will have much to do, to indict a whole people,' especially as convicting juries would be hard to find in the South where, under the Constitution, the trials would have to be held. And hewing to the by-now-familiar hypothesis, he argued, 'The adoption of such a line of policy cannot fail to aggravate the misery of a condition sufficiently miserable now;' moreover, such a policy, if persevered with, 'will retard the work of pacification and

[73] Stephens to Johnson, Fort Warren, Mass., 8 June 1865, Johnson MSS, Series I; Reagan to Johnson, reprinted in Reagan, *Memoirs*, pp. 273–84.
[74] Lewis D. Crenshaw to Mrs Hunter, Richmond, Va., 15 May 1865, Hunter–Garnett MSS.

settlement.'[75] The possibility that the Federal government would prosecute a few leading rebels Campbell ignored; he preferred to assume that imprisonment was temporary and that that would be the extent of the North's need for some Southern leaders to be seen to be punished. Of the prisoners in Fort Pulaski only John A. Seddon ever manifested any fear of worse punishment and this was induced by the trial of Henry Wirz, the Governor of Andersonville, whose superior Seddon had been when Secretary of War.[76]

The complacency of Southern leaders in the wake of defeat and in the face of the imminent declaration of the conqueror's terms was not the outgrowth simply of blind overconfidence. It was rather a combination of unrefuted assumptions and substantial evidence. As representatives of a class equipped with all the accoutrements of noblesse oblige, natural aristocracy and hierarchy, it was difficult for the Confederate politicians to envisage Congress voluntarily removing them from power. Furthermore, if sectional differences were to be healed and the nation reunited, the Southern social and political order could not be tampered with. But if it were to be, the Confederates felt reasonably sure that they could frustrate such intentions. Besides, there was a good deal of evidence to indicate that the Federal government did indeed have conciliatory goals in mind. Therefore, there was no point in adopting a public posture, particularly in the press, which did not nurture optimism and a confidence that self-government and the status quo were to be encouraged and respected by Washington. And since leniency was expected it would be foresighted and discerning as well as expedient to draw attention to hopeful and therefore more meaningful signs while discounting contrary indications.

There were four types of evidence which provided the South's leadership with comforting indications that what it wanted and what it felt was the North's only available policy would merge and crystallize before long. During the last two years of the war, Southerners had been apprised of the general direction in which Federal policy would move by a number of initiatives and experiments undertaken by President Lincoln. Of the latter the attempts to establish legal governments in Tennessee, Louisiana and Arkansas had given clear evidence that Lincoln favored a policy of mercy and did not intend

---

[75]Campbell to Hunter, Richmond, Va., 21 April 1865, Hunter–Garnett MSS.
[76]John A. Seddon to Hunter, Fort Pulaski, 6 September 1865, Hunter–Garnett MSS.

to interfere other than minimally with a State's internal affairs. His private initiatives gave even more assurance on this score, in particular the Hampton Roads Conference of January 1865 and the suggestion to John A. Campbell in Richmond on 4 April that he initiate reorganization by recalling the Confederate legislature of Virginia.[77] Then of course there were also the exceedingly conciliatory terms offered Johnston at Durham Court House, which, although later repudiated by Johnson and Stanton, were nevertheless indicative of the degree of leniency implicit in the Federal position.[78] In view of these precedents, the *Charleston Courier* could announce only a few days after the new President had come into office that in effect the Federal negotiating-position was sufficiently established and its objectives so obvious that no change of personality in its executive department could alter it. 'We do not believe,' said the *Courier*, 'it is the intention of the Government to exercise any harsh measures towards the people of the [Confederacy], . . . simply because the Government, having asserted and maintained its authority over the whole land, can afford to be liberal toward the deluded classes who so unwittingly plunged themselves into the mire of destruction.'[79] Ten days later the *Courier* was convinced that there would be continuity. Happily, 'Those who know [Johnson] best are firmly of the belief that he will determinedly carry out the views of the late President with reference to the important

---

[77] A memorandum on the Conference prepared by Hunter, Stephens and Campbell, the Confederacy's representatives, was published, probably at Stephens' request, in the *Augusta Chronicle*, 7 June 1865. The construction placed on the meeting by the Confederates was that Lincoln was urging the South to surrender before Northern sentiment grew more hostile. He said that many in the North were considering $400 million compensation for the Southern planters' emancipated slaves, though he warned against the radical Republicans and urged the South to realize that he, as the Chief Executive, could 'offer all the power of mercy, and pardon, and influence.' On the subject of the freedmen, Lincoln indicated that his philosophy was one of 'Root hog or die,' but added that the South would have to ratify the recently passed amendment abolishing slavery, 'he hoped within six years.'

Campbell defended himself against the charge of 'overreaching and deceiving [Lincoln] and misrepresentation' in a letter to Hunter of 15 September 1865 from Fort Pulaski, deposited in the Hunter–Garnett MSS. Campbell said that the proposal to recall the legislature was Lincoln's, not his own; 'Mr. Lincoln suggested a method of obtaining peace that I approved and endeavored to assist.'

[78] The *Augusta Constitutionalist* optimistically referred to this as an indication of Administration policy, 21 May 1865.

[79] Editorial, *Charleston Courier*, 18 April 1865.

questions involved in the pending National difficulties.'[80] Consequently when Johnson's proclamations were issued, the *Courier* was able to admit that it was not at all surprised at their leniency.[81]

There were indications, though less explicit, from another source that Federal policy might well be conciliatory. During the early weeks after Lee's capitulation Southern civilians experienced at first hand the influence and the personnel of the United States Army. In the confused state of affairs, State commanders were supreme within their jurisdiction, though this power was limited by the exigencies of the situation. Most commanders felt, however, as did Brigadier-General James H. Wilson, commanding in Georgia, that 'The war having ended it is the true office of the military power of the government to assist in the re-establishment of civil law, not to replace it.'[82] Consequently, following the example of George H. Thomas when in command of most of the Southern States during April, the military allowed civil officials to retain their offices pending the announcement of the Federal terms.[83] They also maintained law and order in an anarchic situation; they supervised repair work on railroads, dispersed relief to the destitute, and reopened educational facilities; and they acted as a liaison between Southern authorities and Washington, offering temporary and conciliatory solutions in a period and situation without precedent.[84]

In the most controversial of all areas for military activity, the question of labor and the freedmen, the military were also harmonious in act and intent. Those General Orders which were issued with regard to freedmen were firm and offered no latitude or special treatment. Freedmen, most Orders warned, should not expect bountiful wages, perhaps not even wages at all, but rather payment in kind; and either of these, because of the surrounding poverty, would be minimal. The government, 'wise and beneficent,' would protect the freedman's freedom and the fruits of his industry; but, continued General Quincy

---

[80]Editorial, *Charleston Courier*, 27 April 1865.

[81]Editorial, *Charleston Courier*, 5 June 1865.

[82]Brig.-Gen. James H. Wilson to Gen. Whipple, Macon, Ga., 15 June 1865, Johnson MSS, Series I.

[83]General Order No. 21, Dept. of the Cumberland, 13 April 1865, referred to in George H. Thomas to Asa Seward of Ringgold, Ga., written from Nashville, Tenn., 30 May 1865, George H. Thomas MSS.

[84]James E. Sefton, *The United States Army and Reconstruction, 1865–1877* (Baton Rouge: Louisiana State University Press, 1967), pp. 5–16.

A. Gillmore's General Order No. 63, as did nearly all the other regulations concerned with freedmen and labor in the Southern departments, 'it is the manifest and binding duty of all citizens whites as well as blacks, to make such arrangements and agreements among themselves, for compensated labor, as shall be mutually advantageous to all parties. Neither idleness nor vagrancy will be tolerated, and the government will not extend pecuniary aid to any persons, whether white or black, who are unwilling to help themselves.'[85] Regulations like this offered reassurance about the limitations on Northern sympathy toward the freedmen, the subject uppermost in Southern minds. So, all in all, the behavior and priority of the occupation forces gave no cause for concern, but rather the opposite. As the _Richmond Times_ commented on 5 May, 'If the feelings manifested by the military authorities, and the conservatism of many of the leading statesmen of the North is an index to the policy of the Government at Washington, the ghastly wounds inflicted by the war may be speedily healed, and we may once more become a prosperous and happy people.'[86]

The _Times_' conclusion was based on more than the actions of the army in the South for there were signs that in Washington the mood was one of conciliation. And there were indications of this in Congress as well as in the Johnson Administration, which after all consisted, with the exception of the President himself, of the personnel of Lincoln's Cabinet. On 11 May, the _Natchez Weekly Courier_ felt confident that 'The present looks hopeful. The time has arrived when reason resumes its sway.'[87] There had been doubts as to Northern magnanimity just after Lincoln's death and again in early May when the President refused to countenance restoration of the Southern Governors and the legislatures, but optimism was the dominant sentiment thereafter. On 27 May the _Richmond Times_ was even complacent enough to announce the requiem of the radical faction of the Republican Party, asserting that, '[They] are no longer among the idols of the North,

---

[85] General Order No. 63, Dept. of the South, 15 May 1865, enclosed in Gen. Q. A. Gillmore to Stanton, 24 May 1865, Letters Received, Records of the Office of the Secretary of War, microcopy 221. Also, for example, General Order No. 45, Dept. of North Carolina, 15 May 1865, cited in _Augusta Constitutionalist_, 24 May 1865.

[86] Editorial, _Richmond Times_, 5 May 1865. See also Editorial, _Natchez Weekly Courier_, 11 May 1865, and Editorial, _Augusta Constitutionalist_, 24 May 1865.

[87] Editorial, _Natchez Weekly Courier_, 11 May 1865.

their popularity has long since departed, and Nemesis claims them all as her own. There are none so poor as to do them reverence, and, cast aside and forgotten by their own section, we pass them by without further comment.'[88] Only the day before, the *Augusta Chronicle* had reported a speech by General Benjamin F. Butler, a radical, in which he had outlined a policy consisting simply of '1st., The abolition of slavery; 2nd. The renunciation of the right of secession and others of minor importance.'[89] And on the 27th, the *New York Tribune*, also radical Republican, had issued its 'appeal . . . to the gentlemen of the South . . . to step forward, without regard to past differences, and lead their fellow-citizens in the work of restoring their several States to their former consideration, security and power.'[90] This the *Richmond Times* was quick to note and, from it, draw optimistic conclusions; further substantiation to its observation of 16 May that the Republican press was displaying a conservative tone.[91]

Andrew Johnson himself was an even better guide to Northern policy, however, since it was expected that he would follow Lincoln's initiative by vesting policy-formulation in the executive department. And the President's tone was in fact very reassuring. The *New Orleans Times* on 9 May released a dispatch from its Washington correspondent who reported that 'he has expressed himself decidedly in favor of recognizing the existence of the States, rather than of holding those that have rebelled, in territorial position. . . . There can be no mistaking his language.'[92] And a letter published by the same paper two days previously drew upon Johnson's antecedents, 'He was born in North Carolina and raised in Tennessee,' to show that he would not be sympathetic to severe policies such as were identified with New England. He 'does not,' said the writer, 'pass his entire time in singing psalms through his nose . . . he has never peddled a clock or palmed off a wooden nutmeg,' so that 'the wonderful effects of New England culture are not manifested in any growth of horns upon his forehead.'[93]

As a Southerner who had been a renegade during the war, Johnson could just as likely have been vindictive or sympathetic once secession had been defeated. Yet by mid-May few in the Confederate camp

[88]Editorial, *Richmond Times*, 27 May 1865.
[89]Editorial, *Augusta Chronicle*, 26 May 1865.
[90]Reprinted in *Richmond Times*, 30 May 1865.
[91]Editorial, *Richmond Times*, 16 May 1865.
[92]Editorial, *New Orleans Times*, 9 May 1865.
[93]*New Orleans Times*, 7 May 1865.

believed that the President would follow anything but a conciliatory
course. The key to this analysis was that the President, in his public
speeches, was asserting that States could not commit treason and that
they had never left the Union. From this premise, a proscriptive policy,
with military rule and broad Federal intervention into a State's political and social arrangements, was felt to be highly unlikely. Southern
observers noted however that Johnson's speeches were laced with
hostile sentiments towards those who had initiated and led the rebellion.[94] They also were aware that the President was talking of basing
his Southern policy on the clause of the Constitution which required
the Federal authorities to guarantee a republican form of government
within the States, an approach which seemed to reassure Confederates
even though the radical wing of the Republican Party was also intending to employ it, but for a rather different purpose.[95]

These potentially unfavorable indications did not however distress
the Confederate leaders and their allies among the newspaper editors.
Their reaction to Johnson's speech to an official delegation from
Indiana, led by its Governor, Oliver P. Morton, illustrated this tendency. It was considered a piece of good news for the Confederate
South, even though the President said, as he had continually done,
that traitors and treason were both 'odious' and deserving of punishment. Reassuring however was the statement that the 'guarantee
clause' restored the States which were indestructible to their place in
in the Union since 'their life breath has been only suspended, and it
is a high constitutional obligation we have to secure each of these States
in the possession of a republican form of government.'[96] This speech
was highly gratifying to a public meeting held by leading Confederate
politicians in Montgomery, Alabama, on 11 May. The speech was
hailed and a letter sent to the President, stating: 'We have been in no
small degree encouraged in addressing you this communication by
your recent enunciation at Washington of the principle that the States
which attempted to secede and permanently sever their connection
with the Union are to remain States still, and are not to be lost in territories or other divisions.'[97]

By mid-May or at least a week before the formal announcement
of the Presidential policy, virtually all of the major newspapers which

[94]Editorial, *Augusta Constitutionalist*, 5 May 1865.
[95]Editorial, *Richmond Times*, 13 May 1865.
[96]Speech to the Indiana delegation, 21 April 1865, Johnson MSS, Scrapbooks.
[97]*Charleston Courier*, 7 June 1865.

were representative of the Southern establishment and which were publishing at this early date (many presses had been destroyed during the war or had been taken over by the occupation forces) were convinced that Johnson would be lenient. By 9 May the *New Orleans Times*, 13 May the *Richmond Times*, 24 May the *Augusta Constitutionalist*, and 25 May the *Augusta Chronicle*, were adopting this view of the situation; and of course the *Charleston Courier* as early as 18 April was hopeful, and by 27 April, based on a recollection of Johnson's Nashville speech accepting the Vice-Presidential nomination, was convinced of the President's likely leniency.

Of course there were some other indications of the kindly drift of the President's thoughts on Southern affairs. A letter from General James H. Wilson to Joseph E. Brown of Georgia which was widely reprinted in the press provided further evidence, when he said, with Presidential approval, that

The President hopes by restoring peace and order, giving security to life, liberty and property, by encouraging trade, arts, manufactures, and every species of industry to recover the financial credit of the State and develop its great resources, that the people will again soon be able to rejoice under the Constitution and laws of the United States and their own State, in the prosperity and happiness they once had. To all good people who return to their allegiance, liberality will be exercised.[98]

But this did not overrule the possibility that even though the mass of Southerners would be treated with magnanimity, their leaders might not be; and there were no reports from Washington to relieve that uncertainty. As late as 31 May even, a Georgian, J. L. Dunning, published a summary of an interview he had had with the President. In this the President had said that he wanted to be generous and encouraging to the majority in the South and hoped reorganization would be instigated by Southerners and, also, that now slavery was

[98] Maj.-Gen. J. H. Wilson to Governor Joseph E. Brown, 9 May 1865, in *Charleston Courier*, 25 May 1865; Stanton to Wilson, 8 May 1865, Telegrams Sent, Records of the Office of the Secretary of War, microcopy 473, reel 89. That this was the intention of the President was also indicated in a letter to him from Joseph E. Brown, in which Brown explained that he had followed Johnson's instructions in his speeches around the State. In these he had advised Georgians to be loyal and abolish slavery. And, he added, 'I have also assured them that you are their friend, that it is not your purpose to crush them, but you wish to build them up.' Brown to Johnson, 24 July 1865, Johnson MSS, Series I.

abolished and 'That fact cordially admitted, the remaining difficulties might be easily solved.' But, Dunning said, the President intended nevertheless to exclude the Confederate leaders from the process of restoration.[99]

This was perhaps a concern but the general contours and drift of the President's expected policy were pleasing; the States' integrity would be respected, self-government would be encouraged, and recuperation rather than prostration was clearly intended. Accordingly the Southern press and politicians were sure of the President's future course and they were confident of its benevolent effects at least two weeks before 29 May when his policy was actually announced. The *Richmond Times* even came out on 16 May with what was tantamount to an endorsement of the President's Southern policy. After observing how conciliatory and conservative the Republican press seemed to be, the editor proceeded to argue that President Johnson would not be harsh and tyrannical because his behavior demonstrated a strong tendency towards leniency, and, presumably, since actions speak louder than words, this overruled some of the hostile remarks in his speeches. Johnson, said the editorial, had approved of the conciliatory policy of the army (he had admittedly rejected the Sherman–Johnston truce but then so would Lincoln); he had allowed General Halleck to extend the Lincoln amnesty to Confederate colonels and officers above that rank; he had freed Southern trade from blockade and encouraged food and capital into the South; and finally he had restored the loyal Virginia government headed by Francis Pierpont and ordered elections held. All of this was indicative of conciliation and respect for the Confederate leadership and the status quo. So,

Let no one, therefore, judge the President rashly or precipitately; let us award praise to his wise and lenient acts, and endeavor to do him justice. We do not believe that this man of the people, thus wonderfully elevated by his own talents and the inscrutable decrees of God, is destined to destroy, by a violent and proscriptive policy, the harmony, peace and fraternal feeling which is already so happily springing up throughout the country.[100]

If this assertion had been made merely in the interest of raising hopes and appeasing fears, there was little need for so complete and commit-

[99]J. L. Dunning, report of an interview with the President, in *Augusta Chronicle*, 31 May 1865.
[100]*Richmond Times*, 16 May 1865.

ted an endorsement. No editor would be so unqualified in praise of his conqueror unless he were very sure that his assessment was correct.

With the Lincoln precedent uppermost in their minds and very aware of the turmoil which would result from a harsh policy, the Confederates saw no evidence in the signs and indications from Washington that there would be a reversal of the line of policy undertaken by the previous President. Moreover they were convinced that a rejection of magnanimity and leniency would be most unwise for both sections, and therefore would not be undertaken. And lastly, of course, they wanted reassurance and tended to overlook evidence to the contrary. There was much in this approach which smacked of self-fulfilling prophecies and wishful thinking. But then the radical Republicans were engaged in the same sort of activity; they also gave Johnson the benefit of the doubt and ignored signs they did not like. In view of the outcome they possibly were indulging in even more optimism and self-delusion than their opponents, the Confederates.

Part 2
Encouraging Southern loyalty, 1865

We are not and we cannot be a 'loyal' people as that term is understood at the North, but better, far better, than all the loyalties that ever were spawned, we are a Constitution-loving and law-abiding people . . . Government has no right to prey into the heart. Political attachment is a matter of the purest supererogation.

Augusta Constitutionalist, 15 June 1866

2

The Provisional Governors

In spite of the uproar caused in the North over the terms offered General Joseph E. Johnston by General Sherman, every one of the Confederacy's Governors embarked upon courses of action during the ensuing weeks which implied a total disregard for this furor and for the Northern feelings which had precipitated it. With the concurrence of the President and his Cabinet, Stanton, the Secretary of War, had issued a stinging rebuke to Sherman for concluding an agreement which was 'a practical acknowledgement of Rebel Government.'[1] Yet, one by one, the Governors of the defeated Confederate States published proclamations calling their legislatures into session or else dispatched emissaries to Washington or to the General commanding in their State, to enquire if restoration could be commenced under the old dispensation. The Governors argued, as did Joseph E. Brown of Georgia in a telegram to the President on 7 May 1865, that 'The complete collapse in the currency and the great destitution of Provisions among the poor makes it absolutely necessary that the legislature meet to supply this deficiency and with a view to the restoration of peace and order by accepting the result which the fortunes of war have imposed upon us.'[2]

This recognition of the need for immediate governmental action towards restoring social order and relieving distress was not solely to demonstrate that the incumbent Southern officials would act responsibly if entrusted with a continued lease on political power. It also served as a pretext for initiatives on their part aimed at taking advantage of the temporary political uncertainty so as to present the North with the fait accompli of effective and functional Southern governments. The Federal government was not caught unaware, however, and department commanders were ordered to ensure that the

[1] Stanton's Memorandum on Sherman–Johnston truce, 18 April 1865, Telegrams Sent, Records of the Office of the Secretary of War, microcopy 473, reel 89.
[2] Joseph E. Brown to Johnson, 7 May 1865, Telegrams Received by the President, Records of the Office of the Secretary of War, microcopy 473, reel 6.

Governors cease and desist.[3] Stanton's telegram of 16 May 1865 to Major-General Edward Canby, commanding in the department of the Gulf, outlined the intended policy:

All political subjects belong exclusively to [the President] for adjustment, and he will take such action from time to time as he may deem most conducive to the peace and interests of the Government. You will prevent by force the assemblage of any persons assuming to act as a Legislature, and to exercise any civil or political authority, jurisdiction or right claimed by, through, or under the Rebel Confederacy or the Rebel State Government.[4]

As a result, calls for meetings of the legislature in Florida, Georgia, South Carolina and Alabama were nullified, and permission for a North Carolina delegation to proceed through the Federal lines on its way to Washington was refused. Only in Mississippi was the military's implementation of these orders hesitating. It was not until after the legislature had met there on 20 May and called a constitutional convention for 3 July that a prohibition was placed on this development, and the Governor arrested and the State officials put under guard.[5] The proscription was even extended to a concurrent development in Mississippi headed by Judge Armistead Burwell, a native Union man, which was intended, so Burwell said, to be 'a mere informal commencement of a movement by the people to throw off an imbecile despotism of which they are well tired.'[6] Inclusion of Burwell's initiative may have been the act of an overzealous officer for the ban was really intended to prohibit efforts undertaken by Confederate officials towards reestablishing their war-time governments. These were to be curtailed until the President had decided about the framework for reconstruction. From Washington alone would the initiative come.

[3] In the Department of the South, General Quincy Gillmore issued General Order No. 63 on 15 May 1865; it can be found in Letters Received, Records of the Office of the Secretary of War, microcopy 221. William A. Graham told David L. Swain of the prohibition in his letter of 11 May 1865, William A. Graham Collection.

[4] Stanton to Edward R. S. Canby, 16 May 1865, Telegrams Sent, Records of the Office of the Secretary of War, microcopy 473, reel 89.

[5] Governor Charles Clark, Proclamation, 6 May 1865, *New Orleans Times*, 11 May 1865; James W. Garner, *Reconstruction in Mississippi* (New York: Macmillan Co., 1901), p. 58, n. 1.

[6] Armistead Burwell, interview with the editors, *New Orleans Times*, 11 May 1865.

Until the President made known his plans, the South was in the hands of the United States occupation forces. Only in Virginia, Arkansas, Tennessee, and parts of Louisiana were there civil governments which had been reorganized by Federal authorities. On 9 May a Presidential proclamation had recognized the war-time government of Francis H. Pierpont, located behind Union lines in Northeastern Virginia, as the official administration for the whole of the State. Tennessee, Arkansas and Union-occupied Louisiana had been reorganized under Lincoln's Ten Per Cent Plan, though none of them had yet been restored to the Union.

In spite of the reestablishment of civil government in these States, martial law had been declared in all of them and was virtually as extensive there as in the rest of the Confederate territories. The military everywhere issued General Orders dealing with lawlessness, the freedmen, military court trials, relief of the destitute, repair of the railroads, and even such minutiae as collection of garbage, registration of prostitutes, and the establishment of speed limits for horses and carriages.[7] In most States, all civil offices were technically vacated, so that authority was vested in the military, and in a number of cases, commanders took positive action to encourage citizens whom they regarded as trustworthy and loyal to take action, on a local scale, leading toward reorganization and civil government. The military did not conceive of its role as punitive or abrasive but instead thought occupation would be temporary, and so their task was to heal open wounds and to cooperate and encourage the people of the South.

Once Southerners realized the fighting was over and the Confederate governments would not continue in office, it did not require military prompting to produce unofficial political action at the local level, though in one instance, Georgia, the State commander, General James H. Wilson, initially forbade political meetings.[8] This activity on the part of the South is easily explained. Political control of the State was in the offing, and there were, essentially, two groups vying for it. On the one hand, there were those who had been persecuted during the war because of their loyalist sentiments or who had previously been prevented by lack of wealth or influence from participating in politics. These were the Union men and the previously excluded

---

[7]Sefton, *The United States Army and Reconstruction, 1865–1877*, pp. 8–11.

[8]Alex N. Wilson reported this to Andrew Johnson after touring Georgia; his letter was sent from Chattanooga on 16 June 1865 and is in Johnson MSS, Series I.

classes whom many radical Northerners hoped could be levered into power so as to provide a loyal and progressive South, free from the reactionary influence of the ante-bellum and Confederate élite. On the other hand, there was this latter group, for which the defeat of the Confederacy presented a direct threat to its continued control of power. Both the creation of the Confederacy and its defeat could be attributed to them, a heavy liability to overcome.

Both groups accordingly began to call meetings to demonstrate their desire and their ability to form a civil government and restore the State to the Union. The Unionists felt that meetings led by, and filled with, men less known and not identified with the Confederate stigma would demonstrate that a new class of leaders existed, was strong, and should be entrusted with power. The Confederates, for their part, concluded that if they could arrange informal public gatherings attended by some leading secessionists but mainly by well-known Whigs or anti-secessionists, then the North would see that prominent men were penitent and loyal, and were now eager to regard the struggle as closed and to take positive steps to restore the South physically and politically. Unfortunately this distinction between secessionist and anti-secessionist, although considered by its progenitors as significant and demonstrative of a desire to be conciliatory, was a mere subterfuge or irrelevance for those in the North who supported Congress' ironclad test oath of past and future loyalty, which had become law on 2 July 1862. Few critics would have been disarmed by the tactic, although possibly those inclined in the first place to trust Southern leadership might have been reassured by it.

Throughout the disorganized Southern States during May and June 1865 there were then two sets of political initiatives – the Confederate, and the Unionist and loyalist – each seeking to impress the President and gain access to the machinery of reconstruction. In Virginia the process was brief. After one meeting organized on 8 May at Staunton Court House by Alexander H. H. Stuart, Pierpont was installed the very next day as Governor.[9] Elsewhere, however, popular meetings were called to demonstrate a desire for self-government and for restoration to the Union, and more often than not, to offer a pledge to 'acquiesce in the situation.' Few resolutions were passed, even in Unionist meetings, which went beyond this simple acquiescence, though from time to time there would be evidence of a recog-

[9]Alexander F. Robertson, *A. H. H. Stuart, 1807–1891* (Richmond, Va.: William Byrd Press, Inc., 1925), pp. 223–33.

nition that slavery had been abolished even if only because the United States Army had effected it at the point of a bayonet.[10]

In spite of the President's earlier prohibition of reorganization attempts instigated by official Confederate authorities, he made it known that he would take steps to restore civil government once he was assured that sullen passivity had given way to spontaneous and active efforts towards political reorganization within the Southern States.[11] Apparently satisfied that in North Carolina at least there had been sufficient political ferment so far, Andrew Johnson on 9 May summoned William W. Holden to bring a delegation to the White House. Holden had been a leading secessionist until the 1860 election but had redeemed himself by standing as peace candidate against Zebulon B. Vance, the incumbent, in the gubernatorial election of 1864. A Democrat and editor of the *North Carolina Standard*, Holden was a man from the humbler classes who was determined to challenge the hegemony of the wealthy planters (he called them 'the oligarchs') who maintained their power under the aegis of the Whig party. He was, therefore, an extremely controversial figure in the State. So, it was not surprising then that, although Johnson had prohibited a Vance delegation from coming to Washington, the determination of that group to prevent Holden's gaining the President's confidence was so unrelenting that they still managed to assemble four representatives in Washington in an attempt to outflank him. One of them, David L. Swain later explained what happened: 'We had a three hours interview the day after the arrival and pressed [the President] most earnestly to allow the Legislature to be convened, either by the Speaker of the Senate, or Gen'l. Schofield.... His mind however, as soon became manifest, was already made up, and all that remained for us to do, was to endeavour to modify a course of policy which we could not control.'[12] The only concession to Swain was that his minority delegation was allowed to vote with the Holden group when the selection of Provisional Governor was made. Of

---

[10]Citations for these general observations cannot be made as too much space would be occupied in doing so. A reading of the Andrew Johnson Papers from May until July 1865 would demonstrate the validity of these conclusions.

[11]The details of the manner in which the Provisional Governors were chosen by the President are not considered here but they can be found in the author's Ph.D. dissertation, 'Southern Politics and American Reunion, 1865–1868,' University of Chicago, 1968, pp. 124–63.

[12]Swain to Graham, Chapel Hill, N.C., 4 July 1865, W. A. Graham Collection.

course Holden was chosen but it had not been without the tacit approval of his opponents. And this was important to Andrew Johnson.

Fundamental to Johnson's policy in his selection of Provisional Governors was a determination that the nominee should be a resident of the State and a politician whose antecedents and likely future course would introduce harmony among the conflicting interests within his State. That meant that he could not be proscriptive or punitive and so, in general, Johnson's appointees were representative of the interests which had traditionally governed in the South. But while compatible with the Confederacy and its leaders, they were nevertheless more moderate and less unequivocal in their support, all of them having been opponents of secession and many of them advocates of an early peace. A policy of harmony and reconciliation between the sections and within the Southern States, such as Johnson embarked upon, could not include the removal from power of those who customarily wielded it. As Johnson proceeded to select Provisional Governors for the remaining States, it became clear that rather than being a proto-type, Holden was indeed an exception in an otherwise discernible pattern.

In Alabama there had been a substantial and reasonably well-organized loyalist opposition to the Confederacy. Located in the Northern counties which had been Democratic before the war, it was led by Judge William H. Smith, Joseph C. Bradley, David C. Humphreys, J. J. Giers and others, but, instead of selecting a Provisional Governor from this group, Johnson chose Lewis E. Parsons. Parsons had been prominent in a post-war movement initiated by ex-Governor Watts and from a meeting of this group in Montgomery on 11 May a delegation had been chosen to proceed to Washington.[13] Parsons was a Whig from the hill-county of Talladega who had joined the Democrats in the late 1850s and aided the cooperationists in 1860. Like Holden, he had headed the peace party during the war. By contrast, Georgia's appointee was not Joshua Hill, the leader of the peace forces, but a lesser-known former Congressman who had shared mess privileges with Andrew Johnson while both were Congressmen in the early 1850s. It was not clear exactly why James Johnson was appointed Provisional Governor. Perhaps it was because Hill was

---

[13] *New Orleans Times*, 18 May 1865. Also *Augusta Constitutionalist*, 4 June 1865 and *Houston Telegraph*, 25 May 1865.

insufficiently conciliatory and too controversial that his claim was rejected. Instead Johnson, who had been put forward as the compromise candidate of the two rival delegations to Washington, one led by Hill and O. A. Lochrane and the other by Johnson himself, was selected by the President as his agent in Georgia.[14]

Unlike James Johnson, Mississippi's Provisional Governor was very well-known. Throughout the 1850s William L. Sharkey had been a Union Whig, prominent in his State and in the section; he had been President of the Nashville Convention of 1850 and Chief Justice of the Mississippi High Court of Errors since 1823. His final claim on the governorship was that he had been arrested by General Van Dorn for refusing to supply goods to Confederate officers; with this exception his loyalty to the Confederacy was untarnished. Coming to Washington in June with the lawyer and politician William Yerger as a delegation from Mississippi's Confederate legislature and its Governor, Charles Clark, the President had let it be understood that because of the source of their authorization, he received them as individuals and not as State representatives. Yet in apparent disregard for this declaration of policy, he appointed Sharkey Provisional Governor.[15] One can surmise that despite their coming to Washington without proper authority, Sharkey and Yerger were nevertheless, as individuals, men with the kind of political record and widespread respect which would make either of them fitting agents of the Presidential policy. But why he did this is unfortunately not known.

The name of the man who was to be South Carolina's chief executive, Benjamin F. Perry, was submitted, along with others, by a delegation from Charleston whose credentials and intentions were as unpromising as those of the Mississippians.[16] But, nevertheless,

---

[14] *Augusta Constitutionalist*, 6 June 1865; O. A. Lochrane to Johnson, Washington, D.C., 16 June 1865, Johnson MSS, Series I.

[15] William Yerger, Speech in the Mississippi Convention, *Journal of the Proceedings and Debates of the Mississippi Constitutional Convention*, 1865 (Jackson: E. M. Yerger Publisher, 1865), pp. 146–7.

[16] The proclivities and intentions of this South Carolina delegation were explained to the President in John F. Poppenheim to Johnson, Charleston, S.C., 18 June 1865, and in two letters from Taliaferro P. Shaffner, to Johnson and to General Mussey, his secretary, both written on 29 June 1865. All are in the Johnson MSS, Series I. In his letter to Mussey, Shaffner, who had been contacted by Poppenheim and had also encountered the South Carolinians in their Washington hotel wrote: 'Some of the leaders in the self styled delegation from South Carolina, have expressed the determination that in case the President did not appoint one of

Perry's record before and during the war was extremely good. A Greenville lawyer, he had fought during the 1850s alongside James Petigru and James L. Orr against the powerful secessionist party in his State, even refusing to capitulate, unlike Orr, when the Democratic Party split in 1860. Once the war began however he did accept office under the Confederate government; he may have considered secession unwise but, like most of the anti-secessionists, Perry's interests and sympathies were ultimately tied to the State and to those who took the State out of the Union.

A different course of action was taken once war broke out by the President's appointees in Texas and Florida; they fled the South. Andrew Jackson Hamilton had been Lincoln's intended Governor of Texas, even though he had been a leading and fiery secessionist in the 1850s. Surprisingly, once in office, Hamilton, of whose loyalty even Gideon Welles had been somewhat suspicious, pursued an unconciliatory often proscriptive policy towards the Confederates, becoming, like Holden, a radical Republican by late 1866.[17] Florida's chief executive, William Marvin, had been a prominent figure in his State's judicial history since its statehood. An authority on marine law and an opponent of secession, he had been proposed as a suitable candidate by a group of New York businessmen who had known him during the war and by a number of Marine Insurance Companies from the same city.[18] As a candidate who could stem the ambitions of a powerful clique of Teasury officials loyal to the radical Chief Justice, Salmon P. Chase, Marvin was Andrew Johnson's unhesitating choice. The President appointed him, and Hamilton also, without meeting with State delegations.

Although the careers and attitudes of Johnson's Provisional Governors differed, the selection of each followed a general pattern. Andrew Johnson's restoration policy aimed to restore not only the Southern States to the Union but harmony to the nation, both within and between the States. Therefore, the Provisional Governors would not be men who had precipitated secession or who intended, now that

the 5 gentlemen named to be Provisional Governor, they would there and then put on their hats and say "Good Morning, Mr. President." In their hotel talk, they are as Secesh as ever and have the least respect for National Supremacy, as any man that I have heard from the South since the close of the war.'

[17] *Diary of Gideon Welles*, ed. Howard K. Beale, II, 316.
[18] Petitions from New York businessmen and Marine Insurance Companies, 6 July 1865, Johnson MSS, Series I.

war had ended, to inaugurate a period of social transformation in their States. They were rather to be those who favored union between the sections before the war and union within their respective States after the war. Furthermore, it would be beneficial if they had been prime movers in Southern war-time initiatives against the Confederate government's prosecution of the war and in favor of producing an early peace. Few of the chosen Provisional Governors met all these requirements, Parsons alone, and Sharkey perhaps, approximating the ideal. The South, Andrew Johnson felt, needed repose and assurance of sympathy. Holden's and Hamilton's proscriptive courses, therefore, were not expected, and possibly not desired, by the President. If he had intended that, then he would have insisted on appointees who could have sworn the ironclad test oath and thereby have avoided Sumner's angry rebuke that the oath 'was a peremptory bar against the Holdens and Perrys and their satellites.'[19]

The type of men whom President Johnson selected for the task of leading the Southern States away from secession and independence and back into a harmonious enduring relation with the States which had remained in the Union was crucial to his entire post-war policy. For not only were the Provisional Governors to play a fundamental role in the process of restoration but more than that they were representative of the type of politicians in the South through whose agency and cooperation he believed reunion could be achieved.

Opponents of secession and critics of the Confederate government, they were moderates within the Southern political establishment. If politicians like them could gain control in their section and proceed to mold its attitudes and interests, the South might then be able to coalesce with men of the center in the North and thus effect a cross-sectional coalition of moderates. Radical Republicans and Copperhead Democrats in the North and secessionists and opponents of the establishment in the South, the latter being potential Southern radicals, had to be excluded from the coalition because they were extremists and advocates of views and policies which would perpetuate friction, whether sectional, social or political. The representatives and advocates of moderation, on the other hand, were to be the agents of reunion, and they would later be the ingredients for the

[19]Charles Sumner to Hugh McCulloch, Boston, 7 September 1865, McCulloch MSS. Obviously Sumner, like the President, did not anticipate Holden's subsequent course of action, although even then it was not until late 1866 that he became a radical Republican.

National Union coalition whose formation in mid-1866 the Philadelphia convention of August 1866 was convened to engineer.[20]

Fundamental to the President's approach to the problem of postwar settlement was a belief that differences between the sections over slavery had been so accentuated by extremists in each section that they had become incapable of negotiation by normal political processes and had instead brought about civil warfare. Consequently, sectional controversy could be brought under control, though perhaps never completely eliminated, only by the confluence of the moderates and the removal of the extremists from power and influence. Stability and harmony would always be in jeopardy until men and measures which were moderate and national gained the ascendency. As the President told a Virginia delegation in February 1866, it 'has been hammer at one end of the line and anvil at the other; this great Government, the best the world ever saw, was kept upon the anvil and hammered before the rebellion, it has been hammered since the rebellion, and there seems to be a disposition to continue the hammering until the Government shall be destroyed. *I have opposed that system always, and I oppose it now.*'[21]

In a word, Johnson was trying to create harmony. Basic to his conception was the emergence of a ruling majority with a power-base among the moderate segments of the political establishment in each section. In addition, the political parties, whose sectionalization in the 1850s had broken irrevocably the political ties binding the nation together, would have to become national once more, both in program and constituency. And finally, issues and policies would need articulation and molding so as to provide the program and ideology upon which the intended harmony could be achieved.

It was an ambitious conception. But it was conservative in tone and intent, and it would forestall the revolutionary possibilities which were becoming quite patent as a result of the emancipation of the slaves and the military victory achieved on behalf of a set of values and a national vision dramatically opposed to those which had prevailed in the Confederate States. If these tendencies had been pursued, a significantly different consensus would have emerged. And it would

[20] The details of this scheme which was central to the President's policy will be discussed in chapter 8.

[21] Speech to the Committee from the Virginia Assembly, 10 February 1866, in Edward McPherson, *The Political History of the U.S. During The Period of Reconstruction* (Washington, D.C.: Philip and Solomons, 1871).

have involved not Southern restoration, but its reconstruction and forcible assimilation into a progressive Northern mold. Assisting this alternative development was the existing sectional alignment based on hostility and conflict as well as the prevailing party situation inside and outside Congress. In attempting to defuse sectional animosities and realign the parties, Johnson was bound therefore to confront these institutional and ideological obstacles. From this, it could be argued that Andrew Johnson was attempting the impossible; he was allowing his goals to outstrip the means available to him and his theory to blind him to political reality. But in his approach to the sectional question as well as to that of race, he was merely acting within the tradition of compromise and conciliation towards the Southern planters which had been the stock-in-trade of American leaders since 1787. And needless to say, it received considerable support in the 1860s as well.

3

Strategies for readmission

a: *The President's intended plan*

Early in September 1865, William H. Seward, the Secretary of State, received a communication from a Georgia Whig, Wylly Woodbridge. Woodbridge had a suggestion to offer regarding Federal restoration policy. 'You once resided in our State,' he wrote, 'and have a mastery over Constitutions – the present is to ask you to have one prepared for us to be submitted to the Convention; if you will send it to me its origin will be a mystery it shall be copied by my own hand, and placed into proper management.'[1] Seward, in reply, thanked the Georgian for his suggestion and concluded, 'It is best however that the proceedings of the State convention should not only appear to be but really be spontaneous. Governor Brown and others from Georgia have been with us here and I am sure that they go away well informed of our views about what is necessary to restore the proper and natural relations between the States lately in armed rebellion and the loyal States, and the people of both.'[2]

Of course, the Southern States could have been prepared for readmission by subterfuges such as Woodbridge suggested. Similarly, though less covertly, the terms for readmission could have been dictated to the defeated Southern enemy. These possibilities, however, were rejected by the Administration in 1865 as later they were also to be by Congress when it presented its own plans during 1866 and 1867. Coercion, it was felt, would be harmful in its effects, for, once the pressure was relaxed, assent given under pressure could be withdrawn or alternatively could quickly give way to an angry uncooperative reaction in the face of such tactics.

The Administration did not contemplate such methods. Instead, Provisional Governors, who had been selected by the President during May, June and July 1865, were to call conventions in their States.

[1] Wylly Woodbridge to Seward, Georgia, 9 September 1865, Seward MSS.
[2] Seward to Woodbridge, Washington, D.C., 25 September 1865, Seward MSS.

The voters and delegates were to be men who had sworn the oath of allegiance required by the 29 May Amnesty Proclamation or, if they were among the thirteen excepted classes, had been personally pardoned by the President. These conventions were then to accommodate State laws and constitutions to their Federal equivalents. Finally, a legislature, Congressmen, and State officials would be elected and the normal State governmental machinery set in independent operation, with acceptance or rejection of the reorganized State's Congressmen remaining at the discretion of the new Congress, elected in the fall of 1864, which would assemble in December.[3]

At the outset, Andrew Johnson wished fervently that the South's actions in the coming months might prove acceptable to Congress. The intention of his policy was after all to demonstrate that the Union could be restored most satisfactorily through the agency of the South's traditional leaders, albeit the more moderate of them, and so the success of the scheme depended upon the Confederates' being able to show they were trustworthy and reliable. This could not possibly happen if the President manipulated the Southern conventions and legislatures, beseiged them with Presidential ultimata, and transformed the Provisional Governors into puppets of the Federal executive.[4] Spontaneity was essential.

Loyalty would not, however, blossom unassisted. Spontaneity had to be tempered by guidance. The South had fought desperately for four years, and time and sympathetic circumstances alone could sow feelings of cooperation among Southerners, even among the unwilling masses, who, supposedly, had been dragged into rebellion. Gratitude for mercy shown and awareness of their own self-interest, Andrew Johnson and William H. Seward felt, would be the silken threads by which the South could be drawn back into the Union. The President would not merely elicit their gratitude because of his magnanimity, but he would also urge them to more positive steps by revealing a

---

[3] This process was itemized in the Presidential Proclamations appointing a Provisional Governor in each State.

[4] Of course the whole process derived all of its authority and power from the Federal Chief Executive and his proclamations appointing State Governors and empowering them to call conventions and hold elections. Johnson did not however want to extend this power beyond the procedural limits of simply setting the process in motion. Substantive matters would be the concern of the residents of the States which were involved in governmental reorganization under the guidance of their Provisional Governor; they would not be subject to Presidential manipulation or interference.

course of action that would be mutually beneficial to both the President and the South. This process the President called 'stimulating Southern loyalty.' He expounded the details of it to Jacob D. Cox, the Governor of Ohio, in an interview early in 1866.[5] Of course, this explanation was for publication and was intended to explain and justify a policy which had already failed. All the same, Johnson's and Seward's correspondence reveals that this was very definitely the intention behind the Administration's restoration policy as originally conceived.[6]

The goal of the restoration mechanism was 'everywhere to stimulate the loyalty of the South themselves, and make it the spring of loyal conduct and proper legislation rather than to impose upon them laws and conditions by external force.'[7] A series of incentives was provided as the means to produce this loyalty. Removal of the Freedmen's Bureau and of martial law, for example, would be offered as immediately obtainable benefits if the Southerners provided protection and good treatment for the freedmen and if they were law-abiding and swift to punish offenders. So, too, certain necessary conditions for the peace of the nation, such as Southern abolition of slavery and nullification of State ordinances of secession, were to be assured by the conventions in return for permission to reinstitute civil self-government in the States. Consequently, without realizing it and without having to submit to overt coercion, the South would implement unpalatable measures which it would consider acceptable because of the benefits that would accrue. The South would thus be stimulated to act loyally, and 'their conduct would determine the matter.'[8]

Pressure of circumstances and a realization of the long-term benefits from cooperation would narrow the options for the defeated South. The President considered the possible courses of action open to Southern leaders to be as few as for the paroled ex-Governor of Georgia, Joseph E. Brown. Of Brown, Johnson had told Stanton, 'I think that his return home can be turned to good account. He will at once go to

---

[5]*Washington National Intelligencer*, 27 February 1866.
[6]In a report of the President's interview with a South Carolina delegation on 24 June 1865, there is an example of the way that Johnson saw his task which closely corresponds with the ex post facto explanation which follows. Johnson was reported to have said on that occasion 'that, as executive, he could only take the initiatory steps to enable them to do the things which it is was incumbent upon them to perform.' *New York Times*, 26 June 1865.
[7]*Washington National Intelligencer*, 27 February 1866.
[8]*Ibid.*

work and do all that he can in restoring the State. I have no doubt that he will act in good faith. He cannot, under the circumstances, act otherwise.'[9] The pressures to behave wisely and in a conciliatory manner were, it was presumed, overwhelming. Telegrams and dispatches from the President and Secretary of State arrived with regularity on the desks of the Provisional Governors during the summer and fall urging them and the members of the conventions and legislatures to realize that these needs and aspirations could be satisfied only by action that was indicative of good intentions and conciliation. Benjamin Perry, for example, understood perfectly well what the South should do, as he demonstrated when he wrote during October to Armistead Burt who was on South Carolina's committee to prepare a code of laws protective of the freedmen:

It is all important that [the code] should be ready to be submitted at the Extra Session. The President wishes to see that protection has been afforded or guaranteed to the freedmen before the military authorities are removed. Congress will require it before our Representatives are allowed to take their seats in that body.

I have no doubt General Gilmore [*sic*] will suspend his Provost Courts as soon as your Code is adopted. Seward writes me that all the troops will be withdrawn as soon as our State Government is organized.[10]

Of course it was not the mere fact of adopting a code and organizing a State government that would ensure the withdrawal of the Freedmen's Bureau and the military forces. They had to be acceptable to the Republicans in the North so that potential opposition would be forestalled, and, from time to time, the President warned the Provisional Governors of this. To Perry he telegraphed in September, 'I hope you will proceed with the work of restoration as rapidly as possible and upon such principles as will disarm those who are opposed to the states resuming their former relations to the federal Government — This is all important.'[11] At the outset, in August, when Mississippi was taking the lead in summoning a convention, Johnson exhorted Sharkey to press the convention to include a measure for qualified Negro suffrage, because 'as a consequence the Radicals, who are wild upon negro franchise, will be completely foiled in their attempts to

[9] Johnson to Stanton, Washington, D.C., 3 June 1865, Stanton MSS.
[10] Perry to Burt, Greenville, S.C., 15 October 1865, Perry MSS (Duke).
[11] Johnson to Perry, Washington, D.C., 2 September 1865, Perry MSS (Ala.).

keep the Southern States from renewing their relations to the Union by not accepting their Senators and Representatives.'[12]

Also stimulating the South and channelling its actions was the realization, pointed out by Governor James L. Orr of South Carolina in his inaugural, that 'If [the freedman] is to live within our midst, none are so deeply interested in enlightening and elevating him as ourselves.'[13] This did not mean necessarily that social or political equality was imperative; civil and legal rights and a fair steady wage under the contract labor system introduced by the Freedmen's Bureau would be the kind of measures required. Another who recognized this need was James Lusk Alcorn, later in 1865 to be United States Senator-elect from Mississippi and, in 1870, Republican Governor. Writing to his wife from Washington during August, he suggested: 'We must make the negro our friend. We can do this if we will. Should we make him our enemy under the promptings of the Yankee, whose aim is to force us to recognize an equality, then our path lies through a way red with blood, and damp with tears.'[14] Urging Holden against appointing to office men who would excite suspicion among those Northerners 'opposing a restoration of State government,' the President warned, 'God grant that the Southern people would see their true interest and the welfare of the whole country and act accordingly.'[15]

Accordingly, there was no need to mention formal terms. The South was not to be faced with the necessity of complying with certain specific requirements which, once met, would satisfy the conqueror and permit the 'wayward sisters' to return to the Union. Instead the conventions called during the fall of 1865 were to recognize in their fundamental law the changes brought about by the war and by the defeat of secession as well as to take over those governmental and social tasks temporarily assumed by the Federal military forces. Once this was done, civil government could be considered effective and the Federal troops withdrawn. With autonomy achieved on these terms,

---

[12] Johnson to Sharkey, Washington, D.C., 15 August 1865, Johnson MSS, Series IIIA.

[13] James L. Orr, Inaugural Address, 27 November 1865, *Charleston Courier*, 2 December 1865.

[14] James L. Alcorn to his wife, Amelia, Washington, D.C., 26 August 1865, Alcorn MSS.

[15] Johnson to Holden, Washington, D.C., 27 August 1865, Johnson MSS, Series IIIA.

the goal of the President's policy and of Southern aspirations would have been reached and, hopefully, Congress would have been sufficiently impressed that the readmission of Southern Congressmen would follow automatically. The purpose of the Administration's program was to restore functional and effective civil governments in each Southern State and then, in turn, to restore each State to its appropriate place in the Federal Union. This was what Seward had told Sharkey in July: 'The government of the State will be provisional only until the civil authorities shall be restored, with the approval of Congress.'[16]

This was the theory of the Presidential policy, but what in practice did it require of the South? In the Proclamations appointing Provisional Governors, the President had stated that the Southern States must repudiate Confederate laws at variance with the Federal Constitution, and this meant that secession was to be nullified and slavery abolished. On the first count, the Mississippi convention, and later those of Georgia and Florida, refused to nullify their secession ordinances, preferring to repeal or rescind them, thereby denying their illegitimacy and failing to repudiate them totally. The President did not reprimand Mississippi for this, but hoped that the course of the forthcoming legislature would enable him to overlook this equivocal stance; and this he also did with regard to Florida and Georgia. On the second, the State conventions recognized slavery as abolished, though a problem did on occasion arise and in Alabama it required a telegram issuing indirectly from the President to secure precise compliance. The dispatch to the Provisional Governor and President of the convention was sent from Washington, with the President's approval, by some leading Alabamians, including General Leroy P. Walker. It also serves as an interesting example of the tactics and devices of Presidential restoration policy. The dispatch warned that

President Johnson is earnestly in favor of a speedy restoration of Alabama to the Union, with all her rights excluding slavery and the claim of the right to secede. If slavery is not abolished, and the claim of the right to secede is not fully ignored he neither has the power nor the wish to restore us. The only obtainable good for Alabama is restoration to the Union. To say only that slavery is abolished by the military power of the United States invites, if [it]

[16] Seward to Sharkey, Washington, D.C., 24 July 1865, 'Correspondence with the Provisional Governors,' *Senate Executive Documents*, 39th Cong., 1st Sess., I, No. 26, 60.

does not, necessitate the continuance of that power in the State to uphold emancipation. To say we abolish it by our own act is to take the matter in our own hands, and relieve us from military rule. If you fall short of this, you antagonize the wise and only hopeful policy of the President, and protract, if you do not perpetuate our exclusion from the Union.[17]

In the State proclamations the President had also indicated that only those who had been amnestied or specially pardoned were to participate in the elections to the conventions. Since all of these had taken the oath, specified in the Amnesty Proclamation of 29 May, to support and defend the laws of the United States, and in particular war-time proclamations respecting slavery, it could be assumed that the electorate and the elected members of the conventions had already agreed to take action in the direction of nullifying secession and voluntarily terminating slavery. The instructions therefore were complete; anything beyond them would be done at the South's discretion or at the President's request.

Events were not to be anticipated and further recommendations, if deemed necessary, would be suggested to the Provisional Governors when the occasion arose. Only to Perry of South Carolina did the President give additional instructions before he left Washington. Perry was informed that his State's convention must revise the electoral system in order to curb the power of the tidewater aristocracy and to open to popular election the major executive offices which were currently appointed by the legislature. When Perry asked Seward in August if there were any further specific instructions, he received a terse retort: 'In reply I have to state that no others have been prepared or have been in contemplation than those which have already been addressed to you, including the letter which accompanied your appointment. It is difficult and perhaps unwise to anticipate questions which may arise under unknown circumstances in many States, which are now under Provisional Governors.'[18] Flexibility was essential. The Administration did not intend to put out a set of explicit demands, compliance with which would guarantee readmission. Instead an attempt was to be made to wed the demands and responses of the South in its conventions to those of the Republican majority in Congress.

To the Provisional Governor of the State whose convention was

[17]F. W. Sykes, L. P. Walker, etc., to Parsons and Fitzpatrick, Washington, D.C., 19 September 1865, Johnson MSS, Series I.
[18]Seward to Perry, Washington, D.C., 6 September 1865, Perry MSS (Ala.).

first to assemble, Mississippi in mid-August, Andrew Johnson did in fact send a telegram extending the government's recommendations. Not only did he suggest that the convention should take it upon itself to abolish slavery, he also urged that it should adopt the anti-slavery amendment to the United States Constitution, at that time not yet ratified. Further, he intimated that the bestowal of a qualified Negro suffrage would be to the State's benefit since it would 'disarm the adversary' in the North and also serve as an example to the other Southern States whose conventions were to follow.[19] Such a measure would not, of course, alter the political balance in Mississippi, since very few Negroes were able to read and write, or pay taxes on real estate valued at $250. Realizing this, Sharkey cabled back that 'Many are in favor of giving them the right to testify, but probably this and the right to suffrage may be left to the Legislature,' and, for the President's information, he added, 'The amendment to the Constitution of the United States is referred by Congress to the Legislatures.[20] Johnson thereupon agreed that the legislature should handle the amendment and made no further mention of the suffrage question.'[21] To this Sharkey again replied, 'The right of suffrage I do not think will be extended to them; indeed there is an inclination to limit the right of suffrage with the white man.' And he then proceeded to tell the President that he felt that the amendment would probably not be ratified at all because of the second section which gave to Congress 'power to enforce this article by appropriate legislation.'[22]

The qualified suffrage suggestion was thereupon dropped. Instead there arose at the North Carolina convention another issue which was not included in the original instructions contained in the 29 May Proclamation. Repudiation of the war debts incurred by the Confederate States has been regarded by historians as the third of a triad of static and final requirements announced by the President, the abolition of slavery and the nullification of secession being the other two. The President's terms, however, were never static and never formal, and repudiation was introduced only at a later date and in response to events. The conventions of Mississippi and Alabama which were

[19]Johnson to Sharkey, Washington, D.C., 15 August 1865, Johnson MSS, series IIIA.

[20]Sharkey to Johnson, Jackson, 20 August 1865, Johnson MSS, Series I.

[21]Johnson to Sharkey, Washington, D.C., 21 August 1865, Johnson MSS, Series I.

[22]Sharkey to Johnson, Jackson, 28 August 1865, Johnson MSS, Series I.

held in August and September were never asked to repudiate, although Alabama did so in any case.[23] It was not until the North Carolina convention that the issue became one of consequence. Initially the convention had voted to table the matter on the grounds that it was an internal as well as a potentially divisive issue. And according to a cable to the convention from Robert J. Powell, the State's agent in Washington, this was also how the President and Cabinet wished the matter to be settled.[24] But while the convention was sitting, the anti-Holden forces, consisting primarily of the wealthy who were, in the main, Whigs, decided to establish their opposition to the Provisional Governor on the issue of repudiation. They would run a gubernatorial candidate pledged to assumption and critical of Holden's presumed fiscal irresponsibility, not to mention his unsoundness on the matter of loyalty to the Confederacy and all its works. Realizing the potency of such a platform and eager to nip the movement in the bud, Holden telegraphed Johnson on 17 October informing him that 'Contrary to my expectations the convention has involved itself in a bitter discussion of the State debt made in aid of the Rebellion. A continuance of the discussion will greatly excite the people and retard the work of reconstruction.'[25] Four days later, after the President had sent an unhesitating and uncompromising dispatch urging repudiation, he received a wire from Holden saying that 'Your telegram had a most happy effect. The [Jonathan] Worth faction is working hard but will be defeated by a large majority.'[26]

Although the President had urged repudiation, he had done so only in order to ensure harmony in the convention and at the same time strengthen the Provisional Governor within his State. Yet, in Washington, repudiation quickly became accepted as a measure which would aid in producing loyalty, undermine the power of the wealthy classes, and encourage a desire to reject Confederate entanglements and obligations. James Johnson, Provisional Governor of Georgia, even decided to include repudiation in his message to the convention on 25 October, and, after a committee had come to him to ask whether he was in earnest in this request, he telegraphed for aid in moving the

[23] *Montgomery Advertiser*, 12 September 1865; *Cincinnati Gazette*, 29 September 1865.
[24] *Cincinnati Gazette*, 20 October 1865.
[25] Holden to Johnson, Raleigh, 17 October 1865, Johnson MSS, Series II.
[26] *Ibid.*, 21 October 1865.

convention towards positive action on the war debt.[27] Both President Johnson and Seward sent instructions that the debt should not be assumed by loyal people, since it had been incurred for a disloyal purpose. After a bitter debate and vehement criticism of the Provisional Governor for his truckling to Washington, the Georgia war debt was repudiated by a margin of 177 to 135.[28] Hearing of the President's unequivocal telegram to Holden, the Florida convention also repudiated on 6 November, reversing its earlier decision to submit the matter to the electorate.[29] Florida's flexibility contrasted with the reluctance of South Carolina to take any action on the State debt, even though Seward and Johnson dispatched a series of importuning communications to Benjamin Perry during the month of November. As a parting shot after the convention had failed to take any action, Perry told the Secretary of State that the debt was too small to be trifled with and too much enmeshed with other State finance to be settled on a separate basis.[30]

The scope of the matters to be considered by Southern assemblies during the fall of 1865 was broadening. But there was not in the South a corresponding growth of compliance. By mid-October the President was discouraged. The South was not responding as intelligently or as forthrightly as he had hoped. Consequently, he ordered Sharkey, Holden, and the other Provisional Governors to remain at their posts until relieved on his own orders. This produced an anomalous situation since all the other features of Provisional Government had been superseded by elected legislatures, State officials, Congressmen, and Governors. Presumably the President wanted to retain control until the States had proved themselves more compliant than they had appeared in their conventions. This new initiative, which was first indicated in November to an official delegation from the North Carolina convention, was accompanied by further recommendations. The legislature was to ratify the anti-slavery amendment and to enact a code of laws protective of the liberated slaves.[31] Just as the President did not confine to North Carolina his decision to retain the Provisional Governor,

[27] James Johnson, Message to the Georgia Convention, 25 October 1865, Executive Minutes, Johnson Official Correspondence.
[28] *Cincinnati Gazette*, 2, 4, 6, 13 November 1865.
[29] McPherson, *The Political History of the U.S.*, p. 24.
[30] *Ibid.*, pp. 22–4.
[31] *North Carolina Standard*, 18 November 1865.

he now wrote to Sharkey, suggesting: 'Let such laws be passed for the protection of freedmen, in person and property, as justice and equity demand. The admission of negro testimony, they all being free, will be as much for the protection of the white, as the colored.'[32] The President was having to itemize the kinds of legislative provisions which would have to be made before the troops' functions could be taken over and the States restored to self-government. This he had hoped the Southern conventions and legislatures would do without Presidential prompting.

As an explanation of this move the President told Sharkey, 'The Argument is, if the convention abolished Slavery in good faith, why should the Legislature hesitate to make it a part of the Constitution of the United States.'[33] Ultimately all the Southern States except Mississippi and Texas ratified, with Alabama's vote ensuring the necessary three-fourths in its favor. Nevertheless, in many legislatures, particularly those of Mississippi and South Carolina, there was much suspicion that the second section of the amendment implied virtually unlimited discretion for Congress in ensuring that the first clause, declaring slavery's abolition, was implemented. Consequently Washington sent numerous telegrams to Sharkey and Perry, assuring them that the clause was restrictive rather than expansive in intent. Eventually South Carolina succumbed; Mississippi however still refused to ratify.

A code enumerating the rights and obligations of the freedmen was produced in only two States during 1865, those which actually were the least compliant, Mississippi and South Carolina. Each of the remaining States promised either that a complete code would be framed at the next session of the legislature or that a committee established by the legislature would report early in the New Year on its findings and recommendations. The President's advice was thereby overlooked, and, even in South Carolina and Mississippi, his requirements were not met with any precision. In late November, he had told Perry, 'I hope that your legislature will adopt a code in reference to free persons of color that will be acceptable to the country doing justice to the white and colored population.'[34]

Yet it was evident that the codes were not acceptable to the country.

---

[32] Johnson to Sharkey, Washington, D.C., 1 November 1865, Johnson MSS, Series III B, Vol. I.

[33] Johnson to Sharkey, Washington, D.C., 1 November 1865, Johnson MSS, Series I.

[34] Johnson to Perry, Washington, D.C., 27 November 1865, Perry MSS. (Ala.).

In the Mississippi code there was one act prohibiting freedmen from leasing or purchasing rural land and this the President instructed General Oliver Otis Howard, Commissioner of the Freedmen's Bureau, to have disallowed.[35] Elsewhere in the North, in newspapers and in Congress, there was widespread condemnation of the restrictive and punitive provisions of this and South Carolina's code. There was even complaint in the South. Governor James Orr of South Carolina considered that 'Some of the provisions are objectionable,' but, he added, 'as a whole I think ample and complete protection, is given to the person and property of the negro.'[36] Nevertheless, he was later quite prepared to recall the legislature on 1 January 1866 in order to repeal virtually the whole code after General Sickles, in his General Order No. 1, had rejected it totally and substituted military jurisdiction. A similar course of action was pursued in Alabama by Governor Robert Patton when he vetoed three acts in the code that had been drawn up by the State legislature during December.[37]

Among the measures being considered for inclusion in the freedmen codes, one in particular was the object of considerable Northern interest. This was the right to give testimony in courts of law, a provision which, it was assumed, would be an indication of good faith towards, as well as a guarantee of the freedom of, the emancipated slave. By the summer of 1866, every Southern State except Arkansas had introduced Negro testimony. But it was never allowed in cases where both protagonists were whites, being confined instead to suits where Negroes were parties. The President had never specified that testimony should be allowed in all legal cases and when some effort in this direction was made he gave no indication that he encouraged it. One of these was brought to the President's attention by a telegram from Andrew J. Fletcher, Secretary of State in Tennessee, explaining that moves were afoot in the State legislature for a bill to introduce Negro testimony in all cases. After some delay, Andrew Johnson replied,

---

[35] General O. O. Howard to Colonel Samuel Thomas, Assistant Commissioner for Mississippi, Washington, D.C., 30 November 1865, in *Jackson Clarion*, 6 December 1865.

[36] Orr to Johnson, 27 December 1865, Johnson MSS, Series I.

[37] The action of Orr and Patton is described in Theodore B. Wilson, *The Black Codes of the South* (Tuscaloosa, Ala.: University of Alabama Press, 1965), pp. 75–7. Louisiana also enacted a code which was considerably less punitive and discriminatory but since Louisana was not under Provisional Government, its code was not directly the President's responsibility.

saying nothing about the desirability of this measure but merely urging and endorsing testimony 'in all cases where they are parties' and observing that action on this would indicate 'that the public judgement was moving in the right direction.'[38] The upshot of this communication was that Tennessee did not pass a bill for testimony in all cases. And it was not until pressure was brought to bear by Governor Brownlow later in 1866 that the measure was eventually passed into law. On another occasion, in September, Lewis Parsons had written with information similar to Fletcher's. The Alabama convention was considering admitting Negro testimony in all cases.[39] This time the President failed to reply. The convention did not act on the matter but decided instead to continue to implement the agreement providing for the legal protection of the freedmen which had been drawn up by Parsons and Wager Swayne, the Assistant Commissioner of the Freedmen's Bureau.[40]

From this it can be seen that the provision of equal rights in the witness-box was not one of the stipulations included in the President's program of restoration. Why he failed to encourage moves towards it in Alabama and Tennessee is hard to explain. Perhaps he assumed this matter would be settled by the Freedmen's Bureau through its jurisdictional arrangements with Southern authorities. But it is not unlikely that what the President was really concerned to provide in the South after emancipation was protection and guarantees for freedmen, and not necessarily equality.[41] It is noteworthy that those sections of the

[38] A. J. Fletcher to Johnson, Nashville, 20 November 1865, Johnson MSS, Series I and Johnson to A. J. Fletcher, Washington, D.C., 9 December 1865, Johnson MSS, Series IIIB, Vol. I.

[39] Lewis E. Parsons to Johnson, Montgomery, 13 September 1865, Johnson MSS, Series I.

[40] On 28 September 1865, Parsons explained to the President that 'A large number of the members were willing to incorporate in the constitution a provision making negro evidence competent or what is equivalent thereto giving to the negro the same rights as the non-voting population of the State are entitled to, and I had at one time strong hopes that this could be done, but the majority seemed to think that the people were not fully prepared for such a decided stand, and thought it best to wait for further developments.' There is additional comment on the proceedings in the convention regarding this issue in a previous letter of 23 September from Parsons. Both are in the Johnson MSS, Series I.

[41] The nature of the President's concern can be seen from a telegram to Sharkey on 17 November. 'Let such laws be passed for the protection of freedmen, in person and property,' he said, 'as justice and equity demand. The admission of negro testimony, they all being free, will be as much for the protection of the white men,

Southern codes which he forbade denied or infringed only the protective features of the legislation; he was not concerned when equality of rights and privileges was refused. Although only Alabama, Mississippi, South Carolina and Louisiana had produced legal codes for the freedmen by the end of 1865, what they had done in them did not in general displease the President. For he was quite sympathetic to the whole assumption behind them, which was that the freedmen should be subject to special legislation.

b: *The Southern perspective*

It is natural to hope that conflicts can be resolved by conciliation and compromise. Somewhere, it is assumed, there must exist a package of proposals, an arrangement, which will satisfy each of the protagonists to a sufficient degree. But it was very difficult to discover a device of this kind which might have resolved the complexities and intricacies of the situation facing the President and Congress in the spring of 1865. Measures which, at first glance, might appear to have possessed these qualities often turned out to be snares. Take, for example, the suggestion of a Negro suffrage, qualified as to education and property-ownership. This was the farthest extent to which Andrew Johnson seemed prepared to go in conciliating the radicals without repulsing the South. He suggested this to Sharkey in a telegram just before the Mississippi convention met in August 1865. This might have satisfied the Republicans by disarming their suspicion of the intentions and attitude of the South, while at the same time, if insisted upon, it might have pressured the Confederates into a realization that concession could not be avoided in the process of regaining their seats in Congress. The suggestion fell on deaf ears however; it was never really discussed. What, asked the South, would the enfranchisement of a few hundred Negroes have added to the strength of the Republicans in Congress? Such a miniscule enfranchisement would make no difference to the Republicans' basic problem of survival as the majority party once the South was readmitted. Of course, this concession could have disarmed

---

as the colored.' This is in the Johnson MSS, Series IIIB, and is cited earlier. His concern also was that the South should not be expected to introduce legislation in regard to the freedmen which went beyond the laws prevailing in the North. His telegram of 15 August 1865 to Sharkey about a qualified suffrage suggested: 'This you can do with perfect safety, and you will thus place the Southern States, in reference to free persons of color upon the same basis with the Free States.' Johnson MSS, Series IIIA.

the Republicans but still that would not deal with the underlying problem of political power. And, besides, argued the Mississippi convention, qualified suffrage would be a concession of principle by the South on the question of Negro suffrage. To yield a qualified suffrage might provide just the necessary leverage for further radical demands, in particular for unrestricted Negro suffrage.

Reconciliation of the sections was not easy to accomplish. Beneath attempts to compromise there swirled currents of partisan and sectional conflict. While the victorious Republican Party was fearful that its Congressional hegemony would be undermined if the South succeeded in returning as a unit allied to the Democrats, the South in turn realized that it was in danger of remaining a defenseless and enfeebled minority within the nation. Conciliatory policies would have therefore to overcome attitudes and propensities which were hostile and unaccommodating. It was to these that Robert S. Hudson, a Whig member of the Mississippi convention, referred when he asked rhetorically why Southern representation in Congress was being so eagerly sought by the South and so bitterly contested by the Republicans. And answering himself, he admitted that 'It is, sir, because there is no confidence, no fellowship, no good in store between the two sections, and great *party* purposes are thereby to be accomplished. Neither section is willing to trust the other, to make laws for a common Union and Government. . . .'[42] And this meant that each side required guarantees and assurances of the other before it could consent to reunion, the defeated South as much as the victorious North. The *Raleigh Sentinel* understood what this meant for its own section when it observed in mid-1866 that 'Guarantees are generally demanded by the weaker from the stronger party. To demand that the weaker party shall give guarantees to the stronger side is an anomaly that should expose the fallacious reasoning that urges a policy so unwise.'[43] And the same imperative was recognized in September 1865 by the Alabama anti-secessionist and Whig, C. C. Langdon when he exclaimed, 'It is you, proud and exultant Radical, who should give the guarantees, guarantees that you will not again violate the Constitution, that you will not again deny to any portion of the people their rights. . . .'[44]

[42] Robert S. Hudson, Speech, *Journal of the Proceedings and Debates of the Mississippi Constitutional Convention* (Jackson: E. M. Yerger, 1865), p. 77.

[43] Editorial, *Raleigh Sentinel*, 14 June 1866.

[44] Langdon's remarks were made in a speech in Brooklyn, New York, on 21 September 1865.

Suspicion was rife. The conflict was still raging and by no means suppressed, no matter how desirable in both sections a conciliatory and speedy settlement was considered. Southerners viewed the suggestions offered them by the President as matters to be treated with circumspection. And even had they been postulated as formal terms rather than recommendations their attitude and response would most likely have been no different. For, whether terms or recommendations, they were not ultimate. Andrew Johnson could not guarantee that even if the South met his terms adequately there might not be worse to follow. The South's leaders also realized that if they indicated loyalty or submission by accepting terms too readily and wholeheartedly, Congress, or even the President, might automatically assume that they were too lenient and too readily acceptable and therefore demand harsher conditions. On the other hand, they argued, if they quibbled and gave the impression that the proposed terms were difficult to adhere to, then the critics of the South would realize that they could require nothing more without producing either a hostile reaction or a failure to comply. Accordingly the South contested every demand made from the North, and every recommendation suggested. Both the President and Congress were to be made to realize that Southern politicians could not be trifled with; the exercise of Northern power in the defeated South was to be shown to have limits. Vulnerable though the South's position appeared to be, it was not therefore without assets and resources, and these were to be exploited.

Although not officially formulated, a series of tactics emerged during 1865 which were adopted as responses to and defenses against Northern demands on the South. First among these was the assumption that concession would weaken the South's ability to resist so that as a result one concession would lead to another. This fear was evident in Lewis Parsons' letter to the President informing him of the failure of the Alabama convention to pass a bill for Negro testimony in all legal cases. Parsons was now in two minds about the need to pass the measure and wrote: 'I fear the extreme men [in the North] will now say we must be kept out until they can see what laws are passed "to secure freedmen in the full enjoyment of all their rights of person and property" — and when the Legislature has done what in its judgement is necessary and proper to that end, they will not think it sufficient and thus the struggle will be prolonged.'[45] In an attempt to clear away his

---

[45] Parsons to Johnson, Montgomery, 23 September 1865, Johnson MSS, Series I.

doubts where terms would become final, Parsons added that he felt
that testimony without distinction of color was necessary, and, by
granting it, the South would thus force the radicals to take their stand
on the issue of Negro suffrage. But nonetheless the doubts existed;
concession might never appease but merely be the pretext for further
demands. William L. Sharkey echoed this uncertainty. Expressing his
surprise at how well the Mississippi convention had acted in spite of
the restrictions imposed upon the State by the United States government, he said: 'There is an opinion here, but too prevalent I fear, that
the North will be content with nothing but the humiliation and depredation of the South, which arises I think to some extent from the
management of the freedmens bureau here.'[46] By the time the legislature met in November, Sharkey's successor, who had been elected
but was not yet installed in office, had to inform the President that
these suspicions had not yet evaporated. Aware of the danger of yielding to Northern demands without the assurance that readmission
would be a reciprocal gain, the legislature was considering a quid pro
quo of Negro testimony in exchange for the removal of the colored
troops. This device would at least ensure that advantage would be
derived from a concession. For the fact of the matter was, Humphreys
told the President, 'Members feel that one Concession will only lead
to others. What assurances can I give on the subject.'[47]

There was no satisfactory assurance the President could give; even
his own proposals were expanding as 1865 wore on. From this stemmed the second of the devices adopted by the South. If the Southern
conventions and legislatures were to go beyond the President's recommendations or in any way strain to conciliate the radical Republicans, they would then simply render the radicals and their views more
credible and respectable. It would also deprive the South of justification in any stand on principle which it might try to take. Consequently
conciliation was ruled out. Limits had to be marked out somewhere
unless the Southern States intended to embark on a crusade to discover
the Holy Grail of compromise, which in all probability, many considered would be found either in Boston or Lancaster, Pennsylvania.
And that would not be compromise, but capitulation. Assessing the
work of the South Carolina convention, the *Charleston Courier* re-

[46] Sharkey to Johnson, Jackson, 28 August 1865, Johnson MSS, Series I.
[47] Humphreys to Johnson, Jackson, 16 November 1865, Johnson MSS, Series I.
    In the convention this tactic had also been urged; in that instance abolition was
    to be traded for readmission.

vealed what was a common attitude on this question: 'It is well known that the sentiments of these gentlemen (Sumner Stevens and Wilson) are extremely unpopular at the North, even among the adherents of their own party; then how can it be expected such sentiments will be entertained at the South by men who have always opposed negro radicalism, no matter in whom it appeared.'[48]

The radicals could safely be ignored; in fact it was politic to do so. Support for this view came also from the *Augusta Constitutionalist* when an editorial complained, 'We bear the evils that we have, but care not to fly to others, whose greater magnitude we can well conceive.'[49] To try to satisfy the radicals was to attempt the impossible. Concurring in this was the *Montgomery Advertiser*. Although concerned that the South should shape its policy with reference to Northern sentiment, the *Advertiser* decided unequivocally that this excluded the radical element. On 8 September, an editorial concluded: 'That there is a difference of opinion in the North as to the rights to be accorded to the South is very evident, and it is but poor policy to be given to those who wish to shut us off from all rights, any aid or help, when they already are little enough disposed to act with favor upon our conduct.'[50] And a week later this was followed by the further observation that 'Men who are bent on obtaining political power by force of Northern innovations alone are not to be expected to be pleased with any thing we do, and our people notwithstanding the good sense they may display in their action may prepare to have the bottled wrath of the negro suffrage faction poured upon their devoted heads next winter.'[51]

This analysis of the radicals' position and of the South's relationship to it effectively excluded the radicals from the arena of political debate. The radicals were not one of the political groupings with which the South had to deal during the restoration-process. Either they were irrelevant because rejected by the vast majority of Northerners or else they were so unconventional and unappeasable as politicians that they could not be negotiated with, least of all by Southerners whose views were diametrically opposed to theirs. In effect, practical political discourse was limited to the framework in which the President addressed himself to the South's leaders. There was little need even for consideration of the views of the moderate majority of Republicans since it was

[48] Editorial, *Charleston Courier*, 26 September 1865.
[49] Editorial, *Augusta Constitutionalist*, 19 November 1865.
[50] Editorial, *Montgomery Advertiser*, 8 September 1865.
[51] *Ibid.*, 16 September 1865.

assumed that most of them would either voluntarily or because of patronage considerations be in support of the President's policy. Under
these circumstances two kinds of proposals were viable recommendations from the President — what could not be avoided because it was an
obvious component of any conceivable scheme for restoring Southern
civil government and what the South chose to acquiese in. It was in
this context that the South would struggle to retrieve as strong a political position as possible, by bargaining, by hedging, by delaying, in
fact by every trick and device available, short of outright obstruction
and rejection of Presidential recommendations.

Widely recommended to the Southern assemblies during 1865,
and universally adopted, was a third tactic. This was that the delegates
should draw up as short an agenda as possible, enact the minimal, and
be circumspect about all else. On 21 September Armistead Burt had
suggested to Perry: 'I hope the Convention possesses the requisite
wisdom for their duties, which are unquestionably of the greatest magnitude. But it appears to me much discernment will be necessary to do
well what should be done, and to avoid all subjects that are not indispensable.'[52] Similar advice to the South Carolinians was offered by the
Augusta Chronicle: 'We hope they will not, on account of the multi-
plicity of matters they are seeking to attend to, get affairs mixed up.
In our opinion the less the State Conventions do, at the present time,
outside of that which is absolutely necessary, the better.'[53]

What the contending forces in the North would construe as adequate evidence of loyalty was so unclear that it was best for the South
to do only what could not be avoided. An involvement in other matters
might produce issues and situations in which certain delegates might
take false steps or become embroiled in divisive disputes, thereby
hindering reconciliation within the State as well as between the sections. Furthermore, such positive moves might be construed as overzealousness on the South's part and indicate that an aggressive determination to retain national influence and power was the prime
Southern goal. Nothing could be gained from a consideration of matters extraneous to the President's suggestions and to the basic mechanics of restoring civil government.

These were not the only considerations involved. Many delegates
at the State conventions hoped that if the subject-matter discussed were

[52] Burt to Perry, Abbeville, S.C., 21 September 1865, Perry MSS (Ala.).
[53] Editorial, *Augusta Chronicle*, 22 September 1865.

restricted it might be possible to regain some of the losses sustained during the war. Abolition, for instance, might yet be softened by grants of partial or even total compensation. The Supreme Court might even declare the Emancipation Proclamation a war measure and, therefore, unconstitutional in time of peace. Perhaps the abolition amendment might not even be ratified by the required three-fourths of the States. In August George W. Williams, a prominent Yorkville planter, informed Benjamin Perry of the prevalence of these views, especially among secessionists: 'I fear there are many of them, who say that you and those who sustain you, in the attempt to restore civil government, are responsible for the abolition of slavery and that if the people of the South will watch and wait, take no oaths and remain as they are, slavery will yet be saved.'[54] Such possibilities, delegates often said, were not beyond the realms of possibility and therefore there was nothing to be gained from premature assumptions that uncompensated abolition was as good as implemented now that the war was over. To expand the area of debate was therefore to accept restrictions and burdens which might still be contestable.

Members of the conventions also realized that the more issues they could set aside until after the legislatures met, or until the States were readmitted, the greater the likelihood that the South would be able to manage those affairs without pressure or interference. Noting that Congress stipulated that legislatures rather than conventions should be the instruments for ratification of the abolition amendment, Sharkey and the Mississippi convention correctly referred the consideration of it to the forthcoming legislative session. The other States were happy to act according to the precise intention of Congress and the U.S. Constitution. All States, except South Carolina, Mississippi and Alabama, deferred the problem of creating a code of laws for the freedmen to the New Year after Congress had reassembled. Until that time small committees were set up to investigate the problem and report when, it was hoped, the State would be readmitted.

A final tactic adopted by the Southern assemblies was to assert to its fullest extent the considerable degree of autonomy which had already been conceded to them. In this way Northern attempts to coerce and cajole could be repulsed as inconsistent with the announced policy and an infringement on State prerogatives. The South, after all, was only partially under military jurisdiction and retained considerable

[54]Williams to Perry, Yorkville, S.C., 7 August 1865, Perry MSS (Ala.).

discretion. This was intended. The President and the Cabinet undoubtedly wished the South to take on the responsibilities of civil
government and intended the section's politicians to be free to demonstrate the extent of their loyalty. Besides, they wanted the Southern
States to return as equals, State sovereignty being after all intrinsic to
the nature of the Federal Union. Terms and propositions could quite
legitimately therefore be rejected or criticized. As George L. Potter of
the Mississippi convention correctly observed, 'It is not dictation.'[55]
His and the other States possessed civil governments and were being
treated as States, not as conquered provinces or territories. And besides, if the conventions and legislatures which were envisaged were
to be popularly elected parliamentary assemblies, freedom of choice
had to be exercised or else the whole scheme was either a farce or a de-
ception.

If the President did not expect differences of opinion and discussion
of his proposals, why then did he not forbid free elections and assemblies? When Hampton Jarnagin, a Whig delegate to the Mississippi
convention, concluded therefore that 'today, so far as humility is concerned we stand as if there had been no rebellion, or if we had been
guilty of no treason,' he was not simply revealing a haughty state of
mind. After all, observed Jarnagin, all participants in the elections,
both candidates and voters, had been pardoned and were therefore
loyal.[56] Similarly independent was Potter who desired the President
to make his policy more clear so that he himself would know precisely
what it was he was contesting. He was suspicious of the opaqueness of
the President's intentions, and pronounced: 'I cannot consent to receive Executive *hints* on this subject. I wish the thing plain and outspoken on his part, that I, in my capacity of a delegate of the people,
may be able to respond in like manner, by way of answer.'[57] Not satisfied with possessing the freedom to adjudicate on the specifics of the
President's propositions, Potter wanted to decide on the manner of
their communication to his State's sovereign convention.

Uncertain whether concessions would produce reciprocal advantages and eager to retain as much local control as possible from the process of restoration and readmission, the men who dominated the State
governments and conventions maneuvered cautiously and greeted

[55] George L. Potter, Speech, *Journal of the Proceedings and Debates of the Mississippi Constitutional Convention*, 1865, p. 135.
[56] Hampton Jarnagin, Speech, *ibid*., p. 112.
[57] George L. Potter, Speech, *ibid*., pp. 58–9.

with suspicion and criticism the recommendations of the President. Consequently the purpose of Presidential restoration was regarded, not as a demonstration of Southern good faith or as a meeting of certain obligations which that section had towards the victorious North, but rather as a political battle, with policy the overriding determinant of action.

Among the members of the Southern conventions and legislatures in 1865 there were some who offered a different kind of advice. They were equally concerned that the South should retain as much autonomy as possible and withstand successfully the threats and designs against it from within and from without. They differed in tactic however, arguing that the wisest course to pursue would be one which involved conciliation of the Republicans by at the least coming up fully to the President's terms and even, if possible, yielding something more which might appease doubters in the Republican Party. The hegemony of the Republicans in Congress and the fact of Southern defeat had to be recognized, and, as a result, attempts made to conciliate the victors. If this were done, the Southern States might, in the long run, gain a greater degree of control over their own affairs than they would by a policy of resistance. These advocates of conciliation as a measure of expediency, 'D.S.'; a reporter from the *Cincinnati Gazette*, referred to as the 'Uriah Heaps' by contrast with the recalcitrants whom he styled the 'Rip Van Winkles.'[58]

The 'Rip Van Winkle' approach predominated, but the conciliators continually interjected warnings in an attempt to stem the drift of sentiment towards defiance and an insistence on unlimited autonomy. In the Mississippi convention the opposition was led by William Yerger, Amos Johnston, and J. W. C. Watson, and their argument was based on two assumptions. The first was indicated in a speech by Yerger in which he exclaimed: 'Really, if I had not known the circumstances under which we are assembled, I would have forgotten that we had passed through four years of war; would have forgotten that we had been compelled to yield, after a contest of gigantic character, every position, which we had taken, and that we were not now — as the fact is — under the absolute military control of the Government of the United States.'[59] It was not automatic that the defeated South would

[58]'D.S.,' Montgomery, 22 September 1865, *Cincinnati Gazette*, 29 September 1865.
[59]William Yerger, Speech, *Journal of the Proceedings and Debates of the Mississippi Constitutional Convention*, 1865, p. 161.

somehow or other be readmitted without an adequate display of co-operation and trustworthiness. Moreover, the autonomy which was experienced under the President's program could be reduced or removed; it was not assured.

Stemming from this was the tactical assumption that even though the President was following a policy at variance with the radicals, that was not in itself a guarantee that the South would be spared the rigor of their demands. Rather the reverse. The conflict which most Southerners saw emerging within the Federal Government made it more imperative for the South to comply, not less. Indeed, Andrew Johnson's policy was based on the premise that a generous program, coupled with warnings of what might happen if the South failed to respond, would be more likely to elicit loyalty and cooperation than one involving coercion and harsh measures. So Yerger warned that, by himself 'The President cannot do it, for he has now to stand up against a clamor that is threatening to overwhelm him. The conservative people of the North cannot do it; they have as much as they can do to withstand the tide of fanaticism, which is seeking to overwhelm us by giving equality and suffrage to the negro.'[60] Yerger's speech was indicative of the difficulties faced by those advocating conciliation. By describing the consequences of non-compliance in such baleful terms and depicting the radicals as an organized and powerful group advocating extreme policies (neither of which was accurate), he hoped to induce conciliation. This tactic however could, and did, backfire because it simply justified the fears of the recalcitrants that conciliation could achieve nothing among men so fervent and so much in the ascendant. Equally, if he had argued that Congress was dominated by conservatives, the recalcitrants would simply have regarded that as a signal that conciliation was unnecessary.

Exhortations to adopt a conciliatory posture appeared in the newspapers as well. In November, the *Jackson Clarion* urged the Southern States to realize that 'there is but one alternative; we must accept the President's plan, with all our rights restored, or reject it, and continue to wait for salvation and deliverance.'[61] Two days later, the *Augusta Constitutionalist* concurred, recommending that 'on all doubtful points to obtain the positive and unmistakeable [*sic*] requirements of his Excellency, the President, and then, with what good grace there may be, to conform to the same, is the whole present duty of the Southern man.'[62]

Yet for every admonition and every criticism, there was a soothing reassurance. Throughout November, the newspapers of the South showered criticism upon the legislatures and conventions for their failure to respond to the promptings and warnings of the President. The *New Orleans Times*, for example, severely reprimanded South Carolina for its opposition to the thirteenth amendment and to repudiation of the war debt. 'We trust the suicidal policy which has been so fatal elsewhere,' scolded the editorialist, 'will not be pursued here. It might lead to harsh measures, and throw doubts not only on the sincerity of our people but on their judgement and political sagacity.'[63] A week later, however, the tone was very different: 'Radicalism may be daring in its conventicles, and defiant in its black-letter pronunciamentos; but in the House of the Nation's life, with the altar of liberty before them, and their hands on that great Covenant, the Constitution, the disciples of an absurd political creed will scarcely dare to condemn the South in its persistence, and brave the President in his policy.' And the editorial concluded that the South's representatives would 'be proudly welcomed back to their long vacant seats.'[64] A similar pattern was evident in the *Augusta Chronicle* during early December. After excoriating the assemblies because 'they ignored the public good to preserve a record of consistency,' there followed in the very same editorial the confident assertion that 'conservatism will yet rule the country. It is the life blood of a Republic; while radicalism is its greatest foe. The people are the power, and they will soon arouse themselves and rebuke radicalism in an unmistakable manner.'[65]

An even more graphic example of this contradictory assessment of the situation and of the policies available to the Southern can be seen in the reports from James B. Campbell who appears to have been acting as a self-appointed liaison with the White House while sitting in both the convention and the legislature of South Carolina. On 18 September when the convention was in session he lamented: 'There is no doubt of their disposition to do what is proper but there is a remarkable ignorance or forgetfulness of our true position. . . . They seem not only to rely upon you for their salvation but to consider it already secure

---

[62] Editorial, *Augusta Constitutionalist*, 16 November 1865.
[63] Editorial, *New Orleans Times*, 1 November 1865.
[64] *Ibid.*, 8 November 1865.
[65] Editorial, *Augusta Chronicle*, 8 December 1865.

forgetful that they must do their full share to aid and strengthen your efforts to maintain the government on their behalf and as a part of the great whole against those who would consign us to hopeless ruin and depredation.' As for himself, however, he added: 'I am disposed to advocate entire acquiescence in whatever you wish.'[66] Three months later after the legislature had refused to heed the pleas of the President and Secretary of State to repudiate the war debt, Campbell was telling Johnson, without any apparent realization that he too had begun to respond in exactly the fashion he had deplored earlier, that 'In private, [repudiation] was the subject of much anxious consideration, and the prevalent opinion seemed to be, that as the Legislature, in consequence of the action of the convention, could do nothing binding it was better to do nothing than to do an act, which being *notoriously* void, our enemies might charge against us as delusive or an attempt to deceive. My mind settled into this opinion, and that if Repudiation becomes a fixed necessity, then, that a convention be called for the purpose.'[67]

Although Southern politicians and public spokesmen were fully conscious that there was a divergence of opinion in the North over reconstruction policy and that conciliation on their part might be in their long-term self-interest, they rarely pursued the line of action suggested by the 'Uriah Heeps.' Instead, like Campbell and the newspapers, they preferred to assert and protect the autonomy which the policy of reunion, pursued by the President and favored by a large number, if not a majority, of politicians, encouraged. So, rather than cooperating with the President, they attempted to elicit concessions from him, the assumption being that in the coming contest with the radicals he needed them more than they needed him. This pattern of thinking was exemplified in a remark by E. S. Dargan in a letter to Alabama's Provisional Governor. In August when Southerners began to discern the contours of a struggle between, on the one hand the President and his moderate Republican supporters and, on the other, the radicals, he wrote: 'I heard you say that President Johnson *needed* the aid of the South to defend the South against Northern *radicalism*. I thought this remark Just. But let me *add*, that the full strength of the South cannot be felt, by him nor in his support, untill [*sic*] he will enable it to come forward to his assistance — He has thrown so much

---

[66]James B. Campbell to Johnson, Charleston, S.C., 18 September 1865, Johnson MSS, Series I.
[67]James B. Campbell to Johnson, Columbia, S.C., 31 December 1865, Johnson MSS, Series I.

embarrassment on the South by his Proclamation [appointing a Provisional Governor] that he weakens and injures himself thereby.'[68]

The South's demand for assurances was also evident in the remarkable behavior of Benjamin F. Perry during the closing session of the South Carolina legislature. After a series of telegraphic entreaties from Washington urging repudiation of the war debt and ratification of the abolition amendment, Seward finally pointed out, with evident irritation, that Perry's fears about the possible scope of the enforcement section of the amendment were 'querulous and unreasonable.' Instead of producing contrition in Perry, the dispatch reassured and delighted him. A few days later, he told the legislature 'I am happy to find that the Secretary of State does not regard those objections as well-founded, but considers them "querulous and unreasonable." '[69]

In every Southern State during 1865, the advice of the 'Uriah Heeps' that self-interest would be served by the exhibition of a degree of repentance and the willingness to yield on some of the issues arising from Confederate defeat and emancipation was heard and considered. A favorable response to this advice would have produced the kind of reaction which the President and those who supported his policy of trusting the Confederates hoped would emerge. But everywhere this approach was defeated; instead, the Southern conventions and legislatures disputed even the minimal recommendations of the President and rejected out of hand any attempts to go beyond them. The Southern States considered that their interest lay in preserving, and even extending, the autonomy which they possessed under the President's policy whereas attempts to conciliate the radicals or to achieve a speedy readmission to Congress would place that autonomy in jeopardy and at the same time might not even be successful.

Fundamental to this course of action was an analysis of the state of Northern politics which was quite different from that of the 'Uriah Heeps.' As far as the 'Rip Van Winkles' could see, the eventual victory of the conservative and moderate forces in the North was assured, and when that occurred, the South would be readmitted to Congress and spared the panaceas of the radicals. If, however, this did not occur, then the South would be prostrate and the United States beyond redemption. The people of the Northern States, it could be assumed,

[68]E. S. Dargan to Parsons, Mobile, 29 August 1865, Parsons Official Correspondence.
[69]Benjamin F. Perry, Message to the Legislature of South Carolina, 8 November 1865, in *Charleston Courier*, 9 November 1865.

were either irrevocably like Wendell Phillips and Thaddeus Stevens or else so weak-willed that they could not, or dared not, stand in defiance of them. It mattered little which was the correct explanation, for either way the South considered it unwise and undesirable to rejoin such a Union. Perhaps the most explicit statement of this position was made at the Mississippi convention by George L. Potter, an anti-secession Whig, formerly from Connecticut and now leader of the State's recalcitrants, when he said:

Whether that extreme party which insists upon free suffrage and perfect equality now controls the legislation of Congress, I cannot tell; but . . . if it possesses the majority, and insists upon the duty of the government to raise this population to equality with the white citizens of the State, then we may assume it as certain that our delegation will not be readmitted. On the other hand if we are in the majority – if the majority consists of men of just constitutional views on this subject – then we will be admitted under the terms of the Constitution, whether we have a free Constitution, or [not].[70]

The outcome would be decided elsewhere; and therefore the obvious course for the South to pursue was to wait until the conservatives were in control of Congress. Only then would readmission be possible; moreover, only then would it be desirable. Temporary accommodations and political concessions were incapable of influencing the struggle between conservatives and radicals for control of the Republican Party. Meanwhile, the South should retain what rights and autonomy it had rather than compromise them needlessly. In view of the prevalence of this attitude, it was not surprising that pressures from the White House, subtle as they were, produced little response and evoked small concern in the executive offices and legislative chambers of the rebellious states. The issue would be settled in the North, and with confidence the South awaited the result. Typical of this attitude, assured but fatalistic, was the comment of the *Houston Telegraph* during October that even if the South's Congressmen were rejected, 'we look to see the administration sustained by the people. We shall be surprised if it is not. . . . It is interesting for us who are out of politics to stand by and see the fighting. The game always shows best to the

[70] George L. Potter, Speech, *Journal of the Proceedings and Debates of the Mississippi Constitutional Convention*, 1865, p. 62.

spectator. In one sense of the word we are the stakes played for, but it does not lessen the interest.'[71]

The assumption and hope of those who urged a policy of conciliation towards the Southern States was that the South's leaders would reciprocate this sentiment and demonstrate that they could be trusted with self-government. Responsibility for the successful accomplishment of a lenient peace and an uncomplicated reunion therefore rested on the Confederates' shoulders. So, exercising the choice, exploring the options, and manipulating the power handed to them, they responded by, in effect, demanding that the North first of all demonstrate its candidness and prove that sectional and coercive policies had been rejected. At that point the South would reciprocate, but not before.

c: *The President's plan implemented*

The success of the President's project for 'stimulating Southern loyalty' depended upon the use made of the available stimuli. For it was by means of the leverage they provided that the politicians of the South could be pressured and prompted into actions and behavior which might relieve Northern anxieties. The devices which the President had at hand were essentially six in number. The first, which he himself had specified in his conversation with Jacob D. Cox, was the army of occupation and its agency, the Freedmen's Bureau. These would be retained in the South until the State governments had taken adequate steps towards assuming responsibility for the protection of the freedmen and the preservation of law and order. Akin to this was a second lever, the withholding of recognition from the Southern civil governments until such time as the performance of those governments was deemed satisfactory. Seward was clearly aware of this when he wrote in July that the Federal government must 'retain military control and authority until the civil power is reorganized and when that is done we may close the work of amnesty and restoration.'[72] Another form of pressure was contained in the assumption that it was in the interest of the South to provide good treatment and protection for the freedmen

---

[71]Editorial, *Houston Telegraph*, 2 October 1865.
[72]William H. Seward to comte de Gasparin, Washington, D.C., 10 July 1865, Seward MSS. Seward's views on post-war Southern policy are explained and defended in letters to Gasparin during 1865 and early 1866, and they are summarized in Glyndon G. Van Deusen, *William Henry Seward* (New York: Oxford University Press, 1967), pp. 427–31. See also the Introduction, pp. 3–4.

in order to ensure harmonious relations between the races and the stability of the labor-force. To refuse to recognize emancipation and the new status and rights of the freedmen would be detrimental to the Southern whites. A fourth incentive was provided by the pardoning power of the President. This device which affected individuals rather than institutions could be employed as a weapon to maneuver leading Southerners away from passivity and recalcitrance and towards cooperation. Yet another stimulus was available in the withholding of readmission to Congress until satisfactory evidence of loyalty was given, though this lever would be of little avail if the Confederate establishment could retain control and obtain autonomy and security without being seated in Congress. And finally the President could stimulate Southerners with the threat, which was by no means idle, of worse conditions and greater demands on them should his own intended policy fail. The existence of radical Republicans, and the possibility that their policies might prevail, were cited by Johnson, as they had been by Lincoln at Hampton Roads, in order to stimulate Southern compliance.

Behind this approach to reunion lay the assumption that the Confederates were disloyal until they had proven themselves otherwise. Thus, although there was obviously an element of quid pro quo in the scheme whereby Federal interference would be relinquished step by step as the South took on responsibilities, it was apparent nonetheless that the Federal government would retain ultimate control and would decide when its supervision could finally be removed. By means of this procedure, the stimuli would be able to operate effectively. Unfortunately, however, there were complications. Alongside the assumptions that the Confederates were disloyal was another which was likely to conflict with it. Implicit in the views of those who, like the President and his Cabinet, advocated a lenient and magnanimous policy towards the rebel States was an inclination to trust the Confederates and a corresponding belief that if obstacles were not put in their way, they would reciprocate and return in good faith to the Union. After all, since most Southerners had been opposed to the war anyway and since the abolition of slavery meant that there were no obvious institutional and economic differences between the sections, there was considerable likelihood, so the argument went, that a cooperative spirit might emerge in the South. Therefore, given these assumptions, trust and encouragement were deemed to be essential ingredients for a successful Southern policy. This outlook was, however, somewhat at variance with the idea of 'stimulating loyalty.' Hopes that they could be reconciled were dashed by the corollary which was that success depended on how the South responded, and naturally this conceded initiative as well as power to the leaders of the rebellion. Reunion and the outcome of Presidential policy were therefore dependent to a great degree on the very people who had supported the attempt to destroy the Union. They were to be the instruments, not the objects, of Federal policy. This was admitted by Seward, who declared that 'According to the constitution those citizens acting politically in their respective states must reorganise their state governments. We cannot reorganise for them.'[73]

Throughout those months in 1865 when the President's policy was being implemented, the two themes of stimulation and channelling and of trust and encouragement appeared to be inseparable and concurrent, even though mutually contradictory. The President certainly acted as if they were compatible. In dispatches to Southern Governors, he continually stressed that each State was responsible for its own reorganization and the troops would be removed 'when in the opinion of the government that peace and order, and the civil authority has been restored and can be maintained without them.' These words appeared in a dispatch of 17 November to Governor Benjamin G. Humphreys of Mississippi, an important communication because it demonstrated how unaware Johnson, and also Seward, were of the dividing line between the two strands of their policy. Continuing his remarks, Johnson told Humphreys that 'No concession [was required] other than a loyal compliance with the laws and Constitution of the United States, and the adoption of such measures, giving protection to all freedmen, or freemen, in person and property, as will entitle them to resume all their constitutional relations in the Federal Union.' The stimulation and pressure being brought to bear on the South was to be as unobtrusive as possible so that, effectively, the Confederates would be unaware that they were moving in the direction required by the President. Furthermore, it was to be understood that there was 'no disposition, arbitrarily, on the part of the Government, to dictate what [the States'] action should be.' Instead the President's task was 'to simply and kindly advise a policy.'[74] That this was his intention he was careful to

---

[73] Seward to Gasparin, Washington, D.C., 10 July 1865, Seward MSS.
[74] Johnson to Humphreys, Washington, D.C., 17 November 1865, Johnson MSS, Series IIIB, Vol. I.

explain in an interview as late as February 1866, a month after his restoration scheme had been rejected by Congress. At that time he was reported to have said that '*His own action in prescribing terms upon which these States should be recognized, in so far as he had prescribed any, not in harmony with their forms of State government, or in so far as it seemed to imply that they would not be recognized as States unless they complied with his conditions, was in reality and meant to be, advisory.*'[75] Painfully convoluted though the statement seems, its meaning was revealed in the last few words: the President did not intend to require or demand but only to suggest and advise.

The President could tell Humphreys that he was merely advising and that passing adequate laws for the protection of the freedmen was not a concession but was simply part of the process of reorganization. But despite these assurances, Humphreys and the other Southern Governors were quite aware that they were being pressured by the restraints and obstacles which the President was employing in order to stimulate them to loyal behavior. And at some point the President would be forced to decide whether he placed greater reliance upon conciliation or upon inducement. In the early months he had indicated that the latter would be insisted on since he would not remove the stimuli until after the Southern assemblies had proved themselves loyal and capable of self-government. During July he had upheld the United States military authorities in disputes over civil–military jurisdiction in North Carolina and Mississippi.[76] He had also forbidden Sharkey a month later to organize a State militia but instead when 'military power is needed to preserve order and enforce the law' to call upon Major-General Slocum, the State commander.[77] Furthermore, he had suggested to Sharkey that his State's convention enact a qualified Negro suffrage so as to conciliate, and even anticipate, radical demands, the radicals being an obstacle to Southern readmission and

[75]*Cincinnati Gazette*, 11 January 1866. The report was filed by Whitelaw Reid, under his nom de plume, 'Agate,' and was an account of an interview with a Senator Smith and a Representative Jones. It is not clear who these men were but perhaps Reid was protecting their identity by giving them pseudonyms.

[76]General Henry W. Slocum to Sharkey, Vicksburg, 25 July 1865, Sharkey MSS; General Thomas Ruger to Holden, 1 and 11 August 1865, Holden Official Correspondence.

[77]Johnson to Sharkey, Washington, D.C., 21 August 1865, Johnson MSS, Series IIIA.

thereby a stimulus to Southern loyalty.[78] Finally, late in July, the President had annulled a mayoral election in Richmond, Virginia, because N. P. Sturdivant, an avowed secessionist, had been elected.[79] But by August Andrew Johnson was confronted with an acute dilemma which he could not leave unresolved.

The President's civil appointees, the Provisional Governors, had to deal with a situation riddled with anomalies. These needed clarification if they were to govern effectively and be able to establish viable governing institutions. Were the military or were the embryo governments paramount in the South? Were the military expected to interfere in, and perhaps thwart, Southern reorganization and attempts at self-government or were they supposed to provide support and aid in this difficult task? Moreover, so Sharkey and the Provisional Governors argued, by continually objecting to the difficulties which the military placed in the way of reorganization, could not the President be put in a position where he would have to resolve the problem one way or the other, and probably to their benefit? So partly as an outgrowth of the practical problems of government and partly as a political device aimed by the Southern Governors at producing a favorable adjudication by the President, the issue came to a head in August when Sharkey and Slocum collided over the proposed Mississippi militia.

The goal of the Presidential policy was to produce effective governments in the South and not to frustrate their emergence. This tended to override the question of the nature of those governments because, after all, the latter was dependent upon the former. The process of reorganization preceded, and therefore took priority over, its content. So it was not surprising that, with the future of his policy at issue, the President was forced to support his civil rather than his military agent in Mississippi. Accordingly, on 30 August in a telegram to Carl Schurz, he countermanded Slocum's General Order No. 22. By this move, he indicated his priorities unmistakably. 'One great object,' the President asserted, 'is to induce the people to come forward in the de-

---

[78] Johnson to Sharkey, Washington, D.C., 15 August 1865, Johnson MSS, Series IIIA.

[79] Johnson to Governor Francis Pierpont, Washington, D.C., 1 August 1865, Johnson MSS, Series IIIA. The President was careful not to offend Pierpont by his interference in the election and wrote to reassure him and gain his approval of the move.

fence of the State and Federal Government. . . . The people must be trusted with their Government, and if trusted my opinion is they will act in good faith and restore their former constitutional relations with all the States composing the Union.'[80] The meaning of this was not lost on the South. Editorials applauded the President.[81] Harvey M. Watterson later told the President, 'your endorsement of [Sharkey's] militia call, electrified the whole South. From that day to this, I have met with no man who has not a kind word to say of President Johnson.'[82]

Actually this decision was not so crucial. The broad outline of the Federal policy and the assumptions behind it were already sufficiently clear before the Sharkey–Slocum affair. That episode simply clinched the matter by clarifying anomalies and removing lingering uncertainties. From the outset it was evident that conciliation, autonomy, self-determination were all explicit in the kind of approach to the rebels pursued by the Federal government in 1865. Moreover, with the supporters of this policy dependent upon the South for success and vindication, the Confederates were quite aware of the power at their disposal. Consequently the initiative was from the outset handed over to the South. No matter how cleverly Andrew Johnson might have manipulated the details of his policy, the context in which he could do so had deprived the President of the leverage which he needed. Furthermore it had also given the Confederates room to maneuver around those very pressures which were intended to provoke them into loyal behavior. With a large degree of self-government already granted and recognized, Southern politicians felt that they had sufficient power and influence that they did not need to concede in order to obtain the rest. Therefore, they began to demand that complete autonomy within their States be recognized by the Federal government before concessions and bargains could be made. Under these circumstances and because of the anomalous and unprecedented conditions existing in the Southern States, the Federal executive branch felt constrained to

---

[80] Johnson to Carl Schurz, Washington, D.C., 30 August 1865, Johnson MSS, Series IIIA.

[81] From that day, the *Jackson News* carried on its masthead an endorsement of Johnson for President in 1868, and the *Raleigh Sentinel* presented over its editorial columns that part of the Johnson–Schurz telegram which stated that 'The people must be trusted with their Government etc. . . .'

[82] H. M. Watterson to Johnson, Vicksburg, 7 October 1865, Johnson MSS, Series. I.

clarify confused situations and jurisdictions along lines which would reassure Southern governors and assemblies and encourage them to be cooperative. Obstacles and threats which the President and his Cabinet had considered essential as devices to 'stimulate Southern loyalty' were therefore frequently removed before adequate loyalty had been demonstrated. Indeed they were being seen as obstacles to, rather than producers of, loyalty.

The internal contradictions and inconsistencies of this policy were becoming apparent. Although aimed at restoring self-government and dependent upon the satisfactory action of the South's leading men, it embodied elements of coercion and pressure. As the government cleared military encumbrances from the path to reunion, Southern politicians were close to achieving autonomy in their own States. With the possibility of continued military rule rapidly vanishing, those other levers which the Federal government held in reserve, the denial of speedy readmission to Congress and the threat of more severe terms from the Republican radical minority, seemed to recede out of sight. Their likelihood, although recognized, was of less consequence when self-government could be obtained at little short-term cost.

So the Federal policy did not change; it imperceptibly shifted emphasis so that it became more clearly a program of conciliation rather than of inducement. There is little doubt that Seward and Johnson were unaware of this, but Southern politicians understood fully what was happening. They realized that the architects of a policy originally incorporating elements of a 'carrot and stick' approach were now withdrawing the stick and conceding the carrot. Stress was placed more on encouragement and conciliation than on pressure and incentive. The cable to Schurz of 30 August was indicative of the President's approach, but there were other instances. Johnson had just previously told Governor Sharkey that 'the Government does not intend to irritate or humiliate the People of the South but will be magnanimous and remove the cause of your complaint at the earliest period it is possible.'[83] This clearly was going beyond simply advising Southern officials, and a month later the President was more categorical. Suggesting to General George H. Thomas that black troops should, where possible, be removed, he indicated that the meaning behind this was that 'If the Southern States can be encouraged I have no doubt in my

---

[83] Johnson to Sharkey, Washington, D.C., 25 August 1865, Johnson MSS, Series IIIA.

own mind, that they will proceed and restore their Governments with-in the next six or seven months and renew their former relations with the Federal Govt.'[84] A final indicator of the shift in emphasis was pre-sented in the lengthy dispatch to Humphreys cited earlier, for Johnson concluded it by stating that 'There must be confidence between the Government and the States – While the Government confides in the people, the people must have faith in the government. This must be mutual and reciprocal, or all that has been done will be thrown away.'[85]

The mutuality and reciprocity indicated here were evidently not the quid pro quos envisaged by the concept of 'stimulating Southern loyalty.' By late summer the government was conceding first and the South reciprocating later, and only if it wished so to do. The process of 'stimulating loyalty' was being reversed. The President had yielded the initiative and was now responding to events in the South rather than directing and channelling them. At times it even appeared that the President was actually cooperating with recalcitrant Southerners in his attempts to reassure and encourage. On one occasion he was guilty of what amounted to collusion in an effort to camouflage evi-dence of Southern disloyalty. With the President's approval, General Leroy P. Walker and other prominent Alabamians sent a telegram from Washington to leading officials in their State, suggesting that

The proper policy is to declare the ordinance of secession void also all laws creating debts for prosecution of the war.

If the latter cannot be done then let there be no action which will excite the Suspicion that it is contemplated to assume the war debt.

It is all important that the action of the Convention should be judicious and free from any possible misconstruction.[86]

It would be incorrect, however, to conclude that the President had gone over to the rebels. Although encouragement and appeasement were becoming conspicuous, efforts were still being made to pressure and cajole the South. But there was no coherence or system in the

[84]Johnson to General George H. Thomas, Washington, D.C., 8 September 1865, Johnson MSS, Series IIIB, Vol. I.

[85]Johnson to Humphreys, Washington, D.C., 17 November 1865, Johnson MSS, Series IIIB, Vol. I.

[86]Leroy P. Walker to Parsons and Benjamin Fitzpatrick, Washington, D.C., 18 September 1865, Parsons Official Correspondence. Fitzpatrick was President of the Alabama convention.

President's dealings with the Confederates. By the fall the Federal policy had gone awry and this can be seen through an examination of four aspects of the mechanism as it worked in practice.

The first symptom of this could be detected in the President's simultaneous adoption of apparently contradictory tactics. While he was yielding on questions such as the bestowal of pardons, the influence and jurisdiction of the Federal troops, and the specifics of the Southern conventions' response to Northern requirements regarding the secession ordinances, war debts, and emancipation, he was increasing the range of matters upon which the South had to act. The thirteenth amendment was added, as was a code for the freedmen; repudiation of the war debts was demanded insistently of South Carolina and Mississippi even though that had not been suggested originally; and finally the Provisional Governors had been retained. Evidently the South had not been sufficiently cooperative or conciliatory, and was being urged to do more. Yet the substance had already been gained by the Southern States and therefore in the context within which the South had to act there were lacking those elements of coercion necessary for inducing compliance. Instead compliance with this most recent insistence and pressure was simply an option with very little relevance. Under these circumstances, the Yuletide imperative from the South Carolinian, A. S. Wallace, 'Make the *requirement* absolute, the state will meet it.' was fruitless because there were no sanctions available to the President. Moreover, Wallace admitted the unlikelihood of success in his next sentence, 'The present Legislature is largely ultra not more than ten or twenty union in the house out of 124. The Senate a like proportion hence the indisposition to meet the requirements of the government.'[87] A policy of reconciliation, with Southern autonomy and confidence in Southern good faith as basic premises, was never likely to provide much chance of success for either absolute requirements or subtle guidance. By the winter of 1865 there was in fact no possibility whatsoever.

The stimulus for Southern compliance which the existence of the radical Republicans had provided was also in disarray. Instead of acting as a reminder that non-compliance with the President's policy would give ammunition to the radicals and increase their strength and number, this threat was in fact twisted around by Southern politicians

[87] A. S. Wallace to Seward, Columbia, S.C., 25 December 1865, Johnson MSS, Series I.

so that the President's policy became a protective shield against the radicals. The President was saving the South from worse possibilities and therefore the radicals' demands could safely be ignored, perhaps even the President's also. Yet there was a flaw in this line of argument. If the President intended to hold the middle ground in the North and force the radical Republicans to give up what were widely regarded as extreme policies, he would have to ensure that he had drawn from the South all those concessions and indications of loyalty which would satisfy the demands of the moderate majority of the Republican Party. He could not let the South fall short. The point to which he felt the conservative Northern majority would require the South to go was, it seems, apparent to Lewis Parsons, for the latter cabled the President in September regretting that the Alabama legislature had failed to grant unqualified testimony rights to the freedmen, since 'If it had been done the fight would have to be made on the precise line where I understand you to have placed it – viz – the right of the people of these States to declare who shall vote. . . .'[88] Another Alabama politician, E. S. Dargan, had earlier come to the same conclusion when he had told Parsons that 'There is no stand we can make against the fanatics of the North but on the question of negro suffrage. We may stand our *hand* at that point, but if overruled then woe is *ours* – and woe is the fate of the American people for ages to come.'[89] This meant however that the Southern States would have to yield virtually all measures short of Negro suffrage before the contest could be joined with any hope of success. But the policy of allowing the South a large measure of self-determination made the need to worry about the radical Republicans less urgent and this was simply intensified by Presidential appeasement. The South was thereby given the option of ignoring the radicals, yet by doing so the necessity and credibility of the radicals' policies was likely to be enhanced.

A third indication that the executive policy was awry lay in the difference of opinion between Johnson and Seward and the Southern politicians as to whether the Southern representatives would be readmitted to Congress in December. In accordance with their policy of 'stimulating Southern loyalty,' Johnson and Seward frequently indicated that denial of readmission might be the consequence of non-

---

[88] Parsons to Johnson, Montgomery, 23 September 1865, Johnson MSS, Series I.
[89] E. S. Dargan to Parsons, Mobile, 29 August 1865, Parsons Official Correspondence.

cooperation. To William C. Rives, Virginia's Whig elder statesman, Seward wrote in November that Congress would not waive its iron-clad oath requirement and therefore the Southern States 'had better send an idiot or a child to Congress who can take it, than to send a wise man who cannot.'[90] Johnson also indicated that he had no control over Congress which was constitutionally empowered to decide on the eligibility of its own membership. Essentially therefore it was Congress, not the President, which would decide when reunion could take place. So, in September, he told J. C. Bolling of Columbia, South Carolina, 'I think the members from Tennessee will be permitted to take their seats – provided the other Southern States elect members who are unmistakeably union in practice and sentiment and so amend their constitutions and pass laws in regard to emancipation and freedom which will give them proper protection.'[91] There was no more optimism in November when the President told the Federal General, James B. Steedman who had written about Alexander Stephens' nomination for the Senate, that 'The information we have here is that all members elect to Congress from Georgia, will not be able to take the Oath of Office. A modification of the Oath by the present Congress is exceedingly doubtful.' And, regarding Stephens, he commented, 'If elected he would not be permitted to take his seat, or, in other words he could not take the Oath required, other difficulties being out of the way. He stands charged with Treason, and no disposition has been made of his case.'[92]

The President in fact seemed to have no expectation that the South would be readmitted in December. This was implicit in the letters already cited and it was unequivocally stated on other occasions. In September he had told Rev. James P. Boyce, a member of the South Carolina convention, 'The proceedings of your convention so far is [*sic*] giving great satisfaction here. I hope that in less than the next twelve months the union of the States will be complete and restored.'[93] The letter to General Thomas of 8 September had concluded with the hope that the Southern States 'will proceed and restore their Govern-

[90]Seward to William C. Rives, in *Montgomery Advertiser*, 9 November 1865.
[91]Johnson to J. C. Bolling, Washington, D.C., 21 September 1865, Johnson MSS, Series IIIB, Vol. I.
[92]Johnson to General James B. Steedman, Washington, D.C., 24 November 1865, Johnson MSS, Series IIIB, Vol. I.
[93]Johnson to Rev. James P. Boyce, 19 September 1865, Johnson MSS, Series IIIB, Vol. I.

ments within the next six or seven months and renew their former relations with the Federal Govt.'[94] And in communications with Sharkey on 1 November and with Perry on 27 November the President had revealed similar expectations.[95]

Southern politicians and public spokesmen were often as pessimistic as the President but in the long run they were reasonably convinced that reorganized governments and elected Federal representatives from the South could not forever be excluded and denied recognition. Even if this were delayed until 1866, they were confident that Northern parties would then be competing for Southern votes or that the opponents of reunion would be rejected by public sentiment as disunionists. Johnson too was thinking along these lines, for there was no urgency in his warnings that Congress alone would determine Southern readmission but instead an assumption that those who attempted to keep the South out of Congress did so at their own peril. The result was that while the President employed the possibility of readmission as a realistic threat to stimulate Southern cooperation, he was at the same time not very concerned as to whether the South tried to comply either with Congress' ironclad test or with the Republicans' demands on other matters. Southerners however were aware of their own autonomy as well as of the government's concern that they determine their own self-interest and act upon it. Had representation in Congress been seen as a means towards attaining autonomy within the South, then it might have acted as a stimulus to Southern loyalty. But autonomy was not dependent upon readmission. Moreover, it might be completely undermined by a readmission conditional on ironclad tests which would disqualify all Congressmen-elect with Confederate records. Therefore, although the role of readmission as a component in the Federal policy became confused, it was unlikely anyway that in this context it could have acted as a stimulus and incentive to loyal behavior.

Finally, the contradictions which were intrinsic to the nature of Northern policy and which were then made apparent and aggravated in its enactment could be seen in Andrew Johnson's own assessment of its progress. He seemed to vacillate in his evaluations. In October he had displayed misgivings about the behavior of the South when he had

---

[94]Johnson to Thomas, Washington, D.C., 8 September 1865, Johnson MSS, Series IIIB, Vol. I.
[95]In Johnson MSS, Series IIIB, Vol. I.

retained the Provisional Governors and increased the procedures needing enactment prior to readmission. By late November just before Congress was reassembling his displeasure was well known. 'Leo,' the *Charleston Courier*'s Washington correspondent, reported that 'the President, has been led to believe that the tendency of political events in the South is reactionary. He will not, therefore, move another step towards restoration till he shall be satisfied of his error in this respect.'[96] Southerners in Washington were carefully reading the political signs, and, reported the *New York Tribune*, 'The loss of Executive confidence, which they admit they discerned, occasions serious apprehensions.'[97] The President was indeed disappointed and in that letter to General Steedman concerning the intended nomination of Alexander Stephens for the Senate election, he manifested unmistakable impatience, observing at one point, 'There seems, in many of the elections something like defiance, which is all out of place at this time.'[98] The government's beneficence was being reciprocated with ingratitude and political shortsightedness. Therefore, in order to minimize the damaging effect of this response on the Federal policy, the President urged Perry to keep South Carolina's Congressmen-elect away from Washington, a move which James B. Campbell endorsed, assuring Johnson later that it was 'a great fortune that the Southern members are not admitted or present to embarrass you, as they would be sure to do by foolish sayings and doings.'[99] Nevertheless there were in Washington, contrary to Campbell's knowledge and the President's warning, many Southern politicians seeking their seats when Congress reconvened.

Distressed though he may have been at these manifestations of Southern recalcitrance and indiscretion, the President, like the newspapers and politicians of the Southern establishment, explained that in general he was considerably encouraged by the trend of events since the surrender. Concurrent with his expressions of displeasure to Steedman, he was reported to have told the Republican Governor of Indiana, Oliver P. Morton, that 'The people . . . thought that the Southern

[96]'Leo,' Washington correspondence, *Charleston Courier*, 21 November 1865.
[97]New York Tribune extract, *Jackson Clarion*, 26 November 1865.
[98]Johnson to Steedman, Washington, D.C., 24 November 1865, Johnson MSS, Series IIIB, Vol. I.
[99]James B. Campbell to Johnson, Columbia S.C., 31 December 1865, Johnson MSS, Series I; Johnson to Perry, Washington, D.C., 27 November 1865, Johnson MSS, Series IIIA.

States moved rather slow, but all things considered, he believed they were doing remarkably well.'[100] And a month later after Congress had rejected the Southern applicants, Johnson was accompanying General Grant's hopeful and generally tolerant assessment of Southern developments with a message to Congress in which he expressed his pleasure that 'the aspect of affairs is more promising than, in view of the circumstances, could well have been expected.' And he continued, 'The people throughout the South evince a laudable desire to renew their allegiance to the government, and to repair the devastations of war by a prompt and cheerful return to peaceful pursuits. An abiding faith is entertained that their action will conform to their professions, and that, in acknowledging the supremacy of the Constitution and laws of the United States, their loyalty will be unreservedly given to the government, whose leniency they cannot fail to appreciate and whose fostering care will soon restore them to a condition of prosperity.'[101]

Although annoyed at the incontrovertible evidence of Southern defiance, the President concluded nevertheless that affairs were proceeding as well as could be expected in the South. This was because the policy of restoration was premised, despite intentions and actions towards stimulating and pressuring the South to loyal behavior, upon 'an abiding faith' that the South's leaders could be trusted and that the only means for producing harmony and reunion between the sections was by a conciliatory policy which would in turn produce a like response from the South. So that, despite evidence of recalcitrance, this approach towards the South's political leaders would have to be persevered in because, in a policy based on conciliation, odd instances of recalcitrance were insufficient to jettison the approach. For only by further conciliation could that antagonism and uncooperativeness be assuaged. However, such an approach would of necessity undermine, if not neutralize, any attempts made to pressure and cajole the South into compliance. The Federal government could not present itself both as a source of encouragement as well as of reproof, restoring autonomy and self-determination and at the same time withholding and restricting them.

Both tendencies could not be coequal and simultaneous; one or other had to take precedence. Yet evidently Andrew Johnson and his

---

[100]Washington correspondence, *New Orleans Times*, 27 November 1865.
[101]'Letter of General Grant Concerning Affairs at the South,' 18 December 1865, *Senate Executive Documents*, 1st. Sess., 39th Cong, I, No. 2, 1–2.

close advisers hoped that this need not be so and felt that they were continuing to pursue both approaches throughout 1865. This was evident from Johnson's Annual Message of December. In this, the President explained that the reintroduction of the Federal government into the South through the courts, the reopening of the ports, and the post office was advantageous to that section. 'Is it not a sure promise of harmony and renewed attachment to the Union,' he said, 'that after all that has happened the return of the General Government is known only as a beneficence?'[102] Yet earlier he had pledged, 'But if any State neglects or refuses to perform its offices there is the more need that the General Government should maintain all its authority and as soon as practicable resume the exercise of all its functions.'[103] The contradiction however was not realized by the President or Seward or by those Northerners who supported a conciliatory policy yet wanted the President to pressure the South on the terms for readmission. Immediately after this contradiction was unwittingly stated in the Message, the President indicated that he had nonetheless given priority to conciliation: 'I know very well that this policy is attended with some risk; that for its success it requires at least the acquiescence of those States which it concerns; that it implies an invitation to those States, by renewing their allegiance to the United States, to resume their functions as States of the Union. But it is a risk that must be taken.'[104]

Without really being aware of it or having made a conscious decision, the Administration stressed conciliation and offered free options, and thereby attained only the form and process of reorganization and restoration in the South. The content of that process could have been molded only by pressure and stimulation, even coercion. This, however, although embodied in the original intention and scheme, was relegated to a secondary position, an inevitability in view of the policy's avowed goals and presuppositions. 'Stimulating Southern loyalty' may have been what the President hoped to do and felt he was doing in his restoration policy; but by initially conceding virtual self-government and presuming that the Confederates could be trusted and conciliated, the Federal government lost the initiative and forfeited its leverage and power to persuade.

---

[102] James D. Richardson, *A Compilation of the Messages and Papers of the Presidents, 1789–1897* (Washington, D.C.; U.S. Congress, 1898), VI, 312–14.
[103] *Ibid.*
[104] *Ibid.*

4
Discretion decentralized

The mechanics of Provisional Government were central to the problem of reunion and restoration. The fashion in which the South was governed while under the direct control of the civil and military power of the United States was probably more important than the details of the formal terms offered by the President. After all, the conventions and legislatures which were called upon to consider the President's stipulations were to be elected from a society which had been organized and governed by Washington and its local agents, the Provisional Governors.

Rather than retain the South under direct military control, the President chose to restore self-government. But it was a 'self-government' so regulated and restricted that Southern politicians could assert simultaneously that their State was sovereign and also that its action was substantially limited both by military occupation and the power of Northern politicians and officials. These same anomalous circumstances ensured that the role and power of the Provisional Governor would also be ambiguous, even confused.

The men who were selected by the President to reorganize Southern governments were endowed with powers more extensive than State Governors enjoyed under normal conditions. David L. Swain noted with exaggeration that 'the Governor is in the full exercise of powers, not merely greater than known to any of his predecessors, but greater than ever were claimed for an English monarch since 1688.'[1] The power of the Provisional Governor was in fact great, even if not as wide as Swain claimed. First of all, his appointive powers were virtually unlimited, the only limitation being that the appointee be pardoned and have the approval of the White House. It was not surprising, therefore, that Governors James Madison Wells of Louisiana and Isaac Murphy of Arkansas, who had been chosen by only a section of their State's electorate under the Lincoln Ten Per Cent Plan, urged

---

[1] Swain to Graham, Chapel Hill, 4 July 1865, W. A. Graham Collection.

Johnson to bestow on them the title of Provisional Governor. Wells, in particular, wanted to be able to build a broader base of power and support than he possessed under the constitution and elections of 1864. Throughout the spring and summer he addressed imploring letters to the President.[2] On 14 October a proclamation appointing Wells Provisional Governor was even written out, but never issued.[3] Murphy was less demanding than Wells and even some other Arkansas politicians, feeling that a proclamation recognizing that Arkansas was no longer in insurrection against the United States would bestow the necessary authority and legitimacy to sustain his own government. He did not wish, however (and this was extremely illogical if the insurrection were ended), that the United States troops be withdrawn, since General Reynolds was contributing greatly to the satisfactory functioning of his government.[4]

Second, the Provisional Governors were given authority as a result of the approval and endorsement of the President. They were his men and he was committed to sustaining his appointees in such a vital work. This bestowed an authority that was beyond the normal scope of State Governors and was a guarantee that they would be treated with respect. If they were not, they could always retort that it was the President of the United States, not merely a local official, who was being defied. A chain of authority had in effect been established which linked the governor with the White House. Of this, William W. Holden reminded the justices of Craven County, when he announced that 'Both the Mayor and Commissioners of Newbern and the County Court of Craven exist by virtue of the Provisional Government, and are dependent on it, as I am on the President.'[5]

With these powers at their disposal, the Provisional Governors could have become commanding officials. Yet they did not, for there were substantial weaknesses in their position. The authority they possessed from the President was a liability as well as a potential asset. Appointed by the Commander-in-Chief of the forces of the victorious

[2] These pleas commenced with a letter to the President of 29 April 1865 to be found in the Johnson MSS, Series I, and were followed by a visit in May to Washington by Wells and Hugh Kennedy, Mayor of New Orleans.
[3] Draft of the proclamation, dated 14 October 1865, in Andrew Johnson MSS, Series I.
[4] Isaac Murphy to Johnson, Little Rock, 8 July 1865, Johnson MSS, Series I.
[5] Holden to the Justices of Person County, Raleigh, 19 December 1865, Letterbook, Holden Official Correspondence.

enemy, the Provisional Governors did not stand vindicated in the eyes of those they were to govern. Besides, they were the instruments for relaying and effecting the United States' requirements of the defeated South. Consequently most Provisional Governors were forced to use their immense patronage in order to conciliate or neutralize their opponents as well as to build a base of support to compensate for their own lack of a popular electoral mandate.

It was impossible for the President's Provisional Governors to function with any effectiveness unless they used the patronage to acquire prestige and local endorsement. In this there was, however, a paradox. A failure to wield the appointing power would have deprived the Provisional Governor of the political leverage and respect necessary to ensure his State's compliance with the President's terms. Yet the very use of that power forced most Governors into accommodation with the policies and ambitions of those they had rewarded with office. These latter tended to be the old ruling classes, often leading secessionists, who were not too eager to repudiate the war debt or acquiesce in uncompensated abolition and nullification of the secession ordinance. Whenever the Provisional Governor had, on the other hand, used the patronage to place in power men who were not of the traditional ruling groups, then organized pressure was often directed at undermining his position. If he was not captured, he was invariably immobilized by the old politicians. Fence-mending within his own State frequently occupied the time and energies of the Provisional Governor, while building bridges between the two sections generally became a secondary consideration.

As far as the President was concerned, the Provisional Governors were *the* vital and essential instruments in the work of restoration; they possessed substantive authority. The Assistant Attorney General, J. Hubley Ashton, explained to Holden in June the depth of this concern:

The President desires to strengthen your hands in the reorganization of society in your state by every means Constitutionally belonging to him. To you, primarily, he looks for the support of law and order in your State, and for the initiation of such as will, at the earliest day possible, place her in proper relations with the Federal Union, and thus restore her to all the blessings of a Government which we proudly think to be as strong as it is merciful.[6]

[6]J. Hubley Ashton to Holden, Washington, D.C., 23 June 1865, Holden Official Correspondence.

The task was two-fold – to reorganize the State and to restore it to its place in the Union. With these duties assigned to the Provisional Governors, there was little remaining for the President to do besides administer assurances and correctives when necessary. Since so much depended on the actions of the Provisional Governor it can be readily understood why the President tended to throw his support to him in any dispute or difficulty that occurred. The President had to encourage the Privisional Governor in his onerous task, while the latter in turn exhorted the citizens of his State, upon whom he relied for cooperation in the reorganization of government. The *Charleston Courier* analyzed the situation correctly with the statement that 'The work of restoration, however, must rest with the people . . . Governor PERRY can only direct he cannot control.'[7] So, in practice, Holden's remarks to the Craven County judges would have to be reversed. All authority in the South under Provisional Government flowed from the President, but it was not administered by him, since the politicians of the Southern States were the arbiters of the fate of that power.

a: *Appointments*

If the mandate granted to the Provisional Governors by the President and his Cabinet was extensive, so also was the discretion in the exercise of it. William W. Holden, defending his course as Provisional Governor in North Carolina, admitted, 'I had no lights to guide me in the work of reorganizing and reconstructing an American state, save the instructions received from time to time from the President; and necessarily these instructions have been only of a general character.'[8] The apparent inadequacy of these instructions was not the result of negligence on the President's part. Rather, it reflected his fundamental desire to redistribute the powers gained during the war by the Federal government and to avoid all tendencies toward Federal dictation and manipulation. Fundamental principles of the Constituion had to be reaffirmed before restoration's 'details and collaterals,' a phrase used by both Lincoln and Johnson, could be discussed.

The specifics of reorganization in the South during 1865, though not the fundamentals, differed from State to State, and the policies employed in many cases were completely dissimilar. The war had 'in

---

[7] Editorial, *Charleston Courier*, 28 July 1865.
[8] William W. Holden, Letter to North Carolinians who asked him to run for Governor, 17 October 1865, in 'Memoirs of W. W. Holden,' *The John Lawson Monographs of the Trinity College Historical Society*, II (Durham: The Seaman Printing, 1911), 66.

its revolutionary progress deprived the people of the [Confederate States] of all civil government.' That was the analysis offered by the Presidential proclamations appointing the States' Provisional Governors. But whether the latter inherited societies devoid of all government or governments devoid of all legitimacy until a Provisional Governor was appointed was a matter open to debate. This basic decision had not been made, and from it flowed many other questions of jurisdiction and authority which the Provisional Governors were, by necessity, to decide unilaterally.

On his return to Georgia in July, James Johnson made speeches to meetings in Savannah, Augusta, and Macon, and at each he explained that, as Provisional Governor, he had no authority except 'to enable you to form a government.'[9] Entailed in that task was the formulation of rules for calling and holding a convention which would then establish civil government. He had no power, he said, to appoint officials or to reinstate those who had served under the Confederacy. Legal affairs as well as the important task of tendering amnesty oaths would have to be handled by the military. Georgia was, in fact, to remain under martial law and without any form of civil government until after the convention. But public pressure, during the two weeks following these speeches and his proclamation of 13 July, forced Johnson to countermand the instructions from Seward and Speed upon which he had based the earlier definition of his own powers. The *Augusta Constitutionalist* in particular excoriated Johnson for his slowness in reorganization (the election of the convention would not be held until 4 October) and for his denial of civil government to the people of Georgia.[10] Therefore, on 7 August he reinstated all Confederate officials who had been amnestied, and appointed civil ordinaries to aid the military in tendering the oath.

The same interpretation of the situation inherited by a Provisional Governor was articulated by William Marvin of Florida. Cooperating very closely with General J. G. Foster, Marvin did not recognize any of the Confederate civil officials, although amnestied officers could administer the oath and judges of election appointed by him aided in the process of electing the convention delegates. Not until after the convention had assembled did Marvin restore the Confederate officials.[11]

[9]*North Carolina Standard*, 14 July 1865; *Charleston Courier*, 12 and 24 July 1865.

[10]*Augusta Constitutionalist*, 5 August 1865.

[11]William Marvin, Testimony, *Joint Committee on Reconstruction*, Part IV, p. 6.

In North Carolina, Holden also assumed that civil government was in abeyance when he took office. Unlike Marvin and Johnson, however, he proceeded to fill the vacant posts with new men, in effect building a government from the foundations. Holden, who was editor of the *North Carolina Standard* and had been prominent in Democratic politics since the 1840s, attempted to raise to power Democrats and those who were outside the political establishment. The Whig party included within its ranks most of the men of wealth and social prestige of North Carolina, and Holden intended to remove its adherents from their entrenched positions in office. William A. Graham, Josiah Turner, Jr, David L. Swain, Zebulon B. Vance, William Dortch, Thomas Ruffin, Benjamin S. Hedrick were the leaders of that party and, even before the Provisional Government, were engaged in a personal and political feud with Holden. Yet, unhesitatingly, throughout June and July, the Provisional Governor appointed about 3,500 officials mainly from the party and classes that previously had not been so favored.[12]

The means whereby Holden could accomplish so much in so short a period of time was similar to that used by the President in dealing with the Southern States. A delegation from each county would come to Raleigh requesting that their county be reorganized. After Holden had received a list of eligible claimants for county offices either through a reliable inhabitant or an agent sent from Raleigh, he would appoint a Justice of the Peace who would in turn select county officers. State appointments were handled directly by Holden, and so was the selection of State railroad and bank officials. It was a thoroughgoing overhaul, a cleaning of the Augean stables, so that a new government with new men would emerge in the State.[13] Holden regarded his scheme as a piece of creative building and he told the President, 'I have thought it best to begin at the foundations and build upwards.'[14] But to others like David L. Swain, it seemed to be merely partisan destruction:

---

[12]Holden to Johnson, Raleigh, 24 July 1865, Johnson MSS, Series I.
[13]A thorough discussion of Holden's patronage policy can be found in Horace W. Raper, 'William Woods Holden, A Political Biography' (unpublished Ph.D. dissertation, University of North Carolina, 1951). Why this has not been published seems difficult to comprehend. A printed biography of Holden is much needed, especially as Governor Jonathan Worth, his successor, already has a biographer.
[14]Holden to Johnson, Raleigh, 24 July 1865, Johnson MSS, Series I.

Gov. Holden takes it to pieces from foundation to turret. He removes all the Justices of the Peace, re-appoints and creates new ones to be removed in turn before the Convention, before they have it in their power to exercise judicial functions. He removed the Commissioners of villages, and what is most remarkable, the Presidents of Bankrupt Banks and ruined Rail Roads...[15]

The very success of Holden's redistribution of the patronage made his defeat at the forthcoming election inevitable. The 'oligarchs,' as Holden called them (and Swain was one), had to ensure Holden's defeat; otherwise the provisional appointments would remain operative after civil government was restored. Swain's criticisms that the changes, since provisional and temporary in intent, were far too sweeping, were unfounded unless Holden were in office for just a short time; and this Swain intended to ensure.

A similar reaction was experienced in 1866 by Hamilton of Texas, though it was less extreme because his use of the patronage power was hardly so proscriptive. Hamilton, a renegade secession Democrat like Holden, felt that his State could only be reorganized if a new spirit permeated it. Instead of a wholesale appointment to office of new men, however, he preferred to delay the convention until early in the new year when society, as well as attitudes towards the freedmen, had become more stabilized and reliable. He suggested that a cautious use of the pardoning power by the President and threats to confiscate 'the property of *a few* of the leading rebels – although never consummated – would have a tremendous effect upon the entire class.'[16] As regards the patronage and the form of the government in Texas, he proclaimed during July that he would create only a minimum number of provisional officers sufficient to run the affairs of State, some of whom were new appointees, others existing officials who were reinstated. This would, at the same time, avoid the disharmony and proscriptions involved in the appointment of new men on a wide scale.[17] He was later, after all, to tell General Horatio G. Wright, the State commander, that

There is no *constitutional* state government. The provisional government of Texas is created by and exists at the will of the President. . . . For the present,

---

[15]Swain to Graham, Chapel Hill, 1 November 1865, W. A. Graham Collection.
[16]Hamilton to Johnson, Austin, Texas, 30 August 1865, Johnson MSS, Series I.
[17]A. J. Hamilton, Proclamation, 25 July 1865, in *New Orleans Times*, 31 July 1865.

the action of the civil authorities created by me is allowed only as a means – to the extent that they can be made available – of aiding the authorities of the general government in preserving public peace and order, and in protecting individual rights and property.[18]

This policy had to be expanded, however, because of the disorganization of society and the inadequate communications throughout the State. So Hamilton had subsequently to admit to the President that he had instituted 'a more formal Provisional Government than would under other circumstances have been necessary.'[19] Basically though, he, like Marvin and Johnson, considered civil government to be inchoate until unrestricted State elections were held. But, unlike Holden, he did not regard it as wise or conducive to harmony to change the personnel of government.

Some Provisional Governors took a totally divergent view of the situation confronting them. Sharkey, Parsons, and Perry considered that the reinstallation of many, and in Perry's case, all, of the Confederate officials until the Provisional Government ended was the most efficient and harmonious course to pursue. Perry explained this reasoning to the President:

I thought it wisest and best to restore to office those who had been chosen by the people, were familiar with their official duties, had taken the oath of allegiance and were pardoned. I had implicit confidence in their honor and plighted fidelity and loyalty. This put in operation, at once, the machinery of civil government, perfected and completed, which the necessities of the State imperiously demanded. It was calculated to sooth and harmonize the people in their pledged loyalty to the Union.[20]

Disruption, disharmony, and maladministration, at such a perilous time, were to be avoided if possible. Consequently, the temptation to restore the officials who held office under the Confederacy was very great. Nevertheless, Benjamin Perry was the only Provisional Governor who restored the government as he had inherited it. Both Sharkey and Parsons, on the other hand, appointed new men only to the upper

[18] Hamilton to General H. G. Wright, 27 September 1865, in Charles W. Ramsdell, *Reconstruction in Texas* (New York: Columbia University Press, 1910), pp. 78–9. See also John L. Waller, *Colossal Hamilton of Texas* (El Paso, Texas; Texas Western Press, 1968), pp. 64–7, although there is more said in this account about the personalities appointed than about the guidelines of appointment policy.
[19] Hamilton to General H. G. Wright, 27 September 1865, Johnson MSS, Series I.
[20] Perry to Johnson, Greenville, S.C., 29 August 1865, Perry MSS. (Ala.).

échelons of government while retaining the minor officeholders who comprised the vast bulk of the patronage of their States. Sharkey reinstated local and judicial officers with the proviso that those who later proved to be disloyal could be removed by the Governor while those who had not taken the amnesty oath or were in the excepted classes would be removed. Furthermore, in both States, citizens were called upon to inform the Provisional Governor of malfunctioning among the officers, Sharkey also reserving to himself the prerogative of appointment in counties where no civil officers existed.[21] In substance, the formula, as Parsons explained it to the President, was that 'All county officers from Justice of the Peace, down, were reappointed by my proclamation, but reserving the right to remove for disloyalty or other good cause. All the higher officials of the county and state were specially appointed.'[22] These proceedings had been approved by the President when he had conferred with Parsons and Sharkey in Washington.

The President also approved and endorsed the proclamation of Benjamin Perry, restoring all incumbents in South Carolina provided they had taken the amnesty oath. After seeing the proposed proclamation, the President requested, as Perry later recounted, that he be kept 'informed as to any difficulty I might meet with in organizing a provisional government [so] I said to him, "I have already, Mr. President, organized a provisional government for South Carolina, by adopting the State Government." To this Johnson merely remarked, "Well . . . you are a most expeditious Governor."'[23] Perry justified his course to the President by reminding him that he had been the last Governor appointed and therefore was compelled to act rapidly so that his State would be ready for readmission in December. In view of the President's opinion that restoration entailed a reorganization of the State so that it could be firmly governed in accordance with the laws and Constitution of the United States, it was curious that he should not reprimand Perry for implying that the process itself was so facile, even so futile, a task. Equally strange was his approval of Holden's proclamation, submitted on 24 July, which expounded a totally different method for restoring a Southern State to the Union.

Taking the amnesty oath was, however, a criterion for retention

[21] William L. Sharkey, Proclamation, 1 July 1865, in *New Orleans Times*, 16 July 1865.

[22] Parsons to Johnson, Montgomery, 24 August 1865, Johnson MSS, Series I.

[23] B. F. Perry, Speech, Greenville, S.C., 1 August 1865, Johnson MSS, box 233.

of, or appointment to, office in all the Provisional Governors' proclamations. Therefore, the President may have assumed with good
reason that loyal men were running Southern governments. In fact,
however, that oath was taken by many Southerners as an unpalatable
necessity, some even calling it the 'I am nasty' oath. Furthermore,
such wholesale restoration as Johnson and Perry, even Sharkey and
Parsons, undertook could not but encourage the retention of old
customs and attitudes of mind. Old politicians, and therefore old
ideas, were still in the saddle. Little that indicated a new spirit could
be expected under such circumstances. Even in North Carolina, where
Holden had attempted to implement a proscriptive and partisan
patronage scheme, little could be perceived in late 1865 that was different from States employing the other form of appointment policy.
These developments were conclusive proof that nothing could be done
to change the South unless the leading politicians were disqualified
from office and disfranchised. If they did not initially remain in control, they could always, as events in North Carolina demonstrated,
recover power and influence later at the ballot-box.

Working within the framework of his own announced policy,
Andrew Johnson did not however countermand the plans for the
distribution of offices which had been suggested by the State executives he had appointed. Once appointed, their dependence on
him was ended. He, and hopefully the citizens of their States, would
thenceforth regard them as heads of sovereign States within the Union.
This, of course, would give encouragement to the South since it was
a demonstration that State sovereignty was in the future to be respected by the leaders of the North. At the same time this policy did,
to an extreme degree, decentralize control over restoration. Most of
the Provisional Governors, as even Holden later discovered, could not
command adequate support or respect within their States unless they
bestowed patronage on, and gained the allegiance of, a broad section
of the electorate. Even Governors Pierpont of Virginia and Wells of
Louisiana, as well as the Provisional Governors, felt it necessary to
coopt the leading men, secessionists if necessary, in order to legitimize
their regimes. This policy would also facilitate harmony and cooperation in the difficult task of restoration, which for most of the Governors and the President was the objective sought.

By necessity, all the Governors in the South during 1865 were
compelled to use their discretionary patronage power on behalf of
those elements that had governed before and during the war. The

extent to which they did this very often determined the support given to them in the Senatorial elections in November and the esteem in which they were held within their State, especially at the time of the convention. When he reappointed all of South Carolina's officials, Perry might have surrendered thereby all of his power to reward and punish by means of the patronage. But he was, in spite of this, extremely influential. Sidney Andrews noted that Perry was 'the leader of the Convention;' 'his position . . . makes his word and wish of very unusual significance.' Small wonder that his election to the Senate in November was overwhelmingly endorsed by the legislature.[24] Sharkey and Parsons too were chosen for the Senate, and exerted considerable influence in their States. That their influence was less than Perry's was perhaps because they did not claim, as Perry did, to have a special relationship and confidence with the President. It was also because, in Sharkey's case, less respect was accorded him on account of his being 'pliable as dough,' unable 'to refuse anything it is in his power to grant.'[25]

Although James Johnson had restored to office the Confederate politicians, he had done so under pressure. He had also invited the wrath of wealthy Georgians by inducing the President to suggest that the war debt be repudiated. And, not least of his crimes, he had shown dissatisfaction with Georgia's performance under his Provisional Government. P. Thweatt, the State Comptroller, told Alexander Stephens of this. 'Many persons,' he confided, 'suppose Johnson to have been doing all he would or can to hold on longer before the subject of the *negro*. I tell you in all candour, that he is very little better, if any, than Charles Sumner — I hardly think he is as liberal in his feelings, towards the white man, as Mr. Seward.'[26] The result was that Johnson cabled the President in late November advising that pardons be suspended because Georgia was so refractory, and concluded pitifully, 'I shall be a candidate for the Senate and of course will be defeated.'[27]

Both Holden and Hamilton were renounced by their States at the end of their terms. Neither had placated the establishment politicians

[24]Sidney Andrews, *The South Since the War* (Boston: Ticknor and Fields, 1866), p. 49.

[25]'D. S.,' Jackson, Miss., *Cincinnati Gazette*, 6 September 1865.

[26]P. Thweatt to Stephens, 19 November 1865, A. H. Stephens MSS.

[27]James Johnson to Johnson, Milledgeville, Ga., 24 November 1865, Johnson MSS, Series II.

even though Holden, for example, had attempted, like all the Governors, to have the Negro troops removed from North Carolina and civil authority declared paramount to the military. But both men had clearly expressed sentiments and pursued policies that were not sufficiently protective of their States and, in particular, of the interests of the leading politicians. They and Johnson had been prepared to inform the President of the defiant uncooperative feeling that permeated their States, and for these failings, they were discountenanced within their respective jurisdictions.

It was the paradox of restoration that those Provisional Governors who were attempting to urge strict compliance with the President's recommendations were those who were unable to elicit such assent because they had shown themselves already to be unacceptable by their patronage policy or by their general demeanor. On the other hand, those like Sharkey, Perry and Parsons, who were well-disposed to the leaders of their States and who therefore could secure compliance with their requests, were ipso facto those who would not be likely to overemphasize, or insist on, the President's suggestions. In his *Reminiscences*, Perry was later able to assert, with pride, that during his Provisional Governorship, 'Every official act I had to perform was that of protection, kindness and mercy. In no instance did it become my duty to oppress, injure or wound the feelings of anyone. On the contrary, I was recognized by the President as a shield between the arbitrary acts of the military and the suffering people.'[28] As defender of the faithful, Perry was liked and approved, but that confidence in him, and the political influence it brought, could not be used to counteract this role or else the very influence that it bestowed on him would also be lost. The dilemma of Johnson, Holden, and Hamilton was, of course, the exact reverse. Yet, in both approaches to the patronage question, the Provisional Governor's power to mold events in the South atrophied, and the President's scheme was undermined at the foundations.

b: *Pardons*

Entwined with the question of patronage was the matter of pardons. Like appointments in the Southern States, the exercise of clemency produced paradoxes and complications. Caution and generosity had

[28] Benjamin F. Perry, *Reminiscences of Public Men With Speeches and Addresses, 2nd Series* (Greenville, S.C.: Shannon and Co., 1889), p. 245.

to be simultaneous features of the President's pardoning policy. How exactly to mingle these facets was problematical. In a conference with William W. Holden, when the North Carolinian was being briefed for his term of office, the President demonstrated his ambivalence and uncertainty. Holden reported that

He said to us he expected to confiscate the estates of the large slave owners who were traitors and proscribed, and divide them among the wool hat boys of the South, who had been impoverished and had been compelled to fight for slavery against their will. Mr. [Robert P.] Dick and myself remonstrated against this in earnest terms. We begged him to be as forbearing and as generous as possible. He said he would be, and especially when asked by the proscribed classes, of whom there were fourteen in the proclamation, for their pardons, he would give immediate attention, and pardon where he could.[29]

Both Holden and Johnson were representatives of the common people of the South and both felt towards wealth and privilege a deep-seated aversion which they revealed publicly during and before the war by means of a hostile rhetoric. But presented with the task of reorganizing and reuniting Southern States and nation, both yielded to the need to conserve, harmonize and stabilize. In essence, they were institutional conservatives whose political orthodoxy usually overcame their rhetoric and emotions.

Without a pardon, Southerners were liable to confiscation of their property, whether it had been abandoned or not, and were unable to participate in public affairs. Most could, if they wished, take the simple Presidential oath of future loyalty, but those in the fourteen exceptions of the Amnesty Proclamation of 29 May had to seek special pardon from the President himself. A tight rein could, therefore, be kept on the leading men of the Confederacy. For others, however, such control would be difficult since, so long as there was a desire to be amnestied and there were qualified officials available to administer the oath, no obstacle to a full pardon really existed. Officials qualified to hear the oath were usually United States military and also, in most States, Justices of the Peace. Persons qualified to swear it were merely those who desired so to do, since there were no questions asked regarding motivation or intention. All the same, in those aspects of the pardoning prerogative where discretion was retained by the govern-

[29]'Memoirs of William W. Holden,' pp. 55–6.

ment of the United States, control, as well as a stimulus to loyalty, could be implemented. 'While the Administration desires to make the operation of that Instrument [the 29 May Amnesty Proclamation] as general as possible,' the Assistant Attorney General told Holden, 'it is obvious that great dangers are to be apprehended from a loose or indiscriminate exercise of Executive clemency.'[30] This was the President's plan, and Holden concurred. Informing Johnson that 'Many of the oligarchs are still unsubdued' and should be kept disfranchised and in suspense about the fate of their estates, Holden added that 'a discreet use of the pardoning power and the patronage of the government will contribute greatly to keep them down, and thus preserve tranquillity and order in the State.'[31]

Pardons were to be given cautiously, carefully, discreetly, but also with generosity and magnanimity. The purpose of the pardoning policy was not to punish, but to release from punishment. The beneficiaries would be Southern rebels who demonstrated repentance, although determination of the time and the justification for that release would be decided by the government. It was never clear, however, either in the councils of the Administration or in the implementation of the policy, whether the prospect of a pardon was to stimulate the currently disloyal to loyal action or whether the bestowal of a pardon was a reward for loyalty already demonstrated. As in the question of the terms for readmission, a policy employing simultaneously both incentives and rewards would cause confusion and contradiction. Failure to clarify the function of the pardoning power caused further dislocations, since, in addition, the pardoning power was not exercised methodically with regard to the antecedents of the petitioner. The Attorney General and the rest of the Cabinet could not decide whether it was preferable to grant pardons to those who had resisted secession until the last moment or to leading secessionists who had repented. The result was that those who petitioned, regardless of past career, were pardoned unless their application was unsatisfactory in format.

Andrew Johnson himself tended to be delighted that prominent precipitators of the rebellion sued for pardon since such an act gave evidence of a spectacular change of heart, and, moreover, a personal petition from a leading secessionist was immensely flattering to the

[30]T. Hubley Ashton to Holden, Washington, D.C., 23 June 1865, Holden Official Correspondence.
[31]Holden to Johnson, Raleigh, 24 July 1865, Johnson MSS, Series I.

President. In general, though, there were no guidelines prepared as to whether anti-secessionists or secessionists, Whigs or Democrats, would be preferred. An application for pardon was construed as evidence of repentance and loyalty, and, at its face value, it was received by the authorities in Washington. This was to place far too great a trust in a device which was open to manipulation by Southerners who desired to be pardoned merely in order to retain their property and political influence.[32]

Complaints such as were aired to Sharkey by W. D. Holder, a Mississippi Whig, arose as a result throughout the South. Holder wrote that 'The action of the President in this respect can be construed only, as intending to favor and encourage the one [secessionist–Democrats] and depress the other [Whigs]. How can the conservative party rally its full strength under such circumstances? Bradford, Watson and myself "are held out in the cold" whilst Phelan, Orr, and others are invited around the Executive hearthstone.'[33]

Alexander Stephens was also concerned. Alfred Dockery of North Carolina told R. J. Powell, Holden's agent in Washington, that 'My son Oliver who came through Georgia recently heard Vice President Stephens say President Johnson confided too much in the Secessionists of the South.'[34] There is no doubt that Stephens and Holder expected that the South would be led during the post-war period by men like themselves who had urged against secession and regretted its occurrence. A conservative party would then emerge at the core of which there would be, in all States except possibly Alabama and North Carolina, the Whigs. The government's pardoning policy was, therefore, looked to as an instrument to build up this conservative coalition. But even before petitions for pardons reached Washington, various

[32]The obvious weaknesses in this procedure were pointed out by 'Marcel' of *The Nation*. In an article entitled 'Hard Swearing As An Instrument of Government,' he considered a system of restoring governmental authority by 'a wholesale administration of oaths, . . . essentially medieval.' And he added, 'since the Government of the United States has become the only one in the country, that under which every man has to live whether he likes it or not, it is safe to say that all the swearing that has been done at the South has not made any perceptible addition either to its strength or security.' In war-time, with a choice of allegiances, oaths had some meaning, but in the transition period they could serve no useful function.
[33]W. D. Holder to Sharkey, Egypt Station, Miss., 23 October 1865, Humphreys MSS. Also see C. B. Nero to Sharkey, Buena Vista, 1 July 1865, Sharkey MSS, for similar views from another Whig.
[34]Alfred Dockery to R. J. Powell, 13 November 1865, Seward MSS.

forces and sentiments in the South had interfered to obstruct and threaten this development.

Although Andrew Johnson alone could pardon a traitor, discretionary power was nevertheless delegated to the Provisional Governors to decide which petitions were to be forwarded to Washington for consideration. This decision was based on the assumption that the Provisional Governor was more aware of local conditions than the Cabinet. Although undoubtedly a correct assessment, this would not be conducive to the maintenance of Federal surveillance over Southern affairs. Many Governors viewed their task much as did Benjamin Perry when he exclaimed, 'I had unlimited discretion in pardoning whom I pleased; that was every one who applied for a pardon.'[35] Provisional Governors could judge whether or not a pardon application should, or would, be forwarded to Washington. Consequently they would decide the vast majority of pardons that were granted. The President and Attorney General rarely questioned the recommendations of the Provisional Governors and chose to exercise control only over those few petitioners who applied directly to the President and independently of the chief executive of their State.

Not every Provisional Governor submitted automatically all the applications that he received. Perry claimed that he had received, and automatically forwarded, two to three thousand petitions and had had only two or three rejected by the President.[36] Jack Hamilton of Texas, on the other hand, wrote the President in October:

The pardon business is to me a source of great responsibility and labor. I have acted on the idea that it was the policy of the Govt. to forgive all sincerely repentant rebels whose sins are pardonable. I have refused where I could not in conscience do so, to recommend. I will not recommend to you for pardon any man that I would not be willing to pardon myself were the power mine.[37]

Provisional Governors could either withhold those petitions that

---

[35] Perry, *Reminiscences*, p. 245.
[36] Ibid., p. 288.
[37] Hamilton to Johnson, Austin, 21 October 1865, Johnson MSS, Series I. Yet according to his biographer, 'Except for some twelve to fifteen, he approved all applications submitted to him.' Waller, *Colossal Hamilton of Texas*, p. 82. I am not sure what to make of this conflicting evidence. Hamilton's own correspondence with the President and the reactions of the establishment leadership to Hamilton's record in office both suggest that Waller is incorrect.

they felt could not be recommended for pardon or they could submit all the applications endorsing them with a recommendation to the President that he grant or refuse them. William W. Holden chose the former method and used the discretion he had over the granting of pardons to mold the Democratic Party and the anti-establishment elements into a ruling coalition. When he left office in December, there were filed in his office some three hundred pardons that had not been sent forward to Washington. These were petitions from men like Vance, Josiah Turner, and William A. Graham who were leaders of the Whig 'oligarchs.' In October he wrote to Robert J. Powell telling him that he had sent to the President 'some six or seven hundred endorsed for pardon from this State. Nearly all of these are friends of ours. I wish the President could find time to sign their pardons. He may need their votes and influence in the coming elections. So far as those who are suspended are concerned, I have done my duty, and I do not fear their opposition hereafter.'[38]

Benjamin Perry merely forwarded all the pardons he received, leaving the matter to the President to decide but at the same time refusing to indicate which he recommended. Presumably he wanted as many as possible pardoned regardless of antecedents or current attitudes. Such a course was dangerous since in late summer the pardoning clerk in the Attorney General's office had told one Governor at least that

you have [Attorney General Speed's] authority for saying the only influence possible to be exerted in the matter of petitions by my agent or attorney, whoever he may be, is to delay the petition. All cases coming under the head of exceptions, and all petty civil officers, having your recommendation, need nothing further. They are approved by the Attorney General.[39]

Three months later David L. Swain concluded that a passive abdication of power into the Governors' hands had taken place, and told William A. Graham that, 'As a general rule, the government pardoned no one, without the recommendation, or assent, of the Prov. Gov'r. and withheld it from no one whom they recommended.'[40]

In the Southern States, however, there were very many political

[38] Holden to Powell, Raleigh, 5 October 1865, Johnson MSS, Series I.
[39] M. F. Pleasants to Francis H. Pierpont, 27 August 1865, in *New Orleans Times*, 5 September 1865.
[40] Swain to Graham, Chapel Hill, 1 November 1865, W. A. Graham Collection.

reasons for Provisional Governors to exert pressure for pardons to be issued. First of all, to obtain a pardon for a leading man in the State would win for the Governor the gratitude and political support of the beneficiary. In this regard, Holden's pardoning and appointment policy weakened him. He did not elicit the aid of any but those who supported him in any case. On the other hand, Sharkey was criticized by the Whigs, C. B. Nero, Absalom West, and William Holder, for appointing secessionists and Democrats. But the Mississippi Governor realized that a base of support that was no more than merely partisan would be vulnerable.[41] Second, many Provisional Governors felt personally stronger if they had the backing of some prominent politicians in the State. Such support, moreover, would indicate that leading men approved of a return to the Union on the terms suggested by Andrew Johnson. For a Governor like Hamilton, who was determined to have his State acquiesce quietly, the aid of an important Confederate leader would be a great boon. He told the President, therefore, that the pardon of John H. Reagan, one-time Confederate Postmaster-General, who, in his letter from Fort Warren in August, had shown conciliation and repentance, would greatly facilitate his own work in Texas:

I have in every way possible, in the most public and solemn form, assured the people of the facts, as they exist, and of what was expected of them by the Government, but I have not been able to convince all, and perhaps least of any those, and they are many, who dislike to be convinced by a political opponent. I know of no man who would accomplish as much, with this class of persons, in Texas, as Mr. Reagan.[42]

Like Joseph E. Brown in Georgia and Robert M. T. Hunter in Virginia, Reagan would demonstrate that the most rebellious could be repentant. In the South this would impress lesser men with the respectability of contrition and cooperation while among observant, critical Northerners skepticism might be allayed by such evidence. Citing these possible reactions as justification, Southern Governors could ask for the pardon of notable and controversial figures as a means of broadening their own support or neutralizing political opposition.

There was a third reason for Provisional Governors to exert pres-

---

[41] Absalom West to Sharkey, 3 July 1865 and C. B. Nero to Sharkey, 1 July 1865, Sharkey MSS; W. D. Holder to Humphreys, 23 October 1865, Humphreys MSS.

[42] Hamilton to Johnson, Austin, 29 September 1865, Johnson MSS, Series I.

sure to procure pardons. Numerous applications for pardon, on as wide a front as possible, would provide unmistakable evidence of cooperation and loyalty. It was considered by many in the South that loyalty existed in direct proportion to the number of persons willing to take the oath and be pardoned. The *Atlanta Intelligencer* expressed a similar sentiment in a July editorial while requesting that an adequate number of officials be appointed to hear oaths sworn: 'Like the Governor, we too are solicitous that our people shall have an early opportunity of demonstrating their willingness to accept the proposed amnesty, and their earnest desire to see Georgia again under civil government—law and order, peace and prosperity, again, prevailing within her borders.'[43]

Every Provisional Governor urged citizens to rouse themselves from their uncooperative lethargy and pouting supineness, so that they could show their gratitude for the benevolence of Northern policy and also manifest a desire to bind up old wounds. This perception was shared by James Conner, a Charleston lawyer and convention delegate, who noticed regretfully that elections might not be held in some of the low-country districts. And so he told Governor Perry that 'A small convention will be a misfortune. The circumstances not being known it will be regarded as evincing an unwillingness on the part of the State to recognize the existing condition of things.'[44] In order to obtain a convention elected by a large constituency, many had to be pardoned to enable them to sit or to vote. Consequently, an unrestricted recommendation for the relief of the excepted classes from their disabilities and the availability of officers to hear the amnesty oath were both essential to ensure a demonstration of feelings in the manner proposed. Such action, however, was easily interpreted by Northerners in the same way that Conner had feared a small convention, chosen by a small electorate, would be. Undue haste was as unacceptable and suspicious as defiant passivity.

A final factor contributing to the Southern Governors' wide and almost indiscriminate use of the power to recommend for pardon was the strength that would be brought to the State if leading men were released from restrictions on their political and economic activity. Thus, those who were in the thirteenth exception because they owned

---

[43] Editorial, *Atlanta Intelligencer*, 23 July 1865.
[44] James Conner to Perry, Charleston, 9 August 1865, Perry MSS (Ala.). General Bennett, the local commander, had refused to comply with Perry's proclamation calling for an election; so the local civilian election managers, fearful of provoking a dispute with the military, had refused to initiate election procedures.

more than $20,000 were unable to aid the State in its efforts to recuperate from the blight of war and emancipation. Because of the supposed entrepreneurial talent as well as the financial assets they possessed, it was considered imperative that these resources should not remain locked up and unexploited by the State and its people. Consequently, pressure to pardon those men, who, in Andrew Johnson's view, were the instigators of the rebellion, was considerable, and usually successful. Hamilton and Holden once again proved themselves exceptions among the Southern Governors.[45]

In general, the impetus for pardons came from the States. 'It is certain,' Perry was told by William Whaley, a member of South Carolina's July delegation to the President, 'that the pardoning power will be very largely used upon your recommendations. . . .'[46] The President merely performed the mechanical act of granting what was already decided by the Provisional Governor. Sometimes when he pardoned those not recommended by the latter, the President incurred their wrath, as, for example, when he cooperated with the requests of Benjamin S. Hedrick, who was the representative of the forces working in Washington against the efforts of Holden's agent Robert J. Powell.[47] The occasions, on the other hand, when the President refused to grant petitions for pardons forwarded by the Provisional Governors were extremely rare. Perry and Holden, in their memoirs, could each enumerate only three or four instances of such a refusal. The power to pardon had been delegated to the agents the President had appointed in each State. Therefore, contrary to the opinion of many contemporaries as well as historians, it was not because Andrew Johnson was overwhelmed by the importunings of the Southern chivalry that he had pardoned so freely, but because by late August, when Pleasants had written to Pierpont, he had in effect bestowed the initiative in the matter on the Southern Provisional Governors.

The extent to which clemency had passed from the hands of the Federal executive could be seen most dramatically in the pardoning of those who, although not amnestied, were elected to Southern conventions. Benjamin Perry noted, in his *Reminiscences of Public Men*, that during his visit to Washington in July the President had said that he would 'pardon such persons as I desired to be members of the conven-

[45] Hamilton to Johnson, Galveston, 24 July 1865, Johnson MSS, Series I.
[46] William P. Whaley to Perry, Charleston, 10 July 1865, Perry MSS (Ala.).
[47] Holden to Johnson, Raleigh, 5 October 1865, Johnson MSS, Series I.

tion, and who would be willing to carry out our views of reform. This was generally known, and was an inducement for the prominent secessionists to become candidates for the convention.'[48]

Governors Holden and Johnson, however, were less certain as to whether unpardoned members-elect could sit. Holden telegraphed the President on 21 September that he had 'decided that as people who belong to the excluded classes cannot vote so they cannot sit in the Convention unless they exhibit their pardons.' Graham had taken issue with this position, so Holden wished for a conclusive opinion from the President.[49] The Presidential reply, however, was mystifying. Its premise was in agreement with Holden but it proceeded: 'If the party comes within any one of the exceptions, they must obtain a pardon before voting or sitting as a member. All those who are aspirants to seats in the convention, and are elected, will be pardoned upon your recommendation and a submission of their names by telegraph.'[50] The same answer was given to James Johnson after the President had replied inconclusively to two enquiries on 9 and 26 September. Earlier Rufus Y. McAden, Speaker of the House of Commons of North Carolina in 1866, had written to William A. Graham on this subject early in August and had concluded, 'My impression is that the Convention will be the proper body to decide the qualifications of members.'[51] And this was what happened.

The electorate voted with little regard for the legal status of candidates since it was assumed that no members-elect would be rejected by the President. Only in Texas did the Provisional Governor ban from candidacy and from the convention any person who had not received his pardon. Elsewhere pardons were forthcoming when requested by Perry, Johnson, Holden, and Parsons. Perry even waited until ten days after the convention had met before he wrote to the President on behalf of the twenty unpardoned South Carolinians.[52] Election to public office had become an obvious means of obtaining a pardon once the conventional machinery had failed. For William A. Graham,

[48] Perry, *Reminiscences*, p. 275.
[49] Holden to Johnson, Raleigh, 21 September 1865, Johnson MSS, Series II.
[50] Johnson to Holden, Washington, D.C., 21 September 1865, Johnson MSS, Series I.
[51] Rufus Y. McAden to Graham, Graham, N.C., 11 August 1865, W.A. Graham Collection.
[52] Perry to Johnson, Columbia, S.C., 26 September 1865, *Senate Executive Documents*, 39th Cong., 1st Sess., I, No. 26, 251.

whose arch-enemy was currently Provisional Governor of North Carolina, a seat in the convention would expedite his pardon, and with this end in mind Josiah Turner, Jr, another leading Whig, wrote to Graham suggesting a delegate named Berry be requested to resign in his favor, 'otherwise you will not be pardoned before the election of Governor, Congress, and U.S. Senators comes off.'[53]

Such control as the President's discretionary pardoning power could have had over the course of events in the South during the months when the conventions were assembling was clearly jettisoned. The President's intention had been not to restrict the freedom of the voters to choose whom they liked, but to define the electorate and restrict its composition. In reply to an enquiry from some supporters of his, who declared that 'the privilege of voting loses half its value, and all its dignity, when the elector is forbidden to cast his vote for the person of his choice,' William A. Graham commented accurately that the President had not wanted to tamper with the elections themselves. 'The President,' he added, 'intended to trust the people. He had taken all the security he deemed requisite against the return of disloyal members when he directed the polls to be purged, and the electors to be sworn, and intended to allow the electoral body thus qualified, a free choice of representatives.'[54]

This procedure however did not work so smoothly nor did it guarantee that elected officials and representatives were loyal and pardoned. Indeed, Mississippi and South Carolina were able to elect Governors who were unpardoned. That was noteworthy but the sequel to it was even more instructive as a demonstration of the low esteem in which pardons were held by late 1865. In response to the elections of Generals Humphreys and Hampton, the President had no hesitation in issuing pardons to both men. In Hampton's case however it was later discovered that on a recount he had lost by a narrow margin to James L. Orr. Not wishing to have obtained the pardon under false pretences, Wade Hampton then requested that it be revoked.[55]

---

[53]Josiah Turner, Jr to Graham, Raleigh, 23 September 1865, W. A. Graham Collection.

[54]Lemuel Lynch, H. N. Brown, etc., to Graham, Orange County, N.C., 12 September 1865, and W. A. Graham's reply, 14 September 1865, W. A. Graham Collection.

[55]Wade Hampton III to Perry, Columbia, S.C., 8 November 1865, Perry MSS (Ala.).

c: *Relations with the military*

The Federal executive's power to influence appointments in the South and to control the flow of pardons had been entrusted to the Provisional Governors. The result was that these prerogatives which could have been used to induce the South to act nationally were subordinated to the political needs and pressures experienced by the Provisional Governors within their States. This was also true with regard to the authority of the United States military forces in the South. There was in the South an unappeasable and impatient desire to gain as much autonomy as possible. Southern leaders assumed that all would be pardoned in time, the troops would have to be removed eventually, and in all probability, the planting class would reassume economic control. Furthermore, all the disabilities that Southern politicians and leaders experienced in the early months after the war would eventually be removed. Yet at every point possible they forced the issue, and usually successfully. The South may have 'played possum' in certain respects, but there was also no mistaking the unequivocal pressure for control of their own affairs exerted by the defeated section's leaders in the anomalous conditions of 1865.

The relationship in each State between the President's civil agent, the Provisional Governor, and his military lieutenant, the officer commanding, was very tenuous and undefined. According to their Proclamations of appointment, the Provisional Governors were to be aided and assisted by the military commanders, who were 'enjoined to abstain from in any way hindering, impeding, or discouraging the loyal people from the organization of a State Government as herein authorized.'[56] Yet concurrently the South was under martial law. Provisional Governors regarded such a state of affairs as an infringement of their own authority as well as upon the State's sovereignty. Besides, the presence of a military force was inimical to good civil government and to local control over indigenous problems, in particular the labor force. Accordingly, there was continual pressure for clarification of the powers exerted by and on the Provisional Governors.

Two States, North Carolina and Mississippi, brought to the attention of the Washington authorities cases involving disputes over military jurisdiction. In late July, William W. Holden complained to General Thomas Ruger, who was to be appointed Governor of Georgia

[56] James D. Richardson, *Messages and Papers of the Presidents, 1789–1897*, VI, 312–14.

in late 1867, that the latter's taking into military custody three citizens of Person County was unwarranted since the civil courts were functioning. Ruger replied that 'without doubt, military tribunals have jurisdiction in all that relates to the preservation of order, including the trial and punishment of those guilty of acts of violence.' The military were even able to take preventive action to maintain law and order, certainly without waiting for requests from the civil authorities, especially in cases involving freedmen.[57] From that interpretation of the role of the military, Holden concluded, it was 'a just inference . . . that you [Ruger] deny the existence of any civil law in the State, or, if there be, you insist that its execution rests solely in the military.'[58] Countering Holden's reductio ad absurdam and attempting to assert that an anomalous, ill-defined situation was not necessarily illogical or impossible to administer, Ruger finally admitted that he did not intend to deny concurrent jurisdiction or the existence of civil law 'but only to maintain that the military tribunal had jurisdiction of the entire subject of the preservation of order.'[59] Such were the parameters of a dispute which was, in various guises, reiterated in other Southern States throughout 1865 and which initially was decided by the War Department in the military's favor.

Meanwhile, in Mississippi a feud raged between Provisional Governor Sharkey, himself a celebrated jurist whose name was then being mentioned to the President in connexion with a position on the Supreme Court, and General Henry W. Slocum, the State commander and later Democratic candidate in New York for Secretary of State.[60] Sharkey was determined to take up with the Federal government every infringement on the authority of the State of Mississippi, hoping, by this tactic, to rid his State eventually of all military restrictions. The first test engineered by Sharkey was the trial of Joseph Jackson, a planter who had murdered a Negro. When Judge Daniel O. Merwin, at Sharkey's command, issued a writ of habeas corpus for Jackson, the judge was arrested by Slocum on orders from the President.[61] Sharkey

---

[57] General Thomas Ruger to Holden, 1 August 1865, Letterbook, Holden Official Correspondence.

[58] Holden to Ruger, 8 August 1865, *ibid.*

[59] Ruger to Holden, 11 August 1865, *ibid.*

[60] Thomas Cottman, a Louisiana politician, told Sharkey he would suggest his name to the President, 7 July 1865, Sharkey MSS.

[61] Stanton to Slocum, Washington, D.C., 13 July 1865, Telegrams Sent, Records of the Office of the Secretary of War, microcopy 473, reel 89.

sent a telegram to Seward, complaining that 'If this be tryable [*sic*] by military authority why not all other crimes and what is use of civil government?' The matter was decided in Slocum's favor, however.[62] Sharkey was still not satisfied. To Seward came more documents on the case until, finally, Attorney General Speed was asked to draw up an opinion on the authority of civil judges in the Southern States. The President, noted Gideon Welles, 'dissented wholly from some of his positions,' considering the military as aids to the Provisional Governor and the civil authorities.[63] Nevertheless, Slocum's proceedings were endorsed.

This anomalousness irritated Sharkey, and also the President. Jurisdictional confusion would make it difficult for Southerners to restore civil government and, in addition, would produce individual exasperation. The military was present to enable Provisional Governors to restore civil authority, not to frustrate them and hinder their work. Sharkey, with a legal mind which abhorred military rule, and the President, with a rigid mind which abhorred inconsistencies, found themselves moving into harness on the issue of civil–military relations. Threatening to resign 'if the civil authority is not maintained in whole by the Federal Government,' the Mississippian decided to press the matter until it was settled one way or the other.[64]

If the Mississippi courts could not take cognizance automatically of all cases relating to disturbances of the peace and law and order, then perhaps a Mississippi military force could apprehend and take custody of lawbreakers, thereby pre-empting the role of the United States forces under General Slocum. Reasoning along these lines Sharkey informed the President, on 20 August, of his call for one company of militia in each county. In Mississippi the move provoked an immediate response from General Peter Osterhaus, commanding at Jackson, to which Sharkey replied: 'I know you have every desire to prevent such occurences, and will use every means in your power to do so, and to arrest the culprits. I know too, that the people are reluctant to give you aid by imparting information to you. But in addition to these

---

[62] Sharkey to Seward, Jackson, 21 July 1865, Telegrams Received, Records of the Office of the Secretary of War, microcopy 473, reel 119.

[63] *Diary of Gideon Welles*, I, 366–7.

[64] D. O. Merwin to Sharkey, Vicksburg, 20 July 1865, Sharkey MSS. These are Merwin's words recapitulating to Sharkey what he had been told to do earlier by the Provisional Governor himself.

robberies [committed very close to Osterhaus' H.Q.], information daily reaches me of the perpetration of outrages committed in various ways in distant parts of the State where you have no military forces.' And, furthermore, said Sharkey, the President had volunteered the suggestion, at the interview he and Yerger had had with him at the White House in June, that 'I could organize the militia if it should become necessary.'[65]

Two days later, replies came from the President. He ordered Sharkey to call on Slocum for whatever force he needed, but advised against organizing a militia at so early a stage in the process of governmental reorganization. There was also a rejoinder from General Slocum in the form of the punitive General Order No. 22. In it Slocum commented that it was absurd for Sharkey to suggest that, because, as the Provisional Governor himself admitted, the citizenry would not offer information that would help the army apprehend lawbreakers, they should then be armed to carry out the task themselves. As a remedy, Slocum threatened to disarm all persons within ten miles of the place where an outrage on a citizen or soldier was committed, and then to arrest and garrison troops on any citizen refusing to aid the military in their search for the culprits.[66] Carl Schurz, who was traveling in the State at the time, wrote to the Secretary of War, advising him to endorse the General Order. 'It seems to me,' he said, 'the Government can do nothing that would be better calculated to secure order and peace in the late rebel States, than to approve this order publicly and emphatically. It would at once put a stop to all vagaries on the part of Provisional Governors.'[67] But, by contrast with his endorsement of Slocum on 22 August and of the military in general during previous, but less focal, disputes with Southern civil authorities, the President reversed his stand and permitted Sharkey to call up militia companies, and these would, without doubt, be manned by young Confederate soldiers.

Sharkey, in fact, never did achieve the supremacy of the civil authority that he had hoped for, but the President had been forced, on a clear presentation of the civil–military issue, to indicate his preference. 'One great object,' he had told Schurz, 'is to induce the people to come

[65] Sharkey to General P. J. Osterhaus, Jackson, 22 August 1865, Sharkey MSS.
[66] General H. W. Slocum, General Order No. 22, 24 August 1865, *Senate Executive Documents*, 39th Cong., 1st Sess., I, No. 2, 62–3.
[67] Carl Schurz to Stanton, Vicksburg, 29 August 1865, Stanton MSS.

forward in the defense of the State and Federal Government.'[68] This, the goal of his restoration policy, might be jeopardized if the military were to be obstacles rather than aids to Southern reorganization. But to Southern leaders, the dispute indicated that the President considered the Provisional Governments as possessing a large degree of autonomy. This autonomy was to be preserved, and even protected, by the United States military.

The satisfactory resolution of the dispute over the Mississippi militia produced demands from the Alabama and Georgia conventions for similar armed police forces. Both were approved by Washington, the President telling Johnson of Georgia that these were seen as evidence that the States were taking upon themselves the responsibility for 'arresting marauders, suppressing crime, and enforcing civil authority.'[69] In fact on the same day that he made his decision in Mississippi, the President cabled Parsons suggesting 'the propriety of raising in each county an armed *posse comitatus* organized under your Militia Law and under such provisos as you need to secure their [i.e. the citizens of Alabama] loyalty and obedience to your authority and that of the Military Authorities to repress crime, and arrest criminals.'[70] The provision of a State militia seemed to have become a necessary step towards, as well as an indication of Southern readiness for, governmental autonomy. For the President concluded his dispatch to Parsons by observing that the militia companies were needful and desirable because they would prevent the emergence of vigilante committees and would foster among Alabamians an active rather than a merely passive loyalty.[71]

Acquisition of a State militia and criticism of the Federal forces did not, however, imply a desire for the complete removal of the United States garrisons. Militia were needed to preserve order in the outlying areas where Federal troops were not stationed and where freedmen were more numerous and in need of policing and control. Furthermore, they would supplement the Federal forces, which, if

---

[68] Johnson to Schurz, Washington, D.C., 30 August 1865, *Senate Executive Documents*, 39th Cong., 1st Sess., I, No. 2, 232; Johnson to Slocum, Washington, D.C., 2 September, Johnson MSS, Series III.

[69] Johnson to James Johnson, Washington, D.C., 5 November 1865, *Senate Executive Documents*, 39th Cong., 1st Sess., I, No. 26, 238.

[70] Johnson to Parsons, Washington, D.C., 1 September 1865, Johnson MSS, Series II.

[71] *Ibid.*

employed in support of the State governments and in line with their interests, were quite acceptable. In fact, because of the disturbed state of affairs, State governments would not have been able to function firmly and authoritatively without the aid of the Federal troops. Even in the quietest and possibly least lawless of Southern States this was acknowledged. Writing from Florida where he was in command, General John G. Foster remarked in December, 'I doubt if the State is ready for civil law, at any rate I know that the great body of the best Citizens look with deep regret upon any withdrawal of the strong arm of the National Government.'[72] From Provisional Governors similar endorsements were forthcoming, Lewis Parsons telling the President that mostly he had 'found a willingness on [the military's] part to aid in the administration of the law, and, as I thought, a desire to allow the civil administration of the government to be resumed in all its forms and force, in accordance with your proclamation.'[73] State officials and men of property were in need of help in law enforcement. What they contested was the supremacy of the Federal forces over the local civil authorities, but not their presence.

The United States Army afforded needful services in keeping order at negligible cost (if not a profit when provisions purchased locally were included), but these tasks could only be performed if there was cooperation from the local population. Cooperation, however, implied approval and acquiescence, yet the troops could not be embraced without reservation because they were, after all, an army of occupation. The less Southerners cooperated and sought to act harmoniously, however, the more the military would be forced to intervene or become coercive. But there were limits to this because, although Holden and Sharkey had not been able to effect an unqualified civil supremacy, it was nonetheless apparent that on balance the civil authorities were to be aided and protected rather than restricted and harrassed by the military. So, taking advantage of this potential in an anomalous situation, the South was able to argue that military prerogatives and innovations made government complicated or unpredictable, that military interference would obstruct the returning good feeling exhibited by Southerners, and that, since the civil courts were functioning and civil

---

[72] General John G. Foster to Assistant Adjutant-General, Department of the Gulf, 11 December 1865, Letters Received, Department of Florida, Vol. III, Records of the Army Commands.

[73] Parsons to Johnson, Montgomery, 2 October 1865, *Senate Executive Documents*, 39th Cong., 1st Sess., I, No. 26, 99.

law being enforced, military interference was redundant. Using these devices and arguments, the South cooperated qualifiedly in those areas where it wished the Army to be effective and restricted the extension of military power where it wanted to retain as complete a measure of autonomy as possible.

Aiding Southern officials in their efforts to circumscribe the military were the views espoused by the generals commanding in the South as to the role and purpose of their troops' presence there. Their instructions from Washington indicated that they were not to hinder the work of restoration being carried out by the Provisional Governors. In May, Stanton cabled Edward R. S. Canby, who was commanding in the Gulf States, that 'The President directs me to express his wish that the military authorities render all proper assistance to the civil authorities in control in the State of Louisiana, and not to interfere with its action further than it may be necessary for the peace and security of the department.'[74] This was reiterated to Southern commanders three months later when the Sharkey–Slocum affair was resolved in favor of the civil authorities.[75] And to this policy the generals, with the exception perhaps of Sheridan, assented approvingly. Finding themselves in an unfamiliar role and in unfavorable circumstances, they were not at all eager to assume more responsibilities than were necessary. Canby represented their feelings when he told Governor Wells, 'I desire to divest myself as soon as possible of all questions of civil administration, and will separate, as soon and as far as I can, all such questions from those that are purely military in their character, and commit them to the care of the proper officers of the civil government.'[76]

It was not simply laziness or the military mind's fear of situations without precedent that suggested such a response. From other generals the rationale for military disengagement was posited on theoretical grounds. General Horatio G. Wright urged his civil counterpart in Texas, A. J. Hamilton, to expand civil authority, especially the court

[74]Stanton to Canby, Washington, D.C., 28 May 1865, in Carl Schurz, 'Condition of the South,' *Senate Executive Documents*, 39th Cong., 1st Sess., I, No. 2, 56.

[75]Johnson to Slocum, Washington, D.C., 2 September 1865, Johnson MSS, Series III; Johnson to General George Meade, Commanding, Division of the Atlantic, Washington, D.C., 31 August 1865, Johnson MSS, Series III.

[76]Gen. E. R. S. Canby to J. Madison Wells, New Orleans, 19 June 1865, in Schurz, 'Condition of the South,' *Senate Executive Documents*, 39th Cong., 1st Sess., I, No. 2, 55.

system, because 'It seems to me that the trial should be made at as early a day as practicable, as their [the civil courts'] success or failure will solve most of the difficulties now existing.'[77] The military's presence was to be temporary, and both Southerners and soldiers realized this. Therefore why wait until the military were about to leave before the civil experiment was made? Agreement with this approach came from the more conservative General Thomas J. Wood, later to command in Mississippi, who reasoned that 'Conquered provinces, controlled by military governments, can no more permanently coexist with republican institutions than water mix with oil. Sooner or later the people of the South must be trusted with their local governments; and in my humble judgement the sooner it is done compatible [with] security and order, the better.'[78]

If the purpose of the military was to assist in restoring civil authority, it should, while encouraging initiatives on the part of Southern officials, also seek to avoid friction and conflict. In November after a particularly unpleasant episode in which the sheriff of Copiah County, Mississippi, had arrested the Colonel of a Colored Infantry detachment and had been sustained by the President, General Osterhaus complained that it was imperative that 'some axiomatic decisions be now made by competent authority, in questions of dispute between the Military and civil authorities, as to their respective spheres and limits of jurisdiction in order to prevent a repetition of collisions of those powers, collisions which have a tendency to create estrangement and sensibility, where harmony and cooperation ought to exist.'[79] And with the civil powers in the South taking the initiative in contesting and assuming areas of jurisdiction, it was obvious that, under the circumstances, attempts to eliminate friction would redound to their benefit.

The need for agreement was nowhere more apparent than in matters relating to the freedmen. It was here that the pressure for civil autonomy was most earnest and persistent. That the Federal forces should insinuate themselves into so sensitive an area was bad enough

[77] General H. G. Wright to A. J. Hamilton, 10 October 1865, Letters Sent, Department of Texas, Vol. IV, Records of the Army Commands.
[78] General Thomas T. Wood to General W. T. Sherman, Little Rock, 25 October 1865, W. T. Sherman MSS.
[79] General Peter Osterhaus to Chief of Staff, Division of the Tennessee, 10 November 1865, Letters Sent, Department of Mississippi, Vol. I, Records of the Army Commands.

for Southern white employers, but since the soldiery in Mississippi, Louisiana, North Carolina and Tennessee were predominantly black, and a goodly number of them former slaves now wearing the blue uniform of the United States Army, the prospect was alarming.[80] The Army as such, however, did not have responsibility for the freedmen; this jurisdiction was delegated to a separate agency, though it was established under the War Department and was manned to a large degree by Army personnel.

The Freedmen's Bureau was to function as a guarantee against the reintroduction of slavery or any kind of peonage and to provide protection and fair treatment to the freedmen. There was no intention of screening freedmen from punishment if they broke the law or of encouraging them to refrain from work. If this were done the objection could then be made that the freedman was incapable of surviving on his own in a state of freedom. Moreover such an exclusive jurisdiction could give rise to a state of affairs such as the South Carolinian secessionist, William H. Trescot, discerned when he noted that 'the Freedmans Bureau is to be a perfect Imperium in imperio and that as far as the negro is concerned he is to be in the State but not of it – the subject of a special Government.'[81]

Bureau officials hoped that they would not have to assert their control to this extent. But this would depend on how Southern courts and Southern employers intended to treat the freedmen. If the indications were favorable, then the Freedmen's Bureau would not need to become an 'imperium in imperio' nor would it need to shield the freedmen. Yet if they were unfavorable, then the Bureau would have to act. But, then, Southern hostility and lack of sympathy toward the freedmen would be compounded by antagonism towards the growing influence of the Bureau and by a feeling that the welfare of the Negro Southerner was none of their concern but solely a problem for the resented 'nigger bureau.'

The policy adopted by the Bureau as early as 30 May when the Commissioner, General O. O. Howard, issued Circular No. 5 was intended to forestall possible polarization.[82] The assumption was that

---

[80]Sefton, *The United States Army and Reconstruction, 1865–1877*, Appendix B, pp. 260–1. In December 1865 there were 86,000 white and 67,500 black troops in the South.

[81]William H. Trescot to Perry, Pendleton, S.C., 6 September 1865, Perry MSS (Ala.).

[82]General O. O. Howard, Commissioner, Freedmen's Bureau, Circular No. 5, 30 May 1865.

civil courts and authorities would eventually be responsible for the protection of the freedman and for guaranteeing his freedom and equality before the law. Therefore the Circular outlined a procedure whereby Assistant Commissioners in the States were to concede authority to the civil courts in cases involving Negroes, provided they allowed them the right to testify. By means of this quid pro quo, Southern authorities were to be prompted into providing the freedmen with equal access and treatment in the courts. From this general policy there emerged a number of working relationships between Provisional Governors and Bureau Assistant Commissioners during the summer of 1865.

Early in August, in Alabama, the first of these arrangements was established. General Wager Swayne handed over Negro cases to those civil courts which recognized Negro testimony and civil officials were coopted to work in Bureau courts to help adjudicate suits retained under Bureau jurisdiction.[83] This latter move was a device both to compensate for the lack of legally trained Army officers available to man Bureau courts and also to conciliate whites in counties hostile to Negro testimony and familiarize them with the idea and practice of blacks testifying in court. In Mississippi a similar agreement was made on 25 September after Sharkey had proclaimed that Negro testimony must be received in State courts; by 31 October General Thomas disbanded all Bureau courts on the grounds that the agreement had been so effective and well observed.[84] The convention in Florida passed a Negro testimony ordinance so that procedures there were more simple than in Georgia where General Tillson established three-man courts consisting of the Bureau agent and two civilians, one chosen by the plaintiff, the other by the defendant, to try minor cases in counties where Negro testimony was not received.[85]

In two States the civil authorities refused to participate in this in-

[83] General Wager Swayne's General Order No. 7 of 4 August 1865 was published in the *Montgomery Advertiser*, 6 August 1865.
[84] Colonel Samuel Thomas to Sharkey, Vicksburg, 24 September 1865, Sharkey MSS. Thomas' General Order ending the Bureau courts was G.O. No. 13. It was strange that Thomas felt the experiment with Negro testimony had worked well because the State Legislature was fiercely divided on the question of Negro testimony and it was around this issue that opposition to Sharkey was organized.
[85] William W. Davis, *The Civil War and Reconstruction in Florida* (Gainsville: University of Florida Press, 1964 [1913]), p. 379; General Davis Tillson, Circular No. 4, 13 November 1865, Telamon Cuyler Collection; Alan Conway, *The Reconstruction of Georgia* (Minneapolis: University of Minnesota Press, 1966), pp. 77–82.

terim arrangement, and interestingly the prohibition came from Governors who were regarded as far more independent of the old regime than Sharkey and Parsons. Pierpont of Virginia would not allow State officials to serve under the Bureau because they 'are prohibited from holding any post ... under the Government of the United States.'[86] He was joined by North Carolina's Holden who announced flatly that Negro testimony could not be accepted in the civil courts because State law did not allow it.[87] And in another State, South Carolina, no transitional arrangement was introduced because the Freedmen's Bureau was closely controlled by the Army and its commander, General Q. A. Gillmore, who insisted that, unless Negro testimony were recognized, the system of Army provost courts, and not Bureau courts, would handle cases involving penalties of less than $100 or six months imprisonment.[88]

The Circular of 30 May had envisaged a series of experimental arrangements between the Bureau and the Provisional Governments intended both as a method of cooperation and as a means of prompting the civil authorities into providing legal rights and equal protection to the freedmen. But in attempting this the Bureau was placing itself in a vulnerable position where its offers could be exploited or spurned; and in fact these were the Southerners' responses. In the first three States, Negro testimony was partially conceded and also influence in freedmen cases still retained by means of civilian representation in Bureau courts; and in the latter three, testimony was not granted at all, leaving the Bureau open to criticism for its exclusive jurisdiction over Negro affairs. It was a case of 'damned if you do and damned if you don't.'

The Bureau was in the impossible position of being responsible for aiding and protecting the freedmen yet having to carry out this function in the context of an overall Federal policy aimed at restoring self-government to the Southern States, towards the attainment of which the Bureau was required to offer aid and encouragement. Needless to say it was the second constraint to which the Bureau invariably responded.

Once it was decided that civil government, even though hedged

[86] Francis H. Pierpont to Colonel Orlando O. Brown, Richmond, 7 October 1865, Johnson MSS, Series I.
[87] William W. Holden to General O. O. Howard, Raleigh, 26 September 1865, Letterbook, Holden Official Correspondence.
[88] General Q. A. Gillmore to Schurz, Savannah, 1 August 1865, in Schurz, 'Con-

and qualified at first, should be reestablished in the South, the United States released energies and encouraged propensities in that part of the country which would stultify any attempt at a thorough reconstruction. Jurisdictional disputes would be rife in a context which required cooperation, and cooperation and harmony in turn would be contingent on concessions and conciliation. With the appointment of Provisional civil governments in the South, there had to be proferred support and power for those governments since they were required to perform unpopular as well as immense tasks. The machinery for establishing and strengthening Southern governments was aimed to ensure that the Provisional Governors and their aides would govern effectively and creatively. In this framework, it was counterproductive to insist on requirements which would circumscribe the Provisional Governments. Accordingly, the incentives available to the Federal authorities as means for encouraging Southern cooperation were jettisoned, leaving, within Federal discretion, few pressures towards, and few rewards for, compliance. Embarking on a policy which established and then proceeded to strengthen civil governments in the South, the Federal authorities provided themselves with an institutional and structural context for reconstruction which meant that, even if terms and requirements had been more rigorously and firmly demanded by the President, it could have made only a marginal difference. Carl Schurz told Andrew Johnson in November that 'It will require measures of a more practical character to prevent the dangers which, as everybody that reads the signs of the times must see, are now impending.'[89] Probably not even Schurz realized how radical these would have to be, for it was the assumptions and context of Presidential restoration, not merely its details, which assured its failure.

dition of the South,' *Senate Executive Documents*, 39th Cong., 1st Sess., I, No. 2, 105.
[89] Schurz, 'Condition of the South,' *ibid.*, p. 35.

5

Misrepresentation

By the beginning of 1866 it was evident that a crisis had emerged in the political relations not merely between the President and Congress, but, more fundamentally, between the North and South. Misunderstanding, or breakdown in communications, cannot alone explain the failure of the President's attempt to forge a reunion of the sections by a policy of conciliation. Rather than misunderstanding, there was misrepresentation, both purposeful and unintended. Each section misrepresented, and was misrepresented by, the other. For it was the nature and composition of each section that were in dispute, not merely what each said and demanded. Differences of substance existed, and these were exacerbated by the political exigencies of the times as well as by the feelings of suspicion and recrimination which abounded on both sides of the Potomac.

From the point of view of the Southern politicians, there were three dimensions to this problem of misrepresentation. They were convinced, first of all, that the North, especially the radical Republicans, disliked and misunderstood Southerners and the South. To compound this, the Southerners felt that the Republicans proceeded deliberately to misrepresent Southern actions and inactions so as to justify harsher measures towards them. This was misrepresentation *of* the South. Second, they felt that the Republicans in Congress were determined either to exclude the Southern delegates, or, if not exclude them, make certain that they would return to the national councils weakened and represented only by men who could take the ironclad oath and who, ipso facto, were unsympathetic to their own section. Representation in Congress by such men would be tantamount to committing perjury as well as political suicide. This was misrepresentation *for* the South. Last, the South was caught in this syndrome of misrepresentation by its own failure to assess correctly the politics of the North. Partly this stemmed from a mistaken preconception as to the policies envisaged by the radicals and partly from a failure to assess accurately the feelings and maneuverings of Northern politicians and voters. Aggravating these errors were the efforts of some Southern journalists and politicians to portray the radicals as enemies of the South whose demands need not be heeded and whose defeat would necessitate a union of all conflicting parties and interests in the South. This was misrepresentation *by* the South.

In isolation, some of these misrepresentations could perhaps have been remedied or removed, but they were symptoms of a total problem which could not easily have been solved. After four years of war, differences, suspicions, and fears still existed which made political accommodations, as in the 1850s, extremely difficult to achieve.

a : *Misrepresentation of the South*

Readmission to the Union depended upon Northern assessments of the feelings and conduct of the Southern politicians during the summer and fall of 1865. Exactly what it was that would convince or satisfy was not known. Haste to return and a ready compliance with whatever was demanded could be interpreted as untrustworthy overzealousness or regarded as genuine eagerness to return. Delay and circumspection could also be given two mutually contradictory interpretations. Samuel Phillips, a North Carolina Whig, demonstrated that most Southerners understood the position in which they stood when he wrote,

Assertions that everybody is loyal will produce no good impression upon intelligent persons observing the progress of things here. It is quite as likely to produce suspicion as the assertion that a large proportion of the people are disloyal. The witness in the first instance will be doubted and that one who must know the contrary (if he knows anything) should make such assertions will be regarded as part of a plot to lull the government.[1]

Northern politicians were thus left with unlimited discretion in their evaluation of the worthiness of the South for readmittance into the Union of States. And sometimes Southerners saw their reliance on Northern satisfaction as a prospect brimming with hopelessness. The *Jackson Clarion* considered in December that there was nothing the South could do to alleviate its condition, since Northern men such as Clinton B. Fisk, Assistant Commissioner of the Freedmen's

---

[1] Phillips to Kemp P. Battle, Chapel Hill, 5 September 1865, Battle Family Papers.

Bureau in Tennessee, believed that 'the Southerners are not repentant, and do not profess to be,' while others like Henry Ward Beecher asserted that they 'would not wish them to profess repentance and would not trust them if they did.'[2]

It was but a short step from the recognition of this helpless dependence to the assertion that there was in the North a relentless determination to exclude the South from Congress which would be achieved by misrepresenting the feelings of its inhabitants. The South was not trying to lull the North into acquiescence in its loyalty. Instead, hostile elements in the North were providing ammunition to persuade men of the need to reject the South because of its disloyalty. Northern newspapers, especially radical ones, intended, so the *Atlanta Intelligencer* believed, 'to excite a political crusade, by and through which they desire more to benefit themselves, and attain power, than to restore peace,' and it concluded: 'This injustice done to the South, is only equalled in its monstrous atrocity by the cool, calculating duplicity attending it.'[3]

The attempt to consolidate a victory by the sword with one by the pen was also noted by Edward Conigland, a North Carolina secessionist and convention delegate: 'But our enemies are using every literary vehicle to defame us, poison the mind of the world against us, that thereby they may excuse their own atrocities, and make us fit subjects for slaves.'[4] As early as June, the *Richmond Times* was even able to expose the conspiratorial quality in this hostile crusade when it declared that, 'The advocates of negro suffrage have been able to offer but one excuse for their infamous doctrine, and that has been, that the continued "disloyalty of the South" renders it necessary that the negro should vote.'[5] Radical measures, especially Negro suffrage, were, therefore, not a genuine antidote to Southern loyalty, but the fabrication of that disloyalty was to be the pretext for these extreme policies. The Southern States began to see themselves as the victims of a predetermined plot to ensure the supremacy in Congress of the radical wing of the Republican Party.

During the summer and fall of 1865 there existed in the South the

[2] Editorial, *Jackson Clarion*, 7 December 1865.
[3] Editorial, *Atlanta Intelligencer*, 9 August 1865.
[4] Conigland to Thomas Ruffin, Halifax, N.C., 4 December 1865, in *The Correspondence of Thomas Ruffin*, ed. J. G. de R. Hamilton (4 vols.; Raleigh, N.C.: Edwards and Broughton C., 1918), IV, 45–6.
[5] Editorial, *Richmond Times*, 20 June 1865.

conviction that the falsity of these misrepresentations could be exposed by the conciliatory action of the conventions. By complying with the President's policy and restoring their State governments, Southerners would demonstrate that assertions that they were disloyal were slanderous and malicious. In July, the *New Orleans Times*, noting the falsehoods propagated by Northern newspapers, informed its readers that 'The South will persist in its renewed loyalty, despite those who would rejoice in the exhibition of "secession feeling," hoping to make such exhibitions serviceable for paltry partisan purposes. We cannot afford to gratify our maligners by giving the color of verity to their unfounded aspersions.'[6]

The deeds of the conventions and of the voters proved, however, to be inadequate in either appeasing or satisfying Northern critics. On occasion, Southern newspapers issued denunciations of the proceedings of the politicians. The *Augusta Chronicle*, for example, on 8 December reprimanded the Southern conventions: 'Assembled in the most eventful period of the history of the States, at a time when all the talent and power of the conventions should have been used to provide for the future; amid all this responsibility, they ignored the public good to preserve a record of consistency.'[7] Next day the Mississippi legislature, in particular, was excoriated by the leading paper of that State, the *Jackson Clarion*:

It appears, therefore, that our legislature in its overtopping anxiety to feed the prejudices of a certain class of our people, and its indifference to the wholesome sentiment of sober, reasonable men of the State, in its insane proclivity to strain at gnats, after having swallowed the camel, has succeeded in fastening upon us indefinitely the negro bureau, placed us in imminent danger of another provisional government, and caused its own legislative authority to be treated with contempt. . . .[8]

These outbursts were infrequent, however; more often there was little disposition to blame politicians or other Southern leaders for the continued criticism of their section. On the contrary, in order to prevent the emergence of opposition parties or coalitions in the South and to discredit Northern critics, blame was placed anywhere but on the South. Whether criticism of the South was merely a reaction by many Northerners to what was considered an inadequate response

[6]Editorial, *New Orleans Times*, 27 July 1865.
[7]Editorial, *Augusta Chronicle*, 8 December 1865.
[8]Editorial, *Jackson Clarion*, 9 December 1865.

to the requirements of the victorious party or whether it was a pretext for the implementation of a preconceived plan of Negro suffrage did not matter. Such assessments had to be countered by assertions of Southern good intentions, if not loyalty.

Most frequently Northern criticism was countered by defenses of the South's course since the surrender. Governor Jonathan Worth, in a speech to the legislature of North Carolina, announced that 'If all these *acts* are held insufficient to entitle us to confidence, we can scarcely hope to do anything which will be held satisfactory.'[9] In Alabama, Robert Patton's inaugural address asserted that the President's policy 'has been unhesitatingly accepted.'[10] The South Carolina convention's proceedings were endorsed and applauded by Benjamin Perry, and the *Charleston Courier*, in an article aimed at countering Northern attacks, stated that the convention, by adopting the President's terms, 'has thus placed itself on an impregnable foundation, and may appropriately claim the support of the good and wise in every section.'[11]

The Southern assemblies, so the argument went, had complied and had conceded as much as could be expected. Even though they had quibbled or refused to cooperate on a number of matters and even though they had been assertive and demanding on others, the issues of the war had been yielded by the Southern assemblies during 1865. Slavery and secession, the main thrust of the President's concern, had after all been repudiated and clear indications of a desire to rejoin the Union they had fought four years to leave had been demonstrated. Of course, they could have yielded more. But, as the *Montgomery Advertiser* observed, assuming that the President's requests had been complied with, 'the line of demarcation between [Johnson's] policy and that of the radical negro equality men of the North is broad and distinct, and beyond that line Alabamians are not going.'[12] Early in 1866 the *Raleigh Sentinel* indicated similar feelings: 'Let us meet fully the requisitions of the President. Congress has no right to ask more. The terms prescribed by President Johnson upon our surrender, cannot in justice and right be added to. The burdens imposed upon us, when

[9]Jonathan Worth, Speech to the Legislature, 16 December 1865, *North Carolina Standard*, 18 December 1865.
[10]Robert Patton, Inaugural Address, 13 December 1865, *Montgomery Advertiser*, 14 December 1865.
[11]Editorial, *Charleston Courier*, 30 September 1865.
[12]Editorial, *Montgomery Advertiser*, 17 December 1865.

fully borne and discharged cannot be increased.'[13] In a later issue, the *Sentinel* added: 'We do not mean that the South should labor to remove all objection. This is impossible – The Radicals do not intend to be satisfied with us. They will prevent the restoration of the States by every possible method.' Complaint was certain to be made, but 'no *good* ground of offense' and 'no *just cause* for complaint or further conflict' should be offered.[14] Misrepresentation was inevitable, it was argued, but it had to be exposed as such and rejected as unjust and overdemanding in intent.

Disloyalty, after all, was a relative concept. The South would always be disloyal as far as the radicals were concerned, unless it met their maximum demands. It would be degrading, Southerners argued, for them to attempt such self-effacement in an effort to disarm the radicals. Besides, eager accommodation might be considered, not as evidence of loyalty, but of dissembling political ambition. The North had already increased its demands throughout the summer, and every time that they had been met, so the *Charleston Courier* noted on 1 December, further requirements had been issued until finally the South would refuse to comply, at which point it could be maintained it was disloyal.[15] To pursue such a will o' the wisp was to invite unneeded troubles. Yet how else could Southern loyalty be demonstrated; neither acts nor words seemed to be adequate. Reluctantly the *Jackson Clarion* had to admit in January 1866 that 'The painful explanation can only be offered that we cannot be trusted – that our whole conduct is such as to falsify our assertions of loyalty long since made.' It mattered little that 'everything important demanded of us as a proof of our sincere loyalty has been surrendered.'[16]

All that could be stated in reply to the querulous dissatisfaction in the North was that the South could be trusted. This was attempted. But pleadings for confidence such as were on two occasions enunciated officially in speeches by Governors Worth and Patton were hardly likely to convince a suspicious North which believed the South had already displayed evidences of disloyal or unsatisfactory conduct. For Patton, in his inaugural, prayed for confidence on the grounds that 'Candor and sincerity are prominent traits of Southern character. Our people never dissemble; they always mean what they say and

[13]Editorial, *Raleigh Sentinel*, 2 February 1866.
[14]*Ibid.*, 27 February 1866.
[15]Editorial, *Charleston Courier*, 1 December 1865.
[16]Editorial, *Jackson Clarion*, 14 January 1866.

do.'[17] And Worth proceeded to argue that 'unfounded distrust will not beget kindness and confidence. We ought to be judged by our acts.'[18] Placed side by side, these two arguments for trust justified the North's lack of it, for it was indeed on Southern actions in the conventions and legislatures that judgement was based.

Another possibility still existed however. If the South could not convince Northern Congressmen of its reliability, then possibly it could eliminate, or at least curb, those in the rebel States who aided and abetted by supplying the evidence on which this hypothesis was based. Precautions against the emergence of an organized opposition to the reinstatement of the South's traditional leaders were taken continually during the months after the surrender. A partisan split among the politicians or the emergence of a political organization among the classes previously excluded from power might be the cause for internal quarreling. This might 'lead to a breach made wider and deeper every day, until the extremest partizan on either side will become the most powerful man of his party, and the most dangerous to the quiet and prosperity of the State. With such tools as these we shall be sure to dig up negro suffrage and worship it, as many did the cotton bag.'[19] The results of such infighting might not be so disastrous as Bartholomew F. Moore, the North Carolina Unionist and Superior Court Justice, forecast, but it would divide the States internally and make criticism legitimate and widespread.

The existence of criticism and dissent within each State would enable Northern politicians to detect more readily Southern weaknesses and disloyalty, since opposition parties would be the first to reveal this information and broadcast it. But simultaneously, the attempt to smother differences and denigrate dissent would remove any stimulus towards more conciliatory or adequate responses to Northern requirements. Unity and a united front were, however, considered essential and took precedence over the possible utility of internal pressure as a means of evincing loyalty. Therefore, the dissatisfaction manifested by critics of the Southern conventions and legislatures had to be curtailed or else defamed. 'Calumny,' noted the

---

[17] Robert Patton, Inaugural Address, 13 December 1865, *Montgomery Advertiser*, 14 December 1865.

[18] Jonathan Worth, Speech to the Legislature, 16 December 1865, *North Carolina Standard*, 18 December 1865.

[19] Moore to Tod R. Caldwell, 14 October 1865, *North Carolina Standard*, 16 October 1865.

Richmond Times, 'when manufactured by aliens, and paid for by the line, rarely inflicts serious injury' but 'the poisonous shafts which have been recklessly hurled by her own children have, we admit, strengthened the hands of that radical faction which is seeking to strip Virginia of her rights as a State, and degrade her to the status of a conquered province.'[20]

Northern vituperation could be dismissed as being based on insufficient understanding of Southern feelings and conditions and as being intentionally biased. But from Southerners themselves the evidence would be convincing. Unless dissent and dissenters could be epitomized as treasonous and dangerous to the success of the South in its attempts to obtain readmission and a restored government, Northern critics would be supplied with a continuous flow of valuable ammunition. The 'cri de coeur' of John O. Steger, a friend of Robert M. T. Hunter, epitomized the danger of Southern dissent:

> But some extreme union men, who were a few weeks since extreme secessionists, and prepared to denounce you as a traitor, are moving heaven and earth to prove that there is no reliance to be placed in southern loyalty or in southern truthfulness. . . . The most painful result of the contest to me is, the demoralization of our people and the disposition on the part of the extreme secessionists to 'befoul their own nests' and turn states evidence against their own people.[21]

Journalists, politicians, candidates for office who advocated a more complete submission than the State had observed, or who endorsed Negro suffrage and kindred anathemas, were denounced and made to feel the brunt of unfavorable public opinion. Simultaneously, among those who held views which were deemed legitimate, every precaution was taken to minimize differences so that hostilities and ruptures did not result. Accordingly, most State conventions nominated official gubernatorial candidates in the winter of 1865 with a view to avoiding a heated campaign. Rarely however was an automatic election ensured, Georgia and Florida alone managing to enjoy such bliss. Where contests developed, Senators and Congressmen, especially the former, were selected after discussions in smoke-filled rooms that would eliminate public dissension and conflict in the legislature or during the campaign.

[20]Editorial, *Richmond Times*, 8 August 1865.
[21]Steger to Hunter, Richmond, Va., 13 August 1865, Hunter – Garnett MSS.

Besides discouraging criticism within the South which would be used as incriminating evidence by the Northern prosecution, the effort to maintain a united front also aided the traditional leaders of the Southern States in their attempt to regain political power. There might be differences between Whigs and Democrats, anti-secessionists and secessionists, but these were submerged temporarily in the interest of precluding the emergence of organized opposition. The result was that in most Southern States the return of the Confederate leaders had been assured, Democrats and secessionists often playing a supportive rather than a prominent role.[22] Where their return had not ensued, as in North Carolina, opposition and dissent were encouraged by those same groups which in other States condemned them as aids to the enemy.

The gubernatorial candidacy of Jonathan Worth was urged against the claims of William W. Holden, a parvenu Democrat, who, as Provisional Governor, had remodeled the State's officialdom. Even though, as Worth himself admitted, 'The impression is made that the Prest. requires the election of Mr. Holden as a condition precedent to our readmission into the Union,' and even though 'It will be hard to resist the effect of the will of the President, as expounded by Mr. Holden, that the issue is Holden and "Go Back" – or Worth and "Stay Out" of the union,' the race was made, the dire consequences notwithstanding.[23]

In response, the *North Carolina Standard*, Holden's paper, tried unsuccessfully to rebut the assertion that if Worth were elected 'the North will see that we prefer the steady light of a fixed star to the uncertain blaze of a comet,' a reference to Holden's inconsistency in advising secession in 1860 and later, in 1863, peace. Undaunted, the *Standard* next accused the Worth faction and its supporter, the *Raleigh Sentinel*, of creating fatal division: 'Six months ago there was not one word of opposition; four months ago the "Sentinel" did not "peep" even about opposition but now men are vieing [*sic*] with each other in

---

[22]In his unpublished Ph.D. dissertation, 'Politics in the Lower South during Presidential Reconstruction, April to November, 1865,' Donald Breese has shown that Whigs were in the ascendancy immediately after the war. Admittedly those who led the South after the war were generally Whigs, but the explanation for their doing so should not be stated on partisan grounds but on the fact that opponents of secession assumed positions of influence and these generally were Whigs.

[23]Worth to B.S. Hedrick, Raleigh, 21 October 1865, Hedrick MSS.

the work of stirring up strife, hindering the Provisional Governor in his work, and raking up old Confederate issues. This is the plain unmistakeable work of traitors – unpardoned, virulent, traitors.'[24] Yet, in 1866, when Holden, out of office, threatened the Whigs, constantly criticizing them and even unwillingly espousing Negro suffrage, it was he who was categorized as a traitor to the South and a 'radical' by the very men who had divided the ranks in 1865. Effectively, therefore, the Confederates were prepared to stir up controversy and provide opposition if it served their interests when they were excluded from office, while they would condemn such activity in others on the ground that it gave aid to the Northern enemy. Retention of power in their State and section by the traditional politicians was evidently the primary reason for discouraging opposition; and the technical leverage and evidence of disloyalty that division might supply to the North was supplementary.

By the beginning of 1866, with dissent outlawed and the Confederates restored, an impasse had been reached. Criticisms of substance from the North were rejected as misrepresentations, while from within the South such challenges were denounced as traitorous. Even the President found himself unable to stimulate or pressure the South's leaders into taking actions which might help resolve their dilemma. Furthermore, Andrew Johnson was unable to admit that the South had failed him and was thoroughly disloyal and hostile. In the fall of 1865 he had often stated his dissatisfaction with the conduct of the South. In March 1866, a friend of his from Tennessee who was not identified by the *Nashville Press* said that he had talked a lot with Andrew Johnson and 'The President is not at all pleased with the conduct of the Southern politicians, newspapers, conventions, and legislatures. On the contrary, he is highly displeased with them. He went to the utmost verge of generosity in order to encourage the rebel leaders to repent and act as national men.[25]

Never in all his public utterances did the President state that he was satisfied with the loyalty of the Southerners. In his message introducing Grant's report on the South he had merely expressed 'An abiding faith' that 'their actions will conform to their professions.' To a delegation of Southern businessmen in September he had said

---

[24] Editorial, *North Carolina Standard*, 17 November 1865.

[25] *Nashville Press*, 20 March 1866, quoted in *North Carolina Standard*, 29 March 1866.

that 'He had confidence in the professions of the people of the South, and of their purpose to restore the Union upon the principles of the Constitution, and he hoped and believed they were ready to come up and rally round the Union and the Constitution.'[26] Even Henry J. Raymond, the President's spokesman in the debate on readmission in the House of Representatives, could only say, 'I hope and believe we shall soon see the day when the people of the Southern States will show us by evidences that we cannot mistake that they have returned in all sincerity and faith to their allegiance to the Union.'[27]

The President's policy required the readmission of the South so that the country would be restored to harmonious working order. He did not need assurance that the Southern States had reconstructed their political system before they could be readmitted. He was prepared to trust them, and he expected cooperation and good treatment for the freedmen to spring from readmission and harmony, and not vice versa. Therefore, evidences of 'returning loyalty' were adequate. He did not need to, and never did, assert that the South was loyal. But still the South had not behaved as well as he had hoped and, besides, the opposition in the North was extremely dissatisfied. Moreover, in January 1866, the South was still patrolled by Federal troops and the Freedmen's Bureau. It even became necessary for Grant, as commanding general of the Army, to issue General Order No. 3 in early 1866 to provide protection for Northern soldiers and Southern loyalists against civil arrest for deeds committed in the course of duty during and after the war.

In view of these occurrences, it was exceedingly difficult for the President to maintain even his minimal stance of confidence in Southern good faith. Yet he was unable to pressure the South since that section considered itself loyal in the eyes of the President and would react if its protector should forfeit his claim to be so by forcing upon it measures that were unpleasant. Furthermore, and more importantly, if it were known that the President believed the South should concede further before being considered ready for readmission, that would be a vindication of Congress' assertion that the South was disloyal and defiant. The President was shackled. His failure to ensure Southern readmission left him with no recourse but either to yield to Congress,

---

[26] *Augusta Constitutionalist,* 21 September 1865.
[27] Henry J. Raymond, Speech in the House of Representatives, 21 December 1865, quoted in *Montgomery Advertiser,* 4 January 1866.

or to defy it and try eventually to defeat it. In the meantime, he deferred making a decision. So, during January and February 1866, there was a stalemate in Northern politics, with the President defending the indefensible and unable to influence the South sufficiently to rescue him from his impotence.

The verdict of the Congress on Southern readmission, the helplessness of the President to influence Southern affairs, and the futility of Southern attempts to gainsay what they believed to be Northern misrepresentation, all combined to effect a passivity and inertia in the South regarding Federal questions. There was nothing for the South to do but wait on events in the North. Whatever was done was misconstrued or could be misrepresented, so it was best to do nothing but tend to matters within the States, to build up the wastes of the defeated land, and to confide to the warring parties in Washington the future of the Republic and of the South. 'In the position in which the South now finds herself,' suggested the *New Orleans Times*, 'nothing can be gained by intemperate and fretful protests. . . . Let her bide her time in hope.'[28] The *Montgomery Advertiser* suggested a moratorium on political activity: 'The threadbare cant of office-holding demagogues about treason, rebellion and confiscation will be hushed by the mighty hummings and heavings of that gigantic machinery which soon will be built up in the South if we go honestly to work about it. . . . Thus shall we deliver the South from oppression and the whole nation from the ruin of anarchy.'[29] And as a postscript to the year following the surrender, the *Augusta Constitutionalist* could declare: 'And so much for a year of activity – this fawning, sneaking, cringing, dirt-eating, "loyal" activity. . . . Let us have a little masterly inactivity by way of a change.'[30] As far as the Confederates could see, Northern demands and misrepresentations had demonstrated the impossibility of cooperation and the distinctiveness of Southern society. Southern separatism was self-evident by early 1866.

b: *Misrepresentation for the South*

The Joint Committee on Reconstruction had been established in December 1865 'to inquire into the condition of the States, which formed the so-called Confederate States of America, and report

[28]Editorial, *New Orleans Times*, 9 May 1866.
[29]Editorial, *Montgomery Advertiser*, 8 February 1866.
[30]Editorial, *Augusta Constitutionalist*, 14 April 1866.

whether they, or any of them, are entitled to be represented in either house of Congress.'[31] Thinking that this was, in essence, a Committee of Elections and Privileges, William A. Graham contacted the chairman, Senator William Pitt Fessenden of Maine, to see if North Carolina's Congressmen-elect could be present during sessions so as to 'guard against ex parte testimony from unknown or irresponsible sources' and offer counter-evidence where possible.[32] Fessenden informed him that the committee was not examining credentials of individual Congressmen; and, besides, it was 'not customary to allow a cross-examination of witnesses before a committee appointed to report on a subject not involving individuals. The committee is supposed to be desirous to ascertain the truth, and capable of making all the examination necessary.'[33] Under the circumstances, then, witnesses called by the committee would be free, so Graham feared, to misrepresent North Carolina and the other States not represented in Congress. Readmission of the Southern States would therefore depend mainly on the testimony of Freedmen's Bureau agents, United States soldiers, and Southern loyalists as well as a sprinkling of orthodox Confederate politicians. And, in a manner of speaking, these men would serve as ad interim substitutes for the duly elected but rejected Congressmen.

It was not because of ill-luck or miscalculation that Southern representation in Congress had been reduced to such calamitous proportions. A definite decision had been reached among the leaders of the South. They preferred to be guided by the Administration's frequent relaxation of the ironclad test oath as a prerequisite for Federal office-holders in the South rather than to take for granted Johnson's and Seward's warnings that they had no control, and desired none, over the qualifications for Congressmen. Consequently the voters and legislatures of the South were allowed to select, with few exceptions, men who could not swear the ironclad oath unless they perjured themselves. But had candidates able to swear the oath been elected, the Southern States would have been represented by those who had opposed, or at least, failed to support, the Confederacy. Not only would that have been equivalent to a repudiation by the South of its four years' struggle and of those who had suffered for it, but it would

---

[31] *Jount Committee on Reconstruction*, p. iii.
[32] Graham to Fessenden, 29 January 1966, W. A. Graham Collection.
[33] Fessenden to Graham, Washington, D.C., 24 January 1866, W. A. Graham Collection.

also have been an endoresement of loyalism in the South. In essence, it would have handed over the major Federal elective offices of the States to men who would inevitably form the core of an opposition party, replete with the power of patronage.

As long as the politicians could retain these positions, even at the expense of temporary exclusion from Congress, the most important goal would have been secured, namely, control of State political power. Southern politicians were agreed on preventing the ironclad qualifications from becoming agents of 'divide and rule' in their States. Misrepresentation in Congress was to be avoided for just the same reasons that criticism within each State was to be discouraged – the grip of the Confederate politicians would be loosened and, ipso facto, so the latter felt, the South as a section would be weakened.

The constituency from which Southern Congressmen were to be selected was not a new one. It was the same as had existed before the war; and unless the principles of representative government were ignored, the 'representatives in Congress should above all things *represent* public opinion in the section.' Continuing, Samuel Phillips, the Whig friend and neighbor of David L. Swain, declared: 'if an erring but repentant constituency exists in a part of the country, which nevertheless is regarded as loyal, let not the loyalty of the erring and repentant representative be questioned.'[34] There should not, in other words, be special concern for a representative's loyalty qualifications over and above those of the people among whom he lived and who had elected him. The ironclad oath was therefore superfluous and a negation of representative government and free elections. It was a war-measure which by 1865 had become obsolete and unjust. If the Southern States were considered loyal and trustworthy enough to hold elections and be readmitted, why, the Confederates remonstrated, did their delegates need to swear a rigid and demanding oath that would in most cases deprive their election of any meaning and prevent their constituents from being represented in Congress?

The inconsistency and illogicality of Federal policy had been detected. This could be resolved only by repeal of the test oath or by a voluntary admission on the part of the Southern people that they were not sufficiently loyal and that, if they wished representation, new constituencies would have to elect their Congressmen. If neither of these things were done, they would have either to succumb to the

---

[34]Phillips to Graham, Raleigh, 10 October 1865, W. A. Graham Collection.

ironclad oath, tantamount to a self-denying ordinance, or else ignore it and hope that the oath would not be implemented. Although a few who could take the ironclad oath were elected from Florida, Arkansas, Louisiana, Tennessee, and Virginia, Southerners in general decided to disregard the requirements of Congress. Had they not taken this approach, the Congressional Republicans would have been hard pressed to exclude them.

The main argument offered as justification for ignoring Congress' proscriptive qualification was that, in their political and economic weakness, the Southern States could not afford to be represented in Congress by any but their most able and experienced statesmen. The Confederate States were in need of defense against the unlimited power of the victorious North. To send men to Congress who could take the ironclad oath would be a mere self-sacrificial gesture since the delegates would be 'mere puppets in the hands of the Republicans.'[35] Strength would be positively added to the Republican Party in Congress, rather than denied it, by the sending of delegates pledged to assail, not protect, the South. Besides, as Samuel Phillips, on one occasion, informed William A. Graham, it was entirely unnatural and perverse to deny office to the talented: 'It will not succeed. I feel great contempt for those who require that the best runners shall be hobbled in order that they may stand some chance in the race, for political honors. . . . What fantastic tricks before high Heaven are there!'[36] Taking of the ironclad, so the argument ran, was not an index of Southern loyalty but a catapult for precipitating into political power those who, under ordinary circumstances, would not have the talent and sagacity to attain so elevated a station. The Southern political and social order was being subverted, and it would be over-thrown if there were Southerners in the Federal legislature who would aid, or at least be unable to withstand, the schemes of the Republicans.

By contrast, it was often argued that by sending its most notable statesmen, the South would be giving a pledge of its earnestness in wanting to be restored. After the election to the Senate of ex-Governor Herschel V. Johnson, a Confederate Senator and president of the convention in 1865, and of Alexander Stephens, Vice-President of

---

[35] Ed. C. Anderson to R. M. T. Hunter, Savannah, 11 October 1865, Hunter – Garnett MSS.

[36] Phillips to Graham, Chapel Hill, 16 September 1865, W. A. Graham Collection.

the Confederacy, the *Atlanta Intelligencer* unblushingly explained Georgia's action: 'Whether or not the selection of Messrs. Stephens and Johnson to represent the State of Georgia in the national councils be acceptable to the people of the North, we have no means of knowing. They are offered as the representatives of a people who are loyal at heart, and who henceforth desire to bear faithful allegiance to the Government. They bear in their persons another "olive branch of peace" from a State whose purposes will be to act out in good faith her promises.'[37] No rationalization was needed and no bravado implied; this was the only fashion in which Georgia was able to demonstrate its readiness to rejoin the Union, ironclad test oaths and Northern priorities to the contrary notwithstanding. It would presumably be deceptive and misleading for Georgia to be readmitted by means of the ruse of selecting ironclad oath-takers since, by this tactic, the State of Georgia would not be readmitted, but merely some masquerading Congressmen from within the State's borders.

On other grounds, too, the admission of the South's prominent political leaders to Congress would be advisable. Francis Pickens, South Carolina's Governor in 1861, told Provisional Governor Perry in October 1865 that 'if the manhood of the Southern States be sent to Congress, it will but add power and strength to [Johnson's] administration.'[38] This argument was premised on the assumption that the President intended to withstand the radicals and would in no way attempt to defeat them by conciliation. Qualifying this recommendation was the advice offered by one of New York's most powerful bankers, John Livingston warned that prominent rebels or secessionists in Congress would so anger Northern opinion that their ability to aid the South or the President would be nullified. They would presumably aid the opposition as much as 'mere oath-swallowers.'[39]

There were essentially two responses from the South to the analysis and warning offered by Livingston. One of them was for the South to recognize the danger referred to. Livingston suggested that the South should compromise by selecting for Congress men who had been reluctant rebels instead of those who had been prominent 'fire-eaters' and secessionists. In the main this was done; but it made little differ-

---

[37] Editorial, *Atlanta Intelligencer*, 2 February 1866.
[38] Pickens to Perry, Edgewood, S.C., 6 October 1865, Perry MSS (Chapel Hill).
[39] Livingston to Perry, New York City, 24 October 1865, Perry MSS (Ala.).

ence as far as Congress was concerned.[40] The other reaction was to ignore Livingston's advocacy of caution and to argue along the lines of Alexander H. H. Stuart. In practice however this was to produce the same kind of Southern representation as the suggestion just discussed. Campaigning aggressively for the Senate and intending to present himself, an anti-secessionist in 1860, as a test-case for removal of the ironclad oath, Stuart declared in his campaign manifesto: 'The question seems to me to narrow itself down to this. Whose views are you to consult in selecting your representative? Are you to seek to

---

[40]The conciliation involved in this maneuver was calculated to benefit the Confederates, as well as to disarm the Republicans. As an indication of this, C. B. Nero's letter to Provisional Governor Sharkey is of interest. Nero argued that his and Sharkey's party should be given power and patronage because it was conciliatory and unionist in reputation; but, as the letter proceeds, it is obvious that the intention of such a move is to create division in the North. So, in spite of Nero's apparent accommodation, the thrust of his argument is nonetheless assertive and threatening. Southern unity and power, he argues, would be better assured by placing Whigs in office, and the upshot of that would be that Northern moderates would be won over and the Northern extremists weakened. So unless the Republicans wished to be undermined in this fashion, they would have to maintain a solid front against all representatives of the Southern establishment, whether Whig or Democrat. Conversely, efforts by Republican moderates to prise Whigs away from Democrats, anti-secessionists from secessionists, would have to be resisted.

In his letter, Nero regretted Sharkey's appointment of secession Democrats and, after asserting that 'The only true Union element in this State [Mississippi] is the Whig party,' he continued:

'The hopes of the Secessionists are greatly revived by such appointments; and already in our own State we hear these rebels exulting in the prospect of a Southern party, and consequently the restoration of slavery.

'Such a party as would result from the appointment of such men can only revive sectional questions which will again end in our defeat by keeping allive [*sic*] the Abolition party.

'Our only hope it seems to me is, in dividing the North which may be done by reorganizing the Whig party upon the following basis:—
    (i) Acceptance of National Sovereignty
    (ii) Cooperation with the government "in making the new labor system efficient to the State and useful to the freedmen."
    (iii) "Opposition to free negro suffrage."'
Conciliatory and national though these sentiments appeared to be, they were nonetheless premised on Southern unity and preservation of the South's internal status quo and on bringing about division and conflict among the Northern Republicans. Tactics rather than goals as well as partisan competition for patronage were the main questions which divided anti-secessionists and Whigs from secessionists and Democrats. C. B. Nero to Sharkey, Buena Vista, Miss., 1 July 1865, Sharkey MSS.

conciliate the radicals or the conservatives? If I am elected, I shall co-operate with the conservatives. The radicals have taken open ground against the policy of President Johnson; I will seek to strengthen his hands, and support him against his enemies. Common prudence, as well as common gratitude, dictates this course.'[41]

Although somewhat similar to Pickens' reasoning, the choice offered by Stuart — help to one's friends or to one's enemies — provided little incentive to discuss which alternative to choose. It was inconceivable that Southern representatives should be chosen at the behest of Thaddeus Stevens when the alternative of aiding the President and his supporters was available. Phrased this way, Southerners would be unlikely to prefer conciliating the radicals. And besides, there was, as Stuart went on to explain, a further incentive to shun concessions to the radicals. 'Each concession,' he said, 'will furnish the groundwork for further demands and we may find in the end that we have conceded until we have forfeited our self-respect and the respect of our adversaries.'[42] In the long run, so it was argued, strength and respect would accrue from a determination to stand firm and refuse to be browbeaten.

Men who had been prominent and were well-known should be sent to Congress, first because lesser men could not be risked at this perilous period in the South's history and, second, because the sending of the former would serve notice to the opposition of Southern refusal to concede as well as constitute an offer of aid to the South's defenders. Besides these arguments, there were also constitutional grounds on which observance of the ironclad was refused. This oath was frequently construed as an ex post facto law and, by Bartholomew F. Moore, in particular, as a bill of attainder, both of which were unconstitutional. Moore also added, on one occasion, the assertion that all bills of pains and penalties, including confiscation, were prohibited by the Constitution; and he cited Marshall and Storey as authorities.[43] On another occasion, he switched from theory to practice as he explained how dysfunctional the oath was:

There is no difference, to the men of common sense, between an enactment by congress, that no man pardoned of an offense shall hold office, because he has committed it, and an enactment that every such man shall swear that

---

[41] Alexander H.H. Stuart, Campaign circular to the electors of the 6th Congressional District, 19 September 1865, Stuart MSS.

[42] *Ibid.*

[43] Moore to Graham, Raleigh, 9 July 1865, W. A. Graham Collection.

he has not been guilty of an offense, and if he swear falsely he shall be guilty of perjury — In both cases the design is punishment; and the operation is to keep alive the pardoned guilt forever to haunt and torture the pardoned man — From such pardons, Good Lord deliver us.[44]

The ironclad oath was one which offered no chance for future deliverance after one of the acts enumerated in it had been committed. It was a test not of present or future loyalty but of past conduct, and therefore was merely a ban rather than a loyalty oath. Such a law could not be conceded legitimacy and, to the many lawyers among those affected by the oath, it was an unconstitutional law and therefore 'no law, and affords justification for nothing.'[45] It should, therefore, not even be obeyed temporarily pending a decision by the Supreme Court. And there were, at that time, a couple of cases before it, most notably the petition of Augustus H. Garland of Arkansas. Stuart had a further objection to the ironclad believing that 'even if it were Constitutional, I have been absolved from its penalties by the pardon of the President.'[46]

To require pardon twice for the same offense was akin to double jeopardy but there was, in any case, no constitutional justification for the ironclad oath, and therefore it should be refused. With a keen realization that it was very likely that the Constitution would be of little benefit to the defeated South and, as far as Southerners could see, of little concern to the radicals, leaders in the South, nonetheless, considered that a relentless insistence on constitutionality might not be in vain if only because it would prevent total neglect and forgetfulness of that sacred document. As William A. Graham argued, a continuous demonstration of the oath's superfluity in times of peace, of its injustice and of its unconstitutionality, might finally force Congress to repeal the two-year-old monstrosity.[47]

These were the cogent objections, adduced by Southern politicians, to selecting men who could take the oath and to even bothering to observe it. A further necessary consideration was the purely practical matter of whether there were men available who could swear the oath, and who were also suitable to become U.S. Senators. Robert

---

[44]Moore to Benjamin S. Hedrick, Raleigh, July 1865, Hedrick MSS.
[45]Graham to William Pell, Hillsboro, N. C., 16 October 1865, W. A. Graham Collection.
[46]Stuart to Henry J. Raymond, Staunton, Va., 19 October 1865, Stuart MSS.
[47]Graham to Pell, Hillsboro, 19 October 1865, W. A. Graham Collection.

M. T. Hunter was asked by Ed. C. Anderson, the mayor of Savannah: 'Can you find any such in Virginia, that are qualified for the struggle that awaits our members in Congress?'[48] Indeed, it was the common lament that there were not men both capable and qualified. This had been argued continually, and sometimes successfully, as a device to have the ironclad qualification for Federal functionaries waived in the South. There were, so the argument ran, few in the South who did not participate in the Confederacy and, were there any who did not, they could not have been significant enough to have held office. Therefore, they would not be capable now of holding a high post such as U.S. Congressman.

Nevertheless, there were capable men who could swear the ironclad in good conscience, but they were rejected by leading politicians because it was dangerous to encourage elements opposed to the Confederacy and to the traditional leadership. A letter to Alexander Stephens from Martin J. Crawford, a Georgia Congressman during the Buchanan Administration and peace commissioner in 1861, explains the way in which such capable and eligible politicians as Joshua Hill and Provisional Governor James Johnson were excluded from consideration. Said Crawford:

I have insurmountable objections to Jim Johnson for he is so thoroughly radical that he would join Sumner and Wilson and go against the President. He can never affiliate with us in any way whatever, it will never do to elect him. Nor will Josh Hill do, although not so radical yet he is heart and soul against the friends of the South and would do all in his power to bring odium upon those who have earnestly desired our separate nationality – it won't do at all, at all – he hates the Democratic party with such intensity that he wouldn't give a cordial support to the President because he is a Democrat. We should have men who would support Johnson earnestly and heartily and yet not hostile to us. My firm conviction is that it is far better not to have Senators at all, than to have such as I have described – Let the election be delayed until we can get such men as are suited to the work. . . .[49]

All means possible were used to encompass the disparagement of such challengers. During the contest for the long-term Senate seat in Georgia some supporters of Stephens, Hill's opponent, published in

---

[48] Ed. C. Anderson to Hunter, Savannah, 11 October 1865, Hunter – Garnett MSS.
[49] Crawford to Stephens, Columbus, Ga., 10 January 1866, A. H. Stephens MSS.

the *Macon Telegraph*, a refutation of Hill's claim to loyalty. They asserted that ability to take the ironclad need not be equated with loyalty. Furthermore, Hill's refusal to aid the Confederacy could be explained, not on grounds of principle, but by his peevish sullenness at failing to win the Governorship in 1861; moreover, this refusal was characterized by silence and inertia rather than active opposition. When Joshua Hill did finally participate in 1863, he aimed at the highest post in Georgia under the Confederacy, so he failed to hold office during the war, but not for want of trying. Stephens' friends asked readers to compare this record with that of the Confederate Vice-President's relentless struggle with Toombs and other secessionists during 1860 and 1861.[50]

This was an unfair characterization of Joshua Hill's intentions during the war, but it provided sufficient fuel to contribute to the Vice-President's overwhelming endoresement as Senator. So too, no doubt, did an anonymous letter, from 'Georgian' which appeared a few days later in the *Atlanta Intelligencer*. 'Georgian' pointed out the danger of even the candidacy of Hill since it would give to the radicals evidence that men like Joshua Hill had support and were numerous when, in fact, he added, and hardly with assurance, 'there is not a corporal's guard' of them.[51]

If men like Joshua Hill were discredited and discouraged, what sort of politicians did run, and successfully, for Congress in 1865? They were certainly men who had featured prominently in the Confederacy – the Vice-President, four generals, five colonels, six cabinet officials, and fifty-eight State and Confederate representatives were dispatched to Washington during the winter of 1865.[52] Yet this defiance was, it seemed, tempered with concession and an awareness of the need for moderation. Most of these representatives, and also their defeated opponents, were neither secessionists nor ironclad oath-takers. Instead, they occupied the middle ground between these two extremes; they were generally Whigs and had been opponents of secession or cooperationists until the break was made. Leading men in their States indeed, but, it was argued, they had been faced with a cruel choice which they had settled in the only realistic fashion; they

[50]*Macon* [Georgia] *Telegraph*, 2 February 1866, reprinted in *Atlanta Intelligencer*, 10 February 1866.

[51]*Atlanta Intelligencer*, 10 February 1866.

[52]John Hope Franklin, *Reconstruction: After the Civil War* (Chicago: University of Chicago Press, 1961), p. 43.

had gone with their State and, being talented and influential, they had achieved high positions in government and the army during the the war.

A sampling of delegations will demonstrate the truth of this. The Alabama Congressional delegation consisted of Bell—Everett Whigs who had opposed secession, Major-General Cullen Battle alone being a Democrat, though not a secessionist.[53] In Mississippi, Sharkey and Alcorn, both Whigs, were the Senators while all the Congressional candidates except the defeated John C. Freeman had been anti-secessionist Whigs, three of the victors having served in the army with notable success.[54] Georgia's Congressmen were Whigs with the exception of Solomon Cohen of Savannah and possibly Hugh Buchanan. Five out of the seven Congressmen had served in the 1865 convention though, of them, Cohen and James D. Mathews, an anti-secessionist Whig, had been noticeable recalcitrants.[55] From North Carolina, along with leading anti-secession Whigs, Bedford Brown, C. C. Clark, and Josiah Turner Jr in particular, there went A. H. Jones who could take the ironclad oath.[56] Virginia sent to Congress four anti-secession Whigs and four who had been inactive previously in politics; and of all these, six were able to swear the ironclad as could the State's Senators, John Underwood and Joseph Segar.[57] And, finally, Arkansas sent anti-secessionists, though surprisingly all three Congressmen and one of its Senators could take the ironclad oath.[58]

In their choice of Congressmen there appeared to be an element of concession and cooperation on the part of the Confederates. This approach synchronized with the intention of the Johnson policy of bringing to the forefront those who had opposed secession, the moderate element in Southern politics, but it was not aimed at meeting the

---

[53] W. L. Fleming, *Civil War and Reconstruction in Alabama* (New York: Peter Smith [1905], 1949), p. 374.

[54] William C. Harris, *Presidential Reconstruction in Mississippi* (Baton Rouge: Louisiana State University Press, 1967), pp. 114–15.

[55] C. Mildred Thompson, 'Reconstruction in Georgia,' *Studies in History, Economics and Law*, LXIV (New York: Columbia University Press, 1915), 155–6.

[56] J. G. de Roulhac Hamilton, 'Reconstruction in North Carolina,' *Studies in History, Economics and Law*, LVIII (New York: Columbia University Press, 1914), 140.

[57] Jack P. Maddex, Jr, *The Virginia Conservatives, 1867–1879: A Study in Reconstruction Politics* (Chapel Hill: University of North Carolina Press, 1970), p. 38.

[58] *Joint Committee on Reconstruction*, Part III, p. 98.

demands of Congress nor did it involve bringing war-time Unionists and loyalists into power. Anti-secessionists and Whigs rather than secessionists were to be at the head of Southern affairs in 1865. The precipitators of the rebellion had to play a subordinate role, not merely because their policies had been found wanting after 1861 but also in the interest of Southern unity and readmission. So, it was the opponents of secession who would be sent to Congress, men such as William A. Graham who was describing himself when he said that

Those deserve confidence most, who reluctantly gave up the Union – for whose preservation their political life had been consecrated – *only* when War was inevitable, and a choice of sides, only, was left – and who during that War, have been uniformly and under all circumstances faithful to the great principles of political and personal liberty [i.e. to the movement for Southern independence].[59]

The *Richmond Times*, in July, explained with more detail why men of these antecedents should represent the Southern States:

We should elect candidates who can cordially and sincerely cooperate with the representatives of the great and constantly increasing Union conservative party at the North. To this result we should look rather than to the possibility of conciliating or disarming the prejudices of the extreme Radical party. *That* would be a most hopeless undertaking, and utterly fruitless of good results. But a delegation of calm, temperate, discreet and true men, who have the entire confidence of our own section, and whose antecedents do not identify them with those of well known and extreme secession proclivities would do much to restore those kindly relations which are now so necessary, are the ones we now need.[60]

In mid-August, most Southern newspapers agreed with this opinion. Moderate Republicans and Democrats would respect the choice of such representatives, regardless of the advice of the Democratic *New York World* that 'The cause of the Constitution does not so much need arguments as votes.'[61] The opinion of the Copperhead *New York News* that the South would be better unrepresented than misrepresented had begun to prevail. Newspapers such as the *Jackson Clarion* and *New Orleans Times*, which in July had stated that the ironclad test

[59] Graham to William N. H. Smith, Murfreesboro, 5 November 1865, W. A. Graham Collection.
[60] Editorial, *Richmond Times*, 11 July 1865.
[61] Quoted in *Augusta Constitutionalist*, 20 August 1865.

could not keep the South out of Congress because there were numerous able men who could qualify to swear the oath, reversed their position after August, claiming that only those who were incapable of holding an office of public trust and who were hostile to the people of the South could meet the requirement.[62] It was preposterous, thought the *Montgomery Advertiser*, 'to suppose the people would elect men to Congress who would swear they did not act, sympathize or feel with [their Southern constituents] ;' and according to William A. Graham, it was equally absurd to assume that 'other motives than reason, justice, and kindness will sway the judgment of the majority in Congress.'[63]

The conviction that moderate and prominent, and therefore representative, men alone should be sent to Congress and would sooner or later be admitted became accepted doctrine in the South in September and thereafter. In spite of the promptings of the President, of Seward, and of the *New York World*, even Southern officials like Benjamin Perry could state in official public gatherings that the test oath was redundant and would not be required. 'I know,' said Perry in a message to the extra session in October of the South Carolina Assembly, 'that this [the ironclad as a prerequisite] is not the policy of the President, and I cannot believe that it will be the avowed policy of the Federal Congress. If the Southern members are present when the role [*sic*] is called by States, they will take a part in the organization of the House, and may vote against the oath being tendered to the members when they are sworn.'[64]

The feeling that misrepresentation was worse than no representation became solidified in the fall, and only one newspaper was prepared, or perhaps able, to recognize the fact that sentiment favoring the ironclad was strong within Congress. The *Richmond Times*, on 21 September, urged that 'it would be better to take a man ignorant of politics, who had been conscripted, against his will, into the Southern army, than the ablest man in the South if he had been prominent in the rebellion.'[65] Not even anti-secessionists should be selected, only

[62] Editorial, *Jackson Clarion*, 30 July 1865.

[63] Editorial, *Montgomery Advertiser*, 17 September 1865 ; Graham to William Pell, editor, *Raleigh Sentinel*, Hillsboro, N.C., 16 October 1865, W. A. Graham Collection.

[64] Benjamin Perry, Message to extra session of the South Carolina Assembly, 24 October 1865, *Charleston Courier*, 28 October 1865.

[65] Editorial, *Richmond Times*, 21 September 1865.

swearers of the oath. Elsewhere in the South, however, the injustice
and unreasonableness of radical demands required rejection of such
terms. But despite these evidences of vituperation, it was felt that the
overall sentiment of Congress and the North was just and reasonable;
so the South should wait unrepresented until this spirit clearly predominated.

There was, beneath Southern suspicion, confidence in the fundamental magnanimity of the North. Therefore, to bide its time was
better policy than to supply eighty Congressmen who would swell the
radical ranks. To the *Raleigh Sentinel*, as for most Southern political
leaders, the alternatives were unmistakable – 'the South would vastly
prefer no voice in Congress in the next five years, rather than submit
to negro suffrage.'[66] If aid could not be given the conservatives in
Congress, it would certainly be denied the radicals. Only able, discreet, representative politicians could be sent to Washington. To
send 'oath-swallowers' was to abandon the issue, not only in Congress
but in the States as well. Indeed, better no representation than misrepresentation. And this was what resulted. Secession was thus a fait
accompli, the Union remained severed, and the traditional politicians
of the South were in power. The ironclad oath had failed to divide the
South.

c: *Misrepresentation by the South*

Although maintenance of their own hegemony and autonomy within
the Southern States was their primary concern after the war, the Confederates were nonetheless fully alert to the possibility that their local
power might be restricted or curtailed at any time until their representatives were readmitted and seated in Congress. Therefore it was
important for them to try to discover what was happening in the North
and how they could most benefit from it so as to facilitate readmission.

As far as they could discern, public figures divided into two categories on the Southern question. First of all, there was the vast majority
which wanted reunion to be speedily accomplished with few restrictions on Southern autonomy and with confidence placed in the
Confederates' ability to act wisely and conciliatorily. Consisting of
the Democrats and the majority of Republicans, proponents of this
approach endorsed a program of the kind introduced by President

[66]Editorial, *Raleigh Sentinel*, 5 September 1865.

Johnson. Offsetting these, however, was a small but influential and vocal group in the Republican Party which was adamant that major changes be made within the South before that section could be considered sufficiently reconstructed to reenter Congress with safety. While they all agreed on the need for Negro suffrage, though often not stating this goal in public, this radical group was at variance over other measures that might accompany this, such as Confederate disfranchisement or disqualification from office, and military rule supplemented by prolonged Southern exclusion from Congress.

Perceiving these divisions in approach to the South and the relative strength and support which each had, the South's political leaders reasoned that readmission on terms and under conditions satisfactory to themselves would be impossible if the second group, the radical Republicans, were in the ascendancy. They were disunionist, hostile, and extreme in their policies, and a reunion between the sections would be possible only if they remained an ineffective minority without control over Republican policy or if they were defeated and eliminated from influence within that party's councils. And in the meantime, their existence was of little concern to the South. If anything it was advantageous that there was division in the North. Moreover the threat of the radicals and their policies could be used on occasion to keep the South united and cohesive. Thus the existence of the radical Republicans could serve as a conceptual device to aid the Confederates in their attempts to keep control over their section, and regain influence in the nation.

Since the radicals were not viewed as an imminent threat and since their views were so antipathetic to the interests of the South, there was nothing to be gained from attempts to conciliate them. There was no necessity, indeed it would be dangerous and inviting trouble, to attempt appeasement in order to neutralize or satisfy their demands. Consequently, the *Montgomery Advertiser* was voicing a widely held opinion when it warned that 'The class of fanatics who are making war upon [Johnson's] restoration policy, would not be satisfied even with our leveling ourselves with them in a wrangle over impracticable issues and isms, and therefore it is hardly necessary to try to shape action so as to please them.'[67] In fact, far from advising concessions either on the President's part or on the South's, the Confederates were convinced that the situation required firmness and uncompromising

[67]Editorial, *Montgomery Advertiser*, 16 September 1865.

determination, leading most probably to a confrontation, whose favorable outcome, they believed, could not be doubted.

This analysis of Northern politics and its likely future development was widely espoused by the newspapers and politicians of the South. As early as June, the *Richmond Times* had prophesied the trend when it remarked that 'Since the [*sic*] President Johnson threw the influence of the administration against the disfranchisement of the gentlemen of the South and the enfranchisement of the negroes, the Jacobins have opened up their batteries upon him.' To counter this, a great conservative party would arise to defeat the radicals and then 'we shall have a union of hearts and hands worth dying for and worth living for.'[68] By October 1865, this party seemed to 'Sumter,' the *Charles Courier*'s New York correspondent, to be a reality. 'Our people,' he said, 'can afford to laugh at the Radicals, however, as long as we have the support of President Johnson and the Democrats and the Conservative Republicans.'[69] And just before this, the *Raleigh Sentinel* had announced: 'We predict that [the President] will either force [the radicals] to be silent or he will drive them to the wall,' and the editorial continued, 'they are evidently becoming alarmed at the growing strength of the President, and hence their unwillingness to break with him.'[70]

Moreover, the South was confident that the President would stand firm, for what doubts may have existed had been dispelled by Johnson's course in the Sharkey – Slocum affair. The Rubicon had been crossed and a courageous, resolute Julius Caesar was imagined to be in the White House. On 11 September the *Jackson News* proclaimed: 'He possesses one decided characteristic of greatness – power of will, and with it, he will crush down all opposition to his policy. With all the lights before us, we do not hesitate to say, as we have said before, that he is our choice for our next President.'[71] Paeans like these were broadcast throughout the South in the fall of 1865. Throughout October, the *Richmond Times* lauded Andrew Johnson, on one occasion describing him as the man 'who had the courage and the manhood to place himself as a breakwater between the Radicals of the

[68] Editorial, *Richmond Times*, 16 June 1865.
[69] 'Sumter,' New York correspondent, *Charleston Courier*, 5 October 1865.
[70] Editorial, *Raleigh Sentinel*, 27 September 1865.
[71] Editorial, *Jackson News*, 11 September 1865, quoted in *Jackson Clarion*, 3 October 1865.

North and the prostrate people of the bleeding South.' So, continued the *Times*, 'The Union of our fathers was not restored by the sword, but by Andrew Johnson.'[72] Five days later, Johnson was 'a statesman of God's creation,' and the *Times* concluded that 'the mad career of this party [the radicals] has been arrested by the strong arm of a patriot President. The signs are unmistakeable that its capacity for mischief is almost at an end.'[73]

In the forthcoming fight against the proponents of disunion and Negro suffrage, the force arrayed with the conservatives seemed to be invincible. In addition, morality, decency, and sound sense were on their side. Describing the radicals with epithets familiar to the South at this time, the *Richmond Times* suggested on 9 September that 'Radicalism, building its platform of fiendish principles upon the vilest passions which disgrace human nature, must strive in vain to perpetuate revenge, intolerance and sectional hate.'[74] Policies which were negative and disruptive, it was assumed, could never become permanent. Their unnaturalness and unwisdom was another argument for their likely rejection. Along these lines Robert M. Patton argued while campaigning for Governor of Alabama: 'The absurd project of conferring the right of suffrage upon an ignorant and semibarbarous population of suddenly emancipated slaves we can never consent to, nor do I believe it would be insisted on by the Northern people when they give it a sober second thought.'[75]

Since this showdown was impending and its outcome confidently anticipated, Southern politicians would be working at cross-purposes if they concerned themselves with palliating the radicals. Instead they felt it incumbent upon themselves to guarantee that the posture of their allies was secure. Accordingly Herschel V. Johnson suggested to the President's Southern envoy, Harvey M. Watterson, that the White House strengthen its position by publishing

a Proclamation to the effect that [the Southern States] are entitled to representation in Congress, provided they should elect Senators and Representatives *constitutionally* qualified to hold seats in the two respective branches. . . .

[72] Editorial, *Richmond Times*, 21 October 1865.
[73] *Ibid.*, 26 October 1865.
[74] *Ibid.*, 9 September 1865.
[75] Robert M. Patton, election manifesto, 10 October 1865, in *Montgomery Advertiser*, 15 October 1865.

It would not only delight the Southern States, but, in my judgment, it would be a stroke of mature policy. For being *constitutionally* qualified, no party in the North can be sustained who will advocate their rejection.

By this maneuver, the issue would be presented clearly: the radicals, by insisting on the ironclad oath for Southern Congressmen, would be stigmatized as men disposed to disregard the Constitution and 'in a word, become the disunion party.' If, in addition to this, the President used his patronage to force the Clerk of the House to place the names of the Southern members on the roll, his position as upholder of the Union and as a focus around which the Northern conservatives could rally would be immensely strengthened.[76]

Among the conservatives who were to rally to the President were, of course, the Confederate politicians. And in order to solidify the support of the South for the head of the Federal government and his policy, many Southerners urged him to extend amnesty to the waverers in their section. There were actually very few of these but the *Houston Telegraph* still insisted that an amnesty proclamation 'would complete the conquest which this strange man has already partially made of the hearts of the Southern people.'[77] And R. M. Brown, a Tennessee friend of the President, advised that 'a General Amnesty would now rally the whole south to your support.'[78] More specific and more enthusiastic was a proposal from Robert M. T. Hunter. As part of a scheme for consolidating a conservative coalition consisting of Democrats, conservative Republicans and Southerners, Hunter urged on Seward the advisability of 'a liberal course to the South,' and proceeded to suggest:

Let [Johnson] declare a general amnesty or if there must be exceptions let them be as few as possible. I think there ought to be none. The more liberal he is the stronger he will be with the South and the Democratic party. The South would then come to him enthusiastically, they will rely on him as a friend and if he should find it necessary to ask of them sacrifices of interest and opinion which did not interfere with their honor they would make them from attachment to him.[79]

During the fall, while advice flowed from the South to the White

---

[76] Johnson to Harvey M. Watterson, 28 October 1865, Johnson MSS, Series I.
[77] Editorial, *Houston Telegraph*, 4 October 1865.
[78] R. M. Brown to Johnson, Nashville, 30 September 1865, Johnson MSS, Series I.
[79] Hunter to Seward, 27 September 1865, W. H. Seward MSS.

House, elections were taking place in some of the Northern States. These, it can be argued, should have indicated to the South that the President's position was less secure and the radicals' stronger than had been assumed. For what appeared to be a widespread endorsement of the President's policy was in fact based very much on temporary political expediency and on caution against prejudging the outcome of the Presidential program before it was completed. Moreover, there was evidence in the Midwest and New England that in instances where Republican Party platforms which opposed the President were introduced, majorities could be obtained for them. These qualifications and provisos notwithstanding, the elections were adjudged in the South as portending no difficulties; but indeed they were greeted with equanimity, even confidence.

To each of the objections to the view that the elections indicated widespread endorsement of the conciliatory policy of the executive, the South had a ready explanation and rebuttal. The first consideration which the South had to bear in mind was that both the Democratic and Republican Party organizations had an interest in demonstrating their adherence to the President's course. The Republicans could not at this early stage before the policy had reached completion judge it a failure and then proceed to cut themselves off from the head of their party and the source of its Federal patronage. To do so would be unwise as well as inexpedient. The Democrats also could derive benefit from supporting the President because thereby they might reenter the political mainstream and begin to expunge the stigma of Copperheadism and war-time recalcitrance.[80] For some in the South, like James L. Orr, who was later to be elected Governor of South Carolina, these organizational imperatives did not, as he told the President, vitiate the fact that the Republican Party conventions 'at the North have endorsed you and your reconstruction policy notwithstanding the radical views of Mr. Thaddeus Stevens.'[81] For others, however, the institutional needs of the party were a guarantee of support for the policy. The *Jackson Clarion* reproduced in its editorial columns a quote from the *New York Herald* which expressed a view it concurred in: 'If either of the political parties desire to obtain the benefit of [the President's] prestige before the people they have

[80]La Wanda and John Cox, *Politics, Principle, and Prejudice, 1865–1866* (Chicago: The Free Press, 1963), chap. iv.

got to rally to his support. Now that both parties stand essentially on the same platform, that party which is the most efficient and shows itself the most earnest in support of his policy will win the race.'[82] So the elections had not been about measures but simply about men, those who were 'in' or those who were 'out.' And patronage would ensure the success of the President's policy.

The second warning against an unqualifiedly enthusiastic reaction to the elections was that, after all, the Democrats had been universally defeated. But once again comfort and evidences of eventual success could be gleaned from what seemed an unfavorable situation. Observing that the Democrats were 'everywhere prostrate,' the *Jackson Clarion* countered with the projection that 'We think the future success of the Republicans will depend altogether on the use they make of this victory. If they allow the Radical negro-suffrage element of the party to control, and take issue with the President and his plan of reconstruction, they will rapidly sink into a minority. Their party conventions in all states but Massachusetts and Minesoto [*sic*] indorsed President Johnson.'[83] Other politicians and spokesmen agreed that the aftermath would determine the significance and meaning of the elections; but there was disagreement about what this would most likely be. Obviously the *Jackson Clarion* expected the moderates to retain control, and this was the assumption usually made in the South. From the *New York Herald*, however, came another view which had many Southern advocates; this was that few Republicans endorsed the President's policy and that 'rather than seek new associations they would follow on, at the back of radicalism, to their own destruction, and the peril of the republic.'[84] A third angle was that suggested by 'Sumter,' the *Charleston Courier's* New York reporter, who felt sure that whether radicals or moderates finally came to dominate, the anticipated ruinous feud between them both would nevertheless break out now that the party was in the ascendancy and this would allow the Democrats to take hold provided Johnson stood firm and insisted on Southern readmission to Congress.[85] Another view of the compensation to be derived from the Democratic defeat was that of the *Rich-*

[81]Orr to Johnson, Anderson, S.C., 2 October 1865, Johnson MSS, Series I.
[82]From the *New York Herald*, quoted in *Jackson Clarion*, 17 October 1865.
[83]Editorial, *Jackson Clarion*, 21 November 1865.
[84]Editorial, *New York World*, 7 November 1865, found in Edward McPherson MSS.
[85]'Sumter,' New York correspondent, *Charleston Courier*, 17 November 1865.

mond Times which argued that 'they may not have won the trappings
and spoils of office, but they have changed the tone of public sentiment
at the North, and compelled the Republican party to abandon many of
its objectionable and proscriptive measures.'[86]

Whatever might develop in the Republican Party during the coming months, the South was confident. Should the party become radical, it would face rejection at the polls, and undoubtedly, even before
that occurred, there would be a massive and perhaps lethal struggle
among radicals and moderates within the party for control. While if
the party remained moderate in tone, it would prevail, and of course
so would the South.

This was the South's appraisal of the configuration of Northern
politics and policies during the fall of 1865, and it was undeniably
optimistic in tone. On occasion, however, there were indications that
the details of this expected pattern of development were not working
out too well. In late November and in December doubt and concern
arose below the Potomac because of a fear that perhaps the President
was yielding his principled position and was indulging in conciliation
of the radicals. And concession, although not involving defeat, did
imply retreat. When Johnson reinstated the Provisional Governors
after the Southern State elections, and insisted on ratification of the
proposed thirteenth amendment, Francis Pickens, South Carolina's
Confederate Governor, drew broad-ranging conclusions: 'From the
new conditions enacted, I suppose it is the intention to keep the State
from being recd into the Union. . . . The truth is the Northern States
have gone so largely Republican rabid, that the President cannot afford to risk an issue with them, and he intends to cling to the Black
republicans by sacrificing the position assumed for the Southern States.
Things look very gloomy indeed for the State.'[87] Congressman-elect
Samuel MacGowan also confided to Perry his worries about the President. Noting that he had not repudiated the ironclad test oath nor
proclaimed that the war was ended and civil authority restored, Mac-
Gowan bemoaned the President's vacillation and timidity. The Southern Congressmen had been given no instructions, he complained, and
'Unless we know this we can't help him, besides I confess to you,
that his reticence alarms me. The state has passed "the amendment"
and I can not see why he delays now, unless it is to make us *repudiate*.

[86] Editorial, *Richmond Times*, 11 November 1865.
[87] Pickens to Perry, Edgewood, S.C., 23 November 1865. Perry MSS (Ala.).

And if we were to repudiate, he might still exact something more – I have gone just as far as I can go.' The fact that the President had not issued a proclamation authorizing his restoration policy was evidence that he had yielded to the increasingly hostile Northern temper and slipped from his alignment with the South. 'I fear,' MacGowan concluded, 'that the Republicans have driven him from [his intended Southern course], or at least have made him exact so much as to make the scheme impossible.'[88] From Georgia, M.C. Fulton informed Alexander Stephens: 'I have grave fears that the President is changing his reorganization programme to suit the Radicals,' a development which could not 'fail to excite a general feeling of disgust and contempt in the minds of the Southern people.'[89]

Of course, concession did not necessarily mean anything more than a tactical recognition that the opposition's demands be met on a limited scale in order to ensure the intended object which in this case, as the *Augusta Constitutionalist* realized, was 'congressional representation to the south.'[90] All the same though, the need to yield these points was evidence that Northern sentiment since the elections had worsened. So Southern confidence was beginning to be mixed with doubt, and this was epitomized in a *Raleigh Sentinel* editorial of 17 November: 'We are not enthusiastic, nor overly credulous or sanguine but we are hopeful. The press and leading men of the South as well as the tone of some in the North, have led the Southern people to believe that reconstruction was a very easy thing and would be quickly over. We have thought otherwise, yet we have fallen into the current of expectation, to give hope to our people. The whole matter is a new thing. It is an experiment.'[91] Facing rebuff and difficulty, the post-war policy of the Confederate leadership, especially its newspapers, was being called into question.

So too was the course of the President and the praise lavished upon him earlier. The rejection of the Southern Congressmen-elect in early

---

[88] MacGowan to Perry, Abbeville, S.C., 18 November 1865, Perry MSS (Ala.). The South Carolina convention had managed to circumvent the pleas of Johnson and Seward for repudiation of the State's Confederate debt, and it was to the possibility that the President might reiterate his demand that MacGowan referred. Actually South Carolina was the only Confederate State to avoid repudiation.

[89] M.C. Fulton to Stephens, Thomson, Ga., 29 November 1865, A. H. Stephens MSS.

[90] Editorial, *Augusta Constitutionalist*, 28 November 1865.

[91] Editorial, *Raleigh Sentinel*, 17 November 1865.

December, an unequivocal indication that reunion would not be straightforward for the South, evoked denunciations of the President. Johnson had been unclear in his instructions to the South; he had misled and confused. The *Jackson Clarion* complained that 'if President Johnson intended to insist on all these as essential conditions to restoration, he should have so stated in official communications to the Provisional Governers.'[92] These feelings about the President's lack of firmness were echoed by the *Raleigh Sentinel* after reading his Annual Message: 'The inviolability of these terms, it seems to us, ought to have been asserted and maintained by the President in his message as well as his power and right to proclaim the restoration of the States as soon as they comply with the terms.' The question now was whether the President 'designs to yield up the whole matter to the revision and adjustment of [Congress].'[93]

Many felt this was quite possible. Governor-elect Jonathan Worth told the North Carolina legislature in mid-December that Provisional Government might be retained even until after his own official term had expired in two years' time.[94] Meanwhile, George S. Houston, Senator-elect from Alabama, was confiding to his colleague, Lewis Parsons: 'I have not at any time had much hope of getting seats early – I think the radicals intend to pass all obnoxious acts that they want before they let the Southern members have seats so that if need be they can overrule a veto.'[95]

Simultaneous with these gloomy forecasts, there were indications from two Southerners who were actually in the capital that events might transpire rather differently. William A. Graham, who was in Washington seeking his Senate seat, wrote to his wife on 10 December that 'the tone of the papers I have seen represent that Northern sentiment is becoming more liberal, and the prospect of the admission of Southern members more hopeful.'[96] Moreover it was quite possible that pressure from the Democrats and moderate Republicans might

---

[92] Editorial, *Jackson Clarion*, 5 December 1865.
[93] Editorial, *Raleigh Sentinel*, 12 December 1865.
[94] Jonathan Worth, Speech to the North Carolina Assembly, 16 December 1865, in *North Carolina Standard*, 18 December 1865.
[95] George S. Houston to Parsons, Athens, Ga., 25 December 1865, Parsons Official Correspondence.
[96] Graham to his wife, Susan, Washington, D.C., 10 December 1865, W. A. Graham Collection.

result in the readmission of some of the delegates from Tennessee, Louisiana, and Arkansas, thus undermining the policy of blanket exclusion of the Southern applicants. Being aware of this, William Yerger was convinced that sentiment was moving favorably after the initial check which had been registered in the rejection of the Southern representatives. And he cabled Governor Humphreys, in a telegram widely publicized over Christmas and the New Year, 'I am satisfied the Southern members will be admitted soon as Congress meets in January.'[97]

Although these weeks were full of uncertainty and worry, Southern confidence never evaporated; the general assumptions about Northern politics were always present. Consequently the *Arkansas Gazette* could argue that 'on the "sober second thought" and after a time, the influences which will be brought to bear, and which, if properly wielded, can do much, will obtain for the South her entire rights under the Constitution.'[98] Equally it was considered absurd to assume that the radicals could prevail. Frank C. Dunnington, a friend of the Johnson family, wrote that 'The Radical column is very solid. They seem to be bent on general ruin. There seems to be no such thing as cooling time with them. . . . I believe that when the President finds it practicable to make a *sharp issue* the majority of the people, North and South, will rally to his support.'[99] And of course there were frequent expressions of confidence in the President, the *Augusta Chronicle*, for instance, asserting on 12 December that 'There is a man in the Presidential chair, Andrew Johnson, who knows how to be magnanimous, and who, determined to be President of the whole country, will order into silence these rampant radicals.'[100]

Optimism about the future was not necessarily premised upon speedy readmission; for many in the South, a more complete salvation could be anticipated after the radicals and disunionists had been driven off. Until this were accomplished, the radicals would be merely outmaneuvered, but never exposed, and never defeated and eliminated. Welcoming a showdown, James B. Campbell forecast that 'It is to be

[97] William Yerger to Humphreys, Washington, D.C., 22 December 1865, Benjamin. G. Humphreys MSS.
[98] Editorial, *Arkansas Gazette*, 16 December 1865.
[99] Frank C. Dunnington to Robert Johnson, the President's son, Nashville, 11 December 1865, Johnson MSS, Series I.
[100] Editorial, *Augusta Chronicle*, 12 December 1865.

the old fight of Gen. Jackson and the People on one side. Bloated, Arrogant politicians on the other — No fear of the result.'[101] And by late December the *Jackson Clarion* was recovering from its earlier un-happiness and beginning to perceive hope in a long-range view of af-fairs. On 23 December it offered its readers some Christmas good cheer:

The fierce and malignant spirit which is daily shown by Wilson, by Sumner and Stevens and echoed by the radical press with tenfold force will recoil upon themselves, slowly, perhaps, but nevertheless certain to destroy those whose aim now appears to be to crush the South, crush the high spirit of her people and bring them on their knees before New England power and fana-ticism. They will fail, but while we believe this we would urge our people to patience. . . . The rise of conservatism to power will be the death blow to Radicalism, for at least a generation, if not forever, and the struggle will be long, but we are assured not doubtful and it is necessary that we bide our time. . . .[102]

In this long-term view of the situation, failure to gain readmission into Congress could be converted from setback into opportunity. Readmission, unless accompanied by the capitulation of the radicals, was merely an episode in an extended struggle. Therefore confidence and hope for the future could be derived from what was merely a tem-porary obstacle. By late December, the South was regaining its as-surance. On 28 December, Samuel Phillips, the North Carolina Whig and associate of Graham and Swain, felt able to suggest: 'I do not pre-tend to know, but it seems very certain to me that all Radicals who do not wish to be "taken" or "killed" will have to evacuate the position taken by Messrs. Sumner, Stevens, etc.' And elaborating further on the forthcoming struggle with extremism, he continued:

As it is, they have seemed to triumph with present results, but it is quite con-ceivable, perhaps not impossible, that they shall bring their *political* fortunes, at least, in collision with the nation before things have become quiet again. . . . I believe, Sir, that I prefer that those gentlemen shall be *encouraged* to raise their banners and display their ranks. Let us have a settlement of those issues with the nation, as well as those of Mr. Rhett. . . . I do not doubt that it will

---

[101]Campbell to Johnson, Columbia, S.C., 31 December 1865, Johnson MSS, Series I.
[102]Editorial, *Jackson Clarion*, 23 December 1865.

come sooner or later, if the issue be only made and the longer it takes to *come*, the more complete and satisfactory its coming will be.

And until the finale arrived, Andrew Johnson, Phillips thought, would have to play the role of skillful angler to the radical fish and 'give it the line, and let it weary itself by its displays of strength and spirit.' Yet it was a dangerous game, and so Phillips, aware of this, concluded: 'Whether the play be worth the candle, is a question of some moment, and I am not so sure of it as to say that I would choose that the Southern delegates should be rejected.'[103] But if the South were still kept out when Congress reassembled in the New Year, then at least there was still a good chance for success and no need for despair.

It was a desperate gamble. Excluded from Congress with the consent of a majority of that body, the South's leaders nevertheless sought vindication and salvation in a showdown with the radicals. The conservative majority in the nation, it was felt, would reject the extremism of the radical Republicans. Although this was a logical assessment of the state of affairs in the North, the likelihood of its occurring in the very near future was not great. In this respect the South misrepresented Northern opinion. Senator John Sherman described the situation in Congress far more accurately than the South ever did during 1865 and 1866 when he told his brother:

The Union party is moderate and reasonable. Johnson cannot do without it unless he is prepared to restore the old domineering and churlish coalition between the aristocracy of the South and the more ignorant elements of the North. Against such a coalition new ideas and education are at war. I believe our people are prepared for conciliation and universal amnesty to the South but they are not prepared to have this administered by the Copperheads of the North. . . . It is better for the South that reconstruction should be dictated by those they have considered their foe for then it is permanent. . . . But I really believe that a coalition between the South and the Copperheads North would preserve the Republican party in all its old sectional bitterness as the only effectual means to war with the sectionalism South.[104]

What this meant was that moderate Republicans placed the survival of their party and section over and above the differences they had with

---

[103]Phillips to Graham, Chapel Hill, N.C., 28 December 1865, W. A. Graham Collection.
[104]John Sherman to General William Tecumseh Sherman, U.S. Senate, 10 November 1865, W. T. Sherman MSS.

the radicals within their party. It might be a long time, years perhaps, if ever, before the Republicans would split apart. In view of this, the South needed to consider cooperation. But if the price of accommodation were the weakening or division of the Confederates, then in all probability the Southern leadership could wait and was prepared to take the short-term consequences, especially if there were a chance that even these might be avoided or alleviated. At all events, 'no union with radicals' was the South's slogan and strategy.

Part 3
Seeking Southern cooperation, 1866

... We have nothing, to which the ambitious can aspire, but office. I say nothing, because the private walks of life are as Wide open in England as here, and afford, in that Country, as well as in this, occupation for much of the Active talent of the Community. But office here is family, rank, hereditary fortune, in short, Everything, out of the range of private life. This links its possession with innate principles of our Nature; and truly incredible are the efforts Men are Willing to Make, the humiliations they will endure, to get it.

Edward Everett to Justice John McLean,
18 August 1828, McLean MSS.

It ought to irritate no honorable men, it will irritate no reflecting men, that the Southern people decline when a measure is submitted for their sanction, to vote for, as if of choice and conviction, their own injury and their own shame.

Richmond Enquirer, *13 November 1866.*

6

Anticipation

In December 1865 the campaign for the readmission of Southern delegates to Congress suffered a major setback. Congress refused to seat the Congressmen who had been selected under the auspices of the Provisional Governments. For a short while, Southerners were dismayed and disappointed. But very little time elapsed before reports came South which, to a large degree, laid their fears to rest. In the New Year, Washington correspondents from Southern newspapers, sympathetic Northern politicians and official lobbyists from various Southern politicians currently in the Federal capital provided the reassuring news that the President and his supporters had not been overwhelmed or cowed into submission but were simply biding their time until a favorable moment presented itself when a clear break with the Republican radicals could be made.[1]

A typical analysis was offered by John. H. Wheeler, a lobbyist for North Carolina, when he suggested that 'The heavy patronage of the President (and to be yet larger, by the Freedmen's bill) doubtless holds them [the radicals] in restraint, but, like two trains at full speed, in opposite directions on the same railway, the collision is only a question of time.'[2] Even before these informed assessments were received from men close to developments in Washington, the newspapers were stating as a matter of indisputable fact the eventuality of a contest with Congress. The *Raleigh Sentinel* was echoing the views of the *Atlanta Intelligencer*, *Richmond Times* and *Charleston Courier* when its editorial

[1] 'Leo,' Washington, D.C., 6 February 1866, *Charleston Courier*, 12 February 1866; Congressman John L. Dawson of Pennsylvania to R. M. T. Hunter, Washington, D.C., 19 December 1865 and 16 February 1866, Hunter–Garnett MSS; Hedrick to Worth, Washington, D.C., 29 January 1866, Jonathan Worth MSS; L. Q. Washington to Hunter, Washington, D.C., 23 January 1866, Hunter–Garnett MSS; Perry to Armistead Burt, Greenville, S.C., 20 April 1866, Perry MSS-Duke). This last letter included Perry's recollection of the President's intentions as they had been outlined to him at a White House interview in February.

[2] John H. Wheeler to Graham, Washington, D.C., 12 February 1866, W. A. Graham Collection.

of 9 January stated that 'During the recess of Congress, the indications have multiplied in the most undisputable manner, that the President is firmly fixed in his determination to defy, and crush, if need be, the radicals, and to bring about the thorough pacification of the country by the complete restoration of the Union.'[3]

No doubt existed as to whether the President would force the issue. The only question was when and how. After being called to the White House on 4 February to discuss the details of an executive proclamation announcing the end of hostilities in all the Confederates States, William L. Sharkey advised Johnson that 'by taking the initiative you make no issue with any party, but simply discharge a duty required by law. If Congress should not sustain you, it is that body that makes the issue with you, not you with them.'[4] Two weeks later, by vetoing the Freedmen's Bureau bill, Andrew Johnson used a different means but nevertheless acted upon the suggestion offered by Sharkey. The veto was intended to reveal unmistakably what Johnson believed were not only the sectional and disunionist intentions of the Republicans' radical wing but also its scheming, through the provisions of the bill, to extend and enlarge the power of the Federal government.

With their expectations met and their fears appeased, the Confederates greeted the veto with joy and relief. The assemblies of North Carolina, Virginia, Louisiana, Mississippi and Alabama met and passed joint resolutions, all praising the President for his 'statemanship,' his 'true patriotism,' and his 'manliness' in protecting 'constitutional liberty.'[5] 'Andrew Johnson,' intoned a *Jackson Clarion* editorial, the sentiment of which was repeated throughout all the Confederate newspapers, 'has arrested the storm with which a fanatical majority intended to overwhelm us. He has pierced the black cloud that has so long hung over us and shown us the "silver lining."'[6]

Matters did not rest with the veto alone, for the President followed it up with an extemporaneous public speech on the White House lawn. Having checked the radicals in Congress, he proceeded logically with an appeal to the electorate to vindicate his action. The strategy was fully understood in the South, the *Atlanta Intelligencer* concluding

---

[3] Editorial, *Raleigh Sentinel*, 9 January 1866. The other editorials were in the *Atlanta Intelligencer* on 7 January, the *Richmond Times* on 5 January, and the *Charleston Courier* on 6 January.

[4] Sharkey to Johnson, Washington, D.C., 5 February 1866, Johnson MSS, Series I.

[5] Copies of these joint resolutions can be found in the Johnson MSS, Series I.

[6] Editorial, *Jackson Clarion*, 23 February 1866.

that 'An appeal must now be taken to the people of the North to elect men to the next Congress who will aid the President in saving the Union from disruption and anarchy. A crisis is now upon the country more imminent than has ever threatened the stability of our Government, and the patriotic masses must rally round and strengthen the hands of the President, or all is lost.'[7] And indeed there was evidence that Northern support for the President's move was considerable. Noting the many public meetings called to register approval of the veto, Governor Humphreys complimented the President and added that 'It is gratifying to find so many conservative men and statesmen of parties in the North have so nobly sustained your effort to restore the Southern States to their Constitutional rights in the Union.'[8]

But the veto had not accomplished the defeat of the radicals; rather it was simply the opening shot in what might be a protracted siege. In private, among themselves, Southern politicians were fearful. Sharkey told William A. Graham that 'It is now "war to the knife, and the knife to the hilt" between the radicals and the President.' Moreover, although 'The Southern people undoubtedly have the body of the people of the North in sympathy with them, as well as the President, . . . he is powerless, except by the veto power . . .' In the meantime, Sharkey concluded, that 'the radicals having really become spiteful against us, . . . we need not hope for admission sooner than next winter, indeed, I think not during this Congress.'[9] A former secessionist from North Carolina, Walter Gwynn, admitted that the veto 'has utterly failed to break the Northern phalanx' and so there was 'but little hope for the South even when restored to political rights.'[10] And a month later, after Johnson had sent in another veto, this time against the Civil Rights bill which, unlike the last, was overridden, Armistead Burt was convinced that Southern Congressmen would not be seated this session, 'and probably not during the present Congress.'[11]

Delighted though Confederates undoubtedly were that Johnson had moved so decisively to defy the radicals and mobilize electoral opinion against them, the immediate future was full of difficulty and uncertainty. A running battle with the radicals would almost certainly

[7] Editorial, *Atlanta Intelligencer*, 27 February 1866.
[8] Humphreys to Johnson, 6 March 1866, Johnson MSS, Series I.
[9] Sharkey to Graham, Washington, D.C., 22 February 1866, W. A. Graham Collection.
[10] Walter Gwynn to Thomas Ruffin, Raleigh, 12 March 1866, in *The Papers of Thomas Ruffin*, ed. J. G. de R. Hamilton, (4 vols.; Raleigh, N.C.: Edwards and Broughton Co., 1920), IV, 52–3.
[11] Burt to Perry, Abbeville, S.C., 19 April 1866, Perry MSS (Ala.).

provoke them into adopting measures and tactics possibly inimical to the South; it would guarantee political instability for a number of months; and, not the least of considerations, it might not be successful. The current status of the South would therefore be undecided and unclear for quite a while. Furthermore, besides these anxieties, concern was expressed from time to time about the quality of the President's leadership in so massive an undertaking. While most Southern newspapers applauded the whole of the President's handling of the Freedmen's Bureau veto, including his subsequent speech on 22 February, dissent was on occasion evident. William D. Holder, a Mississippi Whig, approved highly Johnson's statesmanlike veto message but added that 'in his speech . . . the landmarks of the partisan politician and demagogue cropped out perceptibly, and unfortunately I fear for the good of the country. To say the least of his speech it was in bad taste for the President.'[12] This fear was shared by William A. Graham who a little later regretted 'the President's fondness for stump speaking.'[13]

After the Civil Rights bill veto, there was even more justification for alarm. First of all, the veto was not sustained, a likelihood in any case since the bill had originally passed with a two-thirds majority. And then, there was the uncertainty articulated by the *Richmond Times* that 'While the "civil rights bill" . . . is a far more dangerous and atrocious measure than that heretofore vetoed, we are by no means as confident as we have been of the power of the President to speedily and utterly demolish the strength of the Radical party.' And the *Times* added with concern that the vetoes seemed to be uniting rather than disrupting and dividing the Republicans.[14]

The reason for this latter development was not lost on C. H. Ray, a radical Chicago journalist, who, before the veto, told Lyman Trumbull, the bill's sponsor, that if the President agreed to the bill 'and if he halts at that, and war is made on him because he will not go to the extent of negro suffrage, he will beat all who assail him.'[15] This should not have passed unobserved by Southerners either. For Parsons had

---

[12]W. D. Holder to Humphreys, Satillo, Miss., 19 March 1866, Humphreys MSS.

[13]Graham to Kemp P. Battle, Hillsboro, N.C., 23 August 1866, W. A. Graham Collection. Graham's remark was occasioned by the President's setting out from Washington, D.C. on his campaign tour called the 'Swing around the Circle.' Graham remembered only too well the harmful effects of the 22 February speech.

[14]Editorial, *Richmond Times*, 29 March 1866.

[15]C. H. Ray to Trumbull, Chicago, 7 February 1866, Trumbull MSS.

concluded during the previous summer that the President might concede on all points short of suffrage for the freedmen; and on two occasions prominent Southerners, John Letcher of Virginia and Herschel
Johnson, had concluded that this would be the President's line of
attack, and a wise and, most likely, a successful one at that.[16] Instead
the President had engaged the radicals on a more moderate issue, civil
rights, which was not an advanced and radical measure but a position
adopted by the Republican Party as a whole. Therefore, he had
broken, not with the radicals alone, but with the entire party. This,
however, appeared to be little noticed in the South, not to mention
President Johnson and his supporters.

Doubts about the details of the policy were overwhelmed by the
general feeling of excitement and expectation at the prospects which
the President's overall strategy portended. Fundamental to the policy
was the assumption that although partisan and sectional antagonisms
characterized national life in 1866, there lay beneath them a more
enduring and permanent sentiment which longed for stability, harmony, and an end to the turmoil of the war years. On this, latent, but
currently silent, majority opinion, reunion between the sections and a
lessening of party tensions could be based and brought to fruition.
And it was towards the mobilization of this majority that the President
and his advisers aimed when they forced the issue with Congress
during early 1866. Out of this maneuver they hoped to raise up an
intersectional, interparty coalition which would eliminate, or reduce
to manageable proportions and influence, the extremists on both left
and right within each section. In this strategy, the South would play
a vital part. The Confederate States naturally were essential to the
creation of a coalition able to span the sections and produce reunion.
As a consequence, leading politicians in the South were less concerned
with the details of the scheme than with the implications of it for the
future of their section.*

[16] Parsons stated this to the President in his letter from Montgomery, 23 September
1865, Johnson MSS, Series I; John Letcher to Johnson, Lexington, Va., 24 July
1865, Johnson MSS, Series I; Johnson to Alexander Stephens, Augusta, Ga.,
8 January 1866, H. V. Johnson MSS.

*This was the first post-war attempt to 'nationalize' the Republican Party and it
preceded Hayes' scheme of 1877 by over a decade. The Northern search for an
intersectional party able to produce reunion and stability without jeopardizing
the gains of the war was a fundamental theme in the Reconstruction period, the
1872 Liberal Republican campaign being a second variation on the theme.
Indeed, this should not even be confined to Reconstruction because the
Republican Party ever since the Civil War has been trying to create a Southern

Three aspects of the strategy immediately impressed themselves on the Confederates' minds. First, the position of the Confederate South within the parameters of a program aiming at national reunion implied that the Southerners were loyal, and when, on 2 April, the President finally issued his Peace Proclamation announcing the insurrection ended, it was clear that war-time assumptions no longer applied. 'In a word,' said the *Raleigh Sentinel*, 'the work of reconstruction is complete, so far as it lies in the power of the States and of the President.'[17] This construction was of course far too optimistic; the Proclamation did not supersede loyalty oaths nor did it end military occupation. But the drift of events was clear.

Second, Southern confidence in the correctness and rectitude of its past and present course was strengthened. Aligned with the forces of moderation and harmony, the salvation of the South seemed to be inevitable and natural. In June, Alexander H. H. Stuart confidently informed the Washington and Jefferson Societies at the University of Virginia that 'reaction is the logical sequence of excess' and therefore

base, the latest attempt being the 'Southern strategy – silent majority' offensive undertaken by Nixon during and after the 1968 election. And the similarity of this initiative with Andrew Johnson's is remarkable.

This general theme has been discussed recently by George Tindall in his *The Disruption of the Solid South* (Athens, Ga.: University of Georgia Press, 1972). Tindall, however, cites the Hayes policy as the first plan for gaining a Republican constituency in the South whereas Reconstruction itself, not merely its ending, was a decade-long attempt to achieve this. Republicans of that era were all agreed on this; their differences, and these were crucial, were over the question of whether their Southern foothold should be created by conciliation of the Southern leaders or alternatively by a radical approach removing them from influence and participation in the proposed Republican Party in the South.

[17] Editorial, *Raleigh Sentinel*, 6 April 1866. Southerners assumed that the Proclamation ended military occupation and was tantamount to an official bill of health. There was considerable anxiety when this appeared not to be so; concern had earlier been expressed within the Army and in Congress because, by contrast, they feared that it might be. Actually, in a little-known interview with General O. O. Howard, Johnson explained his purpose which was that 'the proclamation was a *declaration of intent*, and nothing more; that it did not abolish military courts; did not remove martial law, and was not designed to modify the operations of the Bureau in any respect whatever.' Furthermore, the Proclamation 'would be executively interpreted and administered' and 'as the States, or parts of States, gave unquestionable evidence of their entire readiness to do impartial justice, they would be individually and locally relieved from military government; not otherwise, not sooner.' *Cincinnati Commercial*, 3 April 1866, enclosed in William H. Trescot to Orr, 20 April 1866, Orr Official Correspondence. In this last passage, Johnson was referring to the policy of 'stimulating Southern loyalty' and presumably regarded it as still operative.

after being 'the victim of extreme opinions . . . the Union will be restored, and restored on the basis of the wise policy of the President.'[18] Even the *Jackson Clarion* succumbed to this Whiggish doctrine when it pronounced that 'no government was ever successfully conducted whose measures were radical. . . . Radicalism is faction. Faction destroys. It never perpetuates. It pulls down. It never builds up. Moderation, conservatism is what strengthens a government.'[19]

And finally, Southern politicians began to realize that far from being a pariah, their section was at the core of the movement to redeem the nation from the agitation of the previous forty years. 'The President,' the *Clarion* argued, 'is for all – for no particular section. It is true that our condition was the immediate cause that led to his action [but] . . . It was begun and will be continued for *all* the people of the nation.'[20] The case for Southern readmission began to assume a national, even disinterested, dimension. The irony was, however, that the South came into the coalition as a self-conscious unit; indeed, the Confederates argued continually that its security depended upon its sectional identity and cohesiveness.

The attempt to mobilize moderate and conservative sentiment in the North and at the same time to create a coalition which would give this form redounded emphatically to the Confederate South's benefit. The interests of many Northern politicians and the attitudes of a large segment of the Northern population were obviating the need for the Confederates to confront their conquerors. The South, however, could do little to influence events; it was excluded from Congress and its politicians were not affiliated with any Northern political party. All the same, even though the drift of events was favorable and seemed not to require their help, there was extensive discussion among the Confederates as to how the South should present itself, what posture it should adopt. The *Richmond Enquirer* wondered 'what course on our part would best please those who are demanding justice for us at the North. It would not do for us to seem *indifferent* to the struggle, and yet to declare our interest in it may give capital to the enemy.'[21]

For Lewis Parsons, the dilemma was easily resolved. Summoning metaphors and alliterations to his aid, he urged Governor Patton to

---

[18] Alexander H. H. Stuart, *Address to the Washington and Jefferson Societies of the University of Virginia*, 29 June 1866 (Richmond: Richmond Examiner, 1866), p. 24.
[19] Editorial, *Jackson Clarion*, 12 April 1866.
[20] Editorial, *Jackson Clarion*, 7 March 1866.
[21] Editorial, *Richmond Enquirer*, 14 May 1866.

tell the people of Alabama that 'We must *bear* and *forbear*, as best we may, no matter what the provocation may be. . . . If our people are wise they will not toast Jeff Davis unless they wish to aid our enemies to roast him and us.'[22] Parallel with this, Jenkins of Georgia and Worth of North Carolina issued proclamations enjoining the citizens of their States to observe the Federal and State laws, and the governments of both Alabama and North Carolina issued public statements for Northern consumption, the former after a joint select committee of the legislature had investigated charges of lawlessness and ill-treatment of the freedmen which it reported were unfounded.

By contrast, there was the approach advocated by the *Jackson Clarion*, now rather less conciliatory than earlier: 'What is important is that the precise sentiments of our people should be understood – nothing is to be gained by hypocrisy. In the first place, it will not deceive the ruling majority in the national councils, in the next place, if it did, nothing would be gained by the simulated accord of the sections which would thus be effected.'[23] And actions which were unmistakable in their meaning issued from this kind of thinking. Feeling secure and oblivious to Congressional opinion, North Carolina's electorate rejected the 1865 constitution when it was submitted for ratification in the spring of 1866. The Texas constitutional convention, assembling a number of months after the rest of the Southern States, refused to ratify the Thirteenth amendment. And most telling of all, there occurred in Memphis during May a rampage perpetrated by the police against the blacks of that city and in the last days of July a bloody massacre carried out again by police, this time in New Orleans against the black and white members of the reconvened constitutional convention of 1864. These events, far more than injunctions to be law-abiding and conciliatory, stole the headlines in Northern newspapers and left their imprint on the attitudes of Congressmen and others who would decide the South's future.

Regardless of the favorable way political developments were transpiring in the North, actions like these did not help the Confederate cause in any way. Indeed they must have been greeted with horror by

[22] Parsons to Patton, Washington, D.C., 13 April 1866, Patton Official Correspondence.
[23] Editorial, *Jackson Clarion*, 20 April 1866. The *Augusta Constitutionalist* on May 1866 argued similarly that 'Nothing is to be gained now by speaking with bated breath and in oily phrases. The people of the South must assert their rights. . . .'

many of the South's leading politicians who, despite their relief at the news concerning the efforts being made to rouse the 'silent majority,' were revealing privately that they were fearful of the outcome. Throughout the springtime months, the confidence manifested on the surface was balanced by a contrapuntal disquiet.

There were numerous indications of frustration and anxiety. Kemp Battle, North Carolina's Treasurer, wondered 'What course will Johnson take? Will he be soreheaded and lose his self possession, or will he be more cautious? Is there real danger of a collision or attempt at removing him?'[24] General Joseph Johnston reported in June that his own uncertainties had been corroborated after talking in Washington with Boyce, Clemson, and Trescot, three South Carolina secessionists. 'They seemed to have no decided opinions as to the probability of Mr. Johnson's success,' Johnston told Louis Wigfall, and added that all three 'agreed, however, that the Southern people are more discontented now than they were a year ago.'[25] A final observation was provided by the thoughtful but invariably pessimistic Herschel Johnson who noticed that 'The dominant majority in Congress are more compact every day and more fiercely bent on overwhelming the President and destroying the South.' The indications were, he considered, that they would win the fall elections and thus keep the South out of Congress till after the 1868 Presidential contest. Meanwhile, he believed, 'our only hope' was that the Northern Democrats 'will cordially coalesce with the Conservative republicans and sustain [President] Johnson.' This would be hindered, however, unless first, 'Johnson should stop insulting [the Democrats] by characterizing them as Copperheads and traitors and they should forbear and forget the past for the sake of the country.' And second, 'a heavy responsibility rests on the Southern people! How discreet and cautious we should be, to do nothing to weaken Johnson or subject the Northern democrats to the apparently just imputation of too much sympathy with the South.'[26]

Hopeful about the emerging political possibilities yet skeptical about their successful outcome, and then further discouraged by the recent undisguisable demonstrations of racial and political unreliability, the South's politicians addressed themselves to the long-awaited call for a convention at Philadelphia, with ambivalence and anxiety.

[24]Kemp P. Battle to Hedrick, Raleigh, 13 April 1866, B. S. Hedrick MSS.
[25]General Joseph E. Johnston to Louis Wigfall, Baltimore, 1 June 1866, Wigfall MSS.
[26]Johnson to Stephens, Augusta, Ga., 31 May 1866, H. V. Johnson MSS.

7

The South courted

a: *The project*

As the spring of 1866 merged into summer, intersectional politics drifted into stalemate. Fearing opposition within their section and reacting to, as well as taking advantage of, opposition from outside it, the Confederate leaders had succeeded in welding together a united South. In the North, the Republican party had also managed to consolidate itself. This had resulted from a two-pronged strategy, to prevent the possibility of readmitted Southern Congressmen allying with Northern Democrats and to shield the Republican Party from the President's vetoes which were aimed, it was feared, at its destruction. That the South or the Republicans might divide or be divisible was now highly unlikely. Therefore, the possibility of Southern readmission was more frightening to the Republicans and more remote for the South. Fears of what might result unless each of the protagonists, that is, the leaders of the South and their Republican counterparts, prepared to prevent such an outcome in fact helped to consolidate their opponents as well as themselves. Thus it was inconceivable, on the one hand, that the South would want to join any party but the Democratic and, on the other, that their opponents would let them join any but the Republican.

The irony of this situation was noticed by Jonathan Worth in a letter to Benjamin S. Hedrick:

[The Republicans] fear the South will coalesce with the Copperheads and get control of the government – but surely none of them can be so blind as not to see that their course tends to produce alienation and a coalition with any party North offering less rigorous terms. The real Union men of the South [those who like himself and Hedrick had opposed secession, though had gone with their States] generally regard the democracy with bringing on the war and hence they had no affection for that party. If the Republicans really have no intention of restoring the South to the

Union, their course is intelligible . . . and I fear that Congress reflects the will of the Northern people. . . .[1]

Of course it was easy to imagine what the Republicans would have said in reply; even though Worth could accurately assert that Whigs and anti-secessionists were suspicious of the Northern Democrats, there was no question that they hated the Republicans and in the immediate future could not unite with them. So the impasse was effectively complete. Politicians in both sections realized this but, for the restored rulers of the South and for the Northern supporters of Johnson's and Seward's policy, it had to be broken. How else national reconciliation and a restored Union?

When political opposition is perceived to exist, it can be treated in one of two ways. Either cooperation or outright antagonism can be employed as methods of moderating it, the latter alternative also offering the possibility of eliminating that opposition. When presented with the likelihood of disagreement with the radicals, Andrew Johnson chose to disengage himself and counter-attack. He argued along the lines suggested by Robert M. T. Hunter in his letter of 27 September 1865. There Hunter had told Seward:

I suppose there is no doubt but that the radical republicans will oppose the President and yourself particularly most violently. . . . But the President and yourself can throw them into a minority and raise up a national party strong enough to support and sustain a conservative administration. This party may be composed of the moderate Republicans led by yourself, of the Northern democrats and of the whole south if the true policy is pursued. The President may then rally a large party which will be so strongly attached to him that he may rely upon them in all straits and difficulties.[2]

If he was to confront the radicals the President would have to raise up a body of support capable of alarming them and withstanding their assaults. Yet the Democratic Party alone would be inadequate since it was widely regarded in the North as the party

[1] Worth to Hedrick, Raleigh, 14 May 1865, in *Correspondence of Jonathan Worth*, I, 584–5.
[2] Hunter to Seward, Fort Pulaski, 27 September 1865, Seward MSS. It is not suggested here that Johnson was necessarily acting upon Hunter's advice, but Hunter so well expressed the strategy adopted by the President that it is worth quoting. It is also illustrative of how closely Johnson's policy meshed with the expectations of leading Southerners, like Hunter.

of Copperheadism and treason. While in the South, Whigs and anti-secessionists like Jonathan Worth made it obvious that to rely on the Democrats was to rest on a broken reed. 'I abhor the *strong* disunion party of the North,' he said in May 1866, 'quite as much as the *weak, annihilated* disunion party of the South.'[3] A broader base of support would have to be formed such as Hunter had envisaged, and this was what the South, the President, the Secretary of State, and some moderate Republicans and War Democrats had concluded by the spring of 1866.

Even before the break with the radicals, there was a widespread realization in the South that the only hope of deliverance lay in the unyielding firmness of the President and the 'sober second thought' of the majority in the North. The Northern conservatives would thus have to rally to the President in defiance of the extremism of the radicals. Typical of the hopes expressed was the *Raleigh Sentinel's* editorial in late March:

. . . we have avowed our preference, that all old party designations and machinery should, for the nonce at least, be laid aside, and that there should be a universal rally among all conservative men, both North and South, beneath a distinct and significant banner: "THE NATIONAL UNION PARTY," under the leadership of President Johnson.[4]

As early as 4 January the *Jackson Clarion* had called for a new party consisting of those who asserted that the Southern States were States in contrast with those who considered them territories. Although aware that the Democrats were 'hopelessly defeated,' the *Clarion* believed the 'Reunion party' should consist of all elements except the radical Republicans. The latter would then constitute a feeble minority, the 'Reconstruction party.'[5] After the Civil Rights bill veto it was abundantly obvious to Southern observers that a new coalition must arise representative of the conservative elements in the North but not under the aegis of the Democratic organization.* From the *Mont-*

[3] Worth to Hedrick, Raleigh, 7 May 1866, B. S. Hedrick MSS.
[4] Editorial, *Raleigh Sentinel*, 23 March 1866.
[5] Editorial, *Jackson Clarion*, 4 January 1866.

*The word 'conservative' was used by Southerners to describe those elements in the North and in the South which would assert themselves and organize an opposition to the extremes, particularly the radical Republicans in the North but also the secessionists in the South. Copperhead Democrats who were extremists at the other end of the Northern political spectrum were in an ambiguous position; many Southerners did not consider them as

gomery Advertiser came the advice: 'To strengthen the President it would be wise policy to entirely abandon old parties and party names, and to rally all the conservative men of the country, irrespective of former affiliations, to the support of the principles of his administration.'[6]

By May such a course was less an option than an imperative. The *Richmond Times* announced that 'the welfare of the South can only be secured by the erection of a new, conservative party, upon the ruins of the old parties which agitated the slavery question for nearly forty years.'[7] About a week later, its neighbor, the *Enquirer*, urgently admonished the politicians of both sections: 'It is as clear as noon that conservative Republicans, Democrats, Copperheads, Southern men, "rebels" – whatever they all are, and whatever they are called – have got to unite in support of Johnson and the Constitution. That is the end of it. That is the terminus!'[8] An anti-radical coalition was presumed indispensable for the achievement of national, and especially Southern, salvation. Below the Mason–Dixon line, they were regarded as synonymous. Yet conservative in doctrine as such a grouping might be, it could hardly be considered conservative rather than extreme in personnel or intention, with Copperheads and rebels as components.

The need for, and the inevitability of, such a conjunction was so widely believed that some Southern journals in May and June talked

extremists and would approve their inclusion in the conservative coalition being formed under the National Union banner whereas most Northerners could not agree in this, believing them unreliable even traitorous during the war.

These 'conservatives' were essentially the forces for stability and reconciliation; for they were national rather than sectional, cooperative Comprising essentially the War Democrats and the conservative and some moderate Republicans as well as the anti-secessionists now dominant in the South, these were the ingredients for the National Union movement. They were really the forces of the center coalescing to resist the extremes, both conservative and radical (i.e., the radical right and radical left in contemporary terminology).

They considered themselves to be the moderates therefore. In the context of the 1860s, however, 'conservative' was most frequently preferred as a descriptive term and, to avoid confusion, 'conservative' will be used in this chapter more frequently than 'moderate' but the group referred to is the same; the terms in fact could be used interchangeably.

[6] Editorial, *Montgomery Advertiser*, 6 April 1866.
[7] Editorial, *Richmond Times*, 3 May 1866.
[8] Editorial, *Richmond Enquirer*, 8 May 1866.

and wrote as if it were a reality. On 6 May, William H. C. King, the editor of the *New Orleans Times*, applauded the President for deciding to hold a national convention to consider the measures necessary to save the Republic.[9] It is possible that Johnson had intimated his intentions during a personal interview when King had recently been in Washington. At any rate eight days later the announcement of the convention was made by the *Charleston Daily News*, and on 5 June it was greeted in the pages of the *Raleigh Sentinel*.[10] On King's part, it may have been a premature press-release. Elsewhere, it may have been an unwarranted assumption stemming from the implications of the formation of a National Union Executive Committee in Washington during April or it may have been a wish fathering the thought. Somehow though, it was assumed that the appeal to the people made by the President in his 22 February speech had to be followed up by the establishment of a new party organization or by some means at least which could mobilize conservative sentiment in his support.[11] Partisan proclivities in the North might prevail to destroy such a harmonious scheme, but it had to be tried. Unless it were, the South could never in the foreseeable future return to the Union except by becoming Republican or acquiescing in Republican policies.

The attempt to mobilize and organize conservative support was a logical outgrowth from President Johnson's restoration policy of 1865. The premise of his and Seward's policy was that reunion could be accomplished only by a reconciliation promulgated by, and effected through, elements that composed the middle of the political spectrum, a condition that had been lacking in 1861 and productive accordingly of disastrous results. The principles on which that reconciliation was to

---

[9] Editorial, *New Orleans Times*, 6 May 1866.

[10] Both papers were unrestrained in their enthusiasm. This meeting '"to settle all the issues now pending" . . . strikes us as a gleam of sunshine — a ray of hope — a splendid idea, in these trying times . . . ,' said the *Daily News* in an editorial on 14 May 1866. A *Raleigh Sentinel* editorial on 5 June hailed 'the organization of the Constitutional Union party.' Yet at this point all that had occurred was that the National Union Executive Committee had been formed in Washington on 9 April.

[11] Numerous citations can be offered to demonstrate that Southern leaders were convinced that the President needed to organize all the conservatives in the North and South. Lewis Hanes to Worth, Salisbury, N.C., 1 April 1866, Worth MSS; J. Barrett Cohen to Alexander Stephens, Charleston, 9 June 1866, A. H. Stephens MSS. This prognosis was widely entertained in the spring of 1866.

be accomplished were those embodied in the Presidential policy. The men to implement them, the anti-secessionists, were in power in the South, but the support needed in the North was merely potential and had yet to rally and organize itself. For until the President had broken with the radicals and presented the issue clearly there could be no movement in favor of the policy. But should this rallying of the politicians and voters fail to occur, then the President would be isolated and utterly helpless.

On 2 5 June the announcement of a convention to be held at Philadelphia in August was the long-awaited signal for the mobilization of the supporters of the President's policy. The convention would provide the conservative alternative, hitherto unavailable, and also the occasion for unleashing the real sentiments of the masses, hitherto unexpressed. After the February veto had come the speech of the 2 2nd, after the Civil Rights bill veto the Peace Proclamation, and now after indicating his opposition to Congress' proposed Constitutional amendment as its terms for the South on 2 2 June, President Johnson's supporters announced the National Union Convention. Signed by four members of the Washington National Union Club, in particular future Cabinet members Alexander W. Randall and Orville H. Browning, by four conservative Republicans and by two Democratic Senators, the call summoned to the convention all, North and South, 'who sustain the Administration in maintaining unbroken the Union of the States under the Constitution.'[12]

An impressive gathering, for the purposes of rallying the conservatives in support of restoration and the Presidential policy, the National Union convention was the natural outcome, if not the climax and culmination, of Johnson's plan for national reconciliation. But how exactly was it to function and to what precise purpose? The immediate goal was obviously, by means of the fall elections, to eliminate from political discussion all plans countenancing continued disharmony and disunion. But was a political party to be formed and, if so, was it to be a third party or a rearrangement of existing groups? Once the party was formed would it continue beyond the elections or was it merely temporary? Or perhaps the formation of a new party was not in contemplation at all, and the convention was to be simply a show of strength aimed to rally Northern conservative opinion and to pressure the radicals into moderation or capitulation.

[12] McPherson, *The Political History of the U.S.*, pp. 1 1 8–19.

As far as Johnson and Seward were concerned, the purpose of the National Union démarche, was, so the President told Henry J. Raymond,

that the Convention should exert a strong moral influence upon the Union party, and induce the nomination and election to Congress of moderate men — who were for restoring the Union on Constitutional principles, and would admit Southern men into Congress, provided they would take the oath required by law [the ironclad]. It was only in cases where Republicans should nominate extreme Radicals, that he should desire the election of Democrats in their stead.[13]

This project envisaged no new party and no political benefits for the Democrats; instead 'the Union Party, purified of the extreme doctrines of its extreme men, and adhering to the conservative constitutional ground it had always held, was the party which ought to rule the country and restore the Union.'[14]

In effect, the Republican Party, or the Union Party as Johnson preferred to call it, was to be pressured into moderating and desectionalizing itself, so that some, or perhaps all, of the South's representatives could be readmitted and siphoned away from the Democrats to whom they would more naturally gravitate. The party of the North was being forced to become national in order that the defeated section could be restored, and this implied that the South was more national, or at least less sectional, than the party which had defeated the South's attempt to destroy the nation. The Republicans were out of step. They were sectional, disunionist and extreme and they had to accommodate. But not the South, since the opponents of secession, its national men, were now presumed to be in positions of power and influence.

On the Southern establishment the meaning of the Philadelphia convention was not lost. The news that the forces of conservatism were being mobilized against the radicals was of course welcomed with relief as an indication that there was still opposition to the foes

---

[13] Henry J. Raymond, Letter to the *Albany Journal*, 12 December 1867, Johnson MSS, Series XI, Vol. VI.

[14] *Ibid*. In 1880, Raymond published an account of his experiences with the National Union movement, see 'Extracts from the Journal of Henry J. Raymond: Part IV,' *Scribner's Monthly*, June 1880. For more insights and interpretations of the whole episode, the reader may consult Thomas Wagstaff, 'Andrew Johnson and the National Union Movement 1865–1866,' Unpublished Ph.D. dissertation, University of Wisconsin, 1967, and Eric L. McKitrick, *Andrew Johnson and Reconstruction* (Chicago: University of Chicago Press, 1960), chap. XII, part III.

of Southern readmission. More than that, however, was involved, for it was as a means for the speedy reunion of the sections with minimum preconditions that the movement was initiated. Therefore the South, still vitally conscious of itself as a section, was aligned with those groups which identified themselves with the nation and Union – after all, was it not the National Union movement? The South was no longer a pariah but was identified with and included among the forces of moderation and national unity.

The culmination came when the South was invited to attend and participate in the convention at Philadelphia. This was tantamount to diplomatic recognition. And of course, since it was optional, there was no need for the South to be present unless the Confederates considered it to be in their own interest either directly, or else indirectly and as an aid to their allies. This was very different from the last time the South had tried to enter a national assembly. Moreover, unlike the attempt to regain admission to Congress in 1865, there were no strings attached. If anything, Southern attendance was more needful to the organizers than it was to the South. Under these circumstances, the South could expect to obtain reassurances and guarantees before consenting to attend, if any were necessary. And, in fact, they were. There were features in the call and platform of the convention which were unacceptable, in particular the assertion that Congress could decide on the qualifications of its members and therefore could legitimately require the ironclad as a test. Concessions could be demanded, and might well be obtained, from the Northern conservatives by the South.

In a year the South's bargaining-position had improved immeasurably, although, in practice, it had been considerable even before. In 1865 the President's Southern policy had involved elements of conciliation as well as of implicit coercion and pressure. In the implementation of that policy the strictures had been neutralized and frequently obviated. A year later, the President and his Northern allies (that is, the War Democrats and, it was hoped, a number of Republican moderates) had divested themselves of all hint of coercion. The South was being wooed at Philadelphia. Conciliation had become appeasement.

b: *Southern reactions*

The invitation to the Philadelphia convention was extended to the South at a time when the Confederates, while welcoming the President's offensive, had assumed a posture of inactivity and apparent non-involvement in national politics. Inertia and apathy characterized their mood and consequently provided a substantial obstacle to mobilizing interest and enthusiasm for the National Union movement. When, in late July, newspaper editors reflected on the reasons for the unenthusiastic response to the convention, they attributed it, therefore, not to foregone conclusions about the inevitable success of the movement, but to pessimism and disengagement. The *Richmond Times* explained that it was because 'for the first time in eighty years our people have determined to let the affairs of the nation severely alone and to attend to their own business much more closely than they have heretofore done.'[15] A more extensive explanation was offered by the *Jackson Clarion* when it observed: 'Perhaps, after all, this apathy is not wonderful, when we come to reflect upon the matter. In the first place, many of our people have no hope that any exertion, on the part of the conservative men of the nation, would enable us to avoid the threatened evils. – Secondly, many others cannot be diverted from their own schemes of individual interest, and induced to calmly observe the aspect of the coming storm; and lastly, the silent, slow and insidious progress of political usurpation, fails to excite men and call forth corresponding action.'[16] Moreover, there was no need to rush to obtain readmission. As 'a very distinguished source' told the *Clarion*, 'we have already done ourselves great injury by manifesting an impatient desire to get back into the Union, and a prurient anxiety to grasp the hands of those who were so lately in arms against us,' and this oscillation was hardly likely to impress Northerners with the South's reliability or frankness.[17]

Nonetheless, there were a few newspapers and politicians that refused to countenance the National Union initiative. One of those which did stated flatly: 'Our answer is soon given. The CONSTITUTIONALIST is utterly, absolutely, and without reserve opposed to this whole convention scheme.'[18] And a little later, rebutting the optimists, it suggested: 'Don't expect anything from this Convention and you'll not be disappointed.'[19] More common were the sentiments of the *Richmond Times*: 'The call for a "National Convention" is a cheering

[15] Editorial, *Richmond Times*, 1 August 1866.
[16] Editorial, *Jackson Clarion*, 31 July 1866.
[17] Open letter from 'a very distinguished source' advising against Southern attendance at the Philadelphia Convention, in *Jackson Clarion*, 24 July 1866.
[18] Editorial, *Augusta Constitutionalist*, 7 July 1866.
[19] *Ibid.*, 22 July 1866.

sign, but it is nothing more.'[20] Less equivocal was the *Montgomery Advertiser* which deemed it 'the most encouraging sign that has appeared above the political horizon since the war.'[21] Yet, with whatever degree of approval it was greeted, the responsibility of the South was, as the *Richmond Times* warned, that 'we should take every step necessary to render the first attempt at a "National Convention" (since the war) successful.'[22] And since the South was presented with a fait accompli in the request of the organizers of the convention that it send delegates, the issue revolved around the wisdom and expediency of attendance. Herschel V. Johnson explained the problem to Alexander Stephens: 'Ought the Southern States to send delegates? All my instincts and sympathies prompt me to *desire* that they should be represented in the proposed Convention. But I confess to grave doubts as to the propriety of such a step.'[23]

Wrestling with their doubts yet aware of their influence as Georgia's leading statesmen, Johnson and Stephens engaged in an extensive private correspondence throughout July, during which they raised and discussed most of the serious objections to Southern attendance in Philadelphia. The most important of these was the damage that might be done to the unity which then prevailed among the Confederates and their supporters. Attempts to organize meetings and impress a reluctant constituency with the need to rouse itself in order to engage again in national affairs might provoke dissension. The *Montgomery Advertiser* pointed out on 6 July that while the Southern press was 'almost unanimously' in favor of the convention, the matter of sending delegates to it raised considerable doubts.[24] Not only that but there were statements in the official call which many would feel unable to endorse. So Johnson concluded his 2 July letter to Stephens with the verdict that 'the main point is for us to deal with the subject, so as not to divide at home, or give our enememies [*sic*] an advantage at the North. This is a delicate and difficult path.'[25] To this Stephens assented and so did General Augustus R. Wright, the editor of the *Augusta Chronicle*, who, when asking Stephens' advice, commented:

[20]Editorial, *Richmond Times*, 28 June 1866.
[21]Editorial, *Montgomery Advertiser*, 28 June 1866.
[22]Editorial, *Richmond Times*, 28 June 1866.
[23]Herschel V. Johnson to Stephens, Augusta, Ga., 27 July 1866, H. V. Johnson MSS.
[24]Editorial, *Mongomery Advertiser*, 10 July 1866.
[25]Johnson to Stephens, Augusta, Ga., 2 July 1866, H. V. Johnson MSS.

'I will not advocate the movement if by so doing it will tend to dissentions [*sic*] amongst us.'[26]

A lesser, although by no means irrelevant, consideration was the effect that a Southern presence would have on the convention, and therefore on its chances of success. The *Richmond Enquirer* regarded Southern attendance as both unnecessary and likely to jeopardize 'a movement which it otherwise highly applauds.'[27] Meanwhile, from the *Lynchburg Daily News* there issued a plethora of objections. The presence of Southern delegates would probably divide the convention and give rise to animated debate; it would provide the radicals with ammunition for the charge that the National Union movement was merely a device for getting prominent rebels back into positions of national power; and finally 'The truth is, that whoever may be sent will be *accused* of disloyalty, and whether correctly or not, the effects on the prospects of the [National Union] party in the elections North will be the same.'[28] Counterposing these arguments for non-attendance was the observation of the *Richmond Times* that no divisiveness could be occasioned by the presence of Southern delegates because there were no issues to discuss which had not already been settled by the war and, furthermore, the convention could produce no new proposals except to urge the President's policy, and that was well-known and understood by all who would be delegates.[29] More important however was the impression that a refusal to attend might create. General Wright suggested that 'If we stand aloof will it not be taken as an indication of our *continued hostility to the Union*?'[30] Regarded as either aggressive and unrepentant or sullen and defiant, the South's reaction to the invitation presented a dilemma. To the *Richmond Enquirer* there was, however, no difficulty to resolve: 'The South will do *best in cooperation* and *support*, rather than in *participation* and *identification* with the Convention.'[31]

A conclusion similar to the *Enquirer*'s was reached by many when

[26]Stephens to Johnson, Crawfordville, Ga., 3 July 1866, H. V. Johnson MSS; Augustus R. Wright to Stephens, Augusta, Ga., 30 June 1866, A. H. Stephens MSS.

[27]Editorial, *Richmond Enquirer*, 29 June 1866.

[28]*Lynchburg Daily News* editorials, reprtined in *Augusta Constitutionalist*, 12 and 15 July 1866.

[29]Editorial, *Richmond Times*, 28 June 1866.

[30]A. R. Wright to Stephens, 30 June 1866, A. H. Stephens MSS.

[31]Editorial, *Richmond Enquirer*, 27 June 1866.

they began to examine the nature and composition of the National Union movement. Alexander Stephens was quite categorical on this score, and he told Herschel Johnson and the readers of the *Chronicle*:

I have one leading idea about that Convention. If the Northern Democracy favor it — If they sustain the movement or cooperate with it great good will come of it or may come of it and the whole south should be fully represented — But if they do not approve it and do not cooperate with it not much need be expected or hoped from it — The truth is we have but few friends at the North[.] Constitutional liberty have [*sic*] but few friends at the North outside the Democratic organization and while they may cooperate for patriotic ends with the Conservative Republicans they are never going to abandon their organization for any other — This may be counted on as a fixed fact.[32]

Johnson agreed that there was little likelihood that the Democrats could forsake their party but added that on no account should they be encouraged to do so. They should be ready, he believed, to cooperate with any section and any party, which

will advocate the harmonizing of the States, on the Constitutional basis . . . [but] to disband their organization, however patriotic the purpose, they will only weaken themselves — first, by scism [*sic*] among themselves (for it is not to be expected or even hoped, that they will unanimously go over to a fraction of unorganized republicans) and secondly by presenting to the centralists the plausible pretext for saying, they have joined the ('so-called') Southern rebels and traitors, thus making them odious to the Northern masses.[33]

Should the convention produce a new party along these lines, then to the South it might well be disastrous.

To some others the successful creation of such a party would also be greeted with hostility, but for different reasons. Because they suspected that the new organization was simply a cloak for the revival of the Democratic Party, many Southern Whigs resisted involvement in the convention. William Sharkey, a Whig himself, admitted that this was a consideration when he told William A. Graham,

[32]Stephens to Johnson, Crawfordville, Ga., 3 July 1866, H. V. Johnson MSS; anonymous letter from a leading Georgia statesman, clearly Stephens, in *Augusta Chronicle*, 3 July 1866.
[33]Johnson to Stephens, Augusta, Ga., 5 July 1866, H. V. Johnson MSS.

I regret that you are disinclined to attend the convention. . . . Like you I thought it had a squinting towards the reorganization of the Democratic party, and I think some of the more radical of that party, for a time, really hoped to use it for that purpose. Of late such an idea is repudiated by the prominent movers in the matter, and I think will receive no countenance.[34]

Besides these partisan considerations, there was one of a different kind; rarely mentioned publicly in the South at this time but discussed privately, it was that the President was politically a spent force. On one occasion, William W. Boyce confided to J. D. B. DeBow, 'Entre Nous, I think the President is obliged to go by the board. Things were managed so infernally stupid [*sic*] at the South, that the ground has been cut from under the President.'[35] This was mild compared with Herschel Johnson. The convention obviously originated with President Johnson, he pronounced, and 'Who [is] so blind as not to see that it is the object of the movement to unite the democrats and Conservative republicans and the South on him?' Moreover, the Georgia leader continued,

I have no idea that Johnson can be re-elected. He has sown too many seeds of bitterness. The South will support him, if he continues to pursue his present line of policy. But how can the South love him or care for his fate? — All that we can say of him is, that he has not been half so bad and hard upon us, as we expected. The Northern democracy despise him. The Centralists despise him and the Conservatives only tolerate him. Now how is it possible to elect him? – Is it not folly to organize a party in his interest? Were it not better therefore, for the South, to stand aloof and not at this early day to link her destiny with any party movement? If we wait, we shall, in due time, be wooed; concessions will be made to us to obtain our support. Not 'till then shall we begin to have any power.[36]

To this uncertainty about the objectives and nature of the National Union project was added a suspicion concerning the assumptions of its progenitors when Confederates began to scrutinize the terms of the call. Three planks in the platform were certain to cause contention in the South; the inviolability of the Federal debt; the permanence of the

[34]Sharkey to Graham, Washington, D.C., 9 August 1866, W. A. Graham Collection.
[35]W. W. Boyce to J. D. B. DeBow, Washington, D.C., 13 June 1866, J. D. B. DeBow MSS (Duke).
[36]Johnson to Stephens, Augusta, Ga., 5 July 1866, H. V. Johnson MSS.

Union along with the denial of the right of secession; and the right to representation, subject to the judgement of each House over its members' qualifications. This last point was an implicit acknowledgement of the legitimacy of the ironclad oath, and also made it appear that those who could not pass the ironclad test were not welcome at the National Union convention. Herschel Johnson was convinced the call would be divisive in the South and he also questioned 'the right of Randal [*sic*] and others to lay down a platform for the thirty six States.'[37] The reaction expected by Johnson came from the *Augusta Constitutionalist*, widely regarded as the Georgia Senator-elect's mouthpiece. Flaying the platform for its reiteration of 'loyalty,' its insistence on oaths of allegiance to a 'shabby Union or wrangling Government,' and its mouthings about 'traitors' and 'rebellion,' its editor, Salem Dutcher, exclaimed angrily, 'Give us the Federal Constitution, pure and simple — standing serene and beautiful in a majesty that never did any one any harm—suffer us to substitute "law-abiding" for "loyal" — and we are with you. But not otherwise.'[38] And reiterating a frequent theme, the *Richmond Enquirer* commented: 'We submit to the demands and the verdict of force in this matter, but we cannot give the approval of our judgement,' for 'we must preserve our honor — it is all that is left us, and it must not be bartered or compromised.'[39] After all, perhaps concessions on the ironclad test and on other issues relating to reunion were being sought from the South and would be used as precedents by Northern Congressmen. Furthermore, it was not out of the question that the convention's organizers might be attempting to exclude secessionists in particular from participation. So the South should be careful and not rush in precipitately.

In fact, those who were so scrupulous in their analysis of the call really did not want to involve the South in the convention at all. Herschel Johnson asserted in his first letter to Stephens that

The great contest for the restoration of the States to their Constitutional relation to the Union, must necessarily be fought at the North. They are the majority — and they have control of the government. If they do not see fit to admit us to representation, we are powerless. Then, were it not better that we permit them to fight it out, extending to them, on our part, all the moral

---

[37]Johnson to Stephens, Augusta, Ga., 2 July 1866, H. V. Johnson MSS.
[38]Editorial, *Augusta Constitutionalist*, 30 June 1866.
[39]Editorial, *Richmond Enquirer*, 2 July and 27 June 1866.

'aid and comfort' within our power? – that is – 'aid and comfort' to the Conservative party, I mean.[40]

A month or so later just before the convention was to meet, Johnson was still arguing for non-participation, even though he had publicly acquiesced in his nomination as a delegate. In an open letter he complained, 'We can neither say nor do anything that is not converted into a weapon against us. Hence, the policy of entire quiescence, I have thought, is best.' Supporting the conservatives critically was a far better course, since 'In all this, there is an eloquence of submission to wrong and injustice, which, sooner or later, will reach the hearts of good men in all lands.'[41] From the same basic strategy, the *Enquirer* expected a slightly different process to unfold. On 16 July, its editorial reasoned that

It is plain to see that the cooperation of the Conservative men of the North and Northwest, with the people of the South, is inevitable. Since the violent and final feud of the Radicals with the President and his supporters, they need us as much as we need them. . . . They will accord us a real representation instead of the *sham* representation of the test-oath. . . . We may throw away our interests in this matter if *we choose*; but it would be the quintessence of stupidity if we do, for we have the game in our own hands.[42]

The strategy of 'masterly inactivity' was a winning one and should not be compromised. There was proof of that already, noted the *Enquirer*, since non-cooperation and reluctance had already produced from the organizers of the convention assurances about the call as well as a clarification of the test oath for delegates.[43] This would surely continue, and on a larger scale. Meanwhile, said the *Constitutionalist*, why throw away a bargaining-position on a choice in which 'we may take ANDREW JOHNSON or the Radical Congress' for 'such an election is not worth the toss of a straw.'[44] Moreover, 'the haste with which this scheme is pressed would lead one to suppose that it was intended rather for influence on the Northern State fall elections than

[40]Johnson to Stephens, Augusta, Ga., 2 July 1866, H. V. Johnson MSS.
[41]Johnson, open letter to R. A. T. Ridley, 10 August 1866, in *Atlanta Intelligencer*, 19 August 1866.
[42]Editorial, *Richmond Enquirer*, 16 July 1866.
[43]*Ibid.*
[44]Editorial, *Augusta Constitutionalist*, 8 July 1866.

with an eye single to the general good of the whole country.'[45] The scheme had essentially a Northern purpose and Northern components, and the South was brought in only as a supporting actor. As a final word on the project, the *Constitutionalist* predicted that even if the delegates were present at the convention, 'one red-hot, spread-eagle, stars and stripes, slap up, bunkum Yankee speech' would 'set the Southern blood on fire, and then, with the first fire-eating, warhorse talk that answers it, Hope may as well fold her wings and our delegates come home.'[46]

c: *Organizational response in the South*

On 9 July, a month after it had been announced, the *New York Times* commented that 'The Southern press is almost unanimous in its approval of the call for the Philadelphia Convention.'[47] This was a wildly optimistic assessment for there was still, and would continue to be, much skepticism about the specifics of the call. Moreover, it was only gradually and with qualification that papers like the *Constitutionalist* and the *Enquirer* agreed not to oppose Southern participation. Objections to the terms of the call were however frequently waived in the hope that perhaps the general aims of the whole project merited support for it. And perhaps it was this appearance of approval which gave the *Times* its grounds for enthusiasm. But selecting and sending delegates required action and was therefore less easily assented to even than the terms of the call.

The *New York Times*, whose editor, Henry J. Raymond, was deeply involved in the convention, was reporting closely on developments in the Southern States. The report of 9 July might state accurately that Southerners approved of the convention but until mid-July the more detailed conclusions of its correspondents as to the nature and extent of action towards selecting delegates for Philadelphia were gloomy.[48] No activity and even little interest could be observed in South Carolina until James L. Orr's excessively zealous endorsement on 4 July, and only one prominent newspaper, the *Charleston Daily News*, was enthusiastic. Of Georgia doubt was even expressed whether delegates would be sent at all. No prominent Georgia politician save Benjamin H. Hill favored participation and the press was split on the issue.

---

[45] *Ibid.* See also *Constitutionalist* editorial of 10 July 1866.
[46] Editorial, *Augusta Constitutionalist*, 21 July 1866.
[47] *New York Times*, 9 July 1866.
[48] See reports of 'E.C.,' 'Wood,' 'O.R.B.,' and 'Quondam' during these weeks.

Led by the *Augusta Constitutionalist*, the opposition was strong, with the *Atlanta New Era, Savannah News, Macon Citizen, Columbus Sun, Milledgeville Southern Recorder* and most of the country press in train.[49] Most active in urging attendance were the editors of the *Atlanta Intelligencer*, Jared Whitaker and Major J. H. Steele, who were the initiators of public moves to call meetings and address gatherings.[50] And they were joined by the *Augusta Chronicle, Macon Journal and Messenger, Columbus Enquirer*, and *Macon Telegraph*.[51] Virginia also was reluctant; no interest in selecting delegates was shown until a meeting was held in Albemarle County on 2 July. Among the newspapers, the formerly secessionist *Richmond Enquirer* was strongly opposed to participation and so were Lynchburg's *Daily News* and *Republican* and, although approving the call, the *Richmond Whig* as well. Unenthusiastic yet favoring participation was the attitude of the *Richmond Times* and *Petersburg Index*, while unequivocal support for participation was forthcoming only from the remaining Richmond papers, the *Dispatch* and the *Examiner*.[52] Very little eagerness could be discerned in North Carolina where the Whig leadership was noticeably cool towards the project. Curiously however, their main organ, the *Raleigh Sentinel* was enthusiastic from as early a date as 5 June and it became progressively ecstatic as the convention approached. Yet in private the *Sentinel*'s editor, William Pell, was confessing doubt; he told Graham in mid-July, 'It strikes me as the proper course, yet I do not like some things about it.'[53]

Throughout the rest of the South, there was less division, although, with the exception of Mississippi, hardly more action and enthusiasm. According to a report in the *Cincinnati Gazette* of 10 July, Mississippi was in the same condition as Georgia.[54] This was somewhat misleading because in some parts of the State there was a good deal of activity. By mid-July Whig politicians in Hinds, Adams, and Lowndes Counties were actively organizing meetings, and so excited did matters become that two editors, Edward M. Yerger of the *Mississippian* and John L. Power of the *Clarion* went 'armed

[49] *Augusta Constitutionalist*, 22 July 1866.
[50] See *Atlanta Intelligencer* for indications of their activity and encouragement.
[51] *Augusta Chronicle*, 6 July 1866.
[52] The *Richmond Enquirer* reviewed the positions taken by the Virginia press on 29 June 1866 and 2 July 1866.
[53] William Pell to Graham, Raleigh, 14 July 1866, W. A. Graham Collection.
[54] *Cincinnati Gazette*, 10 July, cited in *Flake's Bulletin*, 21 July 1866.

for each other,' both claiming to have been the first to publish the call for a State convention to choose delegates.[55] More prosaic was the course of events in the other Southwestern States and in Florida. Alabama's *Montgomery Advertiser* qucikly endorsed participation; so did the former secessionist Governor, John Gill Shorter, and this initiative was never seriously challenged.[56] In New Orleans, William H. C. King's *Times* took the lead in urging that delegates be selected, probably because King had been instructed by the President to supervise matters in Louisiana. He suggested that, for simplicity, the Democratic Party Executive Committee should appoint delegates but on a bipartisan basis; all the same it was clear that this would not be easy, King telling President Johnson on one occasion that it was difficult to 'manage schemers who can think of nothing but their own and unworthy purposes,' and on another that 'The friends of Dick Taylor,' the irreconcilable Democratic General, were trying to gain influence in the proceedings.[57] In Arkansas, the State's leading paper, the *Gazette*, immediately urged participation, probably because its editor, William E. Woodruff, was recording secretary of the Andrew Johnson Club and was in contact with the President. He was joined by the State's Whigs, in particular Lorenzo Gibson.[58] Finally from Texas and Florida reports were received that sentiment there generally favored attendance, although in Florida there was probably a good deal of apathy and inertia which was reflected in the fact that the delegates were chosen by Governor Walker rather than by public assemblies.[59]

In none of the Confederate States did the convention provoke an unqualifiedly favorable response nor did it prompt decisive action towards participation. In effect, the South drifted into participation. No politicians or presses were prepared to forbid attendance, even had there existed organizations capable of reaching collective decisions and enforcing them. Typical were the attitudes of Johnson and

[55] See Harris, *Presidential Reconstruction in Mississippi*, pp. 229–33; *Jackson Clarion*, 21 July 1866.

[56] Editorial, *Montgomery Advertiser*, 28 June 1866; John G. Shorter to Alexander W. Randall, Washington, D. C., 4 July 1866, cited in *Montgomery Advertiser*, 13 July 1866.

[57] William H. C. King to Andrew Johnson, New Orleans, 8 July 1866, Johnson MSS, Series I.

[58] Editorial, *Arkansas Gazette*, 14 and 28 July 1866.

[59] William W. Davis, *The Civil War and Reconstruction in Florida* (Gainsville: University of Florida Press, 1964 edn.), p. 434.

Stephens. Although men of influence in their State, both referred final judgement to others. Johnson equivocated by saying, 'My impressions however, do not possess the strength of Convictions, and therefore, I cannot say, I would *discourage* such a movement – would rather defer to the general sentiment and policy of our people and cheerfully co-operate if a majority should determine to be represented in the Convention.'[60] Stephens, as was his custom, made his views public yet always added the rejoinder that they were only personal and therefore not binding or authoritative in any way. This indecisiveness, coupled with the refusal to prevent efforts at participation, meant that if a movement were made to call meetings and choose delegates it would have to be accepted and joined or else division would ensue. Consequently, when initiatives were taken, they were never resisted and so they in themselves determined that the State concerned would participate officially at Philadelphia, political reservations notwithstanding. Accordingly, once meetings were called in Georgia, Johnson resigned himself to the new development, saying, 'I think the S. States will go [to] the Convention – the northern democracy are not enthusiastic, as far as I can see and I am far from sanguine of any good. But on the whole, the experiment is worth making.'[61] Like the Georgia Senator-elect, the *Charleston Courier* accommodated, observing, 'It cannot be questioned that much scepticism prevails in reference to the good which this Philadelphia convention undertakes to accomplish, but on the supposition that no positive harm will be done, our delegates have been chosen.'[62] Equally phlegmatic was Lorenzo Gibson of Arkansas when he concluded, 'If it does no good, it can do no harm.'[63]

Contributing to this gradual shifting away from inertia were assurances emanating from certain quarters in the North which assuaged fears about the tone and prerequisites of the convention. On 4 July forty-one Democratic Senators and Congressmen, including Reverdy Johnson, Thomas Hendricks and Garrett Davis, had recommended that Democrats attend the convention. Hardly unequivocal and leaving much to be desired on the part of those who expected a new political organization to emerge from the Philadelphia assemblage, this clearly alleviated some Southern doubts about the attitude of the

[60]Johnson to Stephens, Augusta, Ga., 2 July 1866, H. V. Johnson MSS.
[61]Johnson to Stephens, Augusta, Ga., 20 July 1866, H. V. Johnson MSS.
[62]Quotation from *Charleston Courier*, cited in *New York Times*, 9 August 1866.
[63]Lorenzo Gibson to *Arkansas Gazette*, in *Arkansas Gazette*, 28 July 1866.

Democratic Party.[64] In addition to this, the organizers of the convention were making it clear that the specifics of the call were not intended in any way to deter those who agreed with the general objects and sentiments of the meeting. In particular the ironclad was not a test for participation; this was explained to Alexander Stephens by Montgomery Blair in a lengthy correspondence during mid-July. Blair implored Stephens to attend and extended his importunings to others like him. The Georgian was mollified but was still not sure whether, although now possible, it was expedient for him to appear. However, Blair had already tried to dispose of this objection by pointing out, 'I know of course that we shall be taunted with having traitors in our camp — This I think will do no harm. We are openly fighting for your rights and your presence will not change the issue or affect the question.'[65] Eventually Stephens decided to go and so did Herschel Johnson.[66] Many others were becoming convinced that the Southern States should attend, although the organizers' attempt to apply to the Copperhead Democrats the ban which had been waived for the Southerners did cause some bewilderment and annoyance, the *Richmond Times*, for example, complaining that 'A "Conservative Convention" which excludes any portion of the Northern Democracy from its deliberations will never succeed.'[67]

In general, however, these assurances facilitated Southern participation by removing doubts. More important in propelling the South into action were the many favorable analyses within that section of the intent and composition of the convention. For instance, it was impossible to ignore the fact that Andrew Johnson and Northern conservatives in general were eager for the South to appear at Philadelphia. Therefore, concluded the *Jackson Clarion* on 6 July, 'We cannot remain indifferent while such a momentous issue is in process of solution. [U]nless we cooperate with the good and true men of the North, who are fearlessly and manfully battling for our rights, we may depend upon it that we have not yet tasted the dregs of the bitter cup prepared

[64] McPherson, *Political History of the U.S.*, pp. 119–20.
[65] Stephens to Blair, Crawfordville, Ga., 13 and 23 July, Blair Family MSS; Blair to Stephens, Silver Spring, Md., 17 July 1865, A. H. Stephens MSS.
[66] Johnson of course reneged just before setting off for Philadelphia and explained his reasons in the open letter to R. A. T. Ridley; Stephens left Georgia intending to reach Philadelphia but was taken ill en route and did not appear at the convention.
[67] Editorial, *Richmond Times*, 9 August 1866.

for us.'[68] The *Montgomery Advertiser* agreed: 'The rescue of the South from further spoliation and degredation, and the rescue of the Constitution from utter overthrow are fast becoming bound up in a common cause, and when we see leading Northern men leading in this cause, surely the South should unite with zeal and alacrity.'[69] As an attempt 'to organize a great Constitutional Party' with Southern cooperation, the *Augusta Chronicle* also approved 'the movement' and 'gladly herald [ed] it as a significant indication, from the conservatives of the North, of their determination to uphold and support the President in his patriotic purpose to restore the Union of the States and the rights of the South under the Constitution and Laws.'[70]

When the *Chronicle* used the word 'party' to describe the fruits of the convention, it had suggested something it did not mean. Three days later a clarification was printed: 'It is not as a nucleus for the formation of a party, that we attach importance to this Convention. Nor is it as a tender of sympathy and support to the President, to whom we owe so much for his manly struggle against fanaticism. It has a higher mission and a deeper significance. It is as a gathering of the best people – the representative people of two sections, lately at war, but now earnestly seeking peace – that we attach great importance to the assemblage....'[71] In this perspective also, many waverers were able to accept the safety and necessity of participation. There were no organizational attachments involved; it was simply a gathering in which, as the *Atlanta Intelligencer* explained, 'the South has the deepest interest;' moreover, 'to confer with conservative men from every section . . . in order to meet successfully the organized tyranical [*sic*] bands of Radicals, is her duty.'[72] As a meeting of conservative men, another purpose could be served by Southern attendance, and this was pointed out to Alexander Stephens by R. J. Moses, a former secessionist surprisingly; 'it strikes me as important in having a national organization arrayed' against a sectional one, this will be palpable to feeling as to sight, and is in itself an argument to the people showing *which* is the Union party.'[73]

[68] Editorial, *Jackson Clarion*, 6 July 1866.
[69] Editorial, *Montgomery Advertiser*, 8 July 1866.
[70] Editorial, *Augusta Chronicle*, 3 July 1866.
[71] *Ibid.*, 24 July 1866.
[72] Editorial, *Atlanta Intelligencer*, 10 July 1866.
[73] R. J. Moses to Stephens, 3 July 1866, A. H. Stephens MSS.

Seen in these terms either as a meeting of conservatives or as a device for propagating an anti-disunionist intersectional image, the convention was more easily acceptable; it embodied no threat and it required little commitment from participants. More and more as the convention neared, Southerners conceived of the assembly in these terms; or at least if it were described in this manner, the decision to participate might not appear so irrevocable or long-term, and therefore so difficult.

There were others however who still saw the movement as an organizational matter. The *Raleigh Sentinel* believed the purpose of the convention was to 'concentrate and unite, for a temporary, but vital purpose, all conservative men of all parties, who support President Johnson's policy against the policy of the Radicals.'[74] And Governor James L. Orr was telling the people of South Carolina on 4 July that 'The compact organization of the Conservative men is a necessity to meet successfully the well-organized band of the Radicals, and every man who disapproves of the tyrannical and unjust policy of the latter should join in this national patriotic league.'[75] For these supporters of Southern participation, the attraction of the National Union movement lay not in its being simply a conference or a demonstration but in its having a temporary and limited organizational objective.

There were many, however, who believed that the convention was a device to produce a long-term partisan readjustment, but instead of being deterred by this possibility, they were attracted by it. The *Jackson Clarion* hailed the convention as 'an assemblage of patriotic, conservative men, whose only object is to lay the foundation of a new party, the distinctive policy of which new party, will be to rebuild the fallen fabric of Liberty.'[76] This, needless to say, would require that the Democrats disband their existing organization and integrate themselves into a new party of opposition. The party would not be a third party and this was welcomed by the *Richmond Times* because, as its editors stated, 'without a speedy coalition with the conservative element of the Republican party, the Northern Democracy can do nothing. It has barely strength enough left to stand up, once a

[74] Editorial, *Raleigh Sentinel*, 27 June 1866.
[75] James L. Orr, Address to the People of South Carolina, Columbia, S.C., 4 July 1866, reported in *New York Times*, 12 July 1866 and *Montgomery Advertiser*, 10 July 1866.
[76] Editorial, *Jackson Clarion*, 28 July 1866.

year, just long enough for the Raidcals to knock it down.'[77] Besides, said the *Times*, the South felt no allegiance to 'the old *effete* and moribund parties' which were incapable of defeating radicalism. Instead, 'The exigencies and perils of the hour demand new parties and new leaders.'[78] To Southern Democrats, particularly secessionists like the *Montgomery Advertiser*, the Northern wing of the party had failed to aid the South before and during the war, and by 1866 had even lost influence in the North; so that its metamorphosis into a new party organization was essential before its traditional constituency could be mobilized to any effect.[79] The Georgia secessionist, Judge Richard H. Clark, wrote to the *New York Daily News* beseeching the party to forsake its old organization and 'coalesce under a new name with anybody and everybody who will give, if but only the "widow's mite," toward preserving the blessings of liberty, not only to the subjugated South, but to the people of the victorious North.'[80]

There were yet others, very often pre-war Whigs, who welcomed the prospect of a new partisan alignment. Distrustful of the Democrats, they hoped that if a new second party emerged which was national in scope and conservative in tone, this would not only provide the instrumentality for reunion but would also release the Whigs from the necessity of cooperating with, even joining, the Democratic Party. In Mississippi, one of the few States where Whiggery retained a clear-cut identity and organization, this possibility was quite obviously recognized. But until the new party was actually in process of formation, political alliances and commitments at Philadelphia would be dangerous and self-defeating. Against this James L. Alcorn warned the Mississippi delegates in a public speech of 29 July. At the convention he advised the delegates to demand simply 'an enforcement of your *right* of [Congressional] *representation*,' for 'that enforcement you cannot possibly accomplish, be the support of the Democratic divisions ever so generous, *without the hearty cooperation of the Conservative Republicans*.' Until this occurred any new anti-radical organization would be no more than a different banner for the Democrats to march under. Furthermore, as Johnson, Seward and Raymond were well aware and as some Southerners were prepared to recognize, these Republicans

[77] Editorial, *Richmond Times*, 21 July 1866.
[78] *Ibid.*
[79] Editorial, *Montgomery Advertiser*, 28 June 1866.
[80] Richard H. Clark to *New York Daily News*, 17 July 1866, reprinted in *Atlanta Intelligencer*, 10 August 1866.

had to be, or at least appear to be, at the head of the movement.[81] One who acknowledged this was James Farrow, a former secessionist and now Congressman-elect from South Carolina. Although he realized that 'There is some complaint that the enterprize is launched too exclusively under the auspices of the Republicans,' he rebutted this by arguing that 'it would be well for it to partake more of the *appearance* of Republicanism than Democracy – The great point aimed at should be the *severing* the two factions of Republicans. And this could best be done by allowing plenty of rope to conservative Republicans and letting them appear to lead. Once get them fairly committed and they could then be "worked up" at leisure.' At all events, Farrow believed, party scruples had to be laid aside for 'without a *new organization* we may as well at once I think prepare for Radical ascendency.'[82]

Southern support of and participation in the convention could be justified on a number of grounds, each of which involved a different analysis of the purpose and scope of the assembly. In a sense, the convention was 'all things to all men,' and therefore it was difficult to argue vehemently and successfully against participation. Moreover, when it was apparent that Northern conservatives favored the convention and Southern participation and that the overall objective of it was to repulse the radical Republicans, how could Southerners stand aloof? Also, how could they be passive if, as Benjamin H. Hill explained it, 'This movement at Philadelphia is to save the Constitution?' After all, preventing the fundamental law from being broadly construed was vital to the South's security, and, continued Hill, 'The South sought to save the Constitution out of the Union. She failed. Let her bring her diminished and shattered, but united and earnest counsels and energies to save the Constitution in the Union. Such I always thought was her duty and her safety.'[83] And finally, why should the pessimism of men like Stephens and Johnson as to the possibility of party reorganization prohibit the South from attending and trying to employ its beneficial influence? Even the risk of division within each State could be minimized by cooperating while demanding certain guarantees, rather than by obstructing the movement. These guarantees might be that the State delegation be instructed by

[81] James L. Alcorn, Address to the People of Mississippi, 29 July 1866, in *Jackson Clarion*, 21 August 1866.
[82] James Farrow to Perry, Washington, D.C., 28 June 1866, Perry MSS (Ala.).
[83] Hill to A. R. Wright, 4 July 1866, an open letter printed in *Montgomery Advertiser*, 10 July 1866.

the convention which selected it or that it be mandated to vote only as a unit. The possibility of these provisos contributed greatly to relieving the anxieties of opponents of participation such as the *Augusta Constitutionalist*, the *Richmond Enquirer* and the Virginia Democrats, even though eventually neither State's delegation was bound in these ways.[84]

As a result, skepticism, opposition, and inertia were gradually overcome. There seemed to be no good reason for non-participation, unless an uncompromising stand for 'masterly inactivity' and non-involvement in national affairs were to be adopted. This had not however been taken. Although it was the dominant strain in the Southern posture, Southern politicians still wanted to retain options and a reasonable degree of flexibility. Accordingly, throughout July and early August, meetings and conventions were held in all the Southern States to select delegates to Philadelphia. The method of selection varied from State to State. Because of the shortage of time available before the convention met on 14 August, it was often suggested that the Governor should select the delegates; this however was only done in Florida.[85] Another means of shortcutting lengthy procedures as well as simultaneously keeping the process centralized and under control was for a State convention, whose members were selected locally, to choose the delegates. In Mississippi, North Carolina, and Texas, meetings in each county elected delegates to the State convention, while in the case of South Carolina it was by judicial district.[86] The degree of involvement in the counties however was far from satisfactory, only thirty-two of Mississippi's sixty counties sending representatives and a mere twenty-one out of a total of one hundred and thirty in Texas. North Carolina's county meetings were characterized not necessarily by limited interest but by the control exerted over them by the regular party organizations and the professional politicos.

By contrast, in Georgia and Alabama, meetings were held in every Congressional district, from each of which two delegates were

<hr />

[84]The possibility of obtaining these guarantees and controls over the State delegation seemed a more realistic and less divisive method of assuaging fears about the possible action of a delegation than an obstinate refusal to participate under any circumstances.

[85]Davis, *Civil War and Reconstruction in Florida*, p. 434.

[86]Except where otherwise stated, details on the procedures employed in each State are culled from State newspapers and from the reports in the *New York Times*.

chosen. Then Georgia's at-large members were selected, not on a separate State-wide ballot as had been intended, but instead the at-large nominees of the Macon convention were endorsed, while in Alabama the State convention at Selma was entrusted with this task. In Virginia a variety of procedures were used. Originally, at a meeting in Albemarle County on 2 July, it had been resolved that members of the State committees of the Whig, and of the Breckinridge and Douglas Democratic Parties should convene to suggest a method. This they did on 15 July, and the proposal was that local meetings in counties and cities should elect four delegates at-large and three from each Congressional district. By late July, however, so little had been achieved that the joint committee was forced to reconvene and to select district and at-large nominees itself. At this meeting there was also an intense debate in which the Democrats urged and the Whigs opposed instruction and unit-voting.

Delegates were chosen from Arkansas and Louisiana by small groups of men rather than by assemblies. In the former, William Woodruff and the officers of the Johnson Club consulted with the State's leading Whig, Lorenzo Gibson, and together they chose a delegation. This headed off a separate move by Robert Ward Johnson and the Democratic machine to submit its own slate of delegates and have them authorized by the President, a maneuver which the White House scotched by withholding recognition.[87] And finally in Louisiana, William H. C. King, who was deputed by the President to coordinate selection, suggested that the Democratic Executive Committee choose a non-partisan slate of delegates; this, he felt would be speedy and uncomplicated. There were rivals, however; Christian Roselius' Constitutional Union Association and Cuthbert Bullitt's Andrew Johnson Club, which by July had merged into Roselius' organization, felt that they had sounder credentials for electing a non-partisan delegation. Stealing a march on Bullitt while he was out of town and after giving assurances to the contrary, the Democrats led by H. N. Ogden, the State chairman, elected a slate at the St Charles Hotel in New Orleans on 10 July and then, at a large rally in Lafayette Square on the 24th, had it publicly ratified.[88] Since one

[87] Johnson's maneuver and his plea for recognition can be seen in R. W. Johnson to Andrew Johnson, Pine Bluff, Ark., 23 July 1866, Andrew Johnson MSS, Series I.

[88] This confusing story has been compiled from various news-reports in the *New Orleans Times* and *New York Times* during the first two weeks of July and from

or two of Roselius' and Bullitt's supporters were in the delegation, it appears that they contested the matter no further, though they were obviously extremely angered.

Just as the manner of selection differed, so too did the kind of delegation sent.[89] When Southerners had elected representatives for Congress a year before, they had debated what sort of men they should select; in 1866 the same problem arose. James Farrow posed the question of the hour to Perry: 'Some urging new men without any political antecedents — others urge men of clear record as to past loyalty — and still others urge appointment of those who were conspicuous in support of the war so as to let [the] North see that even those who were prominent in the effort for separation are now Union men.'[90] As a general rule the last of the three possibilities was not followed and instead a combination of prominent anti-secessionists and some lesser-known men was sent, with an occasional noted secessionist for good measure.

Virginia, Alabama, and Georgia were most noticeable in their adoption of this kind of pattern. Regarding the Virginia delegation, 'E.C.' of the *New York Times* commented that it was mainly composed of little-known men and of 1861 moderates like John Brockenborough, Thomas Flournoy, James Barbour, John L. Marye, Jr and A. A. H. Stuart, with Edmund Fontaine a lone secessionist.[91] Alabama sent prominent anti-secessionists, W. H. Crenshaw, George S. Houston, Lewis Parsons and C. C. Langdon as well as 'fire-eaters' John G. Shorter and John Forsyth. At the same time, the Selma convention laid the groundwork for a State-based party to follow up the National Union initiative and this was to be coordinated by General James H. Clanton, a soldier previously uninvolved in politics.[92] Georgia sent the anti-secessionists, Johnson, Stephens, Absalom Chappell and D. A. Walker as at-large delegates, while the remainder of the delegation was also moderate but less well-known.

Bullitt's explanation of how he was double-crossed and outmaneuvered in *New Orleans Times*, 29 July 1866.

[89] The list of Southern delegates can be found in *Washington Weekly Republican*, 24 August 1866, clipping in Johnson MSS, Series XI, Vol. II.

[90] James Farrow to Perry, Columbia, S.C., 23 July 1866, Perry MSS (Ala.).

[91] 'E.C.,' Richmond, Va., 3 August 1866, in *New York Times*, 6 August 1866. 'E.C.' considered Marye a secessionist but his assessment is countered in Jack P. Maddex, Jr, *The Virginia Conservatives, 1867–1879: A Study in Reconstruction Politics* (Chapel Hill: University of North Carolina Pres, 1970), p. 61. Maddex describes Marye as a pre-war Whig.

[92] *Montgomery Advertiser*, 3 August 1866.

Also non-partisan and inclusive were the nominees from Florida and South Carolina. Yet this broadness of scope was reached by a different procedure for both delegations had as their core the State's Congressional representatives. So Florida's Senators, Call and Marvin, headed their delegation, the remainder being selected by the Governor from the four main regions of the State, Middle, West, East, and South. From the Palmetto State as at-large delegates went Senators-elect Manning and Perry, Governor Orr and James B. Campbell who was defeated for the Senate in 1865, while the core of the ordinary delegates consisted of U.S. Congressmen-elect, with distinguished figures like Franklin Moses, David Wardlaw and T. N. Dawkins comprising the remainder.

In the remaining States, the membership was selected primarily on a partisan basis. In Louisiana and North Carolina, Democrats predominated. Deploring the poor quality and tactlessness of his State's delegates, the Whig anti-secessionist Samuel Phillips exclaimed, 'Oh such a convention, such plans, such speeches. . . . What winning ways to make the Radicals despise us, and to increase their numbers' and later, noting the prominence of secessionists in the delegation, 'Edwards, Mordecai, Barringer, Arrington, Manly, Hale, alas! my country!'[93] In Louisiana, irreconcilables like General Richard Taylor, J. Adolphus Rozier, and Charles Gayarré were selected yet so also were Senator-elect Randall Hunt and William H. C. King. On the other hand, the Whigs dominated the Arkansas and Mississippi delegations, William Yerger, George L. Potter, Horatio Simrall, Giles Hillyer being most noteworthy in the latter. And finally, in Texas a delegation was selected on the basis of faction rather than party; the supporters of the recently elected Governor, James W. Throckmorton, dominated the Navasota convention and elected men like Ben Epperson, John Hancock, David J. Burnett and Lemuel Evans, thereby excluding the followers of the more moderate, E. M. Pease, who had been Throckmorton's opponent.

d: *Post-convention assessments*

Delegates from every one of the Confederates States set off for Philadelphia in August 1866. Some, like Alexander Stephens, did not manage to reach the city, but those who did went into the assembly uncertain precisely of what was to happen at the meeting and what was intended

[93]Samuel Phillips to Kemp P. Battle, Chapel Hill, 26 July and 16 August 1866, Battle Family MSS.

of it. There was immense optimism that this gathering could rally the supporters of the President; by contrast there was anxiety that this was a moment and opportunity dire in its consequences if failure accompanied it; and often there was also a conviction that no good could come from an attempt to concoct unity and harmony where neither existed. Perhaps William L. Sharkey's comments to the disbelieving William A. Graham best summed up the spirit in which Southerners viewed the convention:

I regret that you are disinclined to attend the Convention. I hope much good may result from its action, and really believe such will be the case. But this will depend on the way it is managed. . . . If the Convention should turn out to be a failure, I see no hope for the Government, even if there be with the success of the Convention. . . . Everything depends on breaking up the radical party, and I believe it can be done if the Convention should act wisely.[94]

So the Southern States participated. But their participation was minimal. There was no open debating at the convention; the proceedings were staged so that disruptive issues were not aired in the open, but only in closed committees. All speeches were formal and prepared, enunciatory of general sentiments rather than concrete policies. Senator James Doolittle, a Republican of Wisconsin, John A. Dix, a New York War Democrat, Henry J. Raymond, and also James L. Orr addressed the assembly in this spirit. Even so, and despite these careful preparations, discordant notes were audible. The presence of leading Copperheads, Clement L. Vallandigham, Fernando Wood, and Henry Clay Dean, produced fears that the convention would appear ultra, not moderate and conservative, and this would certainly jeopardize hopes that moderate Republicans might lead the movement. A delegation of Southerners, led by George S. Houston of Alabama and accompanied by James Orr and a reluctant Benjamin Perry of South Carolina, was deputed by the organizers to urge Vallandigham to retire.[95] This was done, though not without Dean's objection and the presence of all three on the convention floor and not without grumblings in the South

[94] Sharkey to Graham, Washington, D.C., 9 August 1866, W. A. Graham Collection. Actually Graham did eventually attend.

[95] Lillian A. Kibler, *Benjamin F. Perry, South Carolina Unionist* (Durham, N.C.: Duke University Press, 1946), pp. 444–5; Perry, *Reminiscences of Public Men, 2nd Series*, pp. 297–307; *Montgomery Advertiser*, 19 August 1866. Perry did not mention that Houston went with Orr and himself. The *Advertiser* asserted, however, that he led the delegation.

that these men, staunch allies during the war, should be so shamefully treated, in order to produce an appearance of conciliation. For participating in this maneuver, Perry and Orr were often severely criticized within their section.[96]

Controversial also was the Declaration of Principles drawn up by the Committee on Resolutions. Declaring the sacredness of the national debt and repudiating State war debts, asserting that 'the war has maintained the authority of the Constitution,' and congratulating the Federal soldiers on their gallantry, there was much said that was distasteful to the Southern States and also much left unsaid.[97] The *Richmond Enquirer* snorted: 'Nothing is left us but to spew them.'[98] The *Lynchburg Republican* considered them 'false in fact, insulting in character, and humiliating and disgraceful in their effect on our unfortunate section.'[99] Some, however, were satisfied, including William A. Graham who, along with William Yerger, had been influential in the Resolutions Committee. 'The discussions there,' he said, 'were of the most friendly character, the North conceding whatever we thought vital.'[100] This, however, was not the story told by the Copperhead *New York Daily News*. Exhorting the South not to '*crawl* to conquer,' it added that the Declaration was not solicitous of the South's interests because it reflected only the truckling and accommodation of delegates like Graham, Perry, Orr, and Marvin.[101]

To those in the South who had advised against participation but had acquiesced once the movement for it had begun, the convention's proceedings provided satisfactory vindication of their initial criticisms. Referring to the opening scene of the convention when James Orr and General Darius Couch led their delegations, from South Carolina and Massachusetts, arm in arm into the assembly, the *Richmond Enquirer* asked, 'Did Mr. Orr go to Philadelphia to *confess* that his State lay on an extreme as far out from truth and justice as Massachusetts? That she was an equal offender?' and then concluded by way of an answer:

[96] *Augusta Constitutionalist*, 16 August 1866; Charles Gayarré to James D. B. DeBow, New York City, 25 August 1866, DeBow MSS; Editorial, *Richmond Enquirer*, 15 August 1866.
[97] Editorial, *Richmond Enquires*, 17 August 1866; *Washington Weekly Republican*, 24 August 1866.
[98] Editorial, *Richmond Enquirer*, 18 August 1866.
[99] Editorial, *Lynchburg Republican*, 21 August 1866.
[100] William A. Graham to Kemp P. Battle, Hillsboro, N.C., 23 August 1866, W. A. Graham Collection.
[101] Quoted in *Richmond Enquirer*, 23 August 1866.

'Virginia is for peace and reconciliation. But reluctant and grave in entering upon the fight, she will not be considered a part of any performance which winds up the tremendous tragedy through which we have passed with articificial scenes and ostentatious displays, such as belong to sensation fiction.'[102]

Similar emotions erupted from the *Augusta Constitutionalist* when it exclaimed: 'What a self-abnegatory spectacle was here! What a lying-down of the lion and the lamb together! And what wonder that the sublimest emotions were so appealed to that the delegates melted into "tears"–.'[103] But most vituperative was James P. Hambleton, an anti-secessionist from Georgia who was elected to Congress later that fall. He had been a delegate at Philadelphia and he informed Horace Greeley that the convention 'is not only intensely nauseating but indescribably disgusting. In our heart of hearts we loathe and despise the whole thing as brimful of hypocrisy, duplicity and self-abasement. The Southern heart retches and revolts at the bare mention of the Johnson Seward Raymond pills patented at Philadelphia in the Dix Doolittle wigwarm [*sic*].'[104]

There were others, however, who delighted in the proceedings at Philadelphia. The instigators of the movement were ecstatic. Seward afterwards judged that 'it constitutes an event of historical importance. Certainly, it was one morally sublime.'[105] His feelings were shared by Andrew Johnson. On 18 August at a reception for a representative group of convention delegates headed by Senator Reverdy Johnson, he announced that he regarded it 'as more important than any Convention that has sat – at least since 1787.' And he continued effusively:

The question only is the salvation of the country; for our country rises above all party considerations or influences. How many are there in the United States that now require to be free. They have the shackles upon their limbs and are bound as rigidly by the behests of their party leaders in the National Congress as though they were in fact in slavery. I repeat, then, that your declaration is the second proclamation of emancipation to the people of the

---

[102]Editorial, *ibid.*, 16 August 1866.
[103]Quoted in *Richmond Times*, 24 August 1866.
[104]James P. Hambleton to Horace Greeley, Atlanta, Ga., 27 August 1866, Greeley MSS.
[105]Seward to R. M. Blatchford, Washington, D.C., 21 August 1866, W. H. Seward MSS.

United States, and offers common ground upon which all patriots can stand.[106]

As an attempt not to produce a new party, but to liberate from the restrictions and shibboleths of the old, the convention could be considered a success for the President and his closest advisers, such as Randall, Orville H. Browning, Seward, Dix, Doolittle, and even Raymond.[107]

Newspapers and politicians in the South who had urged Southern attendance at the convention were also enthusiastic. A new party had not been formed and few had expected that, but the principles for a coalition of the anti-radical elements, North and South, had been established. The *Richmond Times* was, therefore, able to announce very optimistically that 'It is now evident that we are standing upon the threshold of a new era in the political history of this country. A new and purified party, uncorrupted by long success and the vice of office, has arisen, which, with the blessing of divine Providence, will yet save this great nation from the horrors and anarchy of revolution.'[108] Even the 'obnoxious resolutions' framed by the convention were justified by the *Times*, since the acceptance of them by the South displayed a spirit of conciliation and an awareness that the Northern delegates and the Southern were engaged in the same enterprise.[109] From the *New Orleans Times*, the *Augusta Chronicle*, the *Atlanta Intelligencer*, the *Richmond Dispatch*, and others, approval was overwhelming — their expectations had been vindicated by the proceedings at Philadelphia.

There were also some who were converted by the convention. Herschel V. Johnson admitted in public that his fears had been exceeded by the good accruing from the convention. In the *Augusta Chronicle*, whose editor, General Augustus Wright, had been amazed while in Philadelphia at the 'strong hold the President has upon the great heart

---

[106] Andrew Johnson, speech to the delegation from the Philadelphia convention, 18 August 1866, in *National Intelligencer*, 20 August 1866.
[107] Randall wrote enthusiastically to the President from the convention on 12 August, O. H. Browning on 13 August, John A. Dix on 16 August — all in Johnson MSS, Series I. Also Seward to Raymond, Philadelphia, 16 August, and Raymond's reply, 19 August 1866, W. H. Seward MSS.
[108] Editorial, *Richmond Times*, 17 August 1866.
[109] *Ibid.*, 18 August 1866.

of the people,' Herschel Johnson wrote that the convention had succeeded in inaugurating a period of good feelings, had established the
principles of a political coalition which would fight the radicals in the
coming elections, and had crystallized the issues before the country.[110]
The South, he advised, should earnestly cooperate even though the
resolutions and certain details were unpalatable, for 'it is the part of
wise and liberal statesmanship to tolerate what it cannot prevent, and
seek, by appeal to reason and patriotism, to mitigate what it cannot
control.'[111] Even the diffident Sharkey was writing to a friend in
Jackson: 'I am delighted to hear that the action of the Philadelphia
Convention is so acceptable to the people. It is producing great
enthusiasm here, and from present appearances, will sweep over the
land like a prairie on fire. My opinion from the first was that it was the
only thing that could save the Government. The President is now
clinching the nail in his trip to Chicago.'[112]

In some Southern States ratification meetings were held, but in none
so frequently as in Georgia where Wright and Jared Whitaker used
their journals as media for advertising these assemblages. They also
wished to use the support of Alexander Stephens, but although this
was not forthcoming, Stephens, in fact, was very gratified at the prospects after Philadelphia and was only disappointed that the newspapers were often still critical. Writing to Herschel Johnson, he
said:

The general result of the proceedings in producing harmony and good feeling — the first step towards restoration — was certainly far beyond my most
sanguine hopes and expectations — and the fact that a Constitutional Phalanx
of Cooperationists was thereby organized for the immediate restoration of
the Govt. [and Congressional readmission without the ironclad qualifica-
tion] was a very great point gained — This is now the great practical issue.
That at least should have received the hearty approval and endorsement of
every lover of Constitutional liberty. If the Conservative elements at the
North organized upon this basis can carry the approaching elections the
Govt. will pass into other hands — In this lies our main if not only hope — I

[110] Augustus R. Wright, letter to *Augusta Chronicle*, Philadelphia, 17 August 1866,
    Augusta Chronicle, 22 August 1866.
[111] Herschel V. Johnson, letter to *Augusta Chronicle*, 1 September 1866, in *Atlanta
    Intelligencer*, 8 September 1866.
[112] Sharkey to a friend in Jackson, Washington, D.C., 30 August 1866, in *Jackson
    Clarion*, 8 September 1866.

mean by *our* the common friends of Constitutional liberty throughout the country North and South.[113]

As a beginning towards cooperation between the sections and as an attempt to present the issues clearly in preparation for the fall elections, little criticism could be leveled at the convention's proceedings. Most of those in the defeated section who had advocated Southern attendance had done so expecting no more than these results.[114] Conservative Northern opinion, even though still channelled into the Democratic Party, would thereby be mobilized and possibly radical candidates defeated in the fall. Basically, it was felt, Northern opinion was favorable to reunion and opposed to radical measures. A convocation such as the Philadelphia convention, no matter that it was rehearsed and stage-managed, would be a visible and tangible sign of the possibilities of cooperation as well as an incentive to take steps to achieve it.

Southern opponents of the scheme, on the other hand, were more hard-headed, themselves thinking and acting sectionally and believing that Northerners were similarly motivated. Usually former secessionists, these politicians and journalists considered the convention as a proposition aimed primarily, not at readmitting or helping the South, but at strengthening Northern politicians in the coming campaign. Given these sectional proclivities, Southern participation would be of little use, in fact it might be harmful. Moreover, the South could not be helped by spectacular displays of synthetic harmony. Declarations of principles mattered nothing; only if the elections could be won and the radicals forced from power would anything be accomplished. The *Augusta Constitutionalist* on 25 August lamented, therefore, that 'proclamations will not salve the sore – speeches will not heal the wound – harmonious Conventions will not minister to the health and well being of the body politic.' Instead, 'give us deeds, Mr Johnson.'[115]

Each group was able to find vindication of its own approach to reunion in the results of the convention at Philadelphia. There did

[113] Stephens to Johnson, Crawfordville, G., 31 August 1866, H. V. Johnson MSS.
[114] For those who urged Southern participation expecting a reorganization of political parties into an anti-radical conservative coalition there was of course disappointment if not immediately after the convention, certainly a month or so later.
[115] Editorial, *Augusta Constitutionalist*, 25 August 1866.

indeed seem to be indications at the convention that the Northern conservatives and supporters of Johnson's policy were reasonably conciliatory and cooperative; equally, there was also evidence of the impossibility of any cooperarion beyond cautious declarations of pious hopes. The elections a few months later were to prove the validity of the pessimistic analysis; but rather than concede that, those who approved of the convention's acts would blame the calamitous 'Swing Around the Circle' and the mismanagement of patronage by the President's lieutenants.

8

'Masterly inactivity'*

The outcome of the struggle between President and Congress for control over the formulation of reconstruction policy was to be decided by the elections of 1866. As a preparation for this decisive contest, the Philadelphia convention was of the utmost importance. Johnson laid the groundwork very carefully. Just before the convention met, Congress was presented with a report from General Gordon Granger on conditions in the South and also with a scathing exposé of corruption in the Freedmen's Bureau compiled by Generals Steedman and Fullerton.[1] Immediately after the convention, the President issued his proclamation of 20 August declaring the insurrection at an end in

---

*This chapter has been previously published, though in a briefer form, as 'The South and Congress' Reconstruction Policy, 1866–67,' *Journal of American Studies*, February 1971.

[1] Granger's report, asserting that the Southerners were well-disposed and only antagonistic and 'disloyal' because of the threats of the radicals, can be found in the *Montgomery Advertiser*, 2 September 1866. Steedman and Fullerton had been sent South by the President to investigate the activities of the Freedman's Bureau. A month or so later Steedman explained to Johnson the line that they would take in their report. On 24 June he wrote:

'The stranglehold which I knew the institution had upon the religious and sympathetic people of the North – thousands of whom honestly believed the negroes would be butchered, if it were not for the protection afforded them by the Bureau – convinced me we would be more likely to produce effect upon the public mind and secure candid attention, by exposing the abuses and frauds, and peculations of its officers, than by attacking the system.

'Our investigations have developed to my mind, clearly, that the Bureau officers, with a very few exceptions constitute a radical close corporation, devoted to the defeat of the policy of your Administration.' Johnson MSS, Series I.

For Johnson, who considered the Bureau necessary and did not wish to remove it until a better disposition was manifested by white Southerners, this line of approach was deemed satisfactory and sufficient to cast doubt upon radical men, if not measures. It was, however, given the President's endorsement of the purpose of the Bureau, a dangerous game to play since, by such exposures, the Bureau might be entirely discredited.

Texas as well as the other States mentioned in the 2 April Proclamation. Then Andrew Johnson embarked by train for Philadelphia, New York, Cleveland, and Chicago on his 'Swing Around the Circle,' an attempt to take 'My Policy' to the people and rally the conservatives of the North for the fight to save the nation in the polling-booths during October and November.

Dignity and enthusiastic crowds attended the procession as far as Cleveland, but, thereafter, especially on the return trip, Johnson's passionate and combative extemporaneous speaking produced entertainment for hecklers as well as rumors of assassination-attempts. Retreating with confusion and denunciation, Johnson appealed to his countrymen's 'brains, and not to your prejudices; to your reason, and not your passions;' yet this ironically engendered the very opposite, passionate derision.[2]

Other occurrences and developments, both before and after the convention met, seriously harmed the prospects of the National Union movement. On 30 July, two weeks before the convention assembled, a particularly violent race-riot had occurred in New Orleans. White policemen had gunned down blacks and whites, who, as members of the 1864 Free State Party convention, were meeting to prepare plans for challenging the Democratic Party, which, since the war, had gained control of the State's governmental machinery. This incident hardly vindicated Johnson's Southern policy or the reliability of the Southerners currently in power. Furthermore, in the North during September it became evident that the Democrats were refusing to accommodate themselves to the intention of the Philadelphia convention and were campaigning on exclusively partisan grounds and using the National Union concept for their own purposes.[3] A final disaster was that all the President's efforts to remove radicals and distribute the patronage to supporters of his and the moderates' conciliatory policy, and these were large-scale during early fall, were more harmful than helpful in his cause. In Maine where the President's followers were aiding the James Blaine–Hannibal Hamlin faction against William P.

[2] Andrew Johnson, Speech at St. Louis, 8 September 1866, in *Montgomery Advertiser*, 16 September 1866.

[3] Unburdening himself to his secretary William G. Moore in 1868, Johnson 'said that had [the Philadelphia convention] received the support of the Democracy, the new party would have succeeded. He said that he could perceive all along the object of certain party leaders which was to use him as they would an orange.' Colonel William G. Moore's Small Diary, 18 March 1868, Johnson MSS.

Fessenden, the latter observed: 'A few men here — old democrats, and a very few flunkies of no political character — are acting as the President's friends, and putting the offices up for sale — asking only that the recipients will agree to support Sweat for Congress. Their offers are spurned with contempt. The thing is highly disgraceful and disgusting, and discreditable to all concerned.'[4] Neither organization Democrats nor Republicans would take offices under such conditions. Instead 'copperheads and flunkies,' men rejected by both regular parties, alone would seek them.[5]

In the South these unfavorable developments evoked alarm and despondency. Newspapers still continued to inspire optimism in the minds of their readers, but privately the politicians were disturbed. To William A. Graham, Herschel Johnson on 25 September unbosomed his fears:

My dear Sir, how dark is [*sic*] our political prospects! I had anticipated much good from the action of the Pha. convention. But it seems that the destructives are gaining, rather than losing, votes. I mourn over the folly, not to use a harsher term, of the President, in some of his speeches, on his late tour to Chicago. Having lost his self-possession, he parted with his official dignity, his prudence and discretion, and going down to the level of blackguards, he bandies epithets, and indulges in bitter denunciation. How unfortunate! I wish he had remained in Washington. He has lost moral power, and seriously damaged the course of Constitutional reorganization.[6]

In similar vein, Alexander Stephens told Johnson, 'the prospect . . . appears gloomier to me than at any period within the last six years.' And he added: 'I was hopeful of better results from the Philada Convention at the North than the facts now warrant us to believe that they will be — While I was hopeful however I was by no means sanguine — I did not think that convention was well managed either in its getting up or in its organization afterwards.' Stephens inclined to the opinion that the President was being misled by advice from some, presumably Seward and Weed, 'who have his confidence but who withhold from him their

[4]William P. Fessenden to McCulloch, Portland, Maine, 7 September 1866, Hugh McCulloch MSS. *Flake's Bulletin*, 7 March 1867, quoted the *New York Evening Post*'s estimate that 2,434 appointments were made in the executive department from September to January.

[5]Fessenden to McCulloch, 29 August 1866, Hugh McCulloch MSS.

[6]Johnson to Graham, Augusta, Ga., 25 September 1866, W. A. Graham Collection.

objects, motives and designs.'[7] But for them, Johnson might have stayed in Washington and waged the electoral battle under the Democratic banner, rejecting beguiling suggestions of interparty coalitions. This, however, was doubtful, besides being based on an inaccurate hypothesis regarding Johnson's political goals.

Others did not have to postulate conspiracy or bad advice; they believed, like Lucius Q. Washington of the *Richmond Examiner*, that 'the President has [not] played his cards well. He irritates but does not crush. He threatens and waits. It is the impression at Washington of good judges that they will impeach and depose him.'[8] In November, Washington's views had changed little: 'Johnson and Seward lack sense badly. I think that foolish trip to pay reverence to a rotten demagogue [Stephen A. Douglas] cost us the fall elections. . . . I hear reports of a general amnsesty but then all the reports of Johnson foreshadowing some wise step turn out wrong and every now and then we have a folly which we were *not* prepared for.'[9]

On one occasion, a newspaper did publicly express its doubts about the President. The *Augusta Constitutionalist* on 16 September considered the President 'a dying man whose life is in the hollow of his hand.' This was 'the weak point in the Presidential policy – that the North sees she is following a wishy-washy lead, and the South is incredulous between precept and example.'[10]

Rarely though were such sentiments seen or uttered in public. There was always hope to be gleaned from every gloomy situation. Besides, there was little purpose in public vituperation against the President since he and his policy were at war with the radicals, and, therefore, there was no alternative but to hope that Johnson would defeat, or at least muffle, the opposition. Particular tactics might fail periodically, but the overall aim could not be conceded as lost. As an example of this, the *Raleigh Sentinel* could draw from the debacle of the 'Swing Around

[7]Stephens to H. V. Johnson, Crawfordville, Ga., 27 September 1866, H. V. Johnson MSS. This same feeling, that the President had been misled by Seward, was revealed by Fessenden in a letter of 11 September to the Secretary of the Treasury, Hugh McCulloch: 'I mourn over Andy. He began by meaning well, but I fear that Seward's evil counsels have carried him beyond salvation. Lost and disgraced humself, Seward seems to have no ambition but to destroy others. Him I cannot excuse or forgive.' McCulloch MSS.

[8]Lucius Q. Washington to Robert M. T. Hunter, Richmond, 23 September 1866, Hunter–Garnett MSS.

[9]Washington to Hunter, Richmond, 17 November 1866, Hunter–Garnett MSS.

[10]Editorial, *Augusta Constitutionalist*, 16 September 1866.

the Circle' the optimistic conclusion that 'with three disgraceful exceptions, the President's tour was one continued and enthusiastic ovation'
and the paper then proceeded to exhort 'the timid and despondent
[to] take courage from the bold and sanguine spirit of the President.'[11]
Or, with the *Richmond Enquirer*, the Southerner could realize that the
Presidential tour had been useful in that it had 'brought to light a feeling of opposition to his patriotic policy, which it will require unprecedented effort to overcome.' Politics appeared to have 'narrowed down
to a mere question of sectional sentiment,' yet, in fact, 'the interests of
the South are wrapped up, at present, in the preservation of the Union
upon the principles of its founders, and President Johnson happens to
be our friend because he is the advocate, not of her interests *per se*, but
of that in which her interests are involved.'[12]

Comfort then could be taken from the realization that, not only the
South, but the whole Union would be ruined, if Johnson's policy
failed. Moreover, the gloomier the situation the more likely Northern
conservatism, 'the sober second thought of the people,' would react to
the continual disjunction of the Union, and to the instability and uncertainty for the commercial and political life of the North which was its
corollary. For the Southern leaders despondency had at all costs to be
avoided, or else, on the one hand, dissension and differences of opinion
as to policy might emerge, and, on the other, humiliating concessions
might be offered or overbearing demands accepted. This, the public
policy of the South's leaders, was delineated in a letter to Governor
Patton from John Forsyth, the ex-secessionist and editor of the *Mobile
Register*:

The general public, North and South, has apparently yielded to a spirit
of despondency about the Fall elections and has given them up to the Radicals. While that result is probable I do not consider it certain. I think
the Southern press ought to encourage our people to more encouraging and
hopeful views. If we live in the shadow of coming proscription and
confiscation, we shall fail to put forth the energies needful to repair the
waste of war. I am pursuing this course, both from policy and conviction.
I believe the time for violent and extreme measures of oppression has past
[*sic*].[13]

[11]Editorial, *Raleigh Sentinel*, 18 September 1866.
[12]Editorial, *Richmond Enquirer*, 11 September 1866.
[13]John Forsyth to Robert M. Patton, Mobile, 6 October 1866, Patton Official
Correspondence.

a: *The Southern response*

Although the South realized that it was defeated militarily and ruined economically and materially, this could not be admitted in public. Submission to Northern demands, whether from President or Congress, was not the only course open to the South. On the contrary, it was unthinkable and to be resisted at all costs until the political leverage and strength which was still available to the defeated section was exhausted. To a considerable extent this would be dissipated if Southerners were allowed to become despondent and dispirited.

The immediate requirement therefore was for the South to resist so as to prevent the exaggeration and exploitation of its inferiority. 'The North and South are bargaining,' the *Augusta Constitutionalist* was later to observe somewhat euphemistically. 'With the North it is arrogance exacting the last farthing. With the South, it is credulity essaying to save some scraps of honor and property.'[14] The *Constitutionalist* was acutely aware of the truism enunciated by the *Raleigh Sentinel* in June that 'Guaranties are generally demanded by the weaker from the stronger party' and offered an elaboration of the relationship between the sections: 'The grand difficulty between the North and South is briefly this: The North asserts the right of conqueror to impose forcibly what it will upon the South. The South admits the power but denies the right. The North asserts its right to compel the South to endorse its own dishonor. The South rejects this interpretation. The argument of force is omnipotent; the argument of stultification feeble.'[15] So, in this state of mind and with this understanding of the relationship between the contending parties, the South's leadership assessed the terms proposed by Congress in the middle of 1866.

Since the opening days of the Thirty-Ninth Congress when the Southern representatives had been denied admission, the Joint Committee on Reconstruction had held hearings on conditions in the South and had labored to produce an alternative program and set of stipulations to supersede the President's policy. The Committee's recommendation was eventually formulated as an amendment to the U.S. Constitution and publicized on 30 April.

The immediate Southern response to the announcement of the intended amendment was one of abuse and anger. The *Richmond En-*

---

[14]Editorial, *Augusta Constitutionalist*, 10 January 1867.
[15]Editorial, *Raleigh Sentinel*, 14 June 1866; Editorial, *Augusta Constitutionalist*, 31 October 1866.

quirer lambasted it as 'a disgrace to the age we live in, and a disgrace even to the worst men that ever dominated a wretched party, since politics became a trade.'[16] A few months later, after Congress had revised the details of the amendment and, in the process stiffened them, the *Enquirer* protested angrily: 'This is *against nature* – It is demanding an *impossibility*. It is requiring the Southern people to sign and seal the bond of *their own infamy*.'[17] After the November elections which had represented a resounding defeat for the President's conciliatory Southern policy and for his schemes for a National Union coalition and concurrently implied an endorsement of the radical wing of the Republican Party, the *Enquirer* reiterated its position, asserting the Northern politicians 'wilfully kept out of view that the *nature* of the objections of the Southern States to the Amendment rendered it impossible that they could vote for it.'[18] Vehement as the *Enquirer* may have been, the last word in vitriol was reserved for the *Richmond Times* which in May announced that the amendment's provisions were 'black and reeking with the marks of Radical hate, and for the South to touch them would be dishonor, degredation and eternal pollution.'[19] Accordingly by February 1867, the amendment had been defeated in the legislatures of all the States of the Confederacy save Tennessee. Elsewhere in the South, only thirty-three votes were polled on behalf of the amendment.[20] Refusing to be diverted from their initial stance of opposition to ratification, the Confederates were consistent as well as united to a degree never experienced before or afterwards during the post-war period in which reconstruction policy was formulated, 1865–8.

The proposal which provoked so unanimous a response was Congress' alternative to Johnson's restoration program of 1865 and it was presented in the form of an amendment to the U.S. Constitution. Known before ratification as the Howard amendment, and after as the Fourteenth, it consisted of four substantive clauses and an enforcement provision. Of the former, the first section defined United States citizens, and then guaranteed their privileges and immunities and affirmed their rights of due process and equal protection – this was in essence a recapitulation of the Civil Rights Act passed earlier in the year. The

---

[16] Editorial, *Richmond Enquirer*, 30 April 1866.
[17] *Ibid.*, 28 June 1866.
[18] *Ibid.*, 13 November 1866.
[19] Editorial, *Richmond Times*, 21 June 1866.
[20] Edward McPherson, *The Political History of the U.S.*, p. 194.

second clause based representation on population rather than on registered voters which the President had wanted, and offered to the States the alternative of enfranchising males of all races or of receiving a representation in Congress reduced in the proportion that those unenfranchised bore to the total population of the State. Reduction on these terms opened up for the South the possibility of conceding a qualified Negro suffrage since individuals merely and not the whole group of which the individuals formed a part were to be the basis for this assessment. The third stipulation was that those who had sworn an oath of office which had required them to uphold the U.S. Constitution and who had subsequently rebelled or aided in rebellion against the U.S. would be disqualified from office, State as well as Federal. Finally, the amendment guaranteed the inviolability of the United States debt while similar debts incurred by the rebellious States were to be repudiated.

Foremost among the objections of the Confederates to the substance of the amendment were the provisions of the third clause. [T]he principal objection to it is, that it disfranchises the best portion of our citizens in order to place political power in the hands of what are called loyal Radicals of all colors.'[21] In saying this the *New Orleans Times* was articulating the grievances of Southern officialdom. Equally aware of the unacceptibility of the disqualification clause were many Northern Republicans who feared that it would prove an insuperable obstacle to ratification. Among these was Joseph Medill, editor of the *Chicago Tribune*, who told Senator Lyman Trumbull: 'The rebel states will never ratify the 3d. section or agree to the enabling act rendering so many persons ineligible to hold any office.'[22] Southern Unionists also were quick to realize this. *Flake's Bulletin* of Galveston, Texas, observed: 'We do not believe there are none intelligent in [the South], save the old office holders. The truth is the objection to this disqualifying clause is more violent than to that of any other section. It is the greed for office which moves many to oppose the amendment. Old political demagogues cannot retire to the shades of political life gracefully.'[23]

Besides removing the incumbents from office and therefore from the enjoyment of political power, the third clause required a corollary, that is, that others be appointed or elected in their place. Since these

[21] Editorial, *New Orleans Times*, 9 November 1866.
[22] Joseph Medill to Lyman Trumbull, Chicago, 2 May 1866, Trumbull MSS.
[23] Editorial, *Flake's* [Galveston] *Bulletin*, 7 November 1866.

would be Southern opponents of the Confederates and therefore in all likelihood Republicans, the South would be regaining admission to Congress at a very heavy price. Not only would the Confederates be losing power in State and nation but they would actually be handing it over as a gift to their opponents in the South and in Congress. Under these conditions, readmission would be a punishment and a disability and hardly an incentive to ratify. The *Richmond Enquirer* pointed this out by suggesting that the amendment

would make any share of ours in the government, already nearly valueless, entirely so, – nay a snare and a source of mischief. It would diminish our representation, confine it to men who would be at best worthless, and provide for the active inquisition of Congress into our minutest local affairs. We cannot be worsted by rejecting it, – for the ruling faction could conceive of nothing to render our remaining power more worthless, or their own domination more cruelly tyrannical.[24]

There seemed to be no conceivable means of limiting the operation of the clause. Samuel MacGowan, a Congressman-elect from South Carolina, and Benjamin Perry, the State's former Provisional Governor, corresponded about this problem, but MacGowan ended the discussion when he remarked, 'You say we can do without representatives in Congress, but we *must* have a state government. What business have they to *direct*, who shall fill our state offices?'[25]

A further substantive objection to Congress' proposal was that it was presented in the form of an amendment to the Constitution. Since the only protection for the South's minority status lay in the restrictions on national power specified in that document, it could not concur in any efforts to undermine them. Of this the *Richmond Enquirer*, for example, was keenly aware: 'There is but little that is in our power. One thing, however, we can do; we can avoid the fatal mistake of our fathers, so far as the constitutional power of defence has not wholly passed away. We can watch with jealousy and zeal the little that is left. If it avails nothing now, it may be valuable hereafter.'[26] The compact of 1787 had broken down in 1861 and the Union had been destroyed by civil war; the task of reunion in 1865 involved therefore renegotiation of the governmental contract along lines which

[24]Editorial, *Richmond Enquirer*, 29 December 1866.
[25]Samuel MacGowan to Perry, Abbeville, S.C., 21 November 1866, Perry MSS (Ala.).
[26]Editorial, *Richmond Enquirer*, 31 December 1866.

would guarantee permanency and prevent disintegration. Amendments such as Congress contemplated in 1866 would alter considerably and permanently the nature of the American Union. Since the intended revision was not in the South's interest, it had therefore to be resisted. It was on these grounds that Alexander Stephens, the South's leading spokesman in 1866, counselled the rejection of the amendment. 'I was in favor,' he said, 'of the seceding states accepting in good faith the results of the war – the abandonment of African Slavery and the doctrine of secession by force. But I am utterly opposed to these States doing anything as a condition precedent to a restoration to them of all their Rights under the Constitution as it now stands amended.'[27] The letter of the Constitution had been insufficient protection prior to 1861; therefore it would be self-destructive for the South to accept even weaker written guarantees as conditions for reentry five years later.

Offsetting these objectionable features of the Howard amendment, there was however one element, that of choice, which could ease the South's predicament. First of all, the amendment was not mandatory; the South could accept or reject it. Furthermore, within the scope of the second clause, there was another choice – Southern representation in Congress would be reduced if complete Negro suffrage were not implemented, and the South could select whichever alternative it preferred. On these options there was unanimous agreement. The adoption of Negro suffrage was never even debated, nor was the choice over ratification. Instead of considering it as evidence of a Northern desire to consult and gain the assent of the South, the leaders of the defeated section rejected it as an insult and a snare. Jonathan Worth, the Governor of North Carolina, asserted that 'If we are to be degraded we will retain some self-esteem by not making it self-abasement. . . . No Southern State, where the people are free to vote, will adopt it.'[28] And later he embellished his argument, telling Hedrick 'As a conquered people we must submit to such terms as our conquerors shall impose, but no generous man ought to expect us to hasten to the whipping post and invite the lash in advance of condemnation.'[29] The *Jackson Clarion*

[27] Stephens to James R. Randall, editor, *Augusta Constitutionalist*, Augusta, Ga., 2 November 1866, A. H. Stephens MSS. Stephens' reference to 'the Constitution as it now stands amended' had in mind the Thirteenth Amendment which had already altered the Constitution since the war.
[28] Worth to Hedrick, Raleigh, N.C., 4 July 1866, B. S. Hedrick MSS.
[29] Worth to Hedrick, Raleigh, N.C., 1 October 1866, B. S. Hedrick MSS.

advised that Southerners 'should not cooperate in our own humiliation.'[30] Since ratification was optional, the amendment would be refused. Perry explained the situation unmistakably in a letter to the President: 'The Amendment will be unanimously rejected by the Legislature. Worse terms may be imposed by Congress, but they will be *imposed* and not *voluntarily accepted.*'[31]

Acceptance of the Howard amendment was, after all, by no means politically imperative. There was, first of all, no guarantee that readmission would be automatic once a State ratified. It was not even clear what exactly constituted ratification – would it involve all the States or just those currently in Congress? Furthermore, with the kind of choice offered to the South, of acceptance or rejection of a particular set of proposals without the suggestion of alternative plans or penalties, there was minimal incentive towards compliance. As a third influence away from cooperation there was the realization in the South that there still remained sources from which relief might come. Andrew Johnson, the Supreme Court, the Northern electorate, the break-up of the Republican Party, all of these embodied possibilities for deliverance from imminent threats. Until all hopes were extinguished and all alternatives exhausted, the South would resist. This was the feeling of the *Raleigh Sentinel* when it observed, 'But what, if we can get no better, ought we to be guilty of the crime of suicide, or welcome death by imbruing our hands in our own blood? While there is hope of the preservation of the Union – of a Government which cost the blood and treasure of our fathers, let the true men of North Carolina, and of the whole land, manfully resist to the end.'[32]

Until early November Southerners had pinned their hopes on the anticipation that the Republicans would suffer reverses in the Congressional elections. With this possibility in reserve, rejection was a safe course to advocate. Without it, one could assume that the South's tactic might change. But this was not so. After the Republican victory, there was no change of policy in the South, not even the suggestion of it. Instead, the outcome was invariably explained in terms other than of defeat for the South. The *Montgomery Advertiser*, for example, said that 'the result of the elections may probably be placed more to the credit of opposition to the Democrats than to a decided expression of

[30] Editorial, *Jackson Clarion*, 20 June 1866.
[31] Perry to Andrew Johnson, Greenville, S.C., 10 November 1866, Johnson MSS, Series I.
[32] Editorial, *Raleigh Sentinel*, 22 June 1866.

disapprobation of the party of restoration.'[33] Moreover, Southerners believed that the Republican victory could have no influence on a response and course of action intrinsically valid, regardless of external pressures and developments. William A. Graham, the North Carolina Whig, wrote on 6 November, 'I have but little hope, from the elections on the other side of the line, which take place today, but hope to see the Southern States, with unfaltering dignity and firmness, reject the proposed amendment of the Constitution.'[34] And the *Richmond Enquirer* a week earlier argued in similar vein: 'We do not propose to reiterate the reasons which make it *impossible* for the South to adopt the Constitutional amendment; but simply to state that they who expect those reasons to be overruled by the result of an election elsewhere, have taken no pains to understand them.'[35]

Yet, strong though Southern objections to the provisions of the Howard amendment may have been, was there not the possibility of unforeseeable events which might make acceptance more self-interested than a continued refusal? Since the direction of Republican policy at the turn of the year was towards far more severe measures and since the mandate for such proposals had been given in the elections, was it not wiser to swallow the amendment thereby demonstrating good faith and possibly preventing worse evils? Both before and after the elections Southerners did, on occasion, contemplate ratification as a tactic which might avoid worse terms, but very rarely was this line of policy adopted.[36] There were too many arguments against such a course. And they were aired fully during the months when the amendment was under consideration.

In considering the expediency of concession on the amendment, the first obstacle which presented itself was that the South's motives in adopting this course might be misunderstood and purposely misinterpreted. First of all, concession might be construed as an indication of vulnerability. Of this the *Jackson Clarion* was convinced and warned that 'the least symptom of weakness or faltering, the first sign of concession on the part of the South, will add new strength to our enemies to enable them to accomplish their present nefarious purpose, and will

[33] Editorial, *Montgomery Advertiser*, 9 November 1866.
[34] Graham to Swain, Hillsboro, N.C., 6 November 1866, W. A. Graham Collection.
[35] Editorial, *Richmond Enquirer*, 1 November 1866.
[36] These instances will be examined in section (b) of this chapter, pp. 247ff.

encourage them to increase and multiply their abominable demands.'[37] A second fear was that concession might simply provide an unfortunate precedent and offer the opportunity for exacting further guarantees and demands. James L. Orr noted this and proposed: 'Our true policy in my judgement is to assent to no further conditions that are tendered by our conquerors. Magnanimity sound policy and justice all unite in condemning the oppressive and proscriptive course adopted by the radicals towards the South. The more palpably our submission to the laws and constitution of the United States and our acquiescence in the disastrous termination of the war is manifested the more exacting, tyrannical and humiliating to us become their demands.'[38]

There was a fundamental flaw in any policy of concession and compromise. Voluntary acceptance of a set of proposals implied that the demands were not yet so unpalatable that they could not under any circumstances be tolerated. Stiffer terms could therefore be safely demanded by the conquerors. The Republicans, the South felt, were probing to discover where the threshold lay. And even though rejection of the amendment could also be taken as justification for further demands it was believed to be a tactic preferable to a series of consessions the limits of which were difficult to perceive. For the point at which the Republicans would be satisfied with Southern accommodation and capitulation was something which the South, in its turn, did not know and was eager to find out. Was there in fact a point of equilibrium at which the South could capitulate no more and the North could ask no more? If that were so, then at that point a stable settlement could be made. But in this experiment in political logistics the South could not participate. To do so would be disastrous.

The South had to stand firm and reject conciliation; yielding would neither appease nor would it produce stability. 'We have tried the conciliatory policy,' said the *Richmond Times*, 'Let us now try what political pluck will do.'[39] And the *Charleston Daily News* regretted that in dealing with the President the previous year and cooperating with him, 'We have sought to dodge the issue,' which was to confront and resist the Republican Party, in particular its radical wing.[40] Conciliation was a policy which would not, under present circumstances, pay

[37] Editorial, *Jackson Clarion*, 25 October 1866.
[38] Orr to Johnson, Charleston, S.C., 11 November 1866, H. V. Johnson MSS.
[39] Editorial, *Richmond Times*, 27 July 1866.
[40] Editorial, *Charleston Daily News*, 26 November 1866.

dividends. The opposition could not be so disarmed, for 'No half-way ground will satisfy them [the radicals] or the great body of their supporters.'[41] In this comment, the *Raleigh Sentinel* had evidently realized, as had many others in the South, that the goals and needs of the Republicans as a party required from the defeated section more than interim concessions and evidences of good faith.

The details of the needs and intentions of the Republicans were discussed by Benjamin Perry. Writing during November in the *New York Herald*, he argued:

I am sure this constitutional amendment can never be adopted by twenty-six States, and I do not believe the Radical leaders ever expected it would be adopted. Now, if adopted, I am confident that it would not satisfy the malignity and revenge towards the South, or their love of power dishonestly and fraudulently obtained. Nothing will satisfy them but universal negro suffrage and the disfranchisement of all prominent Southern men, who do not act with them in carrying out their nefarious purposes. Their object is to establish the permanent rule of the Radical party, secure the next Presidential election, and exclude Northern Democrats, as well as Southern men, from all influence in government.[42]

Therefore, devices such as the qualified Negro suffrage which Andrew Johnson had suggested to the Provisional Governor of Mississippi in 1865 would be insufficient for the Republicans because it would enfranchise at most a few thousand freedmen. The Howard amendment also would be inadequate since it did not ensure Negro suffrage and therefore would not guarantee Republican control of the South by creating an electorate which could outvote the Confederates. A mandatory and unqualified Negro suffrage, it seemed to most Southern politicians, was a prerequisite for the continued supremacy of the Republican Party, and until that was obtained there would be no stability between the sections. 'Negro suffrage,' said James Orr, 'is to be the pet measure of the approaching session and they may manifest the strength which numbers and nothing else gives them by abrogating all of the State Govts. organised under Johnsons policy and establishing territorial or military governments.'[43] In that case, if the Howard amendment could not guarantee the control over the South and the full vote

[41]Editorial, *Raleigh Sentinel*, 15 September 1866.

[42]Perry to the *New York Herald*, late September 1866, Perry Scrapbooks (Chapel Hill).

[43]Orr to Johnson, Charleston, S.C., 11 November 1866, H. V. Johnson MSS.

of the freedmen which the radical Republicans were convincing the party that it had to obtain, then the amendment was insincere as an offer of final terms and might even be a trap. This was what Samuel MacGowan and Perry believed it to be. 'You are right,' MacGowan told Perry, 'the Scoundrels are not in favor of its passage, and never expected it to be adopted. But they expect to make capital out of our refusal. But without regard to consequences, I say let perdition come first.'[44] All the same, neither they nor other Confederates who saw the amendment in these terms were prepared to urge adoption, even for the amusement of seeing the Republicans hoist by their own petard.

Southern thinking in late 1866 was characterized by a lack of trust in the Republican Party's apparent moderation and by a conviction that measures which were more demanding and which were then being aired in the North would be essential for the survival of the party no matter what seemed to be the current policy or negotiating position. In two separate editorials during November the *Charleston Daily News* explained why negotiation with the Republicans was dangerous. Against the suggestion that it would be 'good sense to anticipate the purposes of that party with respect to us, and disarm it by inflicting its policy on ourselves,' the *Daily News* argued that 'This deduction, however is not logical, and the suggestion we cannot accept. We cannot know, nor do they themselves, what the policy is, or what compliance will content them.'[45] And pursuing this argument further, the editorialist added an observation familiar in the post-war South:

The intelligence of that party would be satisfied with concessions. . . . But the instincts of that party are more truly conservative of its organization and existence. They instruct it that it must have an object to antagonize; that one object of exception removed, it must take another; that the want is not of something we will concede — but of something we cannot concede; and to a party to which this is the motive principle, there is no ground for parley.[46]

If it was not clear either to most Republicans or to the South where Northern demands would cease, this was not merely because of an inner and uncontrollable drive for survival within the Republican Party but because events and interests which the party sought to control were not predictable or easily manipulated. The *Richmond Enquirer* embel-

[44] MacGowan to Perry, Abbeville, S.C., 21 November 1866, Perry MSS (Ala.).
[45] Editorial, *Charleston Daily News*, 20 November 1866.
[46] *Ibid.*, 23 November 1866.

lished the argument by saying in a September editorial, 'The cry for negro suffrage is in the hope that negro suffrage would make the Southern States radical. The opposition to Southern recognition is because the Southern States are *not* radical, and it will last until they become so. It will be impossible to conciliate the obstructionists by a compliance *short of that.*' Yet, the *Enquirer* was quick to point out that, 'Negro suffrage, if it were agreed to, tomorrow, would not satisfy them, because its results would disappoint them. Despite their calculations and figuring, it would not gain them a single Southern State.'[47] As a consequence, the Republicans, urged on by the radicals, would have continually to resort to further devices in order to obtain their political objectives.

In the short run, it was felt, a Southern policy of conciliation involving assent to the amendment would only provide the Republicans with the justification and the means for additional guarantees and methods of control while yielding a voluntary consent to fundamental changes in the Constitution and to the removal from power of those currently in office. Nothing would be achieved, not even the possibility of strengthening the moderates and outmaneuvering the radicals. More astute was a long-term policy based on obstruction and non-cooperation.

This strategy was based on two premises. The first was the knowledge that only with extreme difficulty could the Republicans accomplish a political revolution in the South since social influence and control over the labor force which was mainly black would continue in the possession of the politically powerful and wealthy. This was what was implied in the last section of the *Enquirer* editorial cited a few lines earlier. The second assumption was that the Northern electorate, which was basically desirous of national calm and stability and was unsympathetic to the Negro, would deny the Republicans unlimited scope both in time and in measures for achieving reconstruction. They might well balk even at Negro suffrage since only a handful of the Northern States had conceded this within their own borders. When the Northern electorate refused to vote for radicals and protested against Republican policies, then, and only then, would the South know that the limits of Republican demands had been reached.

Throughout 1866, Southern thinking was therefore infused with a conviction that 'masterly inactivity' was the only viable strategy. In September the *Arkansas Gazette* had decided that the South would be

[47]Editorial, *Richmond Enquirer*, 14 September 1866.

advised to remain outside the Union rather than 'enter, as it were, a new government, on terms so derogative of her rights and self respect. She had better wait until returning reason shall possess the minds of the people of the North, or until Providence, in its own good time, shall offer her some means of escape from the present ills that Fanaticism have [*sic*] imposed on her.'[48] Republican excesses, such as the impeachment of the President or a financial crisis, could speed the reaction, but the South could do nothing. By January 1867 there was still no change in attitude and the *Charleston Mercury* assumed that 'With the Executive and the Judiciary, and a powerful conservative element in the North co-operating with us – our true policy is, to look alone to them; and to stand sternly but patiently by their side, and to fall, if fall we must, in one common ruin with them. This, it appears to us, is the course of wisdom – the course of a decent dignity.'[49] Pessimistic and fatalistic this strategy may have seemed but it was based upon the realistic assumption that the power-relationship between the two sections was so out of balance that until a conservative sentiment manifested itself nothing could be gained from readmission. Therefore it was wiser to wait until the Republicans moderated and the Democrats grew stronger before final terms could be negotiated. If before then, however, a set of terms were forced on the South, then there was no alternative but to comply and hope that they could be undermined in their execution. The difficulty was that while waiting for the reaction against the Republicans' radicalism the South had to welcome extreme terms because the more excessive they were and the quicker they became so, the sooner would the Northern reaction be provoked.

In the fall of 1866 there were observable signs, which Southerners perceived, that they might not have to rely on the reaction. It was conceivable that, if the Howard amendment were refused by the South, the Republican Party might disintegrate before the reaction evolved. It was well-known that the amendment had been formulated only after protracted and intense debate in the councils of the Republican Party, and had been agreed upon as a compromise measure which satisfied the moderates without repelling the radicals. Therefore if the South rejected it and Congress had then to produce an alternative, the delicate balance of forces within the party might be destroyed and disintegration ensue. Reliance on the electoral reaction would then no lon-

[48] Editorial, *Arkansas Gazette*, 22 September 1866.
[49] Editorial, *Charleston Mercury*, 30 January 1867.

ger be necessary, since the same effect would already have been accomplished.

With this in mind, the *Richmond Enquirer* felt confident in arguing that 'it is evident [the Republicans] have staked their very existence as a party upon carrying the amendment. If they fail in that they go to pieces like a broken potter's vessel. And they will fail, for *more than ten States* will certainly reject the amendment.'[50] 'Hence,' argued the *Raleigh Sentinel*, 'the anxiety of Congress, that the Southern States should of their own will relieve that body of the difficulty, by passing the Howard Amendment.'[51] And in January 1867 the *Augusta Constitutionalist* was complacently noting that the *New York Times* had at last realized that the Republican Party had 'arrived at a crisis of its fate, in which advance is perilous but retrogression ruin. This is precisely the ground we have occupied for several months, and the North is to be congratulated upon the discovery.'[52] Southern refusal to ratify had placed the Republican Party in a position riddled with pitfalls and problems.

Needless to say, there was an incompatibility in the two analyses of Northern politics which were current in the Confederate South while the Howard amendment was under consideration. If the amendment represented the only program which could keep the party intact and united, it could not at the same time be a stepping-stone for more radical measures which alone could guarantee the survival of the party and its organization. The amendment could not perform both functions. But in terms of Southern strategy towards the amendment, these contradictions did not need to be squared. Non-ratification was the course chosen, and since it was unclear what exactly was the disposition of forces within the Republican Party there was too much risk and no certain gain in ratifying the amendment in the incalculable hope that worse could thereby be averted. Furthermore, non-ratification would enable the Confederates to remain in office, which would have been precluded by adoption of the amendment. And in the meantime the radical Republicans would force the issue, resulting either in the speedy disintegration of their party because of opposition from Republican conservatives and moderates or else, if this did not occur, in the reaction of the electorate against a Republican Party which was

[50] Editorial, *Richmond Enquirer*, 12 September 1866.
[51] Editorial, *Raleigh Sentinel*, 11 December 1866.
[52] Editorial, *Augusta Constitutionalist*, 22 January 1867.

in the control of radicals and advocated radical measures. Somehow or other, the Republicans would encompass their own ruin.

Newspapers therefore could maintain an air of complacent and unyielding defiance, convinced that time was on their side. In private, however, forebodings of woe were expressed but they were mingled with confidence, so that concession was still not considered.

A letter from Lucius Q. Washington, a Richmond journalist and confidant of Robert M. T. Hunter, demonstrated the mixture of uncertainty, fear and confidence experienced by Southern leaders in the months after Southern rejection of the amendment. Writing from Washington in December at a time when Congress was trying to formulate an alternative policy, he observed:

> Matters are not shaped yet. I think, the Radical leaders will have trouble to determine what to do. It is not supposed they can get two thirds of this Congress for the territorializing policy. But that now is the talk of that party. That policy will startle the country I feel assured. Impeachment is hardly possible. I wish they would try it. . . . The amendment being rejected the problem of 'what next' is a puzzle for the Radicals. The President has a strong position. He is firm & confident. I think the situation grave but am far from despairing.[53]

Anxious about the immediate future yet confident that the right decision had been taken, the Southern leadership awaited passively the outcome of the Republicans' deliberations.

b: *Alternatives to inaction*

Electoral defeat for the Northern conservatives in the fall of 1866 did not force on the South a reappraisal of its policies and strategies. Approaches previously adopted were in no need of revision, it was felt; all that had to be accepted was the realization that one of the props of Southern policy had been weakened and could no longer be expected to achieve much. Andrew Johnson's policy of checking the power of the radicals by a head-on confrontation with Congress had failed. In October after the first series of elections had been completed, the *Richmond Times* was of the opinion that the President 'was powerless to enforce his policy.'[54] Two months later the *Augusta Constitutionalist*

[53]Lucius Q. Washington to Robert M. T. Hunter, Washington, D.C., 11 December 1866, Hunter–Garnett MSS.
[54]Editorial, *Richmond Times*, 11 October 1866.

was admitting that 'nothing, however, can save him but a stroke of fate or a coup d'etat,' so his annual message was tantamount to the 'final testament of a dying gladiator.'[55]

Although Southern newspapers were prepared to acknowledge the eclipse of the President's power, they were not recognizing defeat but rather accepting a setback and focusing attention instead on other more realistic sources of hope and deliverance. The South's course was set and, said the *Richmond Times*, even 'if the President deserts his position (of which determination we have seen no indication, but, on the contrary, his declarations and acts disaffirm any such purpose), we are not ready to eat dirt at the bidding of Northern majorities.'[56] The South's leadership was standing firm regardless of what the President decided to do. All the same it was thought unlikely that he would capitulate until all else had failed and no means of resistance remained. For, after all, his two-year fight with the radicals had, in essence, been over a theoretical difference, not simply politics. Johnson had maintained that reunion and loyalty could be secured only by magnanimity and conciliation which would attract, and then extract, feelings of gratitude and cooperation. Coercion, conditions, and terms, on the other hand, would stifle any latent inclinations towards loyalty. Thus, being a theory rather than mere policy, this could not be rejected once the going became rough; in fact, under those circumstances it was even more vital to cling tenaciously to it.

With the President unlikely to change his course though unable to prevail over the Republicans in Congress, Southerners looked elsewhere for succor. It was of course hoped that the Republicans might destroy themselves as the radicals, now increased in number by the elections, tried to pressure the party into adopting a territorial policy for the South. But from another direction also relief was anticipated in December 1866. Just before Christmas, the Supreme Court handed down its decision in the Ex parte Milligan case; this decision struck at military jurisdiction in the South and undermined contemplated radical attempts to treat the Southern States as territories because it stipulated that martial law and military courts could not exist where civil courts were open and functioning without hindrance. Lucius Q. Washington wrote to Hunter on 20 December full of enthusiasm: 'I see or think I see signs the U.S. Supreme Court will oppose the

---

[55] Editorial, *Augusta Constitutionalist*, 5 December 1866.
[56] Editorial, *Richmond Times*, 9 October 1866.

radicals and if so victory is certain. They are beginning to exhibit independence.'[57] For Benjamin Perry this development indicated that the clouds were breaking and he told James Orr that although 'The prospect is gloomy and getting darker as to Federal policy [,] But with the President and the Court against them I think Congress will be checkmated. What can they do without the army and in opposition to the united purpose of the South?'[58] And there was yet another institution which stood in the way of the radicals. Although unsuccessful in the 1866 elections, the Democratic Party was still a major force in Northern politics and its official position on the Southern question synchronized with the stance adopted by the Confederates. With the exception of the *Chicago Times* which soon after the November elections broke rank and advised Southern acquiescence in qualified suffrage, the Democrats urged the South to reject the amendment. To them a reduced, or Republican, representation for the South in Congress was respectively of little or no benefit. Therefore they also had, as the *New York World* put it, 'far more to gain by preserving the Constitution in its entirety, than by a minority representation in Congress. A congressional minority can carry no measure; it can interpose no effectual protection. . . . The only protection remaining to minorities is the Constitution.'[59]

With these forces arranged on its side, the Confederate leadership felt confident in its risky strategy of resistance to the Howard amendment. 'Masterly inactivity' had been implicit in the South's stance since the end of the war; now it was explicit and avowed. Typical of the mood and the strategy prevailing at the end of 1866 were an editorial in the *Jackson Clarion* and the message of Governor Jenkins of Georgia. The *Clarion* advised the South to follow the suggestions of the *New York World* and the *Baltimore Gazette*, 'accepting nothing, rejecting nothing, recognizing no right of the North to enact from us more than has already been conceded, performing no act that might be construed into an assent to Northern dominion, and quietly abide [*sic*] our time.'[60] Likewise, Jenkins, after warning that 'The pending

---

[57]L. Q. Washington to Hunter, Washington, D.C., 20 December 1866, Hunter–Garnett MSS.

[58]Perry to Orr, Greenville, S.C., 29 December 1866, Orr Official Correspondence.

[59]Editorial, *New York World*, 25 October 1866, reprinted in *Atlanta Intelligencer*, 30 October 1866.

[60]Editorial, *Jackson Clarion*, 6 November 1866. The *Clarion* actually changed its

issue may not find a very early solution' and that the South must 'pass through an ordeal thoroughly adapted "to try men's souls,"' demanded: 'we must be true to ourselves, to those who, though not of us, are fighting our battles, and to the country; we must steadily and calmly pursue the course upon which we have started, neither betrayed into error by false representations of the malignant and consequently injurious suspicions of the credulous; nor yielding to humiliating demands, against which justice exclaims, and manhood revolts.' And if that were persevered in, the South would 'in time, live down both detraction and delusion, and achieve a moral victory, far more ennobling and enduring than any triumph of mere force.'[61]

Behind this consensus on the broad policy to be pursued, there was emerging in some quarters a divergent approach towards the North. Ever since the war there had been those who had assumed that the North possessed a different value-system and priorities and that to try to conciliate these was fruitless and self-destructive. Very often secessionists in 1861, these men had been averse to calculating the favorable effect on the North of Southern action. Irreconcilable and defiant, they were frequently the 'Rip Van Winkles' of the 1865 conventions. By late 1866, after being passed over in the elections to Congress and in the nominations to the Philadelphia convention, they began to urge a policy which appeared to be conciliatory. From the editorial columns of the formerly secessionist *Charleston Daily News*, there emerged a line of argument, widely noticed in North and South, called the 'New Southern Spirit.'[62] It endorsed the decision not to ratify the Howard amendment, but nevertheless warned against an unthinking acceptance of the policy of 'masterly inactivity' based and grounded as that was on the assumption that, in a short time, the conservative reaction would develop in the North and with it the South would be saved and swept into power.[63] The beliefs of those, mainly the anti-secessionists, who had dominated Southern politics since the war, had to be exposed

mind and rejected 'masterly inactivity' in early December, editorial, 9 December 1866.

[61] Charles J. Jenkins, Annual Message, 1 November 1866, Executive Minutes, Jenkins Official Correspondence.

[62] For the delineation of this policy see *Charleston Daily News*, editorials on 13, 16, 19, 20, 23, 26 November and 4 and 7 December 1866.

[63] Curiously the policy was frequently interpreted as being submissive and acquiescent in the Howard amendment, yet never was capitulation to or conciliation of the Republicans suggested, and certainly adoption of the amendment was never

as fallacious. It was not simply the temporary and unnatural dominance of Northern politics by abolitionists and radicals which kept sectional hostility and differences alive; there was more to sectionalism than the institution of slavery. Therefore, instead of relying totally on the Northern conservatives and on outmoded constitutional interpretations, the Confederate States were advised to begin realizing that at some point, when terms were clear and final, they would have to submit to the demands of that section which was economically and politically in the ascendant and whose populace endorsed radical Republicanism, even if only as a curb on the South.

This emergent tendency in Southern political thinking lay beneath the surface during the winter of 1866 and it was to emerge as a dominant impulse only in the initial reactions of the South to the Reconstruction Act of March 1867. Before that, however, there occurred from time to time initiatives for compromise on the amendment which seemed to be premature manifestations of the accommodating features of the 'New Southern Spirit.' Acceptance of, or compromise on, the amendment had no part in the *Daily News*' proposition, however. But wherever these moves were discerned, they were met with the scorn and denial of a Confederate leadership which was united on the issue. Nevertheless, there were a number of developments along these lines and they demonstrated that there was, on the one hand, an uneasiness among the Confederates lest their ranks be in any way broken and 'masterly inactivity' scuttled by unilateral overtures to the Republicans and, on the other, an evident anxiety about the wisdom of rejecting so unequivocally a measure which at a later date might regretfully be regarded as moderate.

Nearly every State legislature in the South referred the amendment to its Committee on Federal Relations so that there was never a full-dress debate on the issue, and this no doubt deprived whatever opposition existed of the chance to challenge the decision not to ratify. In three States, however, the Governor recommended ratification but even here the legislature's verdict was as crushing as elsewhere. More moderate and conciliatory than their legislatures, the war-time Union Governors of Virginia, Louisiana and Arkansas urged that the amendment should be endorsed and the justification for this was usually the

contemplated. Often Northerners saw more in the 'new spirit' than was really there and Southern advocates of 'masterly inactivity' chose to see more in order to disparage the suggestion.

only one that would convince the legislators, expediency and the wisdom of averting worse terms.[64] But the ranks held firm, only three votes in Arkansas and one in Virginia being cast for the Governor's proposal. In fact, in Louisiana's case, it was the very fact of Governor Wells' recommending it that considerably contributed to the proposition's defeat, the *New Orleans Times*, hardly an extreme paper, commenting gleefully, 'A Governor without a single supporter in the legislature is without precedent in the political annals of this country.'[65]

Others who as much as hinted at ratification were quickly denigrated or dismissed. The *Charleston Daily News*' new policy was frequently referred to as if it recommended ratification, which of course it did not, and consequently was dismissed contemptuously as defeatist and submissive. When 'Willoughby,' the *Augusta Constitutionalist*'s New York correspondent, suggested in the fall that the South should cease relying on Johnson and the Northern conservatives and instead 'make terms with those who have the power,' his editors very quickly clarified the newspaper's position and assured readers that this was not its policy.[66] Similar treatment was accorded the remark of the Unionist, Joseph Segar, a Senator-elect from Virginia, that the Virginia assembly might adopt the amendment if Congress made it clear that these were its final terms for readmission. This 'absurd story' was vehemently denied by the *Richmond Times*; after all it was tantamount to ingratitude to the Confederate dead, it would involve a risky bargain with the unreliable radicals, and it would scatter the ranks of the Northern conservatives.[67]

On two occasions rumors flew southward that the President was even considering capitulation. In mid-December about the time of

[64] All three States had been reorganized under schemes different from the Johnson program. Narrowly based on a restricted electorate which had excluded the leading Confederates, these State governments were weak and faced by immense opposition both in the legislature and outside it. Arkansas and Louisiana had been reorganized, while the war still raged, under the Lincoln Ten Per Cent Plan, and in Virginia the Pierpont government, which had functioned during the war behind Federal lines in Alexandria, was reinstalled by a proclamation of Andrew Johnson in early May 1865. Given the votes it was apparent that the mood and composition of these assemblies was by 1866 very similar to those under the Johnson scheme.

[65] Editorial, *New Orleans Times*, 8 February 1867.

[66] 'Willoughby,' New York correspondent, 27 September 1866, *Augusta Constitutionalist*, 4 October 1866.

[67] *Richmond Times*, 25 December 1866.

Segar's announcement the *Cincinnati Gazette* printed a report that at an interview with the radical Ohio Congressman, Benjamin Eggleston, the President had 'repeated the hope that the South would be admitted to representation on the adoption of the amendment.' The propriety or otherwise of the conditions in the amendment, he said, it was useless to discuss further; 'It had been agreed upon, and all he could now ask was the guarantee that reconstruction on that basis should be faithfully kept by the party that had offered it.'[68] This story was rarely published in the Southern press, but where it was, as in the *Richmond Times*, there immediately followed a denial of the authenticity of the President's views which was substantiated by information received from reliable sources that the supposed hour-long interview had been in actuality a brief five minute encounter.[69] More worrisome and less easy to discredit was the news that Colonel T. C. Weatherly, a State Senator from South Carolina, was on a mission to the White House during the Christmas vacation. Rumors flew that he intended to discuss compliance with the amendment. And not until after his interview were fears allayed by the information, first, that he had gone to discover precisely what might be the outcome once South Carolina had rejected the amendment and, second, that the President had urged the Southern States to 'remain firm in their position . . . and steadfastly reject it,' though, he hoped, 'being guarded in their reasons assigned for its rejection.'[70]

Rejection of the amendment might be assumed but there was still concern that it would perhaps be wise if some degree of conciliation were manifested or attempted. In Texas where the legislature was considering the amendment, John H. Reagan suggested to Governor Throckmorton that the concession of equal legal rights, including unrestricted testimony, and equal taxation, even an impartial suffrage, would help to convince Congress that, although refusing to endorse the amendment, Texas could be trusted to deal justly with the freedmen. The suggestion was forwarded to Johnson, who replied that he

---

[68] Interview between President Johnson and Benjamin Eggleston, 22 December 1866, in *Richmond Times*, 28 December 1866 and in *Flake's Bulletin*, 1 January 1867.

[69] *Richmond Times*, 29 December 1866.

[70] The explanation of Weatherly's motivation and his authority for going to Washington can be found in *Charleston Courier*, 14 January 1867. Interview between Johnson and Col. T. C. Weatherly, reported by 'Leo,' the paper's Washington correspondent, in *Charleston Courier*, 21 December 1866.

had 'nothing to suggest' except that 'all laws, including Civil rights' be made 'as complete as possible, so as to extend equal and exact justice to all persons without regard to color, if it has not been done.' The legislature, however, ignored the President's advice which Throckmorton had embodied in his message of 31 October.[71] If they did not comply with Southern wishes, the President's promptings were given short shrift.

Also treated with little respect were two other propositions which were raised as possible indices of Southern reasonableness and as devices for causing the Republicans to pause and reconsider the necessity for the amendment. The first of these was proposed by three Southern newspapers, John Forsyth's *Mobile Register*, the *Memphis Bulletin*, and Robert McKee's *Selma Times*. Following the lead of the *Chicago Times*, they proposed that the South should offer some sort of impartial qualified suffrage.[72] More frequently discussed was a quid pro quo involving suffrage and amnesty. But even when the suffrage was qualified and the amnesty universal, it was thought to be unacceptable by the unyielding advocates of non-ratification and 'masterly inactivity.' In the midst of a public debate in the *New York Herald* with Benjamin Perry, Charles Woodward, Pennsylvania's Democratic Chief Justice, suggested a compromise short of the amendment in just these terms. Perry rejected the possibility, saying that a suffrage qualified by education and property like the one Woodward proposed would exclude perhaps one-fifth of the whites already enfranchised and would add only a few Negroes; and this would undoubtedly fail to satisfy the Republicans in Congress. Moreover, it was no bargain, he said, because 'almost everyone has been pardoned.' Of course if the suffrage and amnesty were both universal, it would be rejected by the

---

[71] John H. Reagan to Governor James W. Throckmorton, Palestine, Tex., 12 October 1866, in *Flake's Bulletin*, 30 October 1866; Throckmorton to Johnson, Austin, 29 October 1866, Johnson MSS, Series II; Throckmorton, Message to the Legislature, 31 October 1866, in *Flake's Bulletin*, 7 November 1866. For other contacts with the White House at this time as well as for this, see Claude Elliott, *Leathercoat – The Life and Times of a Texas Patriot, James W. Throckmorton* (San Antonio: Standard Printing Co., 1928), chap. VII. Throckmorton was trying to get the President to remove the U.S. troops from central Texas where they were interfering in black–white affairs and have them stationed on the frontier where Indians were supposedly more in need of control and supervision.

[72] These are cited in *Flake's Bulletin*, 18 November 1866. The *Jackson Clarion*, 1 November 1866, listed other newspapers whose names the *New York Post* had collected.

South because of the suffrage proposition, and would be unacceptable to the North since it would merely restore and legitimize the old politicians and reward them with what might well be pliable Negro votes.[73] Seeming to embody the ingredients for a mutually satisfactory settlement and blending so simply mercy with justice, proposals based on the interrelation between amnesty and suffrage were continually suggested throughout the early years of Reconstruction, yet just as regularly were they rejected as unsatisfactory.[74]

In late 1866, however, this kind of adjustment appeared to be the only hope for producing a settlement which would satisfy moderate Republicans and Southern Unionists and prevent both of them from having reluctantly to align themselves with the radicals and the advocates of 'masterly inactivity' respectively. Therefore the scheme was to be more persistently advocated than its practicability warranted.

More than most Republican moderates in the North, Salmon P. Chase, the Chief Justice and former Secretary of the Treasury, was acutely aware that the initiative was slipping from their grasp. This meant not only that Chase himself might be eliminated from consideration as the next Republican Presidential nominee but that a sectional settlement incorporating a degree of mutuality would thenceforth be impossible. Accordingly on 15 November he visited the White House and suggested that the President reconsider his stand on the amendment and urge the South to ratify. If he found that impossible or impolitic, then Chase recommended that the amendment's controversial second and third clauses be altered and universal suffrage and universal amnesty substituted instead.[75] Simultaneously, Chase was working to produce evidence that the South could respond to overtures such as he had outlined. He was encouraged in this initiative by word from the Unionist, Robert A. Hill, a Federal judge and confidant in

[73] Charles Woodward to Perry, 23 November 1866, Perry MSS (Ala.); Perry to Woodward, Columbia, S.C., 30 November 1866, Scrapbooks, Perry MSS (Chapel Hill). Both were press-cuttings in Perry Collections.

[74] Editorials, *New Orleans Times*, 20 November 1866 and *Jackson Clarion*, 24 November 1866. *Flake's Bulletin*, the Texas Unionist paper, pointed out the danger of universal amnesty and suffrage in an editorial, 1 December 1866. Universal amnesty and suffrage was the pet-scheme of Horace Greeley after it had been proposed in precise terms to the Joint Committee on Reconstruction early in 1866 by Senator William M. Stewart of Nevada. It had been rejected by the Joint Committee for the reason stated in the text.

[75] *New York Tribune*, 19 November 1866, reprinted in *New Orleans Times*, 24 November 1866.

Mississippi, that an assurance that the amendment was final would produce reconsideration, especially if provision were also made for removal of the vital third clause disqualifying existing officeholders.[76] Also encouraging were the observations concerning affairs in Alabama submitted to the Chief Justice on 27 November by Wager Swayne, the son of Chase's colleague, Justice Noah Swayne, who was serving as commander of the U.S. forces in that State. Telling Chase that 'a night attack is sometimes very useful. Please excuse this shot if it is fired in the dark,' Wager Swayne explained that, although the Alabama legislature had adjourned late in November without taking action on the amendment, there were indications that sentiment had moderated during the course of the session and 'at the close of the recess if it is plain that the amendment is a finality, and the only one, it will probably be ratified.' Fearing that possibly he was being a little too optimistic, Swayne retracted with the observation that 'there is a quite general and somewhat outspoken preference for immediate suffrage, with a more general amnesty. The proposition of Mr. Stewart last winter in the Senate, has been concurred in in my hearing here, as generally, and by men locally of as much prominence, as constituted its endorsement in Washington last winter.'[77]

A few days later Chase replied but indicated that he had decided that the initiative should be aimed at securing ratification of the amendment. Swayne had also come to the same conclusion and explained that 'The rapid growth of purpose to enforce at all hazards the Congressional plan of reconstruction, its power and the measures proposed to that end, made an impression here, which made it seem to many of us wise to attempt immediate ratification.'[78] So, with the aid of Governor Robert M. Patton, a moderate who had previously concerned himself more with the State's finances and economic development than with national politics, Swayne proceeded with the intended maneuver. On 6 December, Patton sent in a message reversing his decision of 12 November and advising ratification. His argument was based

---

[76] Robert A. Hill to Chase, Jacinto, Miss., 14 November 1866, Chase MSS. Senator-elect James L. Alcorn of Mississippi later suggested a similar proposal in an open letter reported in *Jackson Clarion*, 29 January 1867.

[77] General Wager Swayne to Chase, Montgomery, 27 November 1866, Chase MSS. Stewart, the Senator from Nevada, had proposed universal suffrage and amnesty but the Joint Committee on Reconstruction had rejected it after only brief consideration.

[78] Swayne to Chase, Montgomery, 10 December 1866, Chase MSS.

purely on expediency, not the merits of the amendment. Even so Patton felt compelled to provide insurance. 'Should you see fit to ratify it,' he told the legislature, 'and our full representation should follow, we may trust to time, and the influence of our representatives to mitigate its harshness. If, on the other hand, admission be delayed, the warning to our sister States may be relied upon to prevent that concurrence on their part which alone can give the measure practical effect.'[79]

The message, Swayne recounted 'produced a marked sensation but no sensible recoil. That night we thought we should succeed, we seemed to be in full possession of the Senate.' The situation was nevertheless very delicate. Swayne felt that 'so vivid was the memory of '60–'61' and so fearful was the prospect of worse measures from Congress, that the legislators would be inclined to concede. This was despite their awareness that 'the people, ignorant, proud, and without mail facilities was not yet up to the necessity, and would be severe upon whoever should act without consulting them.' This, however, was not to be. In the Senate, State Senator Barnes announced that a dispatch had been sent to Governor Parsons, who was in Washington and enjoyed the President's confidences, asking counsel. And Swayne explained, 'It came, emphatic that the Amendment be at once rejected, and that the Legislature meet again in January. I don't believe this had the inspiration of the President, yet it was openly asserted it had. The cry was raised "we can't desert *our* President," and quite soon it was plain that a vote was unavoidable, and that the measure was lost.'[80]

During the Christmas recess, Patton, persevering in what Swayne called 'the new direction,' stumped his constituency in North Alabama and traveled to Washington and New York. From the capital he received overwhelming advice 'to Ratify the Amendment, as a finality' but within his own State there was caution and criticism.[81] Walter H. Crenshaw, the President of the Senate whom Patton had invited to accompany him North, warned that 'this undertaking . . . may cause the Republican party to be more exacting in their demands than they otherwise would.' 'The main purpose,' he continued, 'would be to obtain as mild terms as possible as a finality, and some guarantee that

[79]Robert M. Patton, Message, 6 December 1866, in *Montgomery Advertiser*, 7 December 1866.
[80]Swayne to Chase, Montgomery, 10 December 1866, Chase MSS.
[81]Patton to D. L. Dalton, his personal secretary, New York City, 28 December 1866, Patton Official Correspondence.

no further demands would be made. We should by no means represent that our people are ready to assent to any proposition. Superior power will make them submit to any demand, but it will only be because they feel their inability to prevent its imposition. If possible obtain as a finality, some better terms than the Constitutional Amendment. I do not think our refusal to ratify the Amendment will result in the abrogation of our State Government.' Instead Crenshaw felt Congress would keep the State from representation until after the 1 868 election and this was preferable to adopting the amendment.[82]

Before traveling to Alabama in December, Lewis Parsons advised complete inaction not because, as Crenshaw argued, concession was no guarantee of settlement, but because resistance and non-cooperation alone could bring about the defeat of the radicals. Already, because of Southern non-ratification, the radicals were being forced to extreme lengths and, for their intended measure which was even less satisfactory to the South than the amendment, 'It is thought and believed by our most intelligent friends, they cannot get 2/3 – or 3 5 if there is a full attendance.' Confidently, Parsons pointed out that 'The President is firm and determined it is said and I think he will yet be able to check the enemies of the Constitution in their mad efforts to preserve their own power and ascendancy—for this is all there is of it. They would not make any objection if they thought we could vote for their candidate in 1 868. I hope all the Southern states will stand firmly by the President as long as he stands by the Constitution.' And he concluded phlegmatically, 'It will be time enough for us to consider what else we ought to do when we find there is no hope of securing our rights in that way.'[83]

In the meantime, Patton, undeterred, decided to resubmit the amendment. He had been encouraged by news of the Eggleston interview and of Joseph Segar's announcement, and these offset unpromising reports from Salem Dutcher, the former editor of the *Augusta Constitutionalist*, that there was little disposition in Georgia to follow up Patton's initiative.[84] So, with the issue still in the balance, the legisla-

---

[82]Walter H. Crenshaw to Patton, Greenville, Ala., 10 December 1866, Patton Official Correspondence.

[83]Parsons to Patton, Washington, D.C., 17 December 1866, Patton Official Correspondence.

[84]Salem Dutcher to Patton, Augusta, Ga., 11 January 1867, Patton Official Correspondence. Dutcher had been forced to resign the editorship because both before and after the Philadelphia convention he had been skeptical and opposed

ture prepared to vote on 18 January. This time, Parsons in Montgomery sought an unequivocal verdict from the President, and it came. 'What possible good can be attained by reconsidering the constitutional amendment?' was the Presidential rebuke: 'I know of none in the present position of affairs. I do not believe that the people of the whole country will sustain any set of individuals in attempts to change the whole character of our Government, by enabling acts or otherwise.'[85]

The Patton–Swayne–Chase attempt to create a fissure in the ranks of the exponents of 'masterly inactivity' had been foiled. The President had moved forthrightly and speedily to nip this movement in the bud not simply because of a fear that Southern unity might be endangered but also because he and some of his Southern aides were contemplating a move of their own diametrically opposed to conciliation and in furtherance of their strategy of resistance and confrontation.

On 14 December the President had met with Marvin and Parsons, and then a week later they, along with Sharkey, Congressman Foster of Alabama, and the two Texas Senators, met at Willard's Hotel to arrange, at the President's request, for all Southern Congressmen to gather in Washington on 20 January 1867. But on ascertaining that an insufficient number of them would be there when the Thirty-Ninth Congress convened for its final session, this precise project was abandoned.[86] The general scheme that was behind this move was, however, retained; the only difference would be in the personnel involved. Journeying to Washington in the New Year were a number of Southerners. From North Carolina, a delegation, consisting of the Governor, Thomas Ruffin and David L. Swain, came to protest General Sickles'

to Southern participation. His policy had been based on a lack of confidence in the Northern conservatives and their imminent 'reaction.' Dutcher was therefore a victim of the growing orthodoxy of 'masterly inactivity' and its corollary, reliance on the 'reaction.'

[85] Parsons to Johnson, Montgomery, 17 January 1867 and Johnson to Parsons, Washington, D.C., 17 January 1867, both in McPherson, *The Political History of the U.S.*, pp. 352–3. Later, on 8 February 1868, when he was testifying before the Senate Judicial Committee, Parsons said that Johnson had given no advice or counsel to himself or anyone else regarding the amendment, in *Gettysburg Star and Sentinel*, 8 April 1868, in Edward McPherson MSS. A copy of the telegram from the President is nevertheless in the Records of the Office of the Secretary of War, microcopy 473, reel 1.

[86] *New Orleans Times*, 15 December 1866; O. M. Roberts, 'The Experience of an Unrecognized Senator,' *Texas State Historical Quarterly*, July 1908, p. 99.

General Order No. 15 which prohibited corporal punishment in the Carolinas.[87] Also from that State was a bipartisan broad-based commission selected by Governor Worth to present to Republican Congressmen evidence to counter what they considered to be the misrepresentations of affairs in North Carolina being purveyed by Holden, John Pool and others.[88] James L. Orr, South Carolina's Governor, also came, probably in connexion with the Sickles Order, but not accompanied by Jenkins of Georgia as he had hoped because the latter 'very much question[ed] whether anything would be gained by negotiation or conference with the radicals.'[89] Already in Washington, of course, were Sharkey, Parsons, and Marvin who had all remained in the capital ever since they had presented their Senatorial credentials in December 1865. In close contact with the President they acted as his unofficial advisers and liaison with the Southern States.

As a result of their presence and action in Washington during late January and early February there emerged what came to be known as the North Carolina Plan. Consisting of two parts, the plan proposed, first, an amendment to the United States Constitution, roughly a reiteration of the Howard amendment but eliminating the disqualification provision and adding a clause declaring the Union perpetual, and then, second, an amendment to each State constitution embodying a suffrage requirement, stringently qualified by property and educational prerequisites and excluding none who had previously possessed the vote.[90]

The provisions of the proposal clearly indicated that it fell short of the amendment, since it incorporated a qualified impartial suffrage and excluded any Confederate disqualification, though it did not go so far as to provide for universal amnesty. All the same, it could be said, in the measure's behalf, that it was a Southern initiative and concession in response to the Howard proposal which was unacceptable to the Confederate States. It was as the latter, an attempt to arrive at a

[87] Richard L. Zuber, *Jonathan Worth: A Biography of a Southern Unionist* (Chapel Hill: University of North Carolina Press, 1965), pp. 246–7.

[88] *Ibid.*, pp. 246–52. The commission consisted of Augustus S. Merrimon, Lewis Hanes, Bedford Brown, Nathaniel Boyden, Patrick H. Winston, and James M. Leach. Anti-secessionists and secessionists, Whigs and Democrats were all included.

[89] Jenkins to Orr, Atlanta, 26 December 1866, Orr Official Correspondence.

[90] *New York Times*, 5 February 1867.

mutually acceptable compromise, that the *New York Times* reported the plan on 5 February, the day it was announced: 'The aim of the deliberations of these gentlemen [Sharkey, Orr, Marvin, Parsons, Worth and the President] has been to agree upon some measure as a basis of reconciliation, which will be adopted by the Southern people, meet the views of the President, and at the same time receive the approval of the majority in Congress.'[91] And there were a number who were involved in the formulation of the plan or who were to have a hand in the attempt to get it adopted who also believed it to be a compromise. Bedford Brown and Nathaniel Boyden who were on the North Carolina commission reported that they felt that 'it would be dangerous to the integrity of their party, as a mere party move' for the Republicans to proceed beyond the Howard amendment and they agreed with Lewis Hanes, another member, who, after meeting with Congressmen, told Graham, 'I feel quite sure that the *present* Congress will not pass any law to reorganize the State governments of the South. All the more moderate republicans look upon it as a most dangerous experiment, and not to be adopted except as a *last* resort. One thing they are all determined upon, and that is *impartial* suffrage.'[92] Hanes consequently hailed the North Carolina Plan as 'A plan of pacification and "reconstruction"' which 'I feel confident, cannot be refused by Congress. The Republican party cannot preserve its unity in opposition to it. This, many radicals admitted to us in conversation with them.'[93]

Also in agreement with this assessment were Lucius Q. Washington and Howell Cobb who were in the capital and active. The Virginian, who had given up all hope of relief from the President or the Northern conservatives, reported to Robert M. T. Hunter that Cobb 'will agree readily to the North Carolina Plan—Orr's. His idea is that the South is in the most imminent peril, in danger of utter ruin and yet the people are unconscious of it. I fully concur simply because the opposition are cowed and the President who ought to lead them irresolute and inactive—one who drifts. Cobb is anxious for our people to do something, and we struck out to-day a plan for getting the Radicals, and our men in

[91] *Ibid.*
[92] Bedford Brown and James M. Leach to Worth, Washington, D.C., 13 January 1867, Worth MSS; Lewis Hanes to Worth, Washington, D.C., 20 January 1867, Worth MSS.
[93] Lewis Hanes to Graham, Washington, D.C., 4 February 1867, W. A. Graham Collection.

position to meet soon in Conference.'[94] What that plan was exactly was not clear but presumably it was a procedural one to arrange negotiations on the basis of the North Carolina proposal. The man whose name Washington had connected with the Southern formula, James L. Orr, also considered it to be a compromise. Lamenting, later, after its failure, that North Carolina, the first State to which it was submitted for ratification, had not acted with sufficient speed and enthusiasm, Orr admitted to Alexander Stephens that, but for that, 'I am satisfied it wd have been adopted substantially by Congress as a basis of final settlement.' His hopes for this were high, he explained, because 'My conferences, with moderate radicals satisfied me that there was a sufficient number of them, favorable to less violent measures than proposed by [Congressman Thaddeus] Stevens, to have defeated the extremists.'[95]

This kind of strategy was a departure from 'masterly inactivity;' it involved negotiation, compromise and an offer to the Republicans of a way out of their difficulties as well as a means for saving the South from possible worse terms. But other protagonists of the North Carolina Plan, essentially those who had initiated the move, regarded it as a continuation of 'masterly inactivity' and confrontation. On 3 February, William L. Sharkey wrote about the scheme to his successor, Benjamin Humphreys. He explained that 'The President thinks if these propositions are presented by the South they will break up the [Republican] party. He approves them and desires their adoption.' And earlier in the letter Sharkey had indicated his own view which was that 'the miserable party that is in power is relentless and vindictive towards us, and our only [hope is] to try and bring about a diversion in their ranks.'[96] A slightly different purpose for the plan was suggested by Lewis Parsons, who instructed Governor Patton that 'If this plan, which originated with N.C. should be adopted by that State, and Ala. and Miss. will do likewise, altho the Radicals may and probably will reject it, it will put our friends on much better ground for ultimate success.'[97]

[94]L. Q. Washington to Hunter, Washington, D.C, 15 February 1867, Hunter–Garnett MSS.
[95]Orr to Stephens, Columbia, S.C., 21 February 1867, A. H. Stephens MSS.
[96]Sharkey to Humphreys, Washington, D.C., 3 February 1867, Humphreys MSS.
[97]Parsons to Patton, Washington, D.C., 9 February 1867, Patton Official Correspondence.

As far as the proponents of the plan were concerned, there was clearly a divergence in intention. By one group, it was believed that a positive and conciliatory proposal from the previously passive South might produce an accommodating response from the moderate Republicans which would result in a settlement favorable to the South and satisfactory to the moderates. From the other, a more aggressive intent could be discerned. The presentation of a proposal by the South would cause a crisis within the party's ranks, with the result that the radicals would be discredited and, it was hoped, forced into silence. In effect, both groups were in agreement that the radicals should be stalled and the moderates strengthened by the Southern initiative, but their motivation and assumptions differed, conciliation and settlement contrasting vividly with antagonism and the opposition's disruption.

Yet although intentions differed, so drastically in fact that if there had been further bargaining on the proposal the Southerners would have been hopelessly split, the outcome of the initiative as far as it went was the same for both factions. For even if it had been proposed as a compromise in good faith, the fact was that the Republican Party was agreed in early 1867 that no settlement short of the Howard amendment was possible. Those Southerners in Washington who felt that the moderates could agree to impartial suffrage and no disqualification had simply read the signs inaccurately.[98] By February the moderate Republicans had come to accept the necessity of a mandatory Negro suffrage and a more extensive reorganization of Southern government and politics than the Fourteenth amendment had envisaged. And Congress was involved in the preparation of such a scheme when the North Carolina Plan was announced. Rather than concerning themselves with measures less demanding than the amendment, the Republicans were moving beyond it and were engaged in a violent intra-party

---

[98] Some Republican Congressmen formed the Wentworth Committee to talk with the President about compromise. At the Metropolitan Club in Washington on 13 February, General George Este and William W. Warden, two of Johnson's aides, met thirty to forty Congressmen, moderates mainly, from about eight States. The Johnson men proposed the Howard amendment and impartial suffrage, the Congressmen the amendment and universal suffrage (i.e. the Blaine amendment to the later Reconstruction Act of March). On 14 February after Johnson met the Congressmen himself, he made it clear that neither he nor the South could accept a mandatory universal suffrage, and the negotiation collapsed. See 'Leo,' Washington correspondent, 16 and 17 February, in *Charleston Courier*, 20 February 1867. Also *Richmond Times*, 19 February 1867.

dispute over how far beyond they should go. Accordingly, whether intended as a compromise or as a provocation, the plan would cause immense difficulty and division if it were seriously considered by the Republicans. And so it was never so much as discussed.

And from the South the response was also consensual. At first there had been a disposition to consider the proposition, since it was after all a proposal made by leading Southerners with the approval of the President. The *Sentinel* and the *Enquirer* discussed the scheme, and so did the Mississippi and North Carolina legislative committees on Federal Relations. But both concluded, as did the *Atlanta Intelligencer*, that unless Congress could guarantee that the North Carolina Plan would be its final terms, the States would be advised to take no action.[99] In any case, there was little enthusiasm. In North Carolina where the Plan was to be initiated, the State Treasurer reported that '*Inter nos* Hanes and Boyden etc. could not get our Assembly to adopt the Dixon amendment,' and Worth admitted that once [Thaddeus] Stevens' military bill had been introduced in Congress on 7 February, 'our concession would be so insignificant, that it would subject us to ridicule and contempt.'[100]

Elsewhere there was universal condemnation of what appeared to be an attempt at settlement and the rejection of 'masterly inactivity.' Governor Humphreys retorted to Sharkey's request that Mississippi consider the plan, 'I have no recommendation to make on these propositions, as I disapprove them entirely.'[101] And reasons for this reaction were offered in abundance in the press. The general drift of the argument being that 'There is a weakness in useless effort truly pitiable; there is a vigor in silence truly august,' for the South could do nothing until Congress admitted the finality of its terms.[102] Moreover there were dangers in efforts at conciliation. The *Charleston Mercury*,

[99] Editorial, *Raleigh Sentinel*, 4 February 1867 and *Richmond Enquirer*, 4 February 1867; North Carolina Committee's report is in *Raleigh Sentinel*, 26 February 1867 and Mississippi's in *Jackson Clarion*, 17 February 1867; Editorial, *Atlanta Intelligencer*, 17 February 1867.

[100] Kemp P. Battle to Hedrick, Raleigh, 23 February 1867, Hedrick MSS; Worth to Parsons, Raleigh, 22 February 1867, in *Correspondence of Jonathan Worth*, 'II, 898. A similar telegram was sent the same day to Orr, *ibid.*, p. 897. The North Carolina Plan was sometimes referred to as the Dixon amendment because it had been introduced into the Senate by James Dixon, a Johnson Republican.

[101] Humphreys to Sharkey, Jackson, Miss., 11 February 1867, in *Atlanta Intelligencer*, 20 February 1867.

[102] Editorial, *Augusta Constitutionalist*, 8 February 1867; Editorial, *Charleston Courier*, 8 February 1867. Also Editorial, *Jackson Clarion*, 9 February 1867.

the organ of the 'fire-eating' R. B. Rhett in the late 1850s and early 1860s, advised, even before the Plan was announced, that 'A compromise made with the Radicals, is not worth the paper on which it is written. It would be like all their other compromises – a mere expedient to disarm an opposition they cannot at present master, the better to enable them to master in the future.'[103] A conclusive verdict came from the *Augusta Constitutionalist*. After conceding that the adjustment may well have been the best so far suggested, it condemned it nevertheless as 'utterly futile and foolish' because anything inspired by Johnson and the South would be rejected by Congress. Besides, the South was in no 'position to acquire influence by active interference. Driving, as we do, headlong into every gap of Radicalism causes the party thus assailed to forget squabbles and close ranks; protracts the day of deliverance by healing differences and compelling every cabal to make common cause against our assault; and, worst of all, it is an abandonment of the grandest and strongest line of defence – the power and majesty of *vis inertiae* or passive resistance.'[104]

After refusing, with minimal dissent, to adopt the Howard amendment, the Confederates had witnessed what had appeared to be two attempts to break the ranks of 'masterly inactivity.' But both had in effect consolidated the hold which that policy already had while they had also, by their signal failure, denigrated and disparaged activism. The meaning of the whole episode as far as the Confederates could discover was that Congress seemed to be purposefully opaque and devious in its dealings with the South. The Howard amendment had offered alternatives of which the South had taken full and legitimate advantage; indeed what else could seriously have been expected. Then attempts had been made to accommodate differences. The result was simply that Congress had rejected and rebuffed each Southern move. But there was no alternative. The responses and maneuvers of the Confederates put immense pressure on the Republican Party. Its postwar goals and even its survival as a party were threatened. To resolve the difficulty, legislation was introduced into the lame-duck session of the Thirty-Ninth Congress which would provide finality. Terms would be embodied in a law of the land, and they would be mandatory. This was how it seemed, but the flaws still remained. Within a framework of coercion, options were offered in Congress' Reconstruction Act of 1867. And the Confederates did not take long to discover them.

[103] Editorial, *Charleston Mercury*, 30 January 1867.
[104] Editorial, *Augusta Constitutionalist*, 8 February 1867.

Part 4
Demanding Southern acquiescence,
1867–1868

You are the most competent judges of what degree of influence you can exert over the negroes and *that* would enter, in a controlling consideration, into the question of policy.

Attorney General Henry Stanbery to James L. Orr, Governor of South Carolina, 22 March 1867, Orr Official Correspondence.

9

Reconstruction enjoined – March to July 1867

a: *Submission – Why*

With the passage of the Reconstruction Act in February 1867, the North's terms for Southern readmission had become the law of the land. They could not be avoided. A fundamental reassessment of Southern strategy was imperative. 'Masterly inactivity,' which had never been entirely masterly nor entirely inactive, had to yield to activity, which, if complete and organized, might yet be masterly, at least insofar as affairs in the South alone were concerned. To activate the Southern will toward compliance with a law of the land, which embodied the North's unpalatable terms for Southern readmission, would require energy and resourcefulness on the part of the leaders of the conquered section. The call to action, for a mobilization of Southern will and energies, did, nonetheless, produce compliance speedily and on a broad scale. From the *Charleston Courier* came the warning: 'It is too patent a fact to be disregarded, that inaction can be of no earthly avail.'[1] And in an editorial for the *Augusta Constitutionalist*, 'Junius Brutus' warned that 'to take an active part in political affairs becomes an imperative duty. Everything will be lost by tame submission to tyranny.'[2]

This, however, was not an attempt to rouse the South from torpor in order to offer a positive and cooperative accommodation to terms which were deemed to be justified in function or content. In an open letter, hurriedly produced and then published widely in the Georgia press during the last week of February, Joseph E. Brown urged the calling of a convention to speedily enact Negro suffrage followed by the election of a legislature whose main task would be to ratify the Howard amendment. Immediate compliance with the main features of the Act, Brown anticipated, would bypass its detailed reorganizational procedures, possibly provide some relief from its penalties, and also

---

[1] Editorial, *Charleston Courier*, 16 March 1867.
[2] Editorial, *Augusta Constitutionalist*, 9 March 1867.

ensure the maintenance of Confederate control over the freedmen whom the Act had enfranchised. Brown hoped that moderate Republicans in Congress, unhappy at the extremism of their legislation, would be prepared to reward Southern politicians who had so speedily reconstructed with an alleviation, even withdrawal, of the Act's disqualification and disfranchisement clauses.[3] This was hardly unqualified acceptance of the terms of the Reconstruction Act, but an attempt to bypass its more stringent features by seizing the initiative in its implementation and by manipulating its provisions. Cooperation was not thoroughgoing by conditional and expedient. So it was to be throughout the South in the months after the Act's passage.

The Reconstruction Act of 2 March, actually the first of four such Acts, was probably the most ambitious and far-reaching piece of domestic legislation in the history of the United States.[4] Its overall purpose was to so reorganize the Southern electorate by disfranchising many leading Confederates and later disqualifying them from holding office, and by enfranchising adult male freedmen, that the Southern States would have constituencies and political leaders very different from those which had prevailed previously. They would in fact be a countervailing force to the Confederates and would inevitably vote Republican. A political revolution of this magnitude, engineered as it was from above, was not easy to legislate. It was not surprising therefore that the Reconstruction Act was detailed and complicated.

Dividing the Southern States into five military districts with a General in command of each who was responsible in the last resort for observance of the laws and punishment of offenders, the Act declared that a convention should be held in each State to draw up a new constitution which would incorporate Negro suffrage and that, once a new legislature and State and Federal officials had been elected, the Howard amendment ratified, and the constitution approved by Congress, then the State would be readmitted to the Union. The

---

[3] Joseph E. Brown to Messrs Foster, Faulkner, etc., Washington, D.C., 23 February 1867, in *Atlanta Intelligencer*, 26 February 1867.

[4] The other three Acts were supplemental to the original which because it was mammoth in scope and complex in operation needed continual elaboration and clarification. They were passed on 23 March and 19 July 1867 and on 11 March 1868. For provisions of the first two, and most important, Reconstruction Acts, see Harold Hyman, ed., *The Radical Republicans and Reconstruction, 1861–1872* (Indianapolis: Bobbs-Merrill, 1966), pp. 379–88.

abruptness of this was however to be tempered by a continuity provided by the incumbent Confederate officials who were allowed to remain in power until their State was readmitted. Consequently, the entire procedure prior to readmission could be managed by the Confederate officials, 'provisional' and subordinate to the military though the Act considered them. Although for the most part disfranchised and forced to adopt Negro suffrage, these men were not to be removed until much later in the process when the Howard amendment was ratified and, even at that point, Congress could refrain partially or entirely from implementing the disqualification clause of the amendment.[5]

Movements for immediate action under the Reconstruction Act were initiated by others besides Joseph E. Brown. Governor Pierpont submitted a message to the Virginia legislature on 4 March urging compliance and also dispatched a telegram to State Senator Lewis suggesting that a convention bill be passed in both Houses because 'with liberal action Virginia can get anything she wants.'[6] After very little delay the Senate enacted by a wide majority a measure to call a convention but, with the House of Delegates refusing, a joint delegation was sent to Washington in an attempt to resolve the impasse by enquiring whether Congress in fact wished the initiative under the Act to be taken by the State legislatures.[7] Before an answer was received, two other State Governors had approved action aimed at compliance. Wells of Louisiana proclaimed the Act in force and even affirmed its constitutionality; Alabama's Patton suggested compliance at as early a date as possible since 'to contend against it now is simply to struggle against the inevitable.'[8]

Congress' answer to the problem of how and by whom the reconstruction process was to be set in motion was the passage of the Second, or Supplemental, Reconstruction Act on 23 March. This was an enabling act which required that the military commanders register voters and take control over the whole procedure of calling and holding the

[5] See Larry G. Kincaid, 'Legislative Origins of the Military Reconstruction Act, 1865–1867,' Ph.D. dissertation, Johns Hopkins University, 1968, for details of the measure's passage and the conclusion that this was more a moderate than a radical law.

[6] Francis H. Pierpont, Message to the Virginia Legislature, 4 March 1867, *Richmond Times*, 5 March 1867.

[7] *Ibid.*, 10 March 1867; *Richmond Enquirer*, 12 March 1867.

[8] James Madison Wells, Proclamation, 8 March 1867, in *New Orleans Times*, 8 March 1867; Robert M. Patton to J. P. Ralls, A. L. Woodruff, etc., in *New Orleans Times*, 23 March 1867.

constitutional conventions. Although this legislation took from the hands of Southern civilian officials the initiative in commencing reconstruction, it proffered another option in exchange. In the vote on the calling of a convention, they were given the opportunity within the law of either demonstrating their acquiescence, even their support and cooperation, in the changes envisioned by the Reconstruction Act or of voting against holding a convention and thereby preventing its further implementarion. There was even a third alternative which was to abstain from participation altogether. Either of these two negative alternatives, if skillfully operated, could bring the whole operation to a halt; and actually it was possible for the Confederates even by cooperating, provided they could get control of affairs, to frustrate the countervailing intent of the legislation.

The Confederates had been penalized under the Acts by the disfranchisement of most of their number and they could expect to be deprived of office once the State was readmitted. But over against this were the fears expressed in Congress of what might happen if the South were governed without the assent and participation of its customary rulers and these anxieties forced Congressmen to concede options to the former rebels. The availability of these alternatives invited their destructive use. So, in the first Act, incumbents were to be kept in office while the possibility that disqualifications might be removed was held out as an incentive to cooperate and, in the law of 23 March, the Confederates were conceded the option of giving their assent or of withholding it. Once again, as in the Howard amendment, Congress accompanied a coercive and punitive measure with anomalous provisions for the victim to register or refuse his voluntary consent.

Initially, despite these alternatives, the attitude which was dominant was that submission to the relentless pressure of events would avoid further agitation and debate. That did not imply, needless to say, that the Congressional terms were accepted or endorsed; the Act was regarded by most as unconstitutional, and certainly as unjust and ill-advised. All the same, the point had been reached at which continued contention might be harmful to the South. As Joseph E. Brown pointed out, 'the conquerors dictate their own terms, which are heightened in severity by the delay of the conquered to accept them.'[9] Warning came also from General P. G. T. Beauregard who pointed out that

[9] Joseph E. Brown to Messrs Foster, Faulkner, etc., Washington, D.C., 23 February 1867, in *Atlanta Intelligencer*, 26 February 1867.

'our people should understand that the Radicals can remain in power only so long as the public excitement is kept up.'[10] For too long, argued those who advocated submission, the South had refused to comply, believing that succor was imminent or that the proffered terms were unreasonable. Now, cautioned Thomas J. Wharton of Mississippi, 'we have to deal with things as they *are* – not as we would *have* them.'[11] In fact, to dispute further was the height of foolishness. Another who advised cooperation was James Phelan, also, like Wharton, a Mississippi secessionist, who feared that when 'an extremity is reached at which all reasonable hope expires, of preserving the principle or preventing the wrong further; *firmness* degenerates into *obstinacy*, and passion, dethroning judgement, prompts to deeds, violative of the dictates of that just prudence involved in the law of self-preservation.'[12] Further endorsement for the advisability of cooperation came from Alabama. The wealthy anti-secessionist planter and manufacturer, Robert Jemison, Jr, emphasized that any other course 'would be nothing short of madness';[13] while the *Montgomery Advertiser* was aghast that anyone should contemplate resistance when 'in addition to the large white elements at the North and the South, we would also array the negroes against us, and when even if we succeeded in defeating this measure at the polls we would aggravate the dominant North and make things worse.'[14]

To yield to necessity had now become an act of courage and enlightened honor, not a betrayal of principle or an act of suicide, a considerable change from attitudes of the preceding two years. In urging cooperation, Governor Throckmorton of Texas presented accommodation as a course motivated by the loftiest of sentiments, arguing that 'When a great and gallant people are conquered and overcome, when they are oppressed and spurned, and their very misfortunes are heaped upon them as crimes, and every means are used to make them the instruments of their own torture and humiliation, it requires the

---

[10] Pierre G. T. Beauregard to William H. C. King, 23 March 1867, in *New Orleans Times*, 26 March 1867.

[11] Thomas J. Wharton to John W. Robinson *et al.*, 15 March 1867, in *Jackson Clarion*, 16 March 1867.

[12] James Phelan to W. B. Taylor *et al.*, 25 March 1867, in *Jackson Clarion*, 30 March 1867.

[13] Robert Jemison, Jr, to *Tuscaloosa Monitor*, in *Montgomery Weekly Advertiser*, 23 April 1867.

[14] Editorial, *Montgomery Advertiser*, 15 May 1867.

loftiest courage to overcome the animosities and prejudices of the popular heart, and to combat the terrible surroundings of an outraged public sentiment.'[15] And further examples were legion in the spring of 1867. This kind of argument, used previously to urge non-cooperation, was now advanced in favor of the opposite course. Nothing could now save the South except a wise cooperation with the terms proposed. A realization of the South's predicament dictated action. Policy, expediency, self-interest demanded compliance.

The decision to cooperate with the terms of the Reconstruction Act was not, therefore, a principled stand. The Act bestowing Negro suffrage and specifying the process of readmission was a law of the land and could not be avoided. Moreover, the President had refused to pocket-veto the measure, but instead, after his simple veto had failed, had proceeded to administer the law by selecting the military commanders who would govern the five districts. Therefore, said the *Jackson Clarion*, 'the example of his acquiescence should not be lost;' the South 'has witnessed the defeat of the President, and the assertion of the supremacy of the Legislative Department.'[16] To hope for relief from other quarters, the *Clarion* felt, was illusory. Admittedly, a move was being made from the South to test the constitutionality of the Acts but, said the *Clarion*, to rely on that 'as a plan of *practical relief*' would be 'utterly worthless. It is like the act of the drowning man who grasps at a straw.'[17] To trust completely in salvation from the Court and thus remain passive was highly dangerous, and many advocates of cooperation, such as Fulton Anderson, a Mississippi Whig leader, while prepared to concede a just hope in the Court, nonetheless, urged against total reliance since that might induce inertia.[18]

Northern Democrats, too, were unreliable and to trust in deliverance from them was a dangerous delusion. James L. Orr publicly recalled that on three occasions the South had been misled and betrayed by the Democrats – in 1860–1, in the Philadelphia convention movement, and only the previous winter in their advice to reject the Howard amendment.[19] For its own benefit only did the Democratic Party

[15] Throckmorton to Col. Ashbel Smith, 5 April 1867, in *Arkansas Gazette*, 14 May 1867.

[16] Editorial, *Jackson Clarion*, 30 March 1867.

[17] *Ibid.*, 10 March 1867.

[18] Fulton Anderson to John W. Robinson *et al.*, *ibid.*, 4 April 1867.

[19] James L. Orr, Speech to Charleston Board of Trade, 2 April 1867, *Charleston Courier*, 3 April 1867. Also, Editorial, *Richmond Enquirer*, 2 March 1867.

adopt the cause of the South; self-reliance now was to be Southern policy and the Democrats were to be made to realize that Southern votes and accommodation to their goals would not be automatically available. Besides, the anti-radical forces in the North, whose success was for so long anticipated, had already let the South down. They were weak and despised. Therefore, to continue to wait for a reaction among the conservative Northern elements would be in vain. Even if it did arise, which was unlikely since the conservatives had already tolerated the intolerable on many occasions, it would not come soon enough or totally enough to avert the Reconstruction Acts or topple the radicals from power. A propos this development, *Flake's Bulletin* commented sarcastically, 'We have no doubt an earthquake would accomplish the same result, and be as much within the limits of possibility.'[20]

The unpleasant facts about Northern politics had at last, it seemed, been realized and absorbed in the South. Conservative reaction was a chimera. Radical policies were endorsed, for whatever strange and incomprehensible reasons, by a substantial portion of Northern opinion. Moreover, Negro suffrage, the core project of radical Reconstruction, was 'not only urged on by Congress, but by Northern public sentiment, which is in advance of Congress in extreme demands upon the South.'[21] This admission by the *New Orleans Times* was heretical. It meant that 'the action of Congress is but a faint reflection of Northern public sentiment.'[22] Within the spectrum of Northern opinion, the radicals were in effect no longer radical and, therefore, to accept their proposals was to escape evils far worse which might still be contemplated by Northerners. A similar realization, though expressed in different terms, had been reached by J. Q. A. Fellows, leader of the Constitutional Union Party in Louisiana. In an open letter to the *New Orleans Times*, he said: 'It is certain that every measure of the dominant party is sustained by the masses, both of the people and of the thinking men, because they deem all such measures necessary to preserve and perpetuate the fruits of the victory which has cost so much of treasure and blood.' Even though Fellows was prepared to accept that measures like the Howard amendment and the Reconstruction Acts were 'deemed necessary by the victors' and could not therefore be avoided

---

[20] Editorial, *Flake's Bulletin*, 19 March 1867.
[21] Editorial, *New Orleans Times*, 17 March 1867.
[22] *Ibid.*, 20 March 1867.

by the South, he nonetheless reaffirmed his anti-secessionist orthodoxy by adding that, in spite of the 'revenge [which] activates the mind of some,' 'the great controlling idea [in the North] is that we are one people, one nation, that this idea has been opposed at the South and an attempt made to destroy it.'[23] But Fellows was unusual since few of those who had opposed secession in 1861 were prepared to take the lead in publicly recommending compliance in 1867.

According less credit to Northern conservatism was the *Charleston Courier*. A constitutional revolution had been effected in the North, said the *Courier*, and 'HEREAFTER, HOWEVER PARTIES MAY IN TURN GAIN THE ASCENDANCY AND RULE, THE MAJORITY IN CONGRESS WILL CONSTITUTE IN REALITY THE GOVERNMENT' for 'the truth is, in our judgement, that the practical fact is that with the war the Constitution has perished. . . . Constitutional guarantees are not only no longer respected, but not even recognized.' Northern voters had tolerated irrevocable and dangerous constitutional changes since the war and as a result had 'covered their own freedom with a net, the meshes of which it will be difficult for them to break.'[24] However unfortunate this development, its consequences on the South could not be evaded or wished away. Similar approaches were taken by James L. Alcorn who demanded: 'Let us cease, then, to talk of courts and the constitution,' and also by George P. Cathcart, editor of the *Charleston Daily News*, who argued that the people of the South had

been taught to believe that they have their ancient rights under the Constitution.

This may be true; I do not believe it is. I think the Constitution of the United States should be plastic, as other Constitutions are; that as it was made by *the people*, so too it should be modified to suit varying emergencies and shifting events.[25]

In conceding this point, Cathcart was going beyond the need to submit to necessity, and evidently his colleagues on the editorial board, J. Barrett Cohen and William H. Trescot, wanted it to be made clear

[23] J. Q. A. Fellows to William H. C. King, 20 March 1867, in *New Orleans Times*, 21 March 1867.

[24] Editorial, *Charleston Courier*, 8 March 1867.

[25] James L. Alcorn to *Friar's Point* (Miss.) *Coahomian*, 26 April 1867, in *Vicksburg Herald*, 2 May 1867.

that they did not concur, even though they acquiesced in compliance with reconstruction.[26]

Compliance with the Act did not, however, involve unqualified submission; rather it was tantamount to qualified opposition, since the explicit purpose behind cooperation was to undermine and blunt, rather than fulfill, the intentions of the Republican legislators in Congress. The Negro vote was to be controlled by the politicians rather than to be allowed to act as a counterweight to their influence and power. Furthermore, with incumbent State officials remaining in office until readmission was secured, there was the likelihood that the conventions in most Southern States could be dominated by conservatives, since they still had control of the State's governmental machinery. Negro suffrage might then expand, rather than counter, the sway of the established politicians. That was what submission to the demands of Congress meant.

It was not conducive to the conservatives' interest, therefore, to permit even the consideration of alternatives to action.* Excoriating the *Staunton Spectator* for speaking of choices in this connexion, the *Richmond Whig* exclaimed: 'We had thought that the argument predicated of choice, like that in relation to "honor," had long since been dissipated in the air. There will be a Convention and a Constitution whether we vote for them or against them. If the whites vote them down, the whole reconstruction policy will at once be committed to the faction to which we have referred [the radicals led by J. W. Hunnicutt]. This is a "choice" with a vengeance.'[27] Whites who held office or retained the vote were urged by secessionist Wiley P. Harris, a judge on the Mississippi Supreme Court, to seize the initiative 'since their refusal to act will be a virtual surrender of the civil power into the

[26] *Editorial, Charleston Daily News*, 1 October 1867. Actually Cathcart announced in this editorial that this co-editors had forced him to resign over this difference of opinion.

*The term 'conservative' is used hereafter to describe those who, before the Reconstruction Act was passed, were referred to as 'Confederates.' Initially this group includes both cooperationists and non-cooperationists, but by the fall non-cooperation is its hallmark and policy. Former Unionists, for the most part, worked with the Republican Party, particularly its moderate wing. Not associated with the political establishment and marginal in support of the Southern war-effort, or outrightly opposed to it, these men naturally veered toward the Republican Party when it emerged as the opposition party to the Confederates.

[27] Editorial, *Richmond Whig*, 13 April 1867.

hands of those who will surely employ it to perpetuate their power by further proscriptions.'[28]

The strategy adopted by conservatives in the Southern States during the spring of 1867 depended primarily, not on the configuration of political forces in the North, but on whether the Negro vote could be corralled. In States such as Mississippi, Louisiana, and South Carolina, where a registered majority of blacks was inevitable, the imperative to comply was quickly realized. The *Charleston Mercury* assumed that with these black population majorities they could do no other.[29] And indeed by 24 March the *New Orleans Times* could proclaim with glee, and probably with accuracy too, that 'the difficulty is to find any dissentient, any opponent of the only course left to us, by which the government can be organized.'[30] In Mississippi, too, the *Jackson Clarion* and the *Vicksburg Herald* very quickly pursued a policy of eliciting the opinions of leading men on the question of the day, so as to impress the public mind with an array of authoritative talent, advising compliance with the Act. Former Governors Albert G. Brown and John J. McRae wrote opinions; so did Fulton Anderson, Wiley P. Harris, Amos Johnston, Thomas J. Wharton, Walker Brooke, Henry T. Ellett, and William Yerger.[31] By contrast, the opposition forces advocated a cautious approach to the problem and preferred to rely on the Supreme Court rather than take precipitate action. Leading them were William L. Sharkey and Governor Humphreys, the latter demanding compliance only insofar as obedience to the military and civil authorities in the State was required.[32] By mid-May, however, the *Clarion*'s viewpoint was dominant within the State. And if the non-cooperationist, General William Martin's lament, 'I am so disgusted

---

[28] Wiley P. Harris to John W. Robinson *et al.*, 12 March 1867, in *Jackson Clarion*, 14 March 1867.

[29] Editorial, *Charleston Mercury*, 18 May 1867. A convention would be called in the black majority States so there was no point in not organizing uder the Act in order to get control of its personnel. 'By a proper energy on the part of the white population,' the *Mercury* optimistically predicted, 'we have little doubt that a conservative convention can be elected.'

[30] Editorial, *New Orleans Times*, 24 March 1867.

[31] The *Jackson Clarion* and *Vicksburg Herald* published letters from these influential figures during March and early April. The *Clarion* was by this time under the editorship of Ethelbert Barksdale, a prominent secessionist, and this probably explained its taking the lead in urging compliance after having been an uncompromising advocate of inactivity in late 1866.

[32] Benjamin G. Humphreys, Proclamation, 6 April 1867, Humphreys MSS.

with public affairs, and so terribly disappointed in our own people' was based on accurate observation, it would seem that, behind the lead of Governor Orr and the Charleston secessionists, South Carolina also was taking steps to comply with the Act.[33] This was what the *Charleston Mercury* had expected in these three states. A convention would be voted in anyway by the black majority; the task then for the conservatives was to ensure that they were elected overwhelmingly to it.[34]

The movement towards cooperation had even taken hold in States where white majorities were likely to be registered. The argument was of course the opposite of the *Mercury*'s, whose editors had calculated that a white electoral majority could very easily prevent a convention whereas in a State like South Carolina attempting to do this would be a risky enterprise. Faced with legislation which, because of the 23 March Supplemental Act, would be implemented by a determined Congressional majority whatever the South felt about it and aware that the scheme to test the constitutionality of Congress' laws in the Supreme Court had failed, compliance and involvement in the unfolding of reconstruction seemed to conservative Southern spokesmen expedient and frequently unavoidable. To all intents and purposes, a bandwagon had been set in motion; politicians and newspapers were beginning to change their minds, among the latter the most notable being the *Richmond Whig, Arkansas Gazette*, and *Atlanta Intelligencer*.

Even if initial responses were not altered, it appeared to be wise policy to be active rather than supine. No matter what line of action might be advisable later, all should register, for, without that, choice would be forfeited. So even those who were determined not to cooperate but instead to vote 'No' to the holding of a convention were urging that those eligible should at least register. The *Augusta Constitutionalist*, a journal which was never to alter its early stand against cooperation, was urgent and firm when it demanded 'ORGANIZE, then, ORGANIZE! WARN THE COUNTRY PEOPLE ALL ABOUT, BE

[33] Martin to Perry, Charleston, S.C., 7 May 1867, Perry MSS (Ala.).
[34] It should be noted here that the *Mercury* advised a different course for States with registered majorities of whites. For them, opposition could succeed and thus prevent a convention from being called. The *Mercury* was opposed to compliance, except where there was no option; in both cases the goal was to divert the Reconstruction legislation so that conservatives retained control in spite of it.

COMPACT; BE WARY, BE RESOLVED. THE SUPREME HOUR HAS COME. . . .'[35] The argument behind this admonition was essentially the same as the *Charleston Courier* was to propound later, in August, 'To-day is our own. But who knows what, under the shifting dominion to which we are subject, the morrow may bring;' so the *Courier* advised registering and waiting to see what would transpire.

The unanimity of the movement towards cooperation was, however, more apparent than real; to urge compliance with the Acts to the extent of registering under them did not, in fact, mean cooperation.[36] The editors of the *Richmond Enquirer* were aware that the tactic they recommended might well be construed as cooperation. They urged registration and the formation of a political apparatus which could elect conservative members to the convention, but refused to decide either way on the issue of whether to vote for or against the holding of a convention. Yet this essential was non-cooperation and an editorial of 30 March pointed out that although 'This is called acceptance, endorsement, ratification, and the like. We understand it simply as involuntary admission to arbitrary and irresistible power.' The *Enquirer's* strategy, like the *Courier's*, was simply precautionary, since 'The scheme was made to work slowly, and we shall only render ourselves absurd by vainly trying to hurry it. Besides, it is not, in any view, politic to hasten the denouement, if we could. There are very many who believe that the whole programme will prove in any case a delusion; an attempt to overtake the horizon.'[37] This minimal and preventive compliance was not the same as cooperation; nor indeed was it equivalent to inaction and resistance which was another approach to reconstruction with many advocates and followers. About this latter tactic we shall have more to say later, but in the meantime it is evident that the policy of cooperation undertaken by most leading newspapers and politicians was not so uniform as it seemed, and since it was usually adopted out of expediency it was not likely to prevail if conditions under the Reconstruction legislation changed significantly.

Despite these qualifications, the movement towards cooperation was nevertheless the most striking feature discernible in Southern affairs during the spring of 1867. And there were additional reasons for

---

[35] Editorial, *Augusta Constitutionalist*, 18 June 1867.
[36] Editorial, *Charleston Courier*, 23 August 1867.
[37] Editorial, *Richmond Enquirer*, 30 March 1867.

pursuing this course besides even the compelling necessity of controlling the new Negro vote. One of these was suggested by Walter H. Crenshaw of Alabama when he indicated that 'it is very important to those of us, who are ruled out of office by the Constitutional Amendment, to place ourselves in a position that will probably cause our applications for relief to be favourably considered.'[38] Eager cooperation would, it was assumed, disarm Congressional hostility, and this view was widely held. Julian Selby, editor of the *Columbia Phoenix*, told Benjamin Perry that he had been to Washington and had been assured by some of the radicals, that 'if these propositions were carried out, the members elect would be admitted — even though they had been "rebels"; and also the disfranchising clause would or could be modified after the state were re-admitted.' 'This,' said Selby, 'was my sole reason for adopting the course that the paper has been pursuing.'[39] Similar trust in radical good faith and benevolence was betrayed by David L. Swain who hoped that the government of North Carolina, although 'provisional,' would 'be continued, until Congress may have opportunity, by a two thirds vote, to remove the disability imposed by the Howard Amendment.'[40]

This confidence in the basic responsiveness and decency of the Northern extremists was not universally shared, but it motivated very many, anti-secessionist and secessionist alike. Perhaps it was premised on a judgement that the Republican Party was really in the condition that politicians had previously asserted as a matter of hope rather than fact, that is, that it was in grave peril because of the extremism of its Reconstruction laws. Consequently, a ready compliance would save it and the South from the perils of harsher policies. Others, in contrast, were spurred to action simply by fears of confiscation, either by an enraged Congress should the South not comply, or by a proscriptive radical convention if conservatives did not mold it. Two South Carolinians told Benjamin Perry that protection of private property motivated most politicians to cooperate. J. B. Sitton observed of the political situation in South Carolina during April, 'Nearly every body was rampant for convention, and to get back into the union, and to

[38] Walter H. Crenshaw to Robert M. Patton, Evergreen, Ala., 11 March 1867, Patton Official Correspondence.

[39] Julian Selby to Benjamin F. Perry, Columbia, S.C., 29 July 1867, Perry MSS (Ala.).

[40] David L. Swain to William A. Graham, Chapel Hill, 15 March 1867, W. A. Graham Collection.

save their *lands* from confiscation, by congress.'[41] And Mary Farley
Todd admitted, a month later in August, 'I would be glad if many felt
their loss of property less and their loss of liberty more, and that all
would resolve to stand up rationally for their own Truth and Honor.'[42]

Retention of political control, whether by the support of Negro
votes or by the removal, or avoidance, of individual proscriptions,
was the material goal of those who urged compliance in the spring of
1867. Yet there was a further common denominator among those who
took the lead for implementing the Reconstruction Act's provisions.
In this vanguard were continually to be found secessionists who had
often assumed a subordinate and inconspicuous role since the end of
the war. Except for Virginia, where the Democratic Party, which included most of the secessionists, favored non-cooperation, this generalization held true. Residing mostly in Black Belt or Tidewater counties
with large black populations, the secessionists' ability to regulate the
Negro vote was essential to their local ascendancy as well as to their
power within the State.[43] Furthermore, since those conservatives,
mainly anti-secessionists, who, during the previous two years, had led
the South through fields of 'masterly inactivity,' were now hesitating
in the face of the Reconstruction Act, the opportunity for seizing the
political reins was evident. The anti-secessionists, who had emerged
automatically as the section's leaders in the wake of the defeat of secession and under the encouragement of the Johnson program, could be
thrust aside if the secessionists could now gain control of conservative
policy. The secessionists' political theory, moreover, prepared them
far better for endorsing the terms of the Reconstruction Act. As justification for complying with Congress' mandatory legislation, Albert
Gallatin Brown argued:

We fought as I think, out of the Union and not in it. We fought to maintain
an independent and separate nationality which we had created. And when
we ceased to fight, and gave up our arms we laid them at the feet of the conqueror. From that day to this, we have ceased to have any political rights
which the conqueror was bound to respect.[44]

[41]J. B. Sitton to Perry, Pendleton, S.C., 19 July 1867, Perry MSS (Ala.).
[42]Mary Farley Todd to Perry, Laurensville, S.C., 30 August 1867, Perry MSS
(Ala.).
[43]This conclusion regarding the location and nature of secession sentiment was
reached by Ralph Wooster in *The Secession Conventions of the South* (Princeton,
N.J.: Princeton University Press, 1962).
[44]Albert G. Brown to William H. Allen *et al.*, 22 March 1967, in *Jackson Clarion*,

Although Brown added, 'I am not to be understood in this that he rightfully do with us as he pleases,' nevertheless the assumption was that once terms, final and conclusive, were offered, they could be acquiesced in as the dictate of a victorious foreign enemy.

Those who had precipitated secession had a keen sense of the incompatibility and distinctiveness of the sections. They were in essence hard-nosed in their dealings with the North, unlike their opponents who continued to hope that those Northern interests and sentiments which were conservative of the Union would assert themselves decisively. This difference of approach had often been evident since the surrender, but now it became clearer-cut as two distinct groupings emerged. The *Montgomery Advertiser*, formerly Yancey's secessionist organ, explained the secessionists' outlook : 'Those men had too clear an understanding of the points involved in the contest not to know that when resistance by the sword had failed, nothing was left but to submit as gracefully as they could, and cease to be pugnacious over the "rights" which would only be accorded by the sense of justice and magnanimity of the Northern people. . . .'[45] The terms had finally been presented but they proved difficult for the anti-secessionists to swallow, as had the Howard amendment when proposed in 1866. Among other things they felt aggrieved that, once agian, distinctions had not been made by Congress between secessionists and their opponents; both were under the ban if they had held office and then rebelled. William Marvin, now in New York, told the people of Florida that, because there was no differentiation among those proscribed, 'it is inequitable and unjust.' And, he continued, 'Had I ever adopted the theory of secession, and entertained the notion that the Confederate States had separated from the Union and become an independent power, so as to be capable of being subjugated and conquered in the proper sense of these words, then I could submit to the acts of Congress we have been considering with less sense of humiliation and injustice than I now feel. . . .'[46]

Accordingly, there were many secessionists who were able to ac-

27 March 1867. Brown, like Cathcart of the *Charleston Daily News*, was strongly criticized for his arguments favoring cooperation because they conceded more than was necessary. The constitutional positions presented by each of them effectively denied the South constitutional protection and guarantees.
[45] Editorial, *Montgomery Advertiser*, 30 October 1866.
[46] William A. Marvin, Address to the People of Florida, in *Jackson Clarion*, 28 May 1867.

commodate. Those who responded in favor of cooperation when the *Jackson Clarion* in March and April asked for the opinions of prominent men on the policy to be pursued under the Reconstruction Acts were invariably ex-secessionists. At about the same time, Bejamin Perry subjected his opponents to public scorn when he announced publicly that those in South Carolina who urged cooperation, 'I am happy to know . . . are secessionists, and never were Union men.'[47] Confirmation of this came from a Texan, George Butler, who wrote to Perry that 'now those who were ultra heretofore are willing to bend the suppliant knee to Radicalism and hug the negro to their bosoms.'[48] Furthermore, a correspondent of the *New York Times*, after touring Virginia, South Carolina, Tennessee, and Georgia in early summer, concluded that those who were cooperating were primarily original secessionists who believed that, although harsh, the terms had to be endorsed because they were the conqueror's edict and no better conditions would be offered. Also in this group, so the writer noticed, were men who had found the Confederacy distasteful by comparison with government within the Union. Finally, of course, he noticed many eminent soldiers, the most conspicuous being Generals Beauregard, Taylor, and Longstreet, all of Louisiana, and Early and Lee of Virginia, among those urging that the Reconstruction Acts be considered as final terms and therefore to be complied with.

There were however two important addenda to this analysis which revealed the flaws and weaknesses in the policy of cooperation. First of all, this conservative grouping was not united, even by September when the *New York Times* report was written, on account of 'a certain amount of social and conventional timidity' at the prospect of coalescing politically with Negro voters and acquiescing in Northern Republican terms. Moreover, said the correspondent, the majority of Southerners, those who had never owned slaves and who comprised nine-tenths of the population, were tending 'to become more and more detached from its old political leaders, for they perceive that these can now do nothing for them, whereas they have something to gain by siding with the Republicans. Many fancy that the triumph of the Radicals will secure land to the landless.' Furthermore, 'This class not-

---

[47] Benjamin F. Perry to *Charleston Courier*, *Charleston Courier*, 19 April 1867. Perry, of course, includes himself and other anti-secessionists under the heading of 'Union men,' even though they all eventually sided with and supported the Confederacy.

[48] George Butler to Perry, Maysfield, Tex., 24 June 1867, Perry MSS (Ala.).

withstanding life-long bitter prejudices against the blacks, seems to affiliate readily enough politically with the negro element.'[49] Here lay the major threat to the conservatives; their leadership was being challenged and they had therefore to obtain control not only of the new black voters, but of the mass of whites as well.

b: *Submission – How*

The threat levelled at the Confederates by the Reconstruction Acts was fundamental and irresistible. Besides involving the question of political power, the relationship between blacks and whites, extolled so frequently as being perfectly satisfactory to each, was under fire. If the Negro chose to vote against his employer and former master, then a nail would be driven into the coffin of the Southern cause and its apparatus of apologia. The truth about Southern race relations would then be undesirable. The question for the conservative whites was, of course, whether the attempt to cooperate with the Negroes should be made for fear that it might fail. Perhaps, they surmised, it would be more politic to allow the Southern radicals to bribe and corrupt the new voters into their camp without hindrance or competition. But, in spite of these possibilities, one consideration prevailed; the thought of surrendering the State into the freedmen's and white radicals' hands was, by and large, sufficiently unattractive that it was rarely contemplated in the early months after the first Reconstruction Act.

The course taken by Herschel V. Johnson was typical of many who submitted to a necessity that they deplored. Johnson was categorical: 'I do not *approve* that Bill, and before God I never will. I will not do nor say anything indicating approval or even acceptance of it. I will not attempt or advise acceptance. But under the circumstances that surround us, we must obey it – render the obedience which bayonets impose upon our overpowered people.' For purely expedient and negative reasons he urged compliance: 'The negroes are enfranchised. We must control that element by all proper means, or at least so much of it as will rescue the ballot box from an unfriendly majority against us. . . . If we stand with folded hands and do nothing, the Convention will represent the negroes and that class of worthless whites who will affiliate with them. The result will be deplorable.'[50]

[49]Cited in *New Orleans Times*, 8 September 1867.
[50]Herschel V. Johnson to Alexander H. Stephens, Augusta, Ga., 29 March 1867, A. H. Stephens MSS.

Accordingly, on 13 April, Herschel V. Johnson found himself sitting on a platform with Ebenezer Starnes and Henry Hilliard, and confronted by an audience in which blacks were overwhelmingly predominant.[51] It was under necessity only that he was there. If he had not been there and the radicals were left alone and allowed to superintend the Negroes, Johnson felt it was a frightening and distinct possibility that they would stir them up and incite them against their white employers and protectors. Referring to this ex-Governor Andrew M. Moore told Patton, 'we are standing on a volcano that will burst forth unless the greatest caution is observed.'[52] Nevertheless, quite sure of the direction which this caution would take was the *Montgomery Advertiser* when it observed, 'We think we know whereof we speak, when we give the assurance that the old guard of Alabama do not intend to let so much power go into the hands of their enemies by default.'[53]

The lesser of the evils, it appeared, was the course taken by Herschel Johnson, and, in every State, efforts were made in March, April, and May to wean the freedmen onto the conservatives' side. Joseph E. Brown addressed the first mixed meeting in the South on 4 March in Atlanta and he was soon followed by the most prominent of South Carolinians, Wade Hampton, on 18 March.[54] Hampton's speech urging the freedmen to vote for Southern whites, rather than for 'carpetbagger' émigrés from the North, and offering pledges to aid them in their educational and economic advancement, was seminal in its effect on political waverers throughout the South.[55] Meetings proliferated thereafter. In Richmond on 15 April a mixed gathering was addressed by leading Virginia Whigs, Raleigh T. Daniel, who actually advocated non-cooperation, Marmaduke Johnson, and William H. Macfarland.[56] Throughout Mississippi interracial gatherings favoring cooperation were held during the spring and were addressed by secessionists, Albert G. Brown, J. W. Robb, Ethelbert Barksdale, editor of the *Clarion*, and other prominent figures.[57] Similar developments were occurring in other States. In Arkansas, assemblages of blacks

[51] Herschel V. Johnson, 'Autobiography,' handwritten, H. V. Johnson MSS.
[52] Andrew B. Moore to Patton, Marion, Ala., 1 June 1867, Patton Official Correspondence.
[53] Editorial, *Montgomery Advertiser*, 31 May 1867.
[54] *Atlanta Intelligencer*, 9 March 1867.
[55] *Charleston Courier*, 23 March 1867.
[56] *Richmond Times*, 16 April 1867.
[57] See *Jackson Clarion*, April, May, June 1867.

and whites were called together in late May, sponsored by Generals Gideon Pillow and Thomas C. Hindman. In Alabama's war-time Unionist counties, Governor Patton, Charles S. G. Doster and H. C. Semple organized a series of mixed meetings. And even Jonathan Worth, accompanied by an editor of the *Raleigh Sentinel*, Seaton Gales, spoke to a black audience in Raleigh on 22 April.[58]

Such occurrences, of course, were not sufficient to ensure black support. In fact, some of those who addressed these gatherings were themselves advocates of non-cooperation, and they appeared there mainly to test Negro sentiment for cooperation with the whites and to provide against forfeiture of the Negro vote whatever later might transpire. But it was obvious that unless some formal political organization were instituted whereby an interracial party could emerge, fraternization at public meetings would achieve little. The composition of this party, and its viability, was the crux of the problem of reconstruction in the South during 1867.

In simple terms its components would comprise those whites who wished to cooperate on the basis of the Reconstruction Acts of March interpreted as narrowly as possible and also those blacks who would join them, possibly all of the registered freedmen but more likely a portion of them, thus splitting the Negro vote. More specific, however, was the question of the platform and the party-attachments of the whites. Cooperation implied conciliation of the black vote and of the Republican Party; for a conservative party, led by whites and running on a conservative platform, would nullify the purpose of the Reconstruction Act and would not obtain support from the Negroes. A course had to be steered between what the *Montgomery Advertiser* called the 'Scylla of Northern Radicalism' and the 'Charybdis of Southern Impracticables.'[59] Between those who refused to comply with the Act and those who urged Negro officeholding, Negro jurors, and radical measures in general, a party of the middle-ground had to arise.

In Virginia the *Richmond Whig* suggested that this party of the middle course should be led by moderate Republicans and 'respectable Union men' such as Governor Pierpont, John Minor Botts, and

[58] *Arkansas Gazette*, 11 June 1867; *Montgomery Advertiser*, 2 April 1867 and *Montgomery Weekly Advertiser*, 26 March 1867; *Raleigh Sentinel*, 23 April 1867.
[59] *Montgomery Advertiser*, 15 May 1867. The 'Impracticables' were those Southern conservatives who urged non-cooperation, either by voting 'No' to the convention or by refusing to take any action whatever under the Reconstruction Acts.

Franklin Stearns, and include Negroes and whites favoring reconstruction.[60] But reactions from the Confederate press were derisive. The *Richmond Times* exclaimed:

We should delight to see a sort of political millennium – a new Paradise – where the lion of 'Secession' and the lion of Unionism could live in concert, totally oblivious of all the bitter memories of past dissensions. But no conservative party can ever be formed in Virginia with an 'original Union' head and a 'Secession' tail. The 'reconstructed' voters of Virginia never intend to play second fiddle to the handful of 'original Union men' in this State. Never. Never.[61]

If Flournoy, Baldwin, Stuart, or Goggin, all Whigs and opponents of secession, could lead, then the *Times* would approve, but to require cooperationists to join the Republican Party and follow its lead and platform was unthinkable. Undismayed, the *Whig* reiterated its suggestion after Senator Henry Wilson's visit to Richmond in mid-April.

Believing that reconstruction was likely to be impermanent and possibly impracticable unless a party of whites and blacks, neither radical nor conservative, arose in the South, Senator Wilson and Congressman William D. Kelley traveled to Virginia and Alabama in an attempt to lay the foundation for such a realignment. The proposition was exactly what Lincoln and Johnson had been advocating since early 1865 – a Southern coalition of national men who had supported the Confederacy yet opposed secession and often advocated an early peace, Union men who had been marginal in their support of the Confederacy, and propertied and educated freedmen. Shunning the radical, J. W. Hunnicutt, who controlled the Negroes of Richmond and was developing an exclusively Negro party and, in addition, dismissing the non-cooperationists, among whom were numbered former Governor Wise, and James Mason and Robert M. T. Hunter, this party was beginning to organize in Virginia on the Petersburg Platform of equal political and civil rights, political office for both races, and the repeal of discriminatory legislation.[62] Virginia would be readmitted under the leadership of a moderate Republican organization, which was prepared to join the Sherman–Bingham wing of the na-

[60] Editorial, *Richmond Whig*, 5 April 1867.
[61] Editorial, *Richmond Times*, 12 April 1867.
[62] Editorial, *Richmond Whig*, 23 April 1867. For the position of Wise etc., see Jonathan Worth to Graham, Richmond, Va., 9 March 1867, in W. A. Graham Collection.

tional party and was replete with candidates able to take the ironclad oath.

The cooperation movement burgeoned after 1 July when a meeting in Albermarle County, presided over by prominent Whigs, William F. Gordon, Jr, John J. Bocock, Colonel R. T. W. Duke, and John L. Cochran, decided to negotiate a non-partisan coalition of Republicans and Whigs.[63] Subsequent meetings were held in Amelia, Louisa, Pittsylvania, Prince Edward, and other Whiggish counties during July.[64] The elder statesman of the party, William Cabell Rives, had proposed that Gordon instigate the Albemarle convention as a means of preventing John M. Botts from drawing 'into the hands of a contemptible minority of the white population, by means of the negro vote, the supreme and vindictive control of the affairs of the State.' 'Call them together,' he said, 'under the name of the conservative Union men of the country, or any other denomination you may like better, but don't call them a party.'[65]

The resultant organization was not what Rives had expected. As Gordon explained, 'no matter what shape such an organization might assume it would be regarded as the Democratic party in another form and would be hopelessly defeated in any contest in which it might engage.' In view of the heavy registration of Negroes and radicals, 'the idea suggested itself to some of us that the only hope of saving ourselves from such a consummation [a Negro–white Republican alliance which was opposed to the Confederate establishment] was boldly to unite with the Republican party.'[66] Soon, however, this scheme foundered.

On the one hand, the Democrats, and many Whigs, warned that cooperation with the Republicans would divide the white vote. Senator Wilson, said the *Enquirer*, must be very confident of his claim to white Virginia's affection 'when he advises us to divide off into parties, and fly at each other's throats for his accommodation.'[67] A similar view was presented by the *Times* when it warned that the real danger

---

[63] *Richmond Enquirer*, 3 July 1867.
[64] H. J. Eckenrode, 'The Political History of Virginia during the Reconstruction,' *Johns Hopkins Studies in Historical and Political Science*, XXII, nos. 6, 7, 8 (1904), 75.
[65] William C. Rives to William F. Gordon, Jr, Charlottesville, Va., 17 June 1867, W. C. Rives MSS.
[66] Gordon to Rives, Charlottesville, 1 July 1867, W. C. Rives MSS.
[67] Editorial, *Richmond Enquirer*, 24 April 1867.

was not passivity and non-cooperation but 'the pollution which would follow the taking to our bosom of the blood-stained, crime-blackened, corrupt, merciless party of Senator WILSON of Massachusetts.'[68] On the other hand, this attempt on the part of some of the Confederates to absorb the Negro vote, or at least divide it, helped produce a consolidation of the freedmen behind the faction of J. W. Hunnicutt. By late June, just before the cooperation movement began, the power of the moderate Botts within the Republican Party was visibly on the wane. A gathering in Richmond attended by Pierpont, Senator Wilson, Botts, Hunnicutt, John Jay of New York, and white moderates like John Hawxhurst and L. H. Chandler, was unable to weld the two factions of Botts and Hunnicutt and prepare the party as a unit for alliance with the Whigs.[69] Influence over the Negro vote could only be had by means of affiliation with the radical Hunnicutt faction. That was capitulation, not cooperation.

Thus the movement collapsed with the polarization of Virginia politics. The same pattern developed throughout the South. A moderate coalition between the sections, formed within the Republican Party, had proved impossible of realization in 1866. The failure of the National Union movement was recapitulated a year later with the disintegration of the attempt at interracial and intersectional harmony under the banner of the moderate Republicans and within the terms of the Reconstruction Act. Reconstruction, if controlled by Confederates, depended everywhere upon the formation of a moderate Republican organization. Because this meant division of the white and the black votes, similar movements elsewhere were as unsuccessful as in Virginia.

In Alabama cooperation was widely advocated during the spring, but scant positive action was taken. Instead, the conservatives merely watched and waited while moderate Republicans, mainly former Unionists such as William H. Smith, A. C. Felder, David C. Humphreys, Governor Patton, H. C. Semple, Nicholas Davis, Joshua Morse, and W. J. Bibb attempted to mold an interracial party. Few conservatives agreed with Ben H. Screws, who seemed to be a dissenting co-editor of the *Montgomery Advertiser*, that their presence was needed at the meetings of this group in order to prevent its becoming radical.[70] As

---

[68] Editorial, *Richmond Times*, 26 April 1867.
[69] Eckenrode, 'The Political History of Virginia during the Reconstruction,' p. 73.
[70] *Montgomery Advertiser*, 24 May 1867.

a result, the Republican radicals and moderates subsequently fused and thus left no vehicle by which the conservatives could cooperate. In effect, the policy suggested in the columns of the *Montgomery Advertiser* had tended to prevail among conservatives and that was 'for all Union men, black and white [as opposed to Republicans who were disunionists], to stand aloof, bind themselves to no party, vote for good true honorable men, with the honest interest and purpose of restoring the State to the Union.'[71] And to this Judge Morse gave the angry response: 'We made an active, forward movement then [referring to 1865 and the Johnson program]. It was not active enough, and we failed to reconstruct. Now these same men oppose any action, but content themselves with what they call "dignified submission," compliance and passive acquiescence.'[72]

By contrast, conservatives in Louisiana and Mississippi formed Reconstruction parties led respectively by Fellows and Christian Roselius and by Ethelbert Barksdale and Albert G. Brown. Both were committed to cooperation and both accepted the fact of Negro suffrage, but neither would join the Republicans, hoping instead to entice Negroes to vote for the conservative whites and making no effort to put former Unionists or moderate Republicans at the head of their party. They, therefore, made little headway.[73] In every State there was a disposition among the politicians and the 'respectable' classes to cooperate and vote for a convention. This meant that they were prepared to acquiesce in Negro suffrage. But an acceptable political vehicle by means of which they could engage in reconstruction was lacking. Instead, voters were urged unceasingly to vote for 'good men' regardless of antecedents who would then ally with neither Democrats or Republicans. Presumably 'noblesse oblige' obviated the need for political organization of any sort!

It was in fact extraordinary that there was nothing more than the mere advocacy of the strategy; judging by the lack of discussion of modalities and machinery in public journals and private correspondence, little more than that was even considered. And since there was no discussion of means, not even in private, it must be assumed that

---

[71] Editorial, *ibid.*, 5 June 1867. The term 'Union men' was appropriated by the conservatives to distinguish them from sectional and immoderate politicians.

[72] Judge Morse of Choctaw County to E. LeB. Goodwin, 15 April 1867, in *Montgomery Weekly Advertiser*, 7 May 1867.

[73] *New Orleans Times*, 9 and 12 April 1867; Harris, *Presidential Reconstruction in Mississippi*, pp. 242–4.

engaging in a thoroughgoing canvass and competing with freed slaves and 'mean white radicals' for black and white votes, a majority of which quite probably could not be won, was felt to be too much of a risk and a possible disgrace. Compared to this, suggesting electoral action verbally was easy and comfortable. Also more acceptable was another procedure. To vote against calling a convention or to abstain was more dignified and, even if unsuccessful, did not involve personal humiliation in public or the long-term damage to the Southern political elite of defeat in an open electoral canvass. And, indeed, defeat in the canvass was quite likely, not simply because black and white radical voters would not be easy to manipulate but also on account of the degree of sentiment among the conservatives and their constituents which inclined towards either inaction or voting against a convention. An additional disincentive was that many of the leading conservatives were themselves disfranchised and disqualified from membership in the convention and therefore had nothing personally to gain from a canvass. A final consideration was that although they had been motivated considerably by the need to control reconstruction, especially the new black electorate, most advocates of cooperation had done so on the assumption that the Reconstruction Act was final and mandatory, and would produce settlement. Attempting to reverse the thrust of Congress' legislation would prevent that outcome, for the intent of the Acts was obviously to Republicanize the South. Therefore, cooperation would inevitably result, as the opponents of that policy unceasingly pointed out, in involvement or alliance with the Republican Party.[74]

The direness of the situation, which was apparent to most, but which, because of need, was sublimated temporarily, was described by the *Richmond Enquirer* soon after the first two Reconstruction Acts passed:

There are only two roads to reconstruction. One is, for the Southern States to become unmistakably Radical. Those who are impatient and willing to pay whatever price, should take *that*. The other is, to wait in prudence and quiet,

[74] Regrettably much of this analysis is inferred; there just is not the hard evidence available on which to base a precise statement. Participants in the cooperation policy never explained or examined the reasons why political organization did not develop. They did explain why they did not join the Republican Party but they failed to account for their inability, or refusal, to create the conservative electoral machinery whereby they might have produced a conservative-dominated convention.

a change in Northern sentiment; such a change will remove or overawe the party in power. There is no third course.[75]

By July this was only too evident. Before then, attempts to reconstruct without radicalism, while not engaged in with much conviction or enthusiasm, foundered continually because that moderate coalition which might be productive of intersectional and interracial harmony, but only on the Confederates' terms of course, was forever elusive. The South could resolve the conflict only by capitulation. There was no alternative if readmission to the Union were desired.

c: *Alternatives*

Passage of the first Reconstruction Act in March did not necessarily deprive the South of all redress. The Executive Department had apparently indicated that it would administer the law, but there remained the Judiciary. Ten days after the Act was passed, Governor Worth wrote from Washington, 'At present I think Gov. Sharkie [*sic*], in accordance with the views of the Pres't and Atto. Gen'l, is maturing the only scheme of preserving Constitutional liberty, which is on foot.'[76] That plan was to bring before the Supreme Court an injunction in the name of the State of Mississippi against the President restraining him from executing the Reconstruction Act. By these means there would be provided both an escape from the misery of having to succumb to the Act as well as an alternative course of action. Those, on the other hand, who felt cooperation was advisable, or complete inaction unwise, warned against what the *Jackson Clarion* called 'repose in fancied security.'[77]

Yet the attempt was worthwhile, since there was a possibility that a motion to test the constitutionality of the Act might be entertained. Besides, this move would provide an option since it did not preclude compliance with the legislation pending a decision. But to many, including Sharkey, who initiated the injunction, the judicial action was a part of their determination not to cooperate and, in the event of its failure would produce no change of policy on their part. Agreeing with this was Josiah Turner, Jr, a leading North Carolina Whig. He told Jonathan Worth: 'I am for Judicial resistance to the *last*. . . . I would

[75] Editorial, *Richmond Enquirer*, 13 April 1867.
[76] Jonathan Worth to Graham, Washington, D.C., 12 March 1867, W. A. Graham Collection.
[77] Editorial, *Jackson Clarion*, 10 March 1867.

have you *do nothing* — say *not a word*, give no countenance even to the military move. Sullen silence masterly inactivity is your policy.'[78] Governor Charles Jenkins took a similar approach in his Address to the People of Georgia, informing them that he also proposed to introduce a suit on that State's behalf against the Secretary of War and insinuating unmistakably that he preferred inaction if it failed.[79]

With the aid of Robert J. Walker, Polk's Secretary of the Treasury, Lewis Parsons, and Augustus Garland, Sharkey proceeded with his project. It was intended that Mississippi should not act in isolation but be joined by many other States. Support unfortunately was not forthcoming. The Governors of Alabama, Virginia, and Louisiana were opposed to any course but cooperation under the terms of the Act. North Carolina's Council of State followed the advice of Thomas Ruffin and would not join in the scheme, doubting 'both the power and the inclination of the Court to give us any relief and [thinking] an abortive attempt would impair our influence in the coming elections.'[80] And the Governors of South Carolina and Texas, it soon became apparent, had also decided in favor of cooperation. The Louisiana legislature did resolve not to cooperate in reconstruction and instead to concur in the court-motion but this was insufficient authorization so, as an alternative, Lieutenant-Governor Voorhies canvassed many State executives to initiate action where Louisiana could not.[81] Finally the opinion of Augustus Garland, one of the organizers of the scheme, prevailed: 'To my mind the South should not, by word or deed make herself a party to this proceeding — but should stand still and leave it to those who got it up. After the most careful study and reflection, I conclude, there is nothing of good at all for us in coming in and trying to put it in force.'[82]

This was wise, since, in any case, the response of the Governors had been very unenthusiastic. In fact, there was little confidence altogether, and this did not exclude the scheme's protagonist, William L.

[78] Josiah Turner, Jr, to Worth, 24 March 1867, Worth MSS.
[79] Charles J. Jenkins, Address to the People of Georgia, Washington, D.C., 10 April 1867, *Atlanta Intelligencer*, 16 April 1867.
[80] Worth to Lewis Parsons, Raleigh, 28 March 1867, in *Correspondence of Jonathan Worth*, II, 923.
[81] Resolutions of the Louisiana Legislature, 11 March 1867, *New Orleans Times*, 12 March 1867.
[82] Augustus H. Garland to Stephens, Washington, D.C., 27 March 1867, A. H. Stephens MSS.

Sharkey. Asking for the permission of Governor Humphreys, which was granted, to go ahead in Mississippi's name, Sharkey admitted on 14 March that 'It may turn out that I have made an April fool of myself, though I think not. Indeed I have no doubt about the law, the only doubt that hangs over the question is in the court, some of the judges being very radical.' Even if support were not forthcoming from other States, Sharkey decided nonetheless to go ahead, for 'I shall have nothing to lose, and I shall then, like the girl on her wedding night, lie flat on my back, trust to providence and take whatever comes.'[83]

Nothing very interesting came. The Court would not entertain the case, throwing it out because it was a political matter and because 'a State has no such right to represent its citizens in courts in which the citizens can protect themselves infinitely better than the State can.'[84] This had been anticipated by most politicians, even those anti-secessionists who demanded constitutional guarantees and placed great faith in the Constitution. Alexander Stephens admitted, 'I entertained no hopes for the arrest of [the Acts'] execution from the Supreme Court. I have not been disappointed in the disposition made of the case there.'[85] And Herschel Johnson told Governor Jenkins: 'I scarcely have, even a trembling hope, of the success of your movement. . . . They [The Supreme Court] will hold that, according [to] the fundamental idea of the Bill – to wit, that the State was never out of the Union – the present Govt. of Georgia, organized under the *dictation* of the President, is just as illegal and unconstitutional, as that, the establishment of which, you propose to enjoin. Therefore admitting the unconstitutionality, they will not interpose to uphold one usurpation, to suppress another.'[86]

Needless to say, those who urged cooperation presumed that relief would not be forthcoming from the Court. Walter Crenshaw commented that 'It seems now however to be generally conceded that neither the Supreme Court nor anything else can stand in the way of the will of the Northern people.'[87] And Wiley P. Harris, a Mississippi

[83] William L. Sharkey to Humphreys, Washington, D.C., 14 March 1867, Humphreys MSS.

[84] Opinion of Attorney General Henry Stanbery in *Mississippi* v. *Johnson*, in *National Intelligencer*, 7 May 1867.

[85] Stephens to Thomas G. McFarland, Crawfordville, Ga., 31 May 1867, A. H. Stephens MSS.

[86] Herschel Johnson to Jenkins, Augusta, Ga., 25 April 1867, H. V. Johnson MSS.

[87] Crenshaw to Patton, Evergreen, Conecut Co., Ala., 11 March 1867, Patton Official Correspondence.

secessionist, argued that recourse to the Supreme Court was ridiculous because the Court would not deal with any case involving the political question of whether the South was in or out of the Union.[88] For tactical reasons also, the device of appealing to the Supreme Court was frequently dismissed during these months, first, because the Court would take a long time, maybe a year, to reach a decision and in the meantime the Southern conservatives would have forfeited, or at least failed in, their efforts to control the reconstruction process. A second consideration was that the petition, whether successful or not, would provoke reprisals from the radicals. Eventually, the very fact that there was so great a movement towards cooperation created in itself an obstacle to judicial success because as Herschel Johnson pointed out in May, again to Jenkins, 'I fear the Court is not equal to the occasion. How can timid men be firm, for the right, when such men as Gov. [Joseph] Brown, Orr and others, express the *wish*, that your motion may fail.'[89] Indeed, a month or so earlier when Sharkey had telegraphed Humphreys asking whether he had permission to go ahead on the Mississippi petition, he had admitted 'Our papers and writers God-send to radicals. Crippling me.'[90] Incongruous as it may seem, the Confederates, who had for over six years argued vociferously for constitutional adherence on the North's part and had proclaimed over and again the correctness of their own position, had given up hope in the judicial system as an institution for checking constitutional infringements. Until current political arrangements were reversed, the courts, it was believed, could do nothing.

The referral to the Supreme Court of the North's terms for the defeated South was undertaken at the instigation of men who would not organize under the Reconstruction Acts. Its failure made no difference to their intended course, but to many others it demonstrated that cooperation could not be avoided. Yet, despite occasional defections like the latter, the evidence of a considerable body opposed to their strategy was nonetheless a continual worry for the cooperationists. Gaining control of the Negro vote and thereby of the convention was a difficult enough task; but attainment of these ends was less possible if the conservative whites were divided or a large number unimpressed with the course being pursued. Continued opposition to the

[88] Judge Wiley P. Harris to Messrs Robinson, Helm, Allen, etc., 12 March 1867, in *Jackson Clarion*, 14 March 1867.
[89] Johnson to Jenkins, Augusta, Ga., 11 May 1867, H. V. Johnson MSS.
[90] Sharkey to Humphreys, Washington, D.C., 26 March 1867, Humphreys MSS.

policy of cooperation would therefore help to produce the breakdown of that tactic; and this in turn would vindicate the argument and analysis of its opponents and increase their support. As was so often the case in the post-war South, those who on any particular issue were irreconcilable held the whip-hand.

For many of the non-cooperationists, principle dictated their decision not to reconstruct. In an open letter solicited by the *New Orleans Times*, J. Adolphus Rozier, the leader of the opponents of secession in 1861 and now prominent in the Louisiana Democratic Party, announced that he could not cooperate because

> My theory is to hold fast to the Constitution . . . it is our sheet anchor. . . .
> By our system of government minorities are protected from like oppression of majorities; do away with this and our government becomes anarchical. Acquiescence to that which is so flagrantly violative of many clauses of the Constitution, whether disguised under the plea of necessity, or other new-fangled ideas, virtually declares that instrument obsolete.[91]

Equally principled was the Virginia Whig, Raleigh T. Daniel, who argued that

> The reign of violence cannot last forever. Reason must at some time resume her sway, and with her return, the work of these artificers of ruin, if forced on us against our will must be swept away. Not so if we give it even the semblance of assent; not if they shall be able to quote against us hereafter, the estoppal of *compact*, by which a new class of political rights will have been created, and by which reentrance into the Union, and readmission to representation, will have been acquired.[92]

These positions were firmly grounded on a theory regarding the nature of the American political system as well as on the dangers explicit in the Reconstruction Acts. Alexander Stephens took a different line of approach. In terms of policy only he urged Southerners not to comply with Congress' legislation. Dismissing the assumptions of Daniel and Rozier about the Constitution, he sorrowfully pronounced that 'Liberty secured by constitutional limitations on this continent is in the very throes and agonies of death.' So there was nothing the South could do about it, since 'the Congress plan I take it

---

[91] J. Adolphus Rozier to Hon. Cornelius Fellows, 8 April 1867, in *New Orleans Times*, 9 April 1867.
[92] Raleigh T. Daniel to Robert Ould, etc., in *Richmond Enquirer*, 7 March 1867.

will be carried out whether that portion of the white population amongst us who are not disfranchised join in forming the new organizations or not.' If they did cooperate, Stephens guessed that 'they might save these States now *territorialized* from the lamentable state of things now existing in Ten. and Mo.' But it was doubtful that the white Southerners had 'the wisdom prudence and and discretion' by which even this could be achieved. 'It would require,' he concluded, 'a degree of forbearance, of patience, of concession, or union and harmony amongst themselves that I fear they will never attain.' Even if it were possible, 'It will be only a temporary shield against passing dangers. It will only prolong for a period the advent of that doom which seems to be inevitable indeed already sealed.'[93]

Because public sentiment during the spring was not running in their direction, some non-cooperationists attempted to maintain their point of view and wean opinion away from compliance with the Congressional legislation. Newspapers such as the *Richmond Enquirer*, the *Augusta Constitutionalist*, and the *Jackson Mississippian* continually warned against the course of Joseph E. Brown and General Beauregard, and attacked their constitutional and political positions. On the first count, the constitutional, the *Constitutionalist* on 2 May exposed the logic of Brown's argument for cooperation. Brown had argued that the Act of 2 March was a finality. Despite this assurance, he had warned that confiscation would follow if the Act were opposed. Moreover, the Supplemental Act of 23 March, although not requiring further penalties, had nonetheless proved that the 2 March measure was not final. Furthermore, Brown had sworn an oath to support the Constitution but was urging obedience of a law he himself admitted was unconstitutional, and added to this was his recent acceptance of unconstitutional test oaths and his denial of judicial supremacy. Finally, if, as Brown maintained, the South was in a seceded state and could not appeal to the Supreme Court, did that mean that the North's war to preserve the Union was a blunder as well as fruitless?[94] On the second count, the political, the *Constitutionalist* observed a week later, while cooperation was proving increasingly difficult, that 'We knew very well that Brown was only a way station and those who took the

---

[93]Stephens to J. A. Stewart, Crawfordville, Ga., 2 April 1867, A. H. Stephens MSS. The same viewpoint was expounded in Stephens' letter to Herschel V. Johnson on 30 March 1867, H. V. Johnson MSS.

[94]Editorial, *Augusta Constitutionalist*, 2 May 1867.

Radical train for Brown would not be permitted to tarry long on the track to [Senator Henry] Wilson.'[95]

Although able to snipe at the cooperationists and rebut their arguments, the advocates of non-compliance were, in most States, disorganized and dispersed. Only in Mississippi was there anything approaching organization, and in that State there was formed, and remarkably early too, a political party called the Constitutional Union Party. Led by Whigs William L. Sharkey, Edward M. Yerger, George L. Potter, William H. McCardle and Giles Hillyer, it was organized in mid-June.[96] Of the other States, the situation in South Carolina was typical. Cooperation was widespread and only a lone figure, Benjamin F. Perry, attempted to propagandize for the non-cooperationists' point of view. In the 18 April issue of the *Columbia Phoenix* there appeared a letter from Perry, the first of a series, urging South Carolinians to refuse to submit to reconstruction and Negro suffrage, and choose instead continued military rule. They should vote 'No' in the election for a convention. Any attempts to satisfy the radicals were unavailing for 'there is no faith in tyrants' and the South would not be restored anyway until after the 1868 election. After fighting outside the Union for four years, said Perry, 'Can they not now afford to live four years longer out of that Union, rather than sacrifice their honor, their rights as States, and the great republican principles of freedom?'[97] This was the alternative to legitimizing Negro suffrage by Southern cooperation. In a private letter written during late May, Perry explained his strategy for influencing conservatives to desist from compliance: 'Knowing that the Radicals had scared the Southern people, with *Confiscation* by Congress, from the path of honor and patriotism, I thought I would scare them back again with *Confiscation* by the negroes. . . . My fire has worked admirably. They begin to think they are between "Scylla and Charybdis." I have opened their eyes.'[98]

The non-cooperators need not have worried about inventing devices to induce a swing in sentiment. Cooperation had been entered

[95] *Ibid.*, 11 May 1867.

[96] *Vicksburg Herald*, 30 June 1867. Both Yerger and McCardle were later to leave their imprint on Reconstruction by featuring as plaintiffs in two celebrated habeas corpus cases arising under the Reconstruction Acts.

[97] Benjamin F. Perry to *Columbia Phoenix*, 18 April 1867, in *Charleston Courier*, 19 April 1867.

[98] Perry to F. Marion Nye, Greenville, S.C., 25 May 1867, Perry MSS (Ala.).

into diffidently and out of necessity. It was to meet with rebuffs and obstacles, which were lethal. First of all, as we have seen, organizational difficulties and partisan ties stood in the way of the Southern conservatives' attempts to engage in political action under the laws. Efforts to comply in order to produce conservative-controlled conventions, and therefore in effect to frustrate Congress' intent within the letter of its law, collapsed miserably. The other alternative was to ally with the moderate wing of the Southern Republican Party; this also was to prove too risky, and, after a couple of half-hearted attempts, was ruled out as unacceptable. Therefore, cooperating and voting 'Yes' on the question of whether or not to hold a convention became inexpedient. Non-cooperation, through a 'No' vote or through abstention, consequently appeared to be the more realistic approach by July 1867.

Second, the executor of the Acts was not in sympathy with them. Although Andrew Johnson had told Charles Halpine of the *New York Citizen* on 21 February that he would 'execute all laws scrupulously, and perhaps most scrupulously those which have been passed against my judgement and over my veto,'[99] he very soon reversed this position. On 5 April, General Grant informed Sheridan that 'the fact is there is a decided hostility to the whole Congressional plan of reconstruction at the "White House."'[100] Johnson was privy to the quest for a Supreme Court injunction and had not dissuaded Sharkey and Walker, even though his own Attorney General would be placed in the difficult position of having to argue against the writ. Johnson had nonetheless complied with the requirements of the Act by selecting the military commanders for the Southern Districts and had even gone so far as to overlook some of the more moderate candidates in favor of suggestions from Stanton, the Secretary of War. All the same, it was well known in April and May that the President was not satisfied with the way the Acts were being implemented and had requested Attorney General Stanbery to issue an opinion interpreting the scope of the qualifications for registration and the powers of the military commander. Awareness of this proceeding encouraged Southerners not to register immediately but to procrastinate in the hope of relief or deliverance. The finality of the Reconstruction Acts was therefore put in question, not only by possible stiffer terms from the Congres-

[99] Andrew Johnson, interview with Charles Halpine, 21 February 1867, in *Augusta Constitutionalist*, 28 February 1867.
[100] Ulysses S. Grant to Philip H. Sheridan, Washington, D.C., 5 April 1867, Sheridan MSS.

sional radicals but also by the promise of alleviation from the Executive branch.

Third, initial unwillingness to cooperate was compounded by the way the Acts were functioning in the South. Sheridan explained to his superior, General Grant, what was happening to registration in Louisiana and Texas. 'Politicians,' he said, 'are trying to make it appear that the few white voters registered is on account of the stringency in registration but this is not the case. The whites are waiting until the colored get through. It must not be disguised however that quite a large number of whites will not register because they do not like the military Bill.'[101] It looked as if reconstruction was likely to be swamped by the freedmen, and judging by Sheridan's report, this was a case of the wish fathering the thought. Furthermore, the behavior of the commanders gave cause for alarm. The power of the commanding generals seemed to be limited only by a 'necessary and proper' construction of the Acts. Sickles, in General Order No. 10, virtually suspended South Carolina's legislation concerning indebtedness and assumed extensive control over judicial procedures. General Griffin in Texas issued a jury order which would require registered voters to be impanelled, and that of course included Negroes. Sheridan removed the Attorney General of Louisiana, the Mayor of New Orleans, and an eminent New Orleans judge, and would have removed the Governors of Texas and Louisiana had not Grant advised against so sudden and so provocative a move. And Pope in Georgia, after a dispute with Governor Jenkins in their first communication, had already threatened to have the civil government of Georgia eliminated if it acted as a hindrance to the execution of the Acts.

Reconstruction, it appeared to most Southern conservatives, was not intended, and was not likely, to be moderate. The Act would be construed broadly and few checks imposed on the power of the State commanders or on the governments being created. This was soothing only to those who had advised non-cooperation. After reading Sickles' General Order No. 32 which qualified Negroes as jurors, outlawed segregation in public conveyances, and prohibited the manufacture, sale, or transportation of intoxicating liquors, the *Augusta Constitutionalist* commented with self-satisfaction: 'Let SICKLES continue his patent pills. . . . He is opening the eyes of the timid and enlightening the dreamers of Congressional finality. A little more of this kind of

---

[101]Sheridan to Grant, New Orleans, 4 May 1867, Sheridan MSS.

practice and Dr. Sickles will disgust his patients and force white men to combine for the preservation of their race.'[102]

'Leo,' the *Charleston Courier's* Washington correspondent, was not so sure. He felt the commanders' 'wings must be cut a little, lest they take too high a flight.'[103] For this task the impending opinions of the Attorney General, released in two installments during late May and early June, and finally announced by the Adjutant General on 20 June, would provide aid and authority. The *Charleston Courier* applauded the opinion because it might stabilize reconstruction and mitigate its harshness. 'It became necessary, therefore, not so much as a rebuke in the past as a guidance for the future, that there should be some authoritative exposition of the true measure of [the commanders'] powers and abilities.'[104] But many who urged compliance were skeptical, even angry. The *Charleston Daily News*, unlike its neighbor, the *Courier*, excoriated the President because it expected retaliation from Congress. If Johnson had decided suddenly to change his policy, the *Daily News* complained,

let us at least have some security that he will persevere in his action, and that if, under the opinion of the Attorney General, we refuse obedience to the usurpation of the military commanders, we shall be held harmless for our conduct, that if this construction is repudiated by Congress, . . . we shall not be held responsible for the delay in the work of reconstruction, and the Act will not be amended so as to bear more harshly upon our rights and interests.[105]

Criticism of the President came also from *Flake's Bulletin*. A moderate Republican, Flake believed that Johnson should have requested an explanation of the Act from its proponents in Congress rather than gone ahead independently with an irrelevant one of his own. 'We can a great deal more easily submit to whatever troubles and hardship [the Act] imposes,' he said angrily, 'than to risk others, by uprooting all that has been done.'[106] Reconstruction, he feared, was becoming radical.

Cooperation was becoming more and more difficult and thereby

[102]Editorial, *Augusta Constitutionalist*, 7 June 1867.

[103]'Leo,' Washington correspondent, *Charleston Courier*, 25 April 1867, in *Atlanta Intelligencer*, 1 May 1867.

[104]Editorial, *Charleston Courier*, 21 June 1867.

[105]Editorial, *Charleston Daily News*, 20 June 1867.

[106]Editorial, *Flake's Bulletin*, 28 June 1867. Daniel Sickles had also realized the danger of a special Presidential interpretation of the Acts and he wrote to the

discredited. The course of events in the Military Districts after March and the awareness that revision of the laws, either by Congress or the President, was imminent, provided, for some, a legitimate cause for turning to a policy of non-cooperation, and, for others, a pretext for doing so. The Act of 19 July 1867, which Congress passed in extra session as a rebuttal of the Attorney General's interpretation, decided the issue. Leniency in the execution of the Act was no longer possible. In effect, conservatives could cooperate no longer unless they were prepared to join the radicals. And besides, this latest measure from Congress provided just the scapegoat that the cooperationists needed to blame for their own failure to control the Negro vote. Southern whites and Southern blacks, they argued, had been unable to work together as they naturally would have if radical legislation had not created hostility and forced a division into separate political parties. But in actual fact, for the proponents of cooperation, reconstruction had failed before the July Reconstruction Act.

President warning him against what he thought was developing from the Stanbery instructions. In a letter of 20 June he wrote: 'Allow me to suggest that it will be better to *control* the *execution* of the Reconstruction Acts according to your judgement as to the means employed and measures adopted, than by *Construction* as to the true intent and meaning of the Acts to raise new issues with Congress involving perhaps a contradiction of the views expressed in your Veto Message [that the Reconstruction Act fastened military government on the South] in relation to the Acts and possibly giving supposed occasion for further legislation.' Johnson MSS, Series I. Johnson took no notice of this even though he had asked for any comments Sickles would like to offer when both men met in North Carolina early in June. On 19 June Sickles submitted his resignation because of Stanbery's opinion which was an implied criticism of his role in Military District No. 2 and because his administration would be undermined, if not negated, by so limited a construction of a commander's powers. Johnson rejected the resignation.

10

Reconstruction resisted –
July to December 1867

a: *Non-cooperation*

Doubts about the possibility or desirability of reconstructing under the Congressional Acts were accumulating during late June and July. Commanders noticed this. General Wager Swayne told Chase on 28 June that 'there seems to be a growing feeling against a [constitutional] convention. . . . Our [Republican nominating] convention was an eminent success, and so far there is no appearance of opposing organizations. What we have most to fear is 'No Convention.''[1] A political vacuum was emerging in the South. Conservative whites sensing the unacceptability of the restrictions and demands involved in cooperation were beginning to disengage from reconstruction and instead to adopt a posture which was passive and uninvolved. 'No Convention,' as proposed since April by Benjamin Perry, came, therefore, to be the course generally advocated and the one best suited to the Southern white disposition. Before the July Act was even on the statute books, Sheridan was telling Grant, 'I see a slight tendency on part of politicians to go against Convention and reconstruction. Mississippi is strongly that way. Texas is beginning to look that way and Georgia also. They will have no success in Louisiana.'[2]

That reconstruction was at a crucial stage was also realized by Sickles, who was commanding in the Carolinas. He believed that the manifest disinclination of the whites to cooperate had to be corrected by encouragement. 'A more liberal amnesty,' he told Lyman Trumbul, 'is, in my judgement, essential to the success of the Congressional plan of reconstruction.' With 'the addition made to the loyal vote by the enfranchisement of the colored people,' there was then no need for the disqualification clause of the Howard amendment. Moreover, he said, 'The *people* can surely be entrusted to judge and select from those who

---

[1] General Wager Swayne to Salmon P. Chase, Montgomery, 28 June 1867, Chase MSS.

[2] General Philip H. Sheridan to U.S. Grant, New Orleans, 10 July 1867, Sheridan MSS.

took part in the rebellion the men at once qualified and sincere in their adhesion to the new order of things. Such men, being eligible to office, will have motives to identify themselves with reconstruction, and to support the views of the majority.' After all, 'Now, more than ever men of ability and experience in public business are needed' and their exclusion from governmental and judicial positions 'exposes the experiment of universal suffrage to needless hazards.'[3]

Except in Virginia where belated action and the existence of a strong moderate Republican faction kept hopes alive, the cooperationists were by early July in obvious disarray. And this was compounded by the Third Reconstruction Act passed later that month. In this context, non-cooperation became the obvious strategy. No longer, as the summer wore on, was this policy the property of its initiators alone; it had become Southern strategy by the time voting for the constitutional conventions took place in the fall and winter.

The initiative towards compliance with the Acts had been taken on grounds of expediency and the need to control what seemed to be inevitable, that is, the injection into Southern political life of the enfranchised freedmen. In this thrust the leading men had generally been the seccessionists of 1861 who had until this moment played an inconspicuous role in Southern politics since the war, partly out of desire and partly by necessity. Continuing to believe as they had done before and during the war that there existed neither a harmony of values nor a mutuality of interest between the sections, they had expected little or no help from conservatives in the North but instead had simply waited until the final and mandatory terms were propounded by the dominant political element in that section. Because of their passivity, they had offered little opposition as a group to the activism of 1865 and had concurred in the policy of 'masterly inactivity' in 1866. In contrast, political office and leadership had generally been assumed by their opponents of 1861 who were ideologically far more attached to the Union and often were more national in outlook as well as in economic interest.

Relying on the constitutional protection provided by State rights, the anti-secessionists hoped to ameliorate the South's predicament by cautious cooperation with Northern opponents of sectionalism in the hope that a national consensus could be produced which would restore

[3] General Daniel E. Sickles to Lyman Trumbull, Charleston, S.C., 5 July 1867, in *National Intelligencer*, 10 July 1867.

the Confederates to their place in the Union with minimal short-term or permanent damage. They had therefore been very skeptical about complying with the Reconstruction Act and instead had persevered in their policy of 'masterly inactivity,' refusing to acquiesce in measures which either would hurt themselves directly and immediately and the fundamental law permanently or which would prevent the emergence of a favorable cross-sectional consensus. Accordingly they were leading advocates of non-cooperation, and there was an unyielding firmness about their stance. In spite of the imminent danger, William A. Graham gritted his teeth and announced that 'a half-faced fellowship, a patched-up Union, based on fear, and accompanied with mental reservations, should not be desired.'[4] And with a similar determination, the aged Alfred Huger, Charleston's Unionist Postmaster during the furor over the mailing of anti-slavery tracts in the 1830s, complained that 'to love the Union was my Nature and my inheritance, but it was a Union of Equal Sovereigns! – Can I give my affection to its daily desecration, made more revolting by a hideous and disgusting mockery? and shall I take part myself in this barbarian tragedy?'[5]

The resistance of these men was made more fierce by a feeling that they had been betrayed. Believing themselves to be supporters of union and men of moderation, their efforts at restoring the South had been met by continual rebuffs. The Republicans had persistently refused, in their Southern policies, to distinguish between them and the 'fire-eating' precipitators of the rebellion, and there was still no recognition of these differences in the Reconstruction Act. Yet now that the proposals were reaching their extremity, the secessionists were discovering that they could accept them, and, by this maneuver, might even wrest political control of the South from those who for two years had tried to engineer a moderate settlement. Well, the anti-secessionists would not give up; they would continue to resist. The capitulation of 1861 which was so greatly regretted would not be repeated. Writing after the events in 1867, Jonathan Worth's son-in-law, William H. Bagley, confided to another anti-secessionist, Benjamin Hedrick, 'The plea of policy I listened to in the days of rebellion, and I then determined that I never would do the like again, and would, under all circumstances in the future, vote for those measures only which I

---

[4]Graham to William Pell, Hillsboro, N.C., 10 October 1867, W. A. Graham Collection.
[5]Alfred Huger to Perry, Charleston, S.C., 4 July 1867, Perry MSS (Ala.).

thought right in themselves, and leave the consequences to a "Higher Power." [6]

Whether many others were so aware of the need to redeem past failures did not matter, since it was very obvious that they, like Bagley, considered themselves men of principle, post-war keepers of the Southern conscience and defenders of the American constitutional faith. Yet by the summer of 1867 their opposition on principle to the Reconstruction Act had become expedient, and they were joined by the cooperationists who had been repelled by what that policy implied.

Even though it was in effect a movement to defeat the purpose of the Acts, non-cooperation was nonetheless quite within their provisions, and was even anticipated by them. The Supplemental Act of 23 March which outlined the precise mechanics of reconstruction explained that in the vote to select delegates to the convention, there was a legitimate choice of balloting either 'Convention' or 'No Convention.' A majority for the latter course could, within the law, defeat the call and nullify reconstruction. There was a further way of defeating the Act for, if a majority of the registered voters did not vote, and it mattered not whether the polled vote was 'for' or 'against,' then the convention could not be held. A second chance to defeat reconstruction still remained for if the call for a convention were not defeated, the constitution which it produced could be. The existence of so much choice in the clauses of the Acts was evidence that, in spite of the finality implied in a law of the land, Confederate consent was still desired by the North, and it could still be withheld. But consent and coercion were finely balanced. Was this proposal, like the President's terms and the Howard amendment, voluntary, or was it mandatory? At first it had seemed to be better, out of self-defense and self-interest, to consider the act compulsory, but as the purpose and performance of that law became evident, to assume that choice was offered seemed to Southern conservatives more salutary.

By early July the existence of legal alternatives under the Act, which had earlier been denied or ignored by the advocates of cooperation, was now readily admitted. The free exercise of choice would, after all, permit open discussion on all sides and 'effect an actual, not a sham reconstruction of the Union over the Southern States,' and surely this, suggested the *Augusta Constitutionalist*, was preferable to a drum-head reconstruction, implemented purely for the purpose of making the

---

[6]William H. Bagley to Hedrick, Raleigh, 1 May 1868, B. S. Hedrick MSS.

South radical.[7] Furthermore, the availability of choice, as the *Constitutionalist* well knew, did present the conservatives with the option of rejecting. To vote 'Yes' to holding a convention was to cooperate and to consent, and this was avoidable. Herschel V. Johnson was adamant that the South should withhold its assent. 'It cannot fail to strike the mind of every reflecting man, that the CONSENT of the people to the proposed plan of reconstruction is desired by the dominant party; for, having obtained our consent, they will insist that whatever is irregular is thereby cured, that whatever is unconstitutional is thereby waived, and they absolved from their sins. Then the door of redress, in every form, will have been forever closed.' In effect, 'It is sought to compel us, by appeals to our fears, to consent to a fundamental change in our system of government.' But, Johnson thundered, 'We are overpowered, but not conquered. They can rob us of *freedom*, but never let us *agree* to be *slaves*.'[8] Furthermore, as the *Arkansas Gazette* remarked, 'Congress has allowed [the Southern States] the choice of reconstructing according to a certain plan, or remaining as they are; and surely the exercise of the privilege granted cannot fairly be considered a resistance to law.'[9]

The conservatives were therefore free to consider the Reconstruction Acts in terms of their expediency and to weigh the advantages of cooperation or its opposite. And with similar arguments to those used to urge rejection of the Howard amendment, non-cooperationists explained that cooperation was not a self-interested policy possessing many advantages but rather that it contained many drawbacks and fatal dangers. Cooperationist warnings that representation in Congress would be forfeited by non-compliance were refuted with the argument that the kind of representation obtainable under the Acts was utterly not worth having, in fact should be prevented since it would be radical. The argument that worse might be inflicted was rejected on the grounds that conciliation would only strengthen a declared enemy so that he could more easily hurt the South, and besides the radical governments likely to emerge in the South would probably be more hostile even than Congress. And finally the observation that a convention would be held anyway was no reason for the conservatives to facilitate its creation. These counters and refutations were

[7] Editorial, *Augusta Constitutionalist*, 19 May 1867.
[8] Johnson to John G. Westmoreland, James F. Alexander, etc., Augusta, Ga., 11 July 1867.
[9] Editorial, *Arkansas Gazette*, 8 October 1867.

elaborated in public letters from Perry, Sharkey, Johnson, Graham, Hill, Hampton, and others, during late spring and early summer.

A final consideration raised by the availability of choice was that it removed finality. Senator-elect Alcorn, although deciding to co-operate, noticed this in April and pointed out that those who urged cooperation on the grounds that the Act was mandatory and con-clusive were using 'a logic so subtle as to baffle [the] skill' of 'a literary antiquarian.' The Reconstruction Acts were no more final than the Howard amendment had been.[10] Consequently, it could be argued that final terms were still awaited. On this assumption, Wade Hamp-ton took Congress to task because 'They have not asked the State to return to the Union, nor have they announced the terms upon which it can do so. When they have done these things, it will be time enough for the State to take counsel how to act.'[11]

Postulating and providing choice may have been intended as an incentive to comply but in fact it invariably presented both the means, and the justification for, resistance and rejection.

Arguments asserting freedom of choice and the expediency of employing that choice to reject cooperation and vote 'No' were ubiq-uitious during the summer and fall of 1867. The existence of choice had been overlooked in the dash to cooperate. Also ignored had been the unconstitutionality of the legislation, and this became prominent in the propaganda of the non-cooperationists during late spring and early summer. Few conservatives would have denied this in the spring but the cooperationists preferred to overlook it, while those, usually anti-secessionists naturally who could not so easily dismiss it, took the question to the Supreme Court. But when that failed and an offen-sive was mounted against cooperation in July by Benjamin H. Hill, Herschel V. Johnson, and Benjamin Perry, the argument of uncon-stitutionality was strenuously presented as the overwhelming reason why Southerners should not have anything to do with the legislation. This in effect challenged the motives and principles of those who had been willing to assent to an illegal act. And it drew from the *Mont-gomery Advertiser*, which was advising cooperation, the angry retort that 'the opponents of reconstruction could not be reasonably com-plained of if they would only confine themselves to that mode of op-

[10] Alcorn to *Friar's Point Coahomian*, 26 April 1867, in *Vicksburg Herald*, 2 May 1867.

[11] Wade Hampton to D. W. Ray, Wm. H. Talley, etc., 7 August 1867, in *Charles-ton Courier*, 29 August 1867.

position which the acts of Congress clearly authorize,' but 'in taking this ground they go beyond the limits of discretion which the law prescribes, spurn the law itself as possessing no binding force, and denounce as wilful perjurors those who act in obedience to it.'[12]

Nonetheless, the constitutional argument was persuasive. In an open letter published in Mississippi during October, Sharkey described the infringements of the Constitution which were perpetrated by the Acts. They assumed, 'in short, to abolish all Constitutional government, State and Federal, and to declare them annulled, and that Congress is the supreme power and it might as well have then said, in so many words, all Constitutional government is hereby abolished, and Congress assumes supreme power over the national and State governments.'[13] Even before the July Act, Herschel Johnson marvelled that 'If Congress had taxed its ingenuity to see how many and what grievous infractions of the Constitution it could compress in the fewest words, they could have originated nothing more successful or nefarious than the proposed scheme of reconstruction.' In view of this, how could the threat to impose harsher measures be taken seriously, for 'what more rigorous can human wickedness devise?'[14]

Southern strategies under the Reconstruction Acts cannot be understood without considering a feature of the political structure in the South which had played an influential role in mobilizing public opinion against the Howard amendment and which was still pervasive after the passage of the Reconstruction Act. Incumbent officeholders were as eager to retain power as they had been in 1866. The March Reconstruction Acts stipulated that officials would remain in office and the civil government would be regarded as provisional until the State was reconstructed and restored to the Union. The incentive to cooperate was, therefore, considerable since the reconstruction process could be influenced, if not controlled, by the current State officials. And a prompt cooperation might also be rewarded by relief from disabilities

---

[12]Editorial, *Montgomery Advertiser*, 23 August 1867.

[13]William L. Sharkey to W. H. Worthington, editor, [Columbus] *Mississippi Index*, in *Vicksburg Herald*, 11 October 1867.

[14]Herschel V. Johnson to John G. Westmoreland, James F. Alexander, James P. Hambleton etc., Augusta, Ga., 11 July 1867, H. V. Johnson MSS. Benjamin H. Hill opened his campaign with a speech before General Pope and his staff, Davis Hall, Atlanta, 16 July 1867, and he continued throughout the summer in his 'Notes on the Situation,' published in newspapers throughout the South.

at the hands of a satisfied Congress. This incidentally was in sharp contrast with the Howard amendment which would have disqualified the incumbents immediately and removed all semblance of power from them. But if, under the Reconstruction Acts, it should prove impossible to control or influence appreciably the emerging political order, then not only was there no reason to continue cooperating, but, in fact, every reason actively to prevent the accomplishment of reconstruction and to keep the State out of the Union. Thereby control of the State could be retained and the Howard amendment, which had to be ratified prior to readmission, bypassed. Furthermore, readmission under a radical government and with radical representatives in Congress could be forestalled. There was no need, or desire, for readmission under such terms; retention of office and power within the State was far more important. Officeholders consequently had every interest in voting down, or nullifying, a reconstruction process which, in the end, would destroy their own power.

Little was made in 1867 of the vested interests of Southern State officials, and this was in sharp contrast with the abundance of evidence available in the debate on the Howard amendment. But the statement, early in 1868, of Robert J. Powell, Holden's aide in North Carolina, indicated the reality of this official pressure-group. Requesting Stanton's aid in the removal of 7,000 officeholders prior to the vote on the State's reconstruction constitution, he wrote that 'These rebel officials are not only against us because of their disloyalty, but each has a direct personal interest in keeping the State out. So long as it is kept out, they retain their offices, as soon as it is restored they go out, hence it is a life and death struggle with each and every one of them, so far as offices is concerned.'[15] To the pressure that was already being exerted against cooperation with the Reconstruction Acts was added therefore the self-interest of thousands of individual officeholders.

Although non-cooperation had become almost a necessity by mid-summer, many politicians, nonetheless, justified it as a legitimate preference out of the two alternatives held out by the Reconstruction Acts. Continued military rule or Negro suffrage was the choice, and non-cooperationists indicated, by the course they had adopted, that they preferred the former. In his first letter to the *Phoenix* in April, Benjamin Perry had held out the prospect of military rule as a preferable alternative to the anarchy and disorder involved in Negro suffrage. Undis-

[15] Robert J. Powell to Edwin Stanton, Raleigh, 15 January 1868, Stanton MSS.

mayed, he had pronounced that 'a despotism, wisely, justly, and virtuously administered, is the most perfect government that can be established. It is the government of God. . . .'[16]

A preference for military rule was a more likely response from General Wade Hampton, who announced, in a letter published in mid-August, that 'I think it far preferable the State should remain in its present condition, under military rule, than that it should give its sanction to measures which we believe to be illegal, unconstitutional, and ruinous.'[17] From Herschel Johnson and Alfred Huger likewise, preference was given to military rule. Johnson argued that 'Much as I deprecate military government, it is far preferable to such a government as will probably be inaugurated under the Sherman programme [i.e. the Reconstruction Acts].'[18] And Huger warned that 'we should be careful not to aggravate, by *our own act*, the Evils that surround us – and not hastily escape a "Military Government," administered by intelligence and policy, to embrace such a one as Negro suffrage, with "Agrarianism" as its cardinal principle, *must* provide.'[19]

Military commanders who were white and who could be negotiated with as individuals were preferable to assemblies which, it was assumed, would be dominated by unschooled demagogues. Moreover, in some cases, the commander was known to be moderate, so Humphreys, back in April, could soften the public reaction to non-cooperation by arguing that 'Military power may become intolerable only when it is placed in the hands of the vicious and the unjust, which, happily, is not the case in Mississippi,' where Edward Ord was in command.[20] He, Schofield, Hancock, Meade and Gillem were either Democrats or moderate Republicans and offered, it was hoped, more protection than a radical legislature. Furthermore, if reconstruction

[16]Benjamin F. Perry to *Columbia Phoenix*, in *Charleston Courier*, 19 April 1867.
[17]Wade Hampton to D. W. Ray, Wm. H. Talley etc., 7 August 1867, in *Charleston Courier*, 29 August 1867. The delay prior to publication can be explained by the great concern of the South Carolina cooperationists that a letter from so prominent a man might clinch the defeat of cooperation or certainly weaken it significantly. And at this stage they were not absolutely convinced that cooperation was an ineffective policy to pursue, or that it should be abandoned. In all likelihood, Hampton's letter provoked a crisis in the ranks of the conservatives in S.C. See E. P. Alexander to Perry, Columbia, S.C., 20 August 1867, Perry MSS (Ala.).
[18]Herschel V. Johnson to John G. Westmoreland etc., above.
[19]Alfred Huger to Benjamin F. Perry, Charleston, S.C., 12 June 1867 and 4 July 1867, Perry MSS (Ala.).
[20]Humphreys, Proclamation, 6 April 1867, in *Jackson Clarion*, 6 April 1867.

were not accomplished, the State government, even though 'provisional,' and theoretically subordinate to the military, would remain in effect. Cooperation, on the other hand, meant giving an affirmative answer to a question which Wade Hampton considered to be fundamental and ominous in its ramifications: 'Are the people of the State willing by the adoption of a new and totally different Constitution, to ignore all the teachings of the past, to subvert the whole order of society, to change, in a moment, its whole organization, to commit (if the expression may be used) political suicide.'[21]

Military rule did not, however, turn out to be the panacea anticipated.[22] Nor was it an alternative. With ultimate authority over the implementation and interpretation of the reconstruction legislation, the military commanders were aware that, under the July Act, the mere swearing of the ironclad oath was not conclusive as a qualification for registration and they were also convinced that the registration of the blacks should be as thorough as possible. Thus, they were hardly defenders of the conservatives against 'anarchy' but, in fact, were responsible for ensuring its emergence. In other words, in spite of the apparent choice of either 'no convention' and military rule or of 'convention' and Negro government, the State commanders' mandate from Congress was to provide as surely as possible for a registration so thoroughgoing that defeat of the call for a convention would be virtually impossible.

Congress did not issue its final terms to the South, the Reconstruction Act, with the intention that the South should then be able to nullify them, without even formally rejecting them. And if the conventions or the subsequent constitutions were voted down, the matter would not rest there, for further legislation would be forthcoming either for individual States or the whole section. Choice was a snare — to exercise it would result in swift punishment. The South was to return to the Union; it was not to be allowed to choose to stay out, although it seemed that the alternative did exist. Angrily Charles Jenkins com-

---

[21] Wade Hampton to D. W. Ray etc., above.

[22] It has been suggested to me that Southerners probably preferred military rule because, rather than being flatly unconstitutional like the Reconstruction Act, it was extra-constitutional and governed instead by international law. While this fact about military rule is undoubtedly true, nowhere was there any indication that this was one of the considerations influencing non-cooperationists. Instead, they always argued in terms of the alternatives offered by two evils and of the political advantages of military rule over misrule by the convention.

plained to the President late in November that 'in view of the clear alternative offered in the reconstruction acts by Congress, either to accept their terms, or to remain under military rule, it is a terrible outrage to have still further advantage given to the blacks by the devices and schemes of the military Commander, and to find ourselves denounced as rebels, and factionists.'[23]

Blame for the refusal of the South to vote for conventions was quickly attached, therefore, to the military commanders, rather than to Congress or the President or even the South itself. The *New Orleans Times* argued in September that the problem 'has been the interpretation, the administration of a law, harsh enough of itself, but made a thousand-fold harsher by the mode of its administration. The agents who have directed this administration have been the real and only impediments to reconstruction.'[24] Ironically, so the *Times* mused, Governors Wells and Throckmorton had already been removed (Jenkins, Pierpont, and Humphreys followed in 1868) on the grounds that they had impeded reconstruction, yet they had been deposed by those most guilty of obstruction, the military commanders. Further indication of this awareness was presented by the *Arkansas Gazette* when, after noticing that a majority favoring a convention in July had become a majority opposed in October, it explained that 'the change has been brought about by the efforts of partisan registrars to give control of the body to negroes and violent party men whose aim is to place the state in the condition of Tennessee.'[25]

There was no avoiding the consequences. Not even the military could protect Confederates and those who supported them. The observations of the *Charleston Courier* in July were to be thoroughly vindicated in the ensuing months. The *Courier* had concluded that readmission would not be possible 'until the Southern States are committed hand and foot to the principles and platform of the Republican party [so that] it is due to candor and justice that this should be avowed.'[26] Equally aware at this date was its Charleston neighbor, the *Mercury*, which was now advising even its own State with its black majority not to cooperate, for 'to co-operate with [the Republicans] in the Southern States now, in their flagitious policy, is to be false to the plain

[23] Charles J. Jenkins to Andrew Johnson, Milledgeville, Ga., 22 November 1867, Johnson MSS, Series I.
[24] Editorial, *New Orleans Times*, 19 September 1867.
[25] Editorial, *Arkansas Gazette*, 22 October 1867.
[26] Editorial, *Charleston Courier*, 10 July 1867.

purport of the act – to raise up an antagonism between the races – to aid them in the purpose of ruling the white race, by the black.'[27] Those in Congress who had formulated the Act were in effect failing to obey it. The conservatives alone were trying to remain true to its letter. Therefore, they felt justified in refusing to cooperate in its execution. Moreover, in doing this, they were still acting within the letter of the law because this option was provided in the 23 March Act.

Whether cooperating or not, Southerners could not exclude radicalism from their section. But at least by voting the convention down, the radicals in Congress might be forced into dangerously extremist legislation or might find that reconstruction was too complicated a procedure to continue implementing. Therefore, although it could not prevent the emergence of radical Republicanism in the South, non-cooperation was to remain as conservative policy.

Devices and arguments for promoting this policy were never lacking. Throughout 1867 the advocates of disengagement and non-compliance continually stressed and exggerated the evils and horror which would accompany reconstruction. 'Africanization' and 'Negro supremacy,' not merely equality, became slogans to describe the enormity of the evil being inflicted on the South, as Negro jurors and thousands of Negro voters were created during the summer. General Griffin in Texas noticed as early as May that 'some officials have taken courage [and] are allowing the inference to circulate that no man who ever gave a crust of bread or a drink of water to a rebel soldier can take the required oath. By this they hope to show that the Courts of Justice are practically closed, and thus obtain a modification or a revocation of the [Jury] order.'[28] Many even talked openly of the inevitability of war between the races. Alexander Stephens had, from the outset, anticipated that terrible catastrophe as a consequence of the Reconstruction Acts, and one of his frequent correspondents, the war-time Unionist, J. A. Stewart, took the idea into print in a letter to the *Cincinnati Commercial* during July. 'Too humane,' he said, 'to put us all to death outright by ordering a summary and sweeping extermination, they turn us over to negro majorities previously inflamed by radical teaching, then trust to the Lord to guide their hands in cutting our

---

[27] Editorial, *Charleston Mercury*, 26 July 1867.
[28] General Charles Griffin to General Philip Sheridan, Galveston, Tex., 26 May 1867, Sheridan MSS.

throats.'[29] Something similar was implied in the address of South Carolina's Conservative (anti-reconstruction) convention when it noted that the Reconstruction Acts 'give us war and anarchy' not peace; it was a 'wild and reckless experiment [which] comes home to the hearthstone of every citizen, and involves family and property, society, liberty and even life itself.'[30]

Basic to this strategy of painting, in lurid and grim colors, all the possible evils imaginable in reconstruction was the intention not merely of persuading conservative whites to stand aloof and radical whites to fear for the calamity which they were inducing, but, by the widespread disengagement and inaction thus achieved, to encourage, even to force, the Southern radicals to proceed to extremities. Excesses would redound to the South's benefit, and Sharkey, amongst others, publicly welcomed them: 'Well, let it come; let usurpations be accumulated until their united enormities shall shock the sense of the American people and awaken them to the dangers that surround them. Extremes always bring counter action, and great reforms in government spring from great abuses of power. Such a reform we now much need to restore the Constitution to its purity.'[31]

Cooperation would moderate these developments and would settle Negro suffrage on the South. Resistance was more fruitful. 'For our part,' said the *Augusta Constitutionalist* in October, 'we think the sooner the worst comes, the better. When the Radicals have got to the end of their rope, the rope may determine the end of the Radicals;' and a week later, 'the more infamous the elements composing any Southern convention, the better for the South, at last.'[32] So if the 'No Convention' votes of the conservatives were insufficient to prevent a convention from being held, benefit would still accrue. In October the *Richmond Whig* was emphatic:

Our defeat, considered in connection with all its repulsive concomitants, may have a powerful effect in assisting to give victory to the Conservative masses of the North. Those masses are white and when they see an organized

---

[29] Alexander H. Stephens to Thomas G. McFarland, Crawfordville, Ga., 31 May 1867, and to J. A. Stewart, Crawfordville, Ga., 2 April 1867, and J. A. Stewart to Stephens, Rome, Ga., 25 July 1867, all in Stephens MSS.

[30] Address to the People of South Carolina by the Conservative Convention of South Carolina, in *Charleston Courier*, 9 November 1867.

[31] Sharkey to W. H. Worthington, above.

[32] Editorials, *Augusta Constitutionalist*, 26 October and 2 November 1867.

effort to convert the ten excluded States into black States, for the purpose of opposing and controlling the white people of the South and of establishing negro supremacy in the American Government, can they stand still and let so signal an infamy succeed? We think not.[33]

Unless the results of reconstruction were presented to the North in unequivocal guise, the danger and injustice of it would probably be ignored. Thomas Bragg, a North Carolina secessionist, had realized this soon after the first Reconstruction Act was passed. He told Worth: 'A change at the North is our only hope for civil liberty in this country; and I am quite willing the Radicals should make themselves blacker and blacker, until they become in the sight of all men — especially, all good men — *black and all black!*'[34] The Northern reaction, watched for ever since the summer of 1865, could not long be delayed once Northern self-interest were touched. The earlier measures of the radicals and the ensuing dismantling of the Constitution had not stirred the North to revolt, nor had Negro suffrage. Negro supremacy and black control of ten States could hardly be a negligible consideration in the North. It would be bound to affect that section as well as the South. The Union could not survive half slave, half free. Whereas in the 1850s Negro slavery had been the issue, now it was white slavery. In that case, the *Atlanta Intelligencer* wondered, 'will the white men of the North and the Great West fail to come to the rescue? We answer for them — THEY WILL NOT FAIL.[35] No longer would reaction result from Northern good nature but from Northern self-interest. The secessionist *Charleston Daily News* remarked: 'It is vain for us to speak of conciliation. The black man and the white man today may both desire it, but the law is fixed that members of the same race will and must cling together.'[36]

Negro suffrage had been rejected in the North on every occasion since 1865 when it had been put before an electorate; so surely, William H. Trescot told the Republican Senator, Henry Wilson, Negro supremacy in the South could not be enforced by Northern white men, unless they intended to destroy the Union and even white civiliza-

[33] Editorial, *Richmond Whig*, 26 October 1867.
[34] Thomas Bragg to Jonathan Worth, Smithfield, N.C., 25 March 1867, Worth MSS.
[35] Editorial, *Atlanta Intelligencer*, 12 November 1867.
[36] Editorial, *Charleston Daily News*, 1 October 1867.

tion.[37] Harmony between the sections, so elusive hitherto, could be produced now because, as the *Charleston Mercury* pointed out, 'the white men of the North, as well as of the South, will thus have a *common cause* against negro predominance.'[38] Differences there may have been over slavery; there could be none on race. Racism, therefore, would reunite the divided Union. Nothing else could. This common bond had been fundamental to the assumption that Northerners would renounce the radical Republicans; but now it was inescapably revealed, and the outlines of a returning consensus could be discerned, even felt.

Until the summer of 1867 Southerners had been unable to utilize this common denominator effectively and had not gained the sympathy they had expected. But it was well-known how the Northern States treated blacks, and more sensitive Southerners guessed that one of the chief reasons for the Republicans' desire to aid and protect the Negro in the South was to make sure he did not need to come North.[39] So, after the rejection of Southern representatives by Congress in December 1865, the *Richmond Times* had suggested that 'since we cannot get white men in Congress, let us now try the black.' The strategy was obvious: 'We want negroes to be so thick in Congress that a man standing on the wharf at Acquia Creek, with a favorable wind, could smell them. We want their wool to be knee-deep in the halls of Congress, and we do not want any one there who is not five times blacker than the ace of spades.'[40]

This then was the ultimate deterrent. The reaction at the North would be precipitated by forcing the issue and thus shocking public opinion into repudiating the radicals' pernicious projects. In late July what was known as the South Carolina Plan was evolved, a scheme to divide the spoils with the Southern radical leaders, the white conservatives retaining the offices and control in the State government, the radicals and Negroes receiving the Federal positions. The *Arkansas Gazette* greeted this proposal warmly since it would ricochet against the Congressional radicals on account of the 'violent antipathy to the negro race' in the North.[41] As a consequence, it would soon be

[37] William H. Trescot to Henry Wilson, Hazlewood, nr. Pendleton, S.C., 8 September 1867, W. H. Trescot MSS.

[38] Editorial, *Charleston Mercury*, 26 July 1867.

[39] For a discussion of this feature in Republican policy, see C. Vann Woodward, 'Seeds of Failure in Radical Race Policy,' in Harold Hyman, ed., *New Frontiers of the American Reconstruction* (Urbana, Ill.: University of Illinois Press, 1967).

[40] Editorial, *Richmond Times*, quoted in *Jackson Clarion*, 3 March 1866.

apparent that reconstruction was not a guarantee of the security and stability of the nation, but merely a means of punishing the South by forcing upon it bad government, which would then, of necessity, permeate the national councils and the social fabric of the whole country.

The latency of this reaction was one of the premises upon which these conclusions were based. Those who wished to defeat the call for a convention were constantly on the look-out for evidence that Northern opinion was beginning to turn. Being, in the main, anti-secessionists, they had always expected from the North a rallying in opposition to the radicals, and this could not long be delayed. The wonder was rather that it had not been manifested earlier.

Within a month after the passage of the first two Reconstruction Acts, the election in Connecticut had registered a rebuff to the Republicans. The *Richmond Times* and most other Southern newspapers noticed this but the response was hardly ecstatic: 'It is a mere straw, a cheering sign, a patch of clear sky, amid dark and menacing clouds, and nothing more. Practically, it will in no way change or effect the character of the Fortieth Congress.'[42] Even the non-cooperationists were not terribly impressed. Herschel Johnson a few weeks later observed: 'We are assured by intelligent friends North, that the people are beginning to think, and that a reaction has already begun, which will correct the disorder of the times and save liberty yet I wish I had more hope in this direction — all I *dare* say is, that such a deliverance is *barely possible.*'[43] Even Perry, in his first *Phoenix* letter, noticed the favorable Connecticut returns. But he added quickly that he was opposing the call of a convention not because relief from the North was imminent (though actually he believed it was not), but because endorsing it would not bring relief in any form. He urged non-cooperation even if it took a hundred years for the reaction to come, but, more specifically, he was convinced that restoration would not be attained until after the Presidential election.[44]

As late even as December when the South had been treated to the Republican reverses of September in Maine and California, and of

[41] Editorial, *Arkansas Gazette*, 13 August 1867.
[42] Editorial, *Richmond Times*, 4 April 1867.
[43] Herschel V. Johnson to Charles S. Jordan, Augusta, Ga., 23 April 1867, H. V. Johnson MSS.
[44] Perry to *Columbia Phoenix*, in *Charleston Courier*, 19 April 1867.

October in the Pennsylvania and Ohio elections (and Ohio actually rejected the Howard amendment), there was still no good reason to conclude that salvation had come. In fact, as the *Jackson Clarion*, still attempting to cooperate, had warned, such a defeat would probably elicit more intense efforts by the radicals, not less.[45] In December, Herschel Johnson was cautious and even skeptical. He told Stephens: 'I am of course glad to see the reaction in the North. I believe, judging from the history of Counter Revolutions, that it will be complete,' but he added that it was too late to rescue the South from reconstruction since, before the Congressional elections of 1868, that process would be crystallized and brought to a conclusion.[46] It was a good sign, but it could not overthrow reconstruction. Besides, for the doctrinaire anti-secessionists, only a total reaction was adequate. The anti-slavery amendment was acceptable but further infringements on the guarantees operative in 1860 were not. No half-way counter-revolution would be satisfactory. Therefore, an acceptable salvation was so far off as to be a negligible factor in determining policy.

The move to vote down the conventions in the South was not propelled by a realization that the long-awaited reaction was breaking forth and could deliver the South if it waited patiently. But the evidences of sympathetic activity in the North did provide a rallying-cry and a pretext for inaction.[47] As such it was utilized in the summer and fall. The frantic counter-arguments of the cooperating presses, the *Jackson Clarion* and the *Montgomery Advertiser* for example, indicated that this was effective ammunition. While the *Augusta Constitutionalist* proclaimed in September that 'The GREAT REACTION has set in like a mighty tide from the ocean,' the *Advertiser* earnestly cautioned that, although there certainly was 'an unmistakable revulsion against the Republican party, ... It would ... be the very extreme of madness — nay it would be utter ruin for the Southern States to postpone reconstruction until the Democratic party comes into power and adopts a

---

[45] Editorial, *Jackson Clarion*, 13 November 1867.

[46] Herschel V. Johnson to Stephens, Sandy Grove, Ga., 4 December 1867, A. H. Stephens MSS.

[47] The preceding assessment of the role of the Northern reaction in determining Southern policy under the Reconstruction Acts is at variance with C. Vann Woodward, the most recent writer on this subject. He feels Northern election results were determinative of the change of course, which he asserts, began in the late fall. See Harold Hyman, ed., *New Frontiers of the American Reconstruction*, pp. 135–8.

new set of measures for the purpose.'[48] And this was accurate. Not even an overwhelming endorsement of the Democrats in 1868 could alter the Republican majorities in Congress. And besides, the Democratic Party was unable to help the South in the near future for, after advising cooperation in the spring, the turn of events since had left it, so 'Willoughby' reported, 'all at sea, as respects the means to advance its own fortunes, and its counsels are so divided that it is at present powerless.'[49]

On occasion news of reaction in the North was still able to affect Southern public figures. As an example of the influence which such information could carry whenever the South's position seemed hopeless, as indeed it did in August 1867, the editorial course of the fiery Henry Rives Pollard's Richmond *Southern Opinion* was instructive. On 24 August that paper enunciated the orthodox secessionist view when it said: 'The talk about reaction is silly and senile. It is the talk of the fools who imagine the war to have been a mere accident of partisan contest. It was not so trivial an affair.'[50] Yet, amazingly, three weeks later, after the news of Maine and California, the following editorial appeared: 'The days of Radical domination are numbered. It is very evident from the recent elections that a general political reaction is in progress in the North.'[51]

This change of view did not result in a change of policy, since the *Southern Opinion* was already non-cooperative; but for many it did. Cooperation was proving to be so futile and difficult that any excuse to desist was eagerly snatched. Northern reaction may have been, and probably was, what the *Montgomery Advertiser* considered it, 'for years a stereotyped cry.'[52] For the real reaction was taking place in the South, not the North, and was well underway before September. Before that date, the cooperationists were in total disarray.

A few of them, however, continued along the course they had earlier adopted. A Reconstruction party was eventually formed during late September in Mississippi and right up until their State's conventions were held, the *Montgomery Advertiser* and the *Jackson*

[48] Editorial, *Augusta Constitutionalist*, 6 September 1867; Editorial, *Montgomery Advertiser*, 13 September 1867.
[49] 'Willoughby,' New York City correspondent, 1 August 1867, *Augusta Constitutionalist*, 6 August 1867.
[50] Editorial, Richmond *Southern Opinion*, 24 August 1867.
[51] *Ibid.*, 14 September 1867.
[52] Editorial, *Montgomery Advertiser*, 28 August 1867.

Clarion, for example, continued to urge cooperation. After all, in counties with white majorities, conservative candidates could be elected and might have some marginal effect on the conventions. And in States with a predominance of registered blacks, to argue for inaction and for encouraging the Northern reaction by means of radical political excesses was easier to suggest than to allow actually to happen. But, in general, cooperation was rejected by late summer. If readmission to the Union were to be purchased at a price, and that price was Confederate conjunction with the radical wing of the Republican Party and also cooperation in the enactment of what was envisaged as Negro rule, it was not worth paying. The issue was clear; William A. Graham urged Congress to 'remember that the destruction of a State, which will be the effect of the measure proposed, can never be the means of its restoration.'[53] Such a reconstruction was therefore ill-advised and had little to do with peace terms or justice to the freedmen. It was simply partisan and sectional and consequently put the South under no obligation to consent. And in any case withholding consent was an option quite explicit in the terms of the Second Reconstruction Act. So observance of the law need not involve cooperation.

b: *The politicians fail*

When the President had attempted during the spring to alleviate the impact of reconstruction by calling for an opinion by Attorney General Stanbery on the scope of the Reconstruction Acts, Congress had replied with a reassertion of its intention that the Acts' provisions should be broadly construed. Undismayed by this sequence, Johnson tried again in late August and early September to curb and limit the effect of reconstruction. He demanded Stanton's resignation on 5 August and, after a refusal from the Secretary, suspended him from office.[54] A month later, against the advice of the ad interim Secretary of War, Ulysses Grant, that his removal 'will embolden ['the unreconstructed elements'] to renewed opposition to the will of the loyal masses, believing that they have the Executive with them,' Johnson relieved Sheridan of his command in Louisiana and Texas, and then

---

[53]Graham to William Pell, Hillsboro, N.C., 10 October 1867, W. A. Graham Collection.

[54]He told his secretary Col. William G. Moore that with Stanton's removal, 'the turning point has at last come. The Rubicon is crossed,' though it was rather late to be thinking about points of no return. Moore's Small Diary, August 1867, Johnson MSS.

followed this by doing the same to Pope and Sickles.[55] Concurrently, he issued a proclamation warning 'all persons against obstructing or hindering in any manner whatsoever the faithful execution of the Constitution and the laws,' a move clearly aimed at military commanders, like Sickles, who were overriding or nullifying the decisions of the civil courts.[56] And as a final flourish in this sudden offensive, the President proclaimed amnesty to all Southerners who swore the oath of loyalty, except military or civil officeholders in the Confederate government, those at one time in the United States military, and those still on parole or in prison for war-related activities.[57]

Whether this activity was occasioned, as 'Leo' of the *Charleston Courier* felt, because 'the President has manifested lately an ambition to be President for a while' or because 'Mr. Johnson would like to be the nominee of some party for the President and be elected' was not the central concern.[58] What was important was that the President had evidently vowed to continue his fight against Congress' policies. But for the cooperationists, his actions were disastrous. Although the removal of Stanton and the State commanders and the proclamations of amnesty and civil supremacy could be interpreted as attempts to make reconstruction less punitive and easier to endure, this was not how they were usually construed in the Southern States. There Johnson's attack on the Reconstruction Acts and their administrators held out the hope of eventual relief either by the repeal of the Acts or by their being reduced to impotence through a series of Presidential onslaughts. Consequently the ranks of the cooperators, thinning anyway, were reduced even further. Yet the tangible advantages resulting from the President's action were minimal. Grant was hardly more sympathetic than Stanton, while Canby, so Governors Orr and Worth felt, was far worse than Sickles.[59] And the proclamations achieved virtually nothing, since few were automatically amnestied by it who

---

[55] U. S. Grant to Johnson, Washington, D.C., 17 August 1867, Johnson MSS, Series I. Sheridan commanded the Fifth Military District, Pope the Third (Ga., Fla. and Ala.), Sickles the Second (S.C. and N.C.).

[56] Richardson, *Messages and Papers of the Presidents*, VI, 546.

[57] *Ibid.*, pp. 547–9.

[58] 'Leo,' Washington, D.C., 20 and 23 August 1867, *Charleston Courier*, 24 and 26 August 1867.

[59] Grant interpreted and executed the Acts to the widest possible extent; Orr's and Worth's assessments of Canby can be found in Orr to John W. Burbridge, Charleston, S.C., 5 October 1867, Orr Official Correspondence and Worth to B. G. Worth, Raleigh, 25 October 1867, in *Correspondence of Jonathan Worth*,

had not already obtained pardon. Moreover it was very unlikely that the President's second purpose in issuing the proclamation would be realized, which was that these pardoned individuals should thereupon bring suit for the restoration of their full rights which had been denied by the Reconstruction Acts.[60]

Indeed there was a great deal of skepticism about the benefits likely to accrue to the South from the President's dramatic maneuver. Except for unflinching admirers of Johnson like William H. C. King of the *New Orleans Times* or those such as Edward M. Yerger, now editor of the *Vicksburg Herald*, who would applaud any and every attack on the radicals no matter how unwise or ineffectual, Southerners were exasperated or angry at the President. 'Willoughby' of the *Augusta Constitutionalist* expressed one view when he commented that the President 'has, so to speak, repeatedly led the decent people of the country into a Radical ambuscade, to suffer severe losses. If he will not now press on and rout them from their coverts, let him fall.'[61] Sure that he would not be able to 'press on' and overthrow the Reconstruction Acts and annoyed that the President's quarrel with Congress continually worked to the disadvantage of the South was the *Richmond Whig.* 'He learns nothing and forgets nothing,' said the editors. 'Without a party, without a new policy, with but a fraction of his official term remaining, and in the midst of as great a number of bitter enemies as any public man ever had, we would be false to our interests if we followed him in the conflict in which he is about to plunge almost "solitary and alone." '[62]

This reluctance and criticism were justified since it was clear that not only did Johnson not have any long range schemes in mind, but he was

---

II, 1061. Worth called Canby 'an unostentatious and candid Radical;' whatever this meant, it was certainly uncomplimentary.

[60]The President hoped that the amnesty proclamation would provide a justification for individuals, as opposed to States, to seek judicial redress for the civil rights which the Reconstruction Acts had taken away. If that were successful, voting, and also officeholding presumably, would then be open to the conservatives. In the fall of 1867 General John D. Imboden of Virginia and Sam F. Rice of Alabama did try this method of testing the reconstruction legislation at the lower Federal Court level but without success. Johnson explained his intention in an interview with a Southerner, cited in *Montgomery Weekly Advertiser,* 15 October 1867.

[61]'Willoughby,' New York City, 6 September 1867, *Augusta Constitutionalist,* 10 September 1867.

[62]Editorial, *Richmond Whig,* 28 August 1867.

obviously unaware of the likely effect of his actions on the South. He had conceded in his veto of the 2 March Act that 'It is plain that the authority here given to the military officer amounts to absolute despotism,' yet persistently he had acted in denial of this only to find that Congress had to fix even more securely the admitted despotism.[63] Furthermore, in defending Sheridan's removal, Johnson had refuted Grant's objection that Southern recalcitrance would be encouraged by remarking that 'as intelligent men, they know that the mere change of military commanders cannot alter the law, and that General Thomas will be as much bound by its requirements as General Sheridan.'[64] From these comments it would appear that Johnson understood perfectly what the law entailed and was simply trying to score points against Congress. In that case the conservatives would be his victims, not beneficiaries.

Had President Johnson bothered to consider what best he could do to accommodate the South, he would assuredly have been compelled, in the interest of discretion, to opt for inaction. For the conservatives, all was chaos during the months prior to the elections. Inertia, apathy, and confusion pervaded the leadership. The *Richmond Whig* offered an explanation when it suggested that 'the dread of negro suffrage is producing a panic and paralysis.'[65] But there was more to it than that. Principally the men who had led the South for decades were unable to decide what strategy to pursue. They, in effect, failed to lead.

In the month or so prior to the elections there was a multitude of strategies being pursued, although there still was no division among the white conservatives into organized political parties. All the same, they were taking advantage of all the options lawfully open to them. Some were still advocating cooperation; of them, a few joined the Republicans, while the remainder intended to vote for a convention and also elect conservative candidates. Among the non-cooperationists, on the other hand, was one group which advocated a preference for 'No Convention' alone, while others would vote the same way on the call but would also, as a safeguard in case they were defeated, cast ballots for conservative candidates. Yet another faction of non-cooperationists chose to abstain from the polls altogether, thereby hoping that the required majority of the registered voters would not

[63] Richardson, *Messages and Papers of the Presidents*, VI, 502.
[64] Johnson to Grant, Washington, D.C., 17 August 1867, Johnson MSS, Series I. Actually Winfield S. Hancock, not Thomas, succeeded Sheridan in New Orleans.
[65] Editorial, *Richmond Whig*, 1 July 1867.

participate, and the call be defeated. Some, out of apathy or doctrinal purity, even refused to go so far as to register under the Acts.

The outcome of all these conflicting strategies was that Republican conventions were elected in every Southern State. In some quarters this brought forth approval and relief. The *Augusta Constitutionalist*, for example, rejoiced that white majorities in Georgia and Virginia had failed to defeat the call since this indicated that 'the black vomit is beginning to work its own cure.'[66] To Alexander Stephens, by contrast, this result probably brought a shrug of the shoulders, for he had said in July that 'nothing that we of the South can do or not do can save the country.' Cooperation or non-cooperation amounted to the same thing in the end, Negro supremacy and radical Republican control of the South.[67]

Regret and a wringing of hands, however, were widespread. The *Charleston Mercury* lamented that

The white race had ample power to have prevented every negro convention in the South, if they had pursued the plain and simple policy of registering, and then not voting at the polls. Even in this State, the most desperate of all the Southern States, on account of the heavy negro majority against the white population, the convention would have been defeated, but for the failure of so many white people to register their names.[68]

The *Mercury* was probably accurate in its assertion that a well-organized and urgent campaign for registration and abstention could have defeated the call in each of the Southern States. In the registration there were white majorities in Georgia, Virginia, Arkansas, Texas, and North Carolina. In every one of these States exclusive of Georgia the convention could have been rejected if those whites hoping to defeat it by voting 'No Convention' had instead abstained and prevented a majority being polled. And in Florida and Mississippi only a minority of the registered voters would have participated if those conservatives who cooperated or voted 'No' had instead abstained. By contrast, in Georgia the presence of a compact and numerous white opposition to the conservatives made defeat of the convention call difficult. And Alabama, South Carolina, and Louisiana would have required a really thorough canvass to increase the registration suf-

[66] Editorial, *Augusta Constitutionalist*, 6 November 1867.

[67] Alexander H. Stephens to Herschel V. Johnson, Crawfordville, Ga., 17 July 1867, H. V. Johnson MSS.

[68] Editorial, *Charleston Mercury*, 12 December 1867.

ficiently to make defeat of the call by abstention a viable course of action.[69] But even in these four States conservative success was possible if there had been vigorous organizational activity and a clear policy.

Abstention, however, seemed at the time to be a rather dangerous and questionable policy. There was, after all, an expectation, often expressed, that the freedman might not, because of fear or of the novelty of the privilege, appear at the polls to cast his vote. Therefore, where there were white majorities, provided that they voted solidly and numerously, 'No Convention' would undoubtedly have ensured the defeat of the call, and so abstention was unnecessary. Elsewhere there was circumspection about employing this tactic because it might prove ineffectual if the registrars were able, by fraud and manipulation, to show that those who had abstained had never been registered. And besides, by the time the politicians had begun to consider abstention a possible course of action, there was little time available to instruct the electorate in adopting the new tactic.[70] Unfortunately the non-cooperationists had previously endorsed a policy of voting 'No Convention' and, therefore, as this and abstention were mutually exclusive, a change from the former to the latter would have had to be very efficiently engineered or else those who persisted in voting, even though negatively, would be defeating the purpose of abstention. Thus, there was hesitation and confusion in the ranks of the non-cooperationists during October and early November 1867.

In a process which made available a choice of voting for or against a convention, the initial inclination of those who urged non-cooperation, after it had become evident that the conservatives could not control the black vote, was to vote 'No Convention.' Wade Hampton, Herschel V. Johnson, Benjamin Perry, William A. Graham, and Benjamin H. Hill had all advanced this policy as the assumed, almost orthodox, way of opposing reconstruction. Although asserting the unconstitutionality of the legislation, they preferred to vote negatively under it rather than stand entirely aloof. This would indicate that policy, more than principle or theory, dictated the course of Southern politicians in 1867.

As late as October, in a State with a white majority but a strong body of white radicals, William A. Graham recommended that every-

[69]For registration and voting statistics, see Appendix, p. 348.

[70]The *Arkansas Gazette*, in an editorial on 29 October 1867, had suggested these reasons in defense of continuing with the tactic of voting 'No Convention.'

one should register and vote against a convention, while the leading Whig paper of his State, the *Raleigh Sentinel*, stressed that the essential requirement was the election of conservative delegates, regardless of the vote on the call.[71] But in October, less than a month before most of the elections were to be held, a change began to occur. The Northern elections had been so dramatically favorable that it was felt that a refusal to vote or participate in the reconstruction process would imply a principled nullification of the Reconstruction Acts rather than a contumacious interference with their execution. It could then be asserted that the Acts should be repealed since the South had not recognized them and so they had never been set in motion. They were, in that case, null and void. Any government then set up by the radicals could be contested on the precedent of *Luther* v. *Borden*, a case which had arisen out of the Dorr's rebellion controversy of 1842 in Rhode Island.[72] Furthermore, and probably more important, although it was for obvious reasons little mentioned, was the fact that the whites had been so confused, and so disgusted, by the changes in policy of their leaders and by the thought of voting alongside black people for delegates to a sham convention that their anticipated polling-strength was estimated very low. The conservatives, moreover, were disorganized and had done very little to get out the vote. Speculating after the election, on the causes of defeat, the *Raleigh Sentinel* had concluded that 'they may all be brought under one general head, – that of criminal apathy.'[73]

And so it was in all the States. Therefore, the chances of out-voting the eager and organized white and black radicals were slim. Significant, in any case, would be the amount of abstention by apathetic or outraged white voters, and so defeat of the convention might be achieved more certainly by inaction rather than by negative action and voting 'No Convention.'

Accordingly, political leaders began to advocate abstention partially as an intended strategy and partially because of necessity. On

[71] William A. Graham to William Pell, Hillsboro, N.C., 10 October 1867, W. A. Graham Collection. Editorial, *Raleigh Sentinel*, 6 November 1867. This tactic was urged earlier, in October, as well.

[72] This argument was pleaded in the ex parte McCardle case of 1868, which sought a decision on the unconstitutionality of the Reconstruction Acts, *Luther* v. *Borden* asserted that it was from Congress rather than the courts that a decision should be made in instances where two State governments claimed authority to govern.

[73] Editorial, *Raleigh Sentinel*, 26 November 1867.

4 October the *Augusta Constitutionalist* announced: 'We will retire from a contest where laurels are impossible and leave the field to negroes and white mountebanks who may revel for a time in the triumph of villainy, but shall not revel forever, unless the people of this country are knaves and imbeciles.'[74] Other newspapers changed too, and, among them, were the *Richmond Whig*, the *Danville Times*, the *Atlanta Intelligencer*, the *Vicksburg Herald*, and, on the day of the Georgia election, the *Milledgeville Federal Union*.[75] As an example of vacillation and confusion the case of William A. Graham was instructive. After advising conservatives to vote 'No Convention' in a public letter of 10 October, he urged, in another published on 31 October that 'opposition to the call may be as well, and perhaps more effectually, expressed, by not voting on that question, than by a ballot in the negative; providing there is a general concurrence in action. . . .'[76]

Jonathan Worth, too, urged that 'the only chance to defeat the call, if there be any, is by unanimous non-voting,' but he refused to make public his position for fear of removal on the grounds of obstructing the Reconstruction Acts.[77] On the other hand, both public and formal was the declaration of policy expounded in South Carolina where a Conservative State Convention, held on 6 November, urged voters to stay away from the polls.[78] A sudden burst of activity, with abstention and therefore paradoxically inaction as its goal, had developed in the Southern States during October, but it was too late. Vacillation and changes of policy had so demoralized the electorate that considered action was more than could be expected, especially in a matter that they in any case shrank from and regarded as a fearsome ordeal.

Southern white conservatives had been abandoned by their indecisive leaders. Clear guidance was rarely given. The *Richmond Whig* had been irritated about this in July when its cooperation proposal had been received icily and no alternative suggested. This was a change from the period of secession, the *Whig* noted ironically, when advice

[74] Editorial, *Augusta Constitutionalist*, 4 October 1867.
[75] *Ibid.*, 16 October 1867 mentions the *Richmond Whig*, the *Danville Times*, and the *Charlottesville Chronicle*. The *Atlanta Intelligencer* changed in late October and the *Federal Union* on 29 October.
[76] William A. Graham to J. A. Englehard, Hillsboro, N.C., 25 October 1867, W. A. Graham Collection.
[77] Jonathan Worth to William A. Graham, Raleigh, 28 October 1867, in *Correspondence of Jonathan Worth*, II, 1067.
[78] South Carolina Conservative Convention, Address to the People of South Carolina, *Charleston Courier*, 9 November 1867.

'was not only freely tendered, but pressed upon' the electorate. Now, said the *Whig*,

Some have doubts as to the true policy, some have conscientious scruples, some are tormented with points of honor, and some think that regard for poetry and romance requires that they should invite further suffering and sacrifice. The public mind is distracted. The people want advice—the advice of those whose counsels they have been accustomed to respect. Their advisers are silent. . . .[79]

Few other newspapers would admit the existence of such a break-down of confidence and communication, but the recently amalgamated *Richmond Enquirer and Examiner* did print during October a pitiful letter from 'Conservative,' who complained: 'The white voters are now like sheep without a shepherd. Who shall lead them? They are anxious to do right, but without knowledge of facts they are at a loss what to do. Not one in fifty of them takes a newspaper. . . .'[80] To the *New Orleans Times* as well there came on one occasion in September a letter requesting advice. The editors' response was a headline, 'THE ELECTION — AN IMPORTANT QUESTION' and, accompanying it, was the noncommittal, though absolutely correct, information that a convention would be held if a majority of those registered voted, whether for or against.[81] This was the only tactical advice the *Times* offered its readers prior to the elections! But possibly the reaction of Herschel V. Johnson was typical of most Southern politicians. In July when he had realized that the 'reconstruction programme . . . demonstrates conclusively, that the dominant party are determined, at all hazards, to radicalize the ten proscribed States,' Johnson had informed Stephens, 'I think however, if permitted, I should register, for that would be necessary to put me in position, to oppose the nefarious thing. But there are many good men, who take a different view. So that our division will work our ruin.' Upon acknowledging this he immediately gave up: 'Well, I submit to fate; I fold my arms upon the deck, and make up my mind, that hourly, the ship is approaching the awful precipice and will soon make the fatal plunge to the boiling depths below, when the voice of liberty will be overwhelmed in the mighty

[79] Editorial, *Richmond Whig*, 18 July 1867.
[80] 'Conservative' to *Richmond Enquirer and Examiner*, Halifax County, 1 October 1867, *Richmond Enquirer and Examiner*, 12 October 1867.
[81] *New Orleans Times*, 29 September 1867.

thunders of the cataract. And then, the reign of despotism, dark, vindictive, gloomy unrelenting. "Illium fuit."[82]

A morbid and desperate feeling that the only recourse open to the South was submission to inevitable ruin characterized conservative emotions and attitudes during 1867. Faced with the reality of a Republican organization which was backed by the Union League, Southern politicians, who earlier had decided to do battle with this insurgency, refused to pursue the only possible form of action whereby success could be achieved in the impending conflict. They would not organize. In Alabama, on the day of the election, the *Montgomery Advertiser* complained that the conservatives had nominated only two candidates.[83] An opposition which intended to cooperate in order to control could not expect to achieve much without a party of some sort. Equally, although it was rarely recognized, the non-cooperationists also had to organize. In August, one of them, the *Augusta Constitutionalist*, explained that calling a conservative nominating convention would be fruitless, since 'The temper of the people seems to be averse to conventions or anything so nearly resembling the paraphernalia of old party contests. This apathy, we take it, is not the result of a stolid indifference to the gravity of the situation, but rather a skeptical feeling as to the exact amount of good, real or imaginary, that could possibly accrue.' Moreover, the *Constitutionalist* added, such a gathering might provide a forum, and public at that, for fissures and disagreement to arise and thwart a cause that required unity. A rather curious argument, this was followed up with the equally strange assertion that there was no purpose in creating an organization since there were none among their Republican opponents who could be enticed into the conservative ranks. A third reason was that, if a political machine were created, the politicians would be given an occasion to haggle over patronage and this would engender factions and divisive interest-groups. Finally, said the *Constitutionalist*, organization had to begin in the counties before a State meeting that was representative or useful could be called.[84]

This was a recognition probably of the local variations in policy which would be certain to arise because the Negro vote and the insurgent white vote were not dispersed, but instead were consolidated

[82] Herschel V. Johnson to Stephens, Augusta, Ga., 15 July 1867, A. H. Stephens MSS.
[83] Editorial, *Montgomery Weekly Advertiser*, 24 September 1867.
[84] Editorial, *Augusta Constitutionalist*, 17 August 1867.

in particular areas of each State, and so correspondingly was the strength of the Republican Party. Local situations differed and so therefore did local policies and tactics. Of this the *Montgomery Advertiser* was clearly aware when it observed that, 'In some counties we believe men will be elected who will conform strictly to the letter of the law and not go beyond it. In other counties it is probable that agrarian Radicalism is so far in the ascendent, as to sweep away all chance of defeat[ing]' the call for a convention.[85] In other words, policies that were applicable on a State-wide basis were difficult to formulate. But without directives or guidelines from State politicians, positive action would not be possible in the counties. This decentralization of policy-making decisions was a response to divisive local variations, and perhaps helped explain why conservative leadership was so lacking in the South of 1867.

Attempts at State organization were nonetheless made, but with marginal positive effect. Under the leadership of General James H. Clanton who had earlier, on 11 May, stepped forward to debate non-cooperation with Senator Henry Wilson, Alabama conservatives toyed with the idea of organizing their opposition.[86] After inaugurating the move on 23 July with a meeting in Montgomery, local conventions were held during August, culminating in a State convention on 1 September. Representatives attended from thirteen of Alabama's sixty counties, the majority of them being from a mere five. The outcome of the conclave was a set of resolutions criticizing the Reconstruction Acts and reiterating the platform of the 1866 Philadelphia convention. Nothing was intimated regarding future tactics and nothing announced to guide the electorate. 'A failure in every particular' was the verdict of the reconstructing *Montgomery Advertiser* on this convention which had been dominated by a number of anti-secessionists, in particular Clanton, Judge G. W. Stone, Colonel Michael Bulger, Patton's opponent in the 1865 gubernatorial election, and Robert McKee and Joseph Hodgson, editors of the *Selma Messenger* and *Montgomery Mail* respectively.[87]

In Virginia, county meetings to organize the non-cooperating conservatives were held in mid-September, a month before the elections.

[85] Editorial, *Montgomery Weekly Advertiser*, 24 September 1867.
[86] *Montgomery Weekly Advertiser*, 14 May 1867. W. L. Fleming, *Civil War and Reconstruction in Alabama* (New York: Peter Smith [1905], 1949), pp. 512–14.
[87] *Montgomery Advertiser* throughout August 1867, and 6 September 1867.

Candidates for the convention were selected but no advice offered to the voters as to the policy to be pursued at the polls. It was assumed that a revival of interest and activity after the Maine and California elections in September could galvanize the white registered majority to vote down a convention as well as to select a slate of anti-radical delegates sufficient to control one if it were called.[88] An advocate of these meetings after the Northern elections, which had removed Virginians 'a hundred years further off from universal suffrage than [they] were two weeks ago,' the *Enquirer and Examiner* realized, though too late, that this abortive rallying of the conservative whites had probably ensured that a majority of the registered voters participated.[89] This belated activity had, therefore, been suicidal; without it less than a registered majority would have gone to the polls and thus the convention could not have been held. Regretfully, its editorial of 29 October commented that if more time and attention had been available to consider a way of defeating the convention, 'it would undoubtedly have been best to resist the Convention by abstaining from a vote on the question; thus throwing on its friends, the necessity of out-voting the whole remaining body of registered voters.'[90] But how much time did the *Enquirer* need?!

Georgia politicians had suggested in August that a State convention be held, but all that resulted were local meetings in October to nominate conservative candidates as a safeguard in case the convention call was carried.[91] Herschel Johnson had disapproved of a State-wide convention because, he said, 'In my judgement, it will do no good and this is a sufficient reason why it should not be held. Its effect, I fear, will be to divide us still more, and thus, both increase and expose our weakness.'[92] As in Virginia, no meeting was held until after the election when a new pressure for mobilization was introduced by the need to vote down the constitution which the convention would soon present for popular ratification.

[88] Editorials, *Richmond Enquirer and Examiner*, throughout late September and October 1867.

[89] *Ibid.*, 13 September 1867. The calls for conservative organization and activity were made on 14 and 21 September.

[90] *Ibid.*, 29 October 1867.

[91] C. Mildred Thompson, 'Reconstruction in Georgia,' *Studies in History, Economics and Public Law*, LXIV, 188–9. *Milledgeville Weekly Federal Union*, 6 August 1867.

[92] Herschel V. Johnson to R. S. Hardwick, Augusta, Ga., 23 August 1867, H. V. Johnson MSS.

Conservative conventions were also deemed inadvisable on account of the unity among the radicals that they might provoke. In North Carolina and South Carolina where the Republican Party was well-organized and likely to carry the election, the main hope of relief lay in a split among the members of that party. In Jonathan Worth's State, a moderate faction led by Daniel Goodloe was threatening to break away from the Holdenites. In spite of this, a meeting was called in late September by the *Raleigh Sentinel* and by many citizens of Wake County (Raleigh), favoring cooperation and an attempt still to divide the Negro vote. This policy was rejected by the gathering and a later State convention which was sparsely attended did no more than reiterate this tactic and issue vague resolutions denouncing reconstruction.[93] Many politicians would not participate, including William A. Graham, who instead wrote a letter advising a vote of 'No Convention,' and Jonathan Worth who argued: 'I have feared that anything like organization on our part might arrest the disintegration which I trust is setting in here and abroad among the radicals, and thus result prejudicially to us.'[94]

In South Carolina, however, a convention was held in early November and was attended by Perry, Hampton, James Chestnut, John S. Preston, A. P. Aldrich, William F. DeSaussure, and many other dignitaries. An address was issued; the people were urged to abstain; and a proposition was made to Congress that South Carolina would adopt any Northern State constitution containing a qualified impartial suffrage which was offered as a basis for compromise on the civil and franchise rights of the freedman.[95] The convention came too late to effect the defeat of the call and was criticized strongly by, for example, the *Mercury* because it would annoy the radicals and help them to coalesce their forces and also because the suffrage compromise would mar the effect of the principled stand that was being made in the South against radical reconstruction. Besides, noted the *Mercury*, 'From the conclusion of the war, the curse of the South has been the activity of pragmatical weakness or restlessness.'[96] By September anyway, it was probably too late to accomplish anything by organization except to provoke radical counter-activity.

[93] Hamilton, *Reconstruction in North Carolina*, pp. 249–51.
[94] Jonathan Worth to David F. Caldwell, Raleigh, 28 September 1867, in *Correspondence of Jonathan Worth*, II, 1052.
[95] South Carolina Conservative Convention, Address to the People of South Carolina, *Charleston Courier*, 9 November 1867.
[96] Editorial, *Charleston Mercury*, 4 November 1867.

In Texas, as in Virginia, conservative mobilization produced results which were suicidal. In the Lone Star State the result of the conservative conventions held in January was to guarantee a reconstruction convention which otherwise would certainly have been rejected. To Houston during the first few days of 1868 came two sets of delegates. One group, merchants from Galveston, headed by T. H. McMahon, wanted to put forward Union men on a conservative ticket in order to take the control of the convention away from the radicals. The other faction, consisting of leading Confederate politicians in the State, such as Champe Carter, John H. Reagan, Lemuel D. Evans, James W. Throckmorton, Ashbel Smith, and John Hancock, intended to vote 'No Convention.' There was a white majority in the registration and it had been hoped that, without organization, the convention could be defeated, but the radicals had been able to gain many supporters from the white ranks, thereby destroying this 'No Convention' majority. The conjunction of the two Houston conventions that had been anticipated failed to emerge, and so the conservatives approached the election with two different strategies, the Galveston group advocating voting for, and the Hancock–Reagan faction against, the call.[97] Electoral apathy in Texas was so widespread, however, that about 40,000 white voters refrained from participation even though the politicians had advised them to vote. The result was that the politicians' scheme, which had depended on an aroused electorate, failed utterly. Eleven thousand votes were deposited in opposition to the call, but if these alone had abstained, the convention could not have met. Had the supporters of the Galveston proposal also abstained, the call would have failed overwhelmingly.[98]

The conservative politicians had allowed the election to go by

[97] A detailed account of these conventions can be gleaned from *Flake's Bulletin*. The issues of 5, 20, 23 January 1868 contain the most thorough commentaries. Apparently, according to 'W.,' the correspondent in Houston, Andrew Johnson had an agent, A. P. Sloanaker, in the Hutchins House, canvassing the delegates and urging them to put Union men at the fore and cooperate with the Reconstruction Acts. Unfortunately, more details were not published regarding the authenticity of Sloanaker's authority or his reasons for being there. I have noticed no other instances of Johnson's advising Southerners in such a way.

[98] *Flake's Bulletin* realized this as well. See Editorial of 7 March 1868. Also, Editorial, *San Antonio Express*, 10 March 1868. Commenting on the election, the radical *Express* wryly remarked: 'General Hancock's presence encouraged the desponding rebels; by a spasmodic rally they gave just sufficient votes to guarantee the election of a Constitutional Convention. "God moves in a mysterious way His wonders to perform."'

default. Once the outlines of radical reconstruction in the South had become apparent, and the obstacles to white control of the new Negro electorate manifest, a concerted drive to register as many opponents of the Republicans as possible should have been mounted. These registrants should then have been urged to abstain from voting in the elections. The fact of the matter was, however, that although the conservatives realized in July that they could not control the Negro vote, they did not see that they were losing control of the potential conservative white vote. Those who would not vote with the Republicans frequently stayed away altogether and refused even to register. As a result, by the time the conservatives had evolved the tactic of registration followed by abstention from voting, they were confronted with the reality of an extensive amount of *total* abstention within their constituency. And this, of course, ruined their scheme entirely.

The conservatives' constituents reflected the confusion and bewilderment of their political leaders, and, not knowing which way to turn, decided that complete inaction was the safest course. It was also the most comfortable procedure because it avoided the horror and indignity of an appearance at the registrar's office as well as polling-station alongside the enfranchised Negroes who, with their white allies, were mounting a strong challenge. The strategies of the politicians, however, had required an active electorate and were, therefore, totally unrealistic. So too were the Reconstruction Acts, if their authors had intended the white Southerners to accept them as terms for readmission. A mixture of consent and coercion, they contained the promise of cooperation with the Negro voters mingled with the likelihood that the Southern electorate would become not merely Republican, but radical. Thus the scheme of reconstruction proposed by Congress was confused and confusing, and its implementation did not in any way lessen the contradictions.

Epilogue
The irrelevance of the moderates, 1865–1868

By December 1867 the Confederates faced defeat. Their fight to stay in power and also to retain the constitutional status they and their section had enjoyed before the war had been brought to an end by their inability either to prevent or to control reconstruction. But even in the hour of their defeat, the Southern conservatives refused to submit. The evidence of Northern reaction against Congress' measures were by this time tangible. Moreover, there still remained two opportunities to obstruct reconstruction, and at the very least these would gain time for the Northern conservatives to register their opposition against the Reconstruction Acts and the men who made them.

It was a wild hope and demonstrative of qualities which were far from statesmanlike. The conservatives' reckless and obstructionist motivations were evident in view of the realization widely understood that 'We will not be surprised if the military bills are amended weekly hereafter to meet all contingencies that are probable. A body of men who perjure themselves by enacting such laws as the reconstruction acts, are capable of any enormity.'[1] Yet despite this editorial comment in the *Arkansas Gazette*, the conservatives in that State and in most of the others embarked on a frantic effort to stop reconstruction dead in its tracks. This was to be effected by defeating the new constitutions which had been formulated by the conventions and were then to be submitted for popular ratification. Organizations were hurriedly established to ensure that the constitutions would be defeated by the widespread abstention of those who had registered the previous year. The lesson of the convention elections had been learned; a boycott had to be *organized*, it would not just happen.

In Alabama the strategy succeeded and the constitution failed because of insufficient electoral participation. Moreover, in accordance with the provisions of the Supplemental (Second) Reconstruction Act, the defeat of the constitution also invalidated the elections held

[1] Editorial, *Arkansas Gazette*, 14 January 1868.

simultaneously for State offices. But Congress quickly passed the Fourth Reconstruction Act. Becoming law on 11 March 1868, this measure provided that a majority of the *votes cast only* was required for ratification. No laws which Congress would have to pass in order to ensure the enactment of its reconstruction legislation would create new precedents; they would simply be enabling acts to meet all possible contingencies and loopholes, and therefore they would encounter minimal parliamentary opposition. The need to resort to further legislation was merely a nuisance for the Republicans in Congress, but it did not necessitate a reconsideration of overall intention.

The effect of the new law was automatically to achieve ratification of the State constitution. Not only that but the legislature, State officials and Congressmen that had been elected at the same time were now legitimized and the attempt to arrest the reconstruction process had been foiled. Since the conservatives had abstained, these offices had been filled without exception by Republicans. So this meant that Alabama and also Arkansas, which had held its ratification election in mid-March thereby depriving the conservatives of adequate time to reverse their tactic of boycott, were both thoroughly Republican at all levels of government.

Noticing the effect of the Fourth Reconstruction Act on their intended strategy, conservatives in other States were faced with the same dilemma as they had confronted a year before. Should abstention be continued? Or would it be better to try to influence, even control the composition of State government and Federal representation? The former procedure might allow principle and expediency to fuse, whereas the latter would be expedient only, though naturally expediency would be differently calculated in each case. But there were only these two alternatives available.

For a continuation of a total boycott there were many strong arguments. Pressing for this tactic, Herschel Johnson insisted that to run candidates 'is a waiver of all our objections to [the Reconstruction Act], as a void instrument and ensures the Congressional usurpation in which it originated and strikes from under us our strongest ground of appeal to the Northern Democracy for its appeal [repeal?].'[2] Another argument had been presented by the Alabama Conservative convention when it had appealed publicly for abstention on the ground that 'by our voting with the negro either for or against [the constitution],

[2]Johnson to John B. Gordon, Bartow, Ga., 8 April 1868, H. V. Johnson MSS.

it matters not, ('tis voting with the negro, canvassing with him, canvassing against him or voting against him – this is what [the Northern Republicans] want).' A boycott however 'would hold up to the people of the North and West, the spectacle of eight millions of people, a gallant and chivalrous people, a people of their color, blood and race, having with them a common ancestry and a common history, clinging to the Constitution, and unresisting, about to be stricken down by the merciless decree of Radical ambition and subjected to negro rule and negro equality.'[3] Inaction would speed the Northern conservative opposition of which R. M. T. Hunter could pronounce, 'That it will come I doubt not' for things would become so intolerable in the South that Northern concern for good government and white superiority would unquestionably compel the reaction.[4] Therefore, exclaimed the *Jackson Clarion*, in terms which had by this time become quite familiar, 'Go on, ye madmen. ... Celebrate the installation of the African dynasty, with all your obscene and infernal orgies. You are speeding the blessed day of retribution!'[5] Also confident of the expediency of inaction was the *Charleston Mercury* whose editors warned white Southerners that they 'will be beaten at the polls and ruled, 'but, on the other hand, 'They are not *beaten* at polls, that they *disdain* to attend. They are not *ruled* by any governments they do not recognize as legitimate over them. ... The white race of the South, have only to will the rule of the South; and there is no power on this continent, which can prevent it.'[6]

This was ominous but only too true and explained how inactivity could be persisted in, even though immediate relief was far from guaranteed by it. In Mississippi and Virginia, the former with a registered black majority, the latter with a white, the same kind of assumption resulted in a determined effort to carry to a successful conclusion the other possible tactic. In both these States organization was directed at defeating the constitution and controlling the State government by energetic action and involvement. The Virginia conservatives looked like succeeding on both scores, since control of the State offices had become a distinct possibility through the cooption of moderate white

[3] Address of Alabama Conservative Convention, in *Montgomery Advertiser*, 21 January 1868.
[4] Hunter, speech to Virginia Conservative Convention, in *Richmond Enquirer*, 13 December 1867.
[5] Editorial, *Jackson Clarion*, 29 January 1868.
[6] Editorial, *Charleston Mercury*, 12 December 1867.

Republicans who had resented the influenced within their party of the radical black machine headed by J. W. Hunnicutt. Probably victory was snatched from them by the decision of General Schofield not to submit the constitution which, because of its proscriptive features, had provoked a sufficiently broad opposition as to place its survival in jeopardy.[7] So the election was cancelled. In Mississippi, on the other hand, where a strong cooperation party had existed in 1867 and where the Republicans were poorly organized, a unified conservative campaign had a good chance of success. Under the guidance of James Z. George the argument was advanced that principled objections 'make a lodgement in the mind as a part of our intellectual wealth, but except in rare instances they never arouse to passionate and energetic action.' Passivity would hand over to the radicals the State government while it would stimulate the Northern reaction less than the sight of a beleaguered white population determined actively to save itself.[8] So, by intimidation, fraud, and force, Mississippi conservatives managed to vote down the constitution and reelect the ineligible incumbent State officials of Governor Humphrey's administration, though they did not gain control of the Congressional delegation or the State legislature.

But this effort was of little benefit, since Congress refused Mississippi readmission to Congress and prohibited its participation in the 1868 Presidential election. This was the same treatment that was meted out to Virginia and also to Texas where the convention had been so faction-ridden that reconstruction had been interminably delayed. Elsewhere, there was either division among the conservatives as to whether inaction or action and participation were wiser or else there was confusion when a boycott was initially advised on the constitution issue but rejected on the other elections, and both contributed to a defeat for the conservatives. In no State did they win the most important contest, the ratification election, and only in Georgia did they make substantial inroads into the Republican hegemony, winning, in

[7] By this decision, Schofield, a commanding general who was looked upon with favor by Southern conservatives as a sympathetic interpreter of the Reconstruction Acts, denied them the chance of defeating reconstruction. Whether radical or conservative, the Federal officers were committed to ensuring that the Acts would be administered so as to achieve their aim which was to put the South under Republican State governments.

[8] James Z. George to Fulton Anderson 15 March 1868, in *Jackson Clarion*, 25 March 1868.

that State, close to a majority in the lower house and half of the Congressional delegation.

In a moment of rare candor, the *Raleigh Sentinel* pondered publicly the reasons why, with a white registered majority and a militant campaign, the North Carolina conservatives had failed to win. 'None are more surprized and disappointed than ourselves,' confessed the *Sentinel*'s editors. Electoral fraud was suggested as one explanation of Republican success, but there were deeper reasons than that alone. More important, the *Sentinel* believed, was the organizational effectiveness of the Union Leagues which had been the backbone of the Republican electoral drive. Instrumental also was Republican publicity which had asserted that the constitution was not so detrimental to the whites as the conservatives had claimed. But above and beyond these assets of the opposition, the defection of whites from their traditional conformity with the Southern political establishment was clearly the variable in the development which was most crucial. It was a fact which could not be explained away even by the *Sentinel*'s derogatory comment that they were 'thus ignoring their own color to gratify their pent up malice.' The main location of this opposition was in the non-slaveholding Western counties which had been centers of Unionism during the secession crisis and the war. A final consideration offered by the *Sentinel* was that many had voted with the opposition out of confusion as to whether remaining outside the Union without the constitution or gaining readmission but with the constitution were preferable. And this was an obvious reflection on the disarray and lack of firm, clear leadership within the ranks of the conservatives.[9]

After pursuing two mutually exclusive policies in a half-hearted, confused fashion and suffering thereby political defeat, the conservatives of North and South Carolina, Florida, Georgia, Arkansas, Alabama, and Louisiana saw their States readmitted as Republican into Congress in June 1868. The contests for the constitution and for State and Federal representatives had been merely a confirmation of developments during the previous year. Most significant among these had been the ability of the Southern Republican Party to win the Negro vote and the failure of the Confederates both to elicit the customary deference and support from the white population and to organize their tactics to fit the occasion.

There could be no doubting that the conservatives' attempt to pre-

[9] Editorial, *Raleigh Sentinel*, 28 April 1868.

vent reconstruction had been brought to a conclusion by their defeat on the call for a convention: that was the decisive test, not the vote on the constitution. Not only had the Republicans' reconstruction program gained an irreversible momentum by the calling of conventions in every one of the ten States but at the same time Southern conservatives realized that their attempt to hold their section aloof from alignment with either of the two Northern parties could no longer be sustained. As long as there had existed the possibility that the Northern parties might reorganize and that both were struggling to become national organizations fundamental to which was the inclusion of the South, the latter had had a strong bargaining-position. But with the demise of the Johnson — Seward National Union scheme and with the nationalizing of the Republican Party under the Reconstruction Acts but without the cooperation of the Confederates, there was no alternative but to identify and cooperate with the Democrats. So, in early 1868 the conservatives renamed their existing committees and, with Democratic organizations and as Democrats, they campaigned in the winter and spring elections.

Partisan independence had been something of a chimera anyway, but to many among the Confederates it was preferable to an overt and binding commitment to the Democrats. On a number of counts, the Northern Democrats had failed the South from 1860 to 1864, and there was a good degree of resentment towards that party. This feeling was especially strong among those who had resisted secession and had either been members of the Whig Party or, if Democrats, had, in their efforts to preserve the Union, received little or no encouragement from the Northern wing of their party. To these men, the anti-secessionists, the Democratic Party was the party of secession and disunion, and they resisted vehemently an attachment to the Democrats once the war was over. Yet, from the close of the war until the readmittance of their States in 1868, it was they, the anti-secessionists, who had been in control of Southern politics. The defeat of the conservatives in 1868 had coincided with their unwilling conjunction with the Democrats; and so, with these two developments, the failure of the anti-secessionists' approach to reunion was evident.

That approach consisted of a number of ingredients. The anti-secessionists had risen to positions of leadership after the war because, as opponents of secession and often of the actions of the Confederacy itself, they were the natural representatives of the defeated section since they had not been closely identified with the movement for Southern independence and were consequently more able to reconcile themselves to reunion. But reunion did not mean capitulation or the acceptance of degrading terms. As believers in the reality of the interests and sentiments which tied together the people of all sections of the country, they considered that it would be a travesty to force one section to submit to the special interests and prejudices of the other. Under those conditions, the Union would be one in name only and lacking in mutuality, attachment and cohesion. Therefore, in order to restore the Union, negotiation and compromise were essential. But of course, as they saw the situation, that would mean concession by the North in order to accommodate and reassure a weakened and reluctant South, rather than the other way around.

A second feature of the anti-secessionists' outlook was, as has been suggested, a distrust of the Democrats, both because of the Northern Democrats' dismal performance in the early 1860's and because, for many of them, the Democrats had been the opposition within the South to the Whigs and to the Union. Consequently, the anti-secessionists placed a great deal of reliance on the National Union movement which they hoped would bring about a partisan reorganization sufficiently different from the existing parties with their sectional and war-time identifications. And since the anti-secessionists had been closely identified with the Johnson restoration policy, they would naturally become leading figures in the National Union coalition. Presumably it was to this end that former Provisional Governors Sharkey, Marvin and Parsons were retained by Johnson as Southern advisers in Washington. Where reliance was not placed on the National Union movement as such, it was manifested in the powerful conviction that the conservatives in the North would rise up against the sectional disunion policies of the Republicans and thus provide the kind of leadership and policies in Washington which alone could make possible a Union based on harmony of interest and attitudes. And that would be a Union the South could join.

A third facet of the anti-secessionist approach was their worry that since they had opposed Southern independence they had to prove themselves loyal to their section in peace-time. They could not afford to fail the South. Having frequently been advocates of an early peace as well as opponents of secession, they had to produce a post-war settlement which did not involve humiliating concessions or patched-up differences. It was therefore difficult, even in 1865, for those of them who favored it, to urge strongly that concession and accommodation should be attempted. In a sense, they had to be more Southern than the secessionists had been.

The fourth of the ingredients was that the anti-secessionists were responsible for the South's future at a time when divisions of a fundamental nature were appearing in the Southern political and social system. During the Confederacy there had been no political parties but after the war it was apparent that a reaction against the men who had brought defeat and death to the section was quite possible. Equally the Northern parties, especially the Republicans, might try to divide the South. And not least to be reckoned with were differences among the Confederates, between secessionists and anti-secessionists. The unity of the South under its traditional leadership was therefore an essential, not only for keeping control over the section but for obtaining the best terms from the North.

The anti-secessionists were in a situation therefore which was precarious and delicate. At the head of Southern affairs at a moment which was fraught with danger for the Confederates, they had to move warily if they were to save themselves and their section. They were trying to steer a course between the secessionists on the one hand, and the Southern loyalists and Unionists who were potentially the allies of the Northern Republicans on the other, and they were also attempting to align themselves with the National Union movement which was a party of the center and the organizational manifestation of the Northern reaction. In this predicament where their salvation lay in the hands of others and where positive offensive action might provoke or crystallize opposition, the anti-secessionists found themselves continually opting for a tactic of inaction. Masterly inactivity therefore became the overall strategy of the Southern leadership in the face of Northern demands and as a way of giving time to the conservative reaction against the policies of the radicals.

It was ironical that the kind of response which was most convenient and advantageous to the moderates within the Confederate leadership was one which in fact resulted in a refusal to comply with Northern terms and therefore in a prolongation of the eventual reconciliation between the sections.

If this was the propensity and logic of the anti-secessionists' stance, then it was given encouragement by the course taken by Congress in its approach to the problem of reunion and post-war settlement. Andrew Johnson had taken a conciliatory line towards the South in 1865 and then had placed himself at the head of a movement which would pecipitate the reaction; for this he was strongly criticized by Congress. Yet the Republican majority in Congress adopted a procedure which was not very different from the President's. They too pursued a course of conciliation; they too sought to encourage the South to manifest a cooperative spirit and to abide voluntarily by the terms they proposed. Both the Fourteenth Amendment and the Reconstruction Act had devices built into them whereby the Confederates could register their voluntary assent. Admittedly, the options were narrower and the pressure to cooperate greater than in the Johnson scheme, and they were to become even more so in the Republicans' second proposal, the Reconstruction Act. But assent and voluntary compliance were there nonetheless. And these provisions simply supplemented and never counteracted the tendency towards inaction and delay already evident in Southern policy.

Here again there was irony in the situation. Those in the Republican Party who insisted on an approach to the South based on cooperation, consent and conciliation were the moderates. They believed that a Union based on a forced and reluctant settlement was undesirable and likely to be impermanent. And in each of the two struggles to produce a Republican policy for the South, the moderate Republicans managed to gain acceptance for their own stipulations as to the manner in which the terms were to be presented and enacted.[10] So, in both cases, the fate of the proposal lay in the hands of those who were supposed to be its objects. Firm and unpalatable to the Confederates the measures may have been, the implementation of them was always characterized by the approach of the moderates. And since the propositions were tough, especially in the Reconstruction Act, they made non-cooperation and rejection of the terms more, not less, likely. Even

[10]This point is buttressed by Larry G. Kincaid, 'Legislative Origins of the Military Reconstruction Act, 1865–1867,' Ph.D. dissertation, Johns Hopkins University, 1968. Even though the Reconstruction Act embodied what were considered radical measures, such as military rule, Negro suffrage, and State governmental reorganization, its success was dependent upon Confederate cooperation and acquiescence, and furthermore readmission to Congress was to be the immediate and undelayed result of Southern reorganization. Both these last points were moderate and based on a view that reunion was to be conciliatory and speedy. By late 1867 and the Third Reconstruction Act of 2 July it was clear that reconstruction would be mandatory and that the States would be kept out of the Union indefinitely unless they cooperated – this was more in line with radical thinking.

though moderates might have argued that the Confederates should see the handwriting on the wall and should, in their own interest, capitulate and end the friction, the Confederates, led as they were by antisecessionists, argued the reverse position. Since choice was available and since the harder the terms the more imminent the reaction, therefore the wiser and preferable course was to reject and resist. Not until 1868 when it passed the Fourth Reconstruction Act did Congress make its terms final and unavoidable. And even then it did not state unequivocally that this was so but instead manipulated the legislative machinery to its fullest extent in order to make it impossible for the Confederates to defeat the measure by clogging up its complicated processes.

For three years, Federal policy towards the South was based on the principle of reconciliation. All that changed were the details of that reconciliation and they became progressively more demanding and left fewer options for the Confederates. But there always remained, written into the terms, the ultimate option – non-compliance. Johnson's 'carrot and stick' approach was therefore never jettisoned in favor of a policy which was mandatory. That did not mean that such a procedure was never advocated. Reconstruction at the Confederates' expense and without their consent and cooperation was continually urged by the radicals. But although some of their policies, such as Negro suffrage, became incorporated into Congress' proposals, those proposals themselves were never made final and unavoidable.

As a result, moderates who were dominant in both sections attempted to reconcile their differences by mutual accommodation. The outcome, after three years in which moderate men and conciliatory measures had prevailed and had had the field to themselves, was that the sections were polarized.

Polarization had been the reality, however, in 1865. But the moderates, in the North particularly, though in the South as well, had refused to recognize this and had instead argued that sectional differences could best be healed by reconciliation and by policies aimed at producing harmony. Even in this context, harmony could not be achieved between the moderates who dominated each section. For harmony could only be attained through a policy in which the victorious Republicans removed the ambiguity involved in conciliation, and simply demanded terms and enforced them coercively.

The removal from power and influence of the Southern political and economic elite was a prerequisite for harmony between the sections.

By refusing to consider this, but rather preferring to do what was in effect the opposite, the moderates were attempting the impossible; their assumptions were unrealistic and their policies impracticable. After the civil war practical policies required that the fundamental divergence between the sections, and the effect four years of war had had on attitudes and interests within them, be fully comprehended. Bargains and compromises simply ignored the reality of the situation and could only be palliatives. And in fact, rather than being easier and less troublesome, even they, when attempted, proved difficult to arrange. So, in the process nothing but confusion, frustration and antagonism resulted.

What was ignored in this approach was the fact that the Union had been torn apart and that four million black people had fought for and won their freedom from slavery; this was a radical situation and it demanded a radical solution. Anything else was dangerous and delusive, and, in the long run, it would fail. The events of 1865–1868 demonstrated that, with moderates in power in both sections and dominating national politics, conciliation failed, *even in the short run*. For the paradox of situations where society is polarized and the existing tensions have become unmanageable is that it is at those times more than at any other that policies looking towards reconciliation, compromises aimed to resolve differences, and efforts at creating synthetic harmony become imperative for the moderate. And by then it is obvious that his approach to the problem is inapplicable and bound to end in disaster sooner rather than later.

APPENDIX: Registration and voting statistics for the Southern State Constitutional Conventions, 1867–8

State	Registration			For			Against		
	White	Black	Total	White	Black	Total	White	Blk.	Total
Ala.	61295	104518	165813	18533	71730	90283	5583	—	5583
Ark.	—	—	73784	—	—	27576	13558	—	13558
Fla.	11914	16089	28003	1220	13080	14300	203	—	203
Ga.	96333	95168	191501	32000	70283	102283	4000	127	4127
La.	45218	84436	129654	—	—	75083	—	—	4006
Miss.	—	—	139690	—	—	69739	—	—	6277
N.C.	106721	72932	196873	31284	61722	93006	32961	—	32961
S.C.	46882	80550	127432	2350	66418	68768	2278	—	2278
Tex.	59633	49497	109130	7757	36932	44689	10622	818	11440
Va.	120101	105832	225933	14835	92507	107342	61249	638	61887

From these figures can be deduced the margin between the votes polled and the majority necessary to call a convention:

Ala.	96866: 82907 + 1		Miss.	76016: 69845 + 1
Ark.	41134: 26892 + 1		N.C.	125967: 98437 + 1
Fla.	14503: 14002 + 1		S.C.	71046: 63716 + 1
Ga.	106410: 95751 + 1		Tex.	56129: 54565 + 1
La.	79174: 64827 + 1		Va.	169229: 112967 + 1

Source: McPherson, *The Political History of the U.S.*, p. 374.

A Note on Sources

Since this book is based almost exclusively on evidence from written manuscript collections and from newspaper series, a bibliography which would list those secondary works consulted in the course of research performs no useful function.

Nevertheless, to acquaint himself with the scope of the topics and subject-matter investigated by historians of Reconstruction and with the different interpretative approaches they have employed, the reader would do well to consult the very full bibliography in James Randall and David Donald, *The Civil War and Reconstruction*, revised second edition (Boston: D. C. Heath and Co., 1969) or David Donald's paperbound bibliography, *The Nation in Crisis, 1861–1877* (New York: Appleton-Century Crofts, 1969). For the variety of interpretation, there are about six major articles, namely: Howard K. Beale, 'On Rewriting Reconstruction History,' *American Historical Review*, 1940; John Hope Franklin, 'Whither Reconstruction Historiography?,' *Journal of Negro Education*, 1948; Bernard Weisberger, 'The Dark and Bloody Ground of Reconstruction Historiography,' *Journal of Southern History*, 1959; Kenneth Stampp, 'The Tragic Legend of Reconstruction,' in *The Era of Reconstruction, 1865–1877* (New York: Vintage Books, 1965), chap. 1; Vernon Wharton, 'Reconstruction,' in Arthur Link and Rembert Patrick (eds.) *Writing Southern History* (Baton Rouge: Louisiana State University Press, 1966); and finally, Larry Kincaid, 'Victims of Circumstance: An Interpretation of Changing Attitudes Toward Republican Policy Makers and Reconstruction,' *Journal of American History*, 1970.

Hereafter, this note on sources will be confined to a discussion of the primary materials consulted and will refer only tangentially to the works of historians and biographers.

A: *Written correspondence*

This consisted primarily of the private correspondence of leading Confederates. Some of this was located in the files of Confederates who held public positions, usually Governor, and these were deposited in State archives departments. Also in these official collections were letters of an administrative nature as well as those which were personal or political; though actually the dividing-line was not so clear-cut in the post-war South where administrative actions were inevitably concerned with relations to the Federal military forces or to the central question of reunion and read-mission. A third category of manuscript material was the correspondence of the President and members of the Johnson Cabinet, prominent Generals, and influential, and usually moderate, Republican Congressmen. These were scanned for communications from Southern Confederates, for scraps of evidence about government policy both executive and legislative, and for indications of the role and views of the military who were involved in Southern policy and administration.

The most useful of all these were obviously the Johnson Papers, which are an essential source for the period, not simply because Johnson was at the center of events but also because he was so meticulous and systematic in the preservation of his correspondence, even refusing to burn letters that correspondents wanted destroyed. Also full of insightful commentary and suggestion about the course the South should pursue were the papers of Herschel V. Johnson, Alexander Stephens, Benjamin Perry and William A. Graham, as well as the official papers of Jonathan Worth, Benjamin Humphreys, William L. Sharkey, and Lewis Parsons. The Perry and Worth MSS were scattered in two or three collections but the most full and rewarding were those in Montgomery and Raleigh respectively.

Some of the other collections possessed features which were very interesting and useful even though the papers as a whole were not too satisfying. Notable among these were the Seward Papers which, although suprisingly thin in Southern Correspondence, did contain draft letters by the Secretary himself defending and explaining his reunion policy; the W. T. Sherman Papers which included a running discussion of political affairs between the soldier and his brother, the moderate Senator; the Hunter — Garnett Papers which, while remarkably lacking in general political comment, did contain a lot of letters demonstrative of the family's feelings after the surrender when Robert was arrested and also a number of observations from the Federal capital written by L. Q. Washington who was a lobbyist and later a journalist with the *Richmond Examiner*; and, finally, the Chase MSS, which revealed the continuing interest of the Chief Justice in the question of reunion, especially through his activity with Swayne in trying to obtain a reconsideration of the Howard (Fourteenth) amendment during the winter of 1866. This collection also demonstrated very plainly that, by 1867, Chase was aiming at becoming the moderate Republican or Democratic candidate for President, whereas previously he had been identified with the radical wing of the Republican Party.

Listed by their location, the collections used were:

Library of Congress:

Jeremiah S. Black MSS	Jacob D. Cox MSS
Blair Family MSS	Jabez L. M. Curry MSS
Salmon P. Chase MSS	James R. Doolittle MSS

William Pitt Fessenden MSS
Ulysses S. Grant MSS
Horace Greeley MSS
Andrew Johnson MSS
Reverdy Johnson MSS
Robert E. Lee MSS
John L. Letcher MSS
Hugh McCulloch MSS
Edward McPherson MSS
James M. Mason MSS

William Cabell Rives MSS
John M. Schofield MSS
Philip H. Sheridan MSS
William Tecumseh Sherman MSS
Edwin M. Stanton MSS
Alexander Hamilton Stephens MSS
George A. Trenholm MSS
William H. Trescot MSS
Lyman Trumbull MSS

Southern Historical Collection, Chapel Hill, N.C.:

James Lusk Alcorn MSS
Battle Family MSS
Campbell–Colston MSS
William A. Graham Collection
(in typescript – prepared for
publication by J. G. de R.
Hamilton)

Benjamin Franklin Perry MSS
David L. Swain MSS
Jonathan Worth MSS

Perkins Library, Duke University:

Pierre G. T. Beauregard MSS
Bedford Brown MSS
Armistead Burt MSS
James D. B. DeBow MSS
H. W. DeSaussure MSS
Benjamin S. Hedrick MSS
William W. Holden MSS

Herschel Vespasian Johnson MSS
Benjamin F. Perry MSS
Daniel E. Sickles MSS
Alexander H. Stephens MSS
George H. Thomas MSS
Henry Wise MSS

University of Georgia Library, Athens:
James Johnson papers in Telamon Cuyler Collection
Joseph E. Brown letterbook (typescript) in K. M. Read Collection

Rhees Library, University of Rochester, Rochester, N.Y.:
William H. Seward MSS

South Carolina Library, University of South Carolina, Columbia:
Wade Hampton MSS
Benjamin F. Perry MSS

Alabama Department of Archives and History, Montgomery:
Lewis E. Parsons Official Correspondence
Robert M. Patton Official Correspondence
Benjamin F. Perry MSS

Georgia Department of Archives and History, Atlanta:
    Charles J. Jenkins Official Correspondence
    James Johnson Official Correspondence

Mississippi Department of Archives and History, Jackson:
    Charles Clark Official Correspondence
    Benjamin G. Humphreys Official Correspondence
    William L. Sharkey Official Correspondence

North Carolina Department of Archives and History, Raleigh:
    William W. Holden Official Correspondence
    Jonathan Worth Official Correspondence

South Carolina Archives Department, Columbia:
    James L. Orr Official Correspondence

Archives of the Ohio Historical Society, Columbus:
    Lewis Campbell MSS
    William H. Smith MSS

Alderman Library, University of Virginia, Charlottesville:
    Robert M. T. Hunter MSS (microfilm)
    James L. Kemper MSS
    Alexander H. H. Stuart MSS

B: *Newspapers*

In a study which aimed to include all of the Southern States, not just one as previous political histories of the Reconstruction South have done, a thorough reading in the newspaper-files would have been endless. Also the return on the time spent would have diminished rapidly. Consequently, I decided to select one newspaper for each State and, where the run was incomplete, to supplement it with others. In each instance, I chose as far as I could estimate, the most influential journal. Another consideration was the newspaper's availability on microfilm or in the Library of Congress because I did not have the funds which would enable me to spend the time necessary to read newspapers on my three trips from Washington to the Southern States. In fact, this process of selection worked out well and I was able to gain access to those papers which I wanted; complete runs however were not always available, simply because they did not exist.

    In selecting newspapers as a source for Confederate political views, I was aware of one major methodological objection which could be raised, and that was the degree of representativeness and of influence which newspapers possessed. Although it was a universal complaint among traveling observers from the North that Southerners had little contact with Northern newspapers and read very few of their own, newspapers in the South were nonetheless very important. In a hierarchical society, it matters little that a newspaper has a small circulation; in fact, this is almost inevitable. What was important was the close link with politicians and the highly political tone and interest of the Southern newspapers. Indeed, very often the editors were involved in political action themselves.

On his three tours of the Southern States in 1865 and 1866, Whitelaw Reid, himself a newspaperman, noticed the vital role which Southern newspapers played. It was apparent to him that the newspapers were a crucial link in the chain of Confederate command and rule. Citing a Lynchburg paper's editorial in late 1865 which stated that 'No man can fail to see that our future is pregnant with the most momentous issues, and that it will require the union of all right-thinking men to save our country from the blasting curse of a false and most destructive radical sentiment pervading it,' Reid noted that the newspaper urged 'the union of all the old parties' (*After the War*, p. 338). The papers evidently understood their role in ensuring that partisan differences within the Confederate establishment had to be submerged so as to provide a united front against opponents both within and without the South. So it seems clear that newspaper editors believed it was very important for them to use their journals to align public sentiment with the aims of the politicians and so to sew up fissures and patch differences and misunderstanding wherever they appeared.

In more concrete terms, links with the political leadership were easy to perceive. A number of papers were closely associated with a particular politician; for example, Herschel V. Johnson was closely associated with the *Augusta Constitutionalist*, as was Stephens with the *Augusta Chronicle* and Graham with the *Raleigh Sentinel*. During and before the war there was close identification between the *Montgomery Advertiser* and Yancey, the *Charleston Mercury* and R. B. Rhett, the *Milledgeville Federal Union* and Joseph E. Brown, the *Richmond Enquirer* and Henry Wise, the *Richmond Examiner* and Hunter, and finally the *Richmond Whig* obviously declared its partisanship and alignment with A. H. H. Stuart and others of that party. Furthermore newspaper editors could frequently be seen addressing public meetings, attending Confederate and conservative gatherings, in fact taking an obvious and identifiable role in political activities, and throughout the text of this book their names have appeared. Notably engaged in political activity were Trescot, Cohen and Cathcart of the *Charleston Daily News*; William H. C. King of the war-time Free State organ, the *New Orleans Times*; Augustus Wright of the *Augusta Chronicle*; Ethelbert Barksdale, editor of the *Jackson Clarion* after the fall of 1866 and John L. Power, his predecessor; William Woodruff of the *Arkansas Gazette*; William Pell and Seaton Gales of the *Raleigh Sentinel*; Jared Whitaker and J. H. Steele, editors of the *Atlanta Intelligencer*; and finally, Samuel G. Reid of the *Montgomery Advertiser*. The political role of the Southern newspaper in the pre- and post-war period is, I think, incontrovertible, whether 'political' be defined as partisan or as I prefer it to be used, as describing the role of government in the distribution of power and rule throughout a society. After the war, the newspapers tried to discourage politics in the former sense, but their decision to do so was political in its wider meaning.

There were some newspapers which I consulted which were not Confederate at all, and an explanation here is in order. *Flake's Bulletin* was the only Texas newspaper with anything like a complete run to which I could get access. The *Houston Telegraph*, the *San Antonio Express*, and the *Texas State Gazette* were either too fragmented or were not on microfilm. But since the *Bulletin* was consistently critical of the Confederates, although later it was not a radical Republican paper, I read it throughout the three years 1865–8 as a sample of a non-aligned viewpoint. It was also a newspaper which was very thorough in its news-reportage and therefore, although its editorial policies were not what I had initially wanted, it was quite satisfactory in all other respects. Finally, I have to account for my reading of the *Cincinnati Gazette, Chicago Tribune,* and *New York Tribune* for the spring and summer of 1865, and also of the *New York Times* for the summer of 1866. The first three papers were all radical-Republican and all contained editorials which would indicate the tone of Northern radical opinion just as the war closed. In addition they all sent reporters south in the wake of the Northern armies in March, April, May and June 1865 and their descriptions of the Southern mood are used in Chapter 1. All of them, especially the *Cincinnati Gazette*, reported the Southern constitutional conventions of 1865. Finally, the *New York Times* followed very carefully the developments in the South in response to the Philadelphia convention call.

The newspapers I consulted and the dates of their availability were:

Alexandria Gazette. March 1867–September 1867.

Arkansas Gazette. April 1865–December 1868.

Atlanta Intelligencer. June 1865–December 1867.

Augusta Chronicle and Sentinel. March 1865–November 1866.

Augusta Constitutionalist. April 1865–December 1868.

Charleston Courier. April 1865–December 1868.

Charleston Daily News. April–December 1866; January–October 1867.

Charleston Mercury. January–December 1867.

Chicago Tribune. March–July 1965.

Cincinnati Gazette. March-December 1865; January–April 1866.

Flake's (Galveston) *Bulletin.* January 1866–June 1868; semi-weekly, June–December 1868.

Houston Telegraph. Tri-weekly, January–December 1865.

Huntsville Advocate. January–December 1868.

Jackson Clarion. July 1865–December 1868.

Milledgeville Federal Union. Weekly, August 1867–December 1868.

Montgomery Advertiser. April 1865–March 1867; weekly, March 1867–April 1868

New Orleans Times. April 1865–December 1868.

New York Times. July–August 1866.

New York Tribune. March–July 1865.

North Carolina Standard. April–December 1865.

Raleigh Sentinel. April 1865–December 1868.

Richmond Enquirer. April–December 1866; January–July 1867; January–September 1868.

Richmond Southern Opinion. Weekly, January–November 1868.

Richmond Times. April 1865–December 1866.

Richmond Whig. May–December 1867; January–December 1868.

San Antonio Express. October 1867–April 1868.

Vicksburg Herald. March 1865–September 1866; January–October 1867.

C: *Miscellaneous written sources*

Two manuscript collections, which I used at an early stage in the research when the topic was not what it eventually became, were the Records of the Army Commands, 1865–66, Record Group 98 and the Records of the Secretary of War, Record Group 107, (Letters Received, Main Series, 1801–1870, microcopy 221 and Telegrams Collected by the Office of the Secretary of War [Bound], 1861–82, microcopy 473). Both were in the National Archives, the former in ledger books, the latter available only on microfilm. From time to time, data gleaned from these sources happened to be of use in the book, and citations are given where this occurred.

D: *Printed sources*

The printed materials which I used comprised the following categories: (i) Official documents such as the Reports and Executive Documents issued by the Senate and House of Representatives (commonly known as the Congressional Set). There were a series of reports on conditions in the South in 1865 by Carl Schurz, General U. S. Grant, Benjamin C. Truman as well as the testimony taken by the Joint Committee on Reconstruction during the winter of 1865–6. Among these compilations, were also the Secretary of War's Annual Reports and the Correspondence of the Provisional Governors with the executive branch during 1865. (ii) Compendia of documents such as Edward McPherson's *The Political History of the United States of America During Reconstruction, Appleton's Annual Cyclopedia*, and James D. Richardson's *A Compilation of the Messages and Papers of the Presidents*, Vol. VI. (iii) Sources for Southern bibliographic data, such as Samuel Ashe and Edward McCrady on the Carolinas, 1892, Reuben Davis on Mississippi, 1889, and William

Garrett for Alabama, 1872. (iv) Autobiographies and memoirs of Southern Governors and Congressmen and of Federal Cabinet members and military leaders. (v) Printed collections of the Correspondence of Jonathan Worth and Thomas Ruffin, which were compiled by J. G. de R. Hamilton. (vi) Biographies of Southern political leaders, notably Herschel Johnson, Benjamin H. Hill, Benjamin Perry, Jonathan Worth, Alexander Stephens, James L. Alcorn, and Joseph E. Brown. The list of biographies of prominent Southerners is very thin indeed, and a number of those just cited leave a lot to be desired. (vii) Finally, monographs, books and articles by historians dealing with various aspects of the major themes of the Reconstruction period. The bibliography for those works is vast and the aids and listings mentioned earlier will acquaint the reader with its scope and content. Those works which I consulted most frequently were the State studies carried out initially by members of the Southern school in the first two decades of this century and in most cases subjected to revisionist interpretation since World War II.

E: *Unpublished monographs*

Because they are not listed in bibliographies of printed sources, I would finally like to mention the Ph.D. dissertations I consulted. They were: Donald H. Breeze, 'Politics in the Lower South during Presidential Reconstruction, April to November 1865,' University of California at Los Angeles, 1963; Robert L. Harris, 'The South in Defeat: 1865,' Duke University, 1956; Horace W. Raper, 'William Woods Holden: A Political Biography.' University of North Carolina, 1951; Thomas Wagstaff, 'Andrew Johnson and the National Union Movement, 1865–1866,' University of Wisconsin, 1967; and Larry G. Kincaid, 'Legislative Origins of the Military Reconstruction Act, 1865–1867,' Johns Hopkins University, 1968. The last two I read only after the dissertation had been written and the manuscript of this book was in the hands of publisher's readers. To a large extent, their findings agree with those I have advanced concerning both the National Union scheme (with its culmination in the Philadelphia convention) and the characteristics of Congressional reunion policies.

INDEX

torians and 8f.; and Negro suffrage 18, 71, 146, 169, 275;
general aims of 7, 12, 21, 36,
46n., 60, 292; on state of
South after war 20, 24f., 36;
and Southern readmission 13,
49f., 60, 82, 101, 146f., 159,
161, 168–81; and Johnson's
Southern policy 36, 41, 65f.,
71, 81, 96, 103f., 175f.; South
and, 1865 48, 84f., 90–4,
96, 104, 144, 148f., 151, 159,
161f., 164, 166, 169–81; and
Johnson's national strategy,
1866 185–91, 195, 229n.,
230, 232f.; and Philadelphia
convention 65, 196–200, 208,
214–17, 221f., 226f.; and
Fourteenth Amendment 235f.,
241–52, 255, 258, 260ff.,
265; and Reconstruction Acts
6n., 273, 275, 281, 301,
317f., 321f., 324, 330, 339,
345

moderates: individuals mentioned
7, 255, 312; and conciliation of
the South 9, 160n., 177, 180,
344ff.; and Johnson's Southern
policy 92, 94; and radical Republicans 174; and Philadelphia
convention 199ff., 222; and
Fourteenth Amendment 243–6,
255, 261–4; and Reconstruction Acts 6n., 270, 277n., 288,
290; South and 85, 160n.,
175, 195

conservatives (usually included in
moderate Republicans): and conciliation of the South 6, 166,
168; and Philadelphia convention 197, 199, 205, 215ff.;
South and 94, 170, 172, 193;
and Fourteenth Amendment
246

in the South after 1867: individuals mentioned 64, 72, 153;
role and actions of 270, 277,
277n., 285–92, 299f., 305,

308, 311, 314ff., 325–8,
331f., 334ff., 340f.
Reynolds, Gen. John F. 111
Rhett, R. B. 179, 265
Rhode Island 328
Rhodes, James Ford 7n.
Rice, Sam F. 324n.
Richardson, James D. 109n., 132n.,
323n., 325n.
Richmond 46, 99, 247, 286, 288,
290, 310, 321
Richmond Dispatch 210, 225
Richmond Enquirer, news-reports and
notices 271n., 297n.; and
Southern attitude in early 1866
191; and Philadelphia convention 197, 204, 207ff., 210,
218, 223f.; and Fourteenth
Amendment 183, 233ff., 237,
240, 243f., 246, 264; and Reconstruction Acts 274n., 280,
289, 292f., 298
Richmond Examiner 210, 232, 321
Richmond Southern Opinion 321
Richmond Times, news-reports and
notices 224n., 263n., 271n.,
286n.; expectations of Presidential policy 36, 42, 48f., 50n.,
51f.; and Southern readmission
146, 151, 166f., 174f., 318;
and Andrew Johnson 170f.,
185, 186n., 188, 247; and
Philadelphia convention 197,
202f., 204, 210, 213, 215f.,
225; and Fourteenth Amendment 235, 241, 247f., 252f.;
and Reconstruction Acts 288ff.,
318f.
Richmond Whig 210, 277, 279,
287f., 316f., 324f., 329f.
Ridley, R. A. T. 208n., 213n.
'Rip Van Winkles' (recalcitrants in
Southern conventions, 1865)
89, 93, 250
Rives, William Cabell 105, 289
Robb, J. W. 286
Roberts, O. M. 259n.
Robertson, Alexander F. 30n., 60n.